Rancière and Music

Critical Connections

A series of edited collections forging new connections between contemporary critical theorists and a wide range of research areas, such as critical and cultural theory, gender studies, film, literature, music, philosophy and politics.

Series Editors
Ian Buchanan, University of Wollongong
James Williams, Deakin University

Editorial Advisory Board

Nick Hewlett
Gregg Lambert
Todd May
John Mullarkey
Paul Patton
Marc Rölli
Alison Ross
Kathrin Thiele
Frédéric Worms

Titles available in the series
Badiou and Philosophy, edited by Sean Bowden and Simon Duffy
Agamben and Colonialism, edited by Marcelo Svirsky and Simone Bignall
Laruelle and Non-Philosophy, edited by John Mullarkey and Anthony Paul Smith
Virilio and Visual Culture, edited by John Armitage and Ryan Bishop
Rancière and Film, edited by Paul Bowman
Stiegler and Technics, edited by Christina Howells and Gerald Moore
Badiou and the Political Condition, edited by Marios Constantinou
Nancy and the Political, edited by Sanja Dejanovic
Butler and Ethics, edited by Moya Lloyd
Latour and the Passage of Law, edited by Kyle McGee
Nancy and Visual Culture, edited by Carrie Giunta and Adrienne Janus
Rancière and Literature, edited by Grace Hellyer and Julian Murphet
Agamben and Radical Politics, edited by Daniel McLoughlin
Balibar and the Citizen Subject, edited by Warren Montag and Hanan Elsayed
Rancière and Music, edited by João Pedro Cachopo, Patrick Nickleson and Chris Stover

Forthcoming titles
Simondon and Digital Culture, edited by Yuk Hui, Erich Horl and Jeremy Gilbert

Visit the Critical Connections website at
edinburghuniversitypress.com/series-critical-connections.html

Rancière and Music

Edited by João Pedro Cachopo, Patrick Nickleson and Chris Stover

EDINBURGH
University Press

Edinburgh University Press is one of the leading university presses in the UK. We publish academic books and journals in our selected subject areas across the humanities and social sciences, combining cutting-edge scholarship with high editorial and production values to produce academic works of lasting importance. For more information visit our website: edinburghuniversitypress.com

© editorial matter and organisation João Pedro Cachopo, Patrick Nickleson and Chris Stover, 2020, 2022
© the chapters their several authors, 2020, 2022

Edinburgh University Press Ltd
The Tun – Holyrood Road,
12(2f) Jackson's Entry,
Edinburgh EH8 8PJ

First published in hardback by Edinburgh University Press 2020

Typeset in 11/13 Adobe Sabon by
Servis Filmsetting Ltd, Stockport, Cheshire,

A CIP record for this book is available from the British Library

ISBN 978 1 4744 4022 6 (hardback)
ISBN 978 1 4744 4023 3 (paperback)
ISBN 978 1 4744 4024 0 (webready PDF)
ISBN 978 1 4744 4025 7 (epub)

The right of João Pedro Cachopo, Patrick Nickleson and Chris Stover to be identified as the editor of this work has been asserted in accordance with the Copyright, Designs and Patents Act 1988, and the Copyright and Related Rights Regulations 2003 (SI No. 2498).

Contents

List of Examples   vii
Acknowledgements   viii
Notes on Contributors   x

Introduction   1
João Pedro Cachopo, Patrick Nickleson and
Chris Stover

Part I: Music and Noise

1. *Musique concrète* and the Aesthetic Regime of Art   27
   Loïc Bertrand

2. 'Rip it up and start again': Reconfigurations of the
   Audible under the Aesthetic Regime of the Arts   47
   Daniel Frappier

3. A Lesson in Low Music   71
   Patrick Nickleson

Part II: Politics of History

4. Wandering with Rancière: Sound and Structure
   under the Aesthetic Regime   97
   Martin Kaltenecker

5. Staging Music in the Aesthetic Regime of Art:
   Rancière, Berlioz and the Bells of *Harold en Italie*   117
   João Pedro Cachopo

vi   Contents

6. Rancière on Music, Rancière's Non-music   138
Katharina Clausius

7. Coloured Opera and the Violence of
Dis-identification   156
William Fourie and Carina Venter

Part III: Politics of Interaction

8. Musical Politics in the Cuban Police Order   177
Kjetil Klette Bøhler

9. Rancière and Improvisation: Reading Contingency
in Music and Politics   207
Dan DiPiero

10. Rancière's Affective Impropriety   230
Chris Stover

Part IV: Encounters and Challenges

11. Rancière, Resistance and the Problem of
Commemorative Art: Music Displacing Violence
Displacing Music   265
Sarah Collins

12. Stain   290
Murray Dineen

13. On Shoemakers and Related Matters: Rancière and
Badiou on Richard Wagner   312
Erik M. Vogt

14. Roll Over the Musical Boundaries: A Few
Milestones for the Implementation of an Equal
Method in Musicology   334
Danick Trottier

Afterword: A Distant Sound   353
Jacques Rancière

Works Cited   366
Index   390

Examples

5.1 Hector Berlioz, *Harold en Italie*, second movement ('Marche de pèlerins chantant la prière du soir'), mm. 16–27.   123
8.1 2-3 rumba *clave*, piano *tumbao* and *güiro* rhythm (0:00–0:14).   187
8.2 The repeating *coro* and implied 2-3 rumba *clave* (0:15–0:18).   188
8.3 Carcassés's first *guia*, with implied 2-3 rumba *clave* (0:19–0:23).   189
8.4 Carcassés's second *guia*, with implied 2-3 rumba *clave* (0:27–0:31).   190
8.5 Carcassés's third *guia*, with implied 2-3 rumba *clave* (0:35–0:41).   192
8.6 Carcassés's fourth *guia*, with implied 2-3 rumba *clave* (0:44–0:49).   192

Acknowledgements

This book had its inception in the summer of 2015, when Murray Dineen planned to propose a seminar on musical perspectives on Rancière for the 2016 American Comparative Literature Conference. Always supportive of younger scholars with similar interests, Murray invited Patrick Nickleson to help him plan and organise the session. João Pedro Cachopo and Chris Stover were among the first authors to submit and were quickly added to the timetable. Over post-seminar drinks, Murray suggested that the papers could easily form the critical mass for a book, and thus the initial plans for this volume were formulated.

As such, we should first thank Murray for his support, kindness and vision. We next thank the wonderful contributors; working with each of them was a great pleasure. The volume came together alternately quite quickly, and then very slowly, over a three-year period, and the contributors were always readily available and responsive when the three co-editors were in the throes of rapid bursts of progress. We also thank Kirsty Woods and Carol Macdonald at Edinburgh University Press, who have been hugely supportive and have kept us (largely) on schedule, series editors Ian Buchanan and James Williams, who offered helpful and enthusiastic feedback, and the anonymous readers of our original proposal, whose comments and suggestions helped shape the project through its early stages.

Last, but certainly not least, we would like to thank Jacques Rancière. When we initially discussed the book, we quickly raised the possibility of asking Rancière to contribute, perhaps by commenting directly on the place of music in his work. Authors who have published translations of Rancière's work, or secondary literature on Rancière, frequently acknowledge his kindness and support of their projects. He was similarly supportive of our project and available from the start through its conclusion: indeed, he was the book's first full reader, as he read every essay in the volume before crafting his deeply personal, thoughtful and moving afterword.

Notes on Contributors

Loïc Bertrand is a French writer, artist and researcher. After studies in anthropology (Paris 8 Saint-Denis) and religious sciences (École Pratique des Hautes Études, Sorbonne), he spent several years working on experimental and improvised music. He is currently completing his PhD, under the direction of Martin Kaltenecker (Paris-Diderot), on 'An Archaeology of Sound Art'.

Kjetil Klette Bøhler is a Senior Researcher at Norwegian Social Research (NOVA), Oslo Metropolitan University. He has published articles on the politics of Cuban and Brazilian music. Bøhler is currently completing two books entitled *Groove Politics* and *Pleasurable Nationalism*, which examine different politics of Cuban popular dance music, and a third book that investigates the surplus value that musical sounds bring to political street protests in contemporary Brazil entitled *Musicking Politics in a Changing Brazil: 2016–2020*.

João Pedro Cachopo is a Marie Skłodowska-Curie Fellow with a joint affiliation to the University of Chicago and the Universidade Nova de Lisboa, where he is a researcher at CESEM – Centre for the Study of the Sociology and Aesthetics of Music. His work spans the fields of musicology, philosophy and cinema studies. He is the author of *Verdade e Enigma: Ensaio sobre o pensamento estético de Adorno* (Vendaval, 2013), which received the First Book Award from the Portuguese PEN Club in 2014. His writing has appeared in journals such as *The Opera Quarterly* and *New German Critique*.

Katharina Clausius is an Assistant Professor of Comparative Literature and Intermedial Studies in the Département de littératures et de langues du monde at the Université de Montréal. She received her BMus (Honours) from Western University, MA from Columbia University, and PhD from the University of Cambridge. Her research focuses on word and music studies, comparative musicology, and the intersection of aesthetics and politics.

Sarah Collins is a Senior Lecturer in Musicology at the University of Western Australia. She is the author of *Lateness and Modernism: Untimely Ideas about Music, Literature and Politics in Interwar Britain* (Cambridge University Press, 2019), and *The Aesthetic Life of Cyril Scott* (Boydell, 2013); and editor of *Music and Victorian Liberalism: Composing the Liberal Subject* (Cambridge University Press, 2019). Her research has been published in the *Journal of the Royal Musical Association*, *Twentieth-Century Music*, *Music & Letters*, *Musical Quarterly* and elsewhere.

Murray Dineen is an Emeritus Professor at the University of Ottawa, where he taught in the School of Music until 2019. His research interests include Leftist thought about music, music and affect, Adorno, music aesthetics and philosophy, and music theory. He has received numerous grants from, among other bodies, the Social Sciences and Humanities Research Council of Canada. He is at work on a study of music and the New Materialism.

Dan DiPiero is a musician and Visiting Assistant Professor of American Studies at Miami University of Ohio, where he teaches American popular culture and music history. His current book project investigates the relationship between improvisation in music and in everyday life through a series of nested comparisons, including case studies on the music of Eric Dolphy, John Cage and contemporary Norwegian free improvisers Mr. K.

William Fourie is a Research Fellow at the Africa Open Institute for Music, Research and Innovation, Stellenbosch University. His research is concerned with musical modernism in post-apartheid South Africa and colonial geopolitics of knowledge. Aside from academic publications, he explores these themes in praxis through his work as a curator of new music festivals.

Daniel Frappier is a doctoral student in art history at the Université du Québec à Montréal. His thesis explores the interplay of influences between painting and music through Rancière's notion of 'becoming-passive', and is supported by the Fonds de recherche du Québec and the Social Sciences and Humanities Research Council of Canada. His master's thesis was awarded the Prix des professeurs by the Département d'histoire de l'art et d'études cinématographiques at the Université de Montréal.

Martin Kaltenecker is Associate Professor of Musicology at University Paris Diderot. He has been a fellow at the Wissenschaftskolleg zu Berlin, and is one of the founders of the contemporary music review *Entretemps*. His publications include *Avec Helmut Lachenmann* (Paris, 2001), *L'Oreille divisée. Les discours sur l'écoute musicale aux XVIIIe et XIXe siècles* (2010), and he co-edited the volume *Pierre Schaeffer. Les Constructions impatientes* (Paris, 2011). His current project is a study of melodic writing in twentieth-century music.

Patrick Nickleson is a postdoctoral researcher at Queen's University. His work focuses on questions of authorship and historiography in contemporary musics. His writing has appeared in *Twentieth Century Music*, *University of Toronto Quarterly*, *Intersections* and *Performance Research*. His translation of Rancière's 'Autonomy or Heteronomy: The False Alternative' was recently published in *Perspectives of New Music*, and his monograph *The Names of Minimalism: Authorship and the Historiography of Dispute* is forthcoming with University of Michigan Press.

Jacques Rancière is Emeritus Professor of Aesthetics and Politics at the University of Paris VIII, where he taught from 1969 to 2000 in the Department of Philosophy. His work crosses over the fields of social history, politics, aesthetics, film studies and literature. He is notably the author of *Le Maître ignorant: cinq leçons sur l'émancipation intellectuelle* (Fayard, 1987), *La Mésentente: politique et philosophie* (Galilée, 1995), *Malaise dans l'esthétique* (Galilée, 2004) and *Aisthesis: scènes du régime esthétique de l'art* (Galilée, 2011). His most recent book is *Les Temps modernes. Art, temps, politique* (La fabrique, 2018).

Chris Stover is a Research Fellow at the RITMO Centre for Interdisciplinary Study of Rhythm, Time and Motion and affiliate faculty in the Department of Musicology at the University of Oslo. His work has appeared in *Perspectives of New Music*, *Music Theory Spectrum*, *Media and Culture*, *Music Theory Online*, *The Oxford Handbook of Making Time in Music* and elsewhere. He is currently finishing a monograph on temporal-relational processes in African and Afro-diasporic musics and is co-editor of the forthcoming volume *Making Music Together: Analyzing Musical Interaction* (University of Chicago Press). He is also an internationally active trombonist and composer.

Danick Trottier is Professor of Musicology at the Université du Québec à Montréal and regular member of the Observatoire interdisciplinaire de création et de recherche en musique. Trottier has published articles in journals such as *Circuit*, *Dissonance*, *Filigrane*, *Intersections*, *Kinephanos*, *Les cahiers de la SQRM*, *Perspectives of New Music*, *Speculum Musicae* and *Volume ! La revue des musiques populaires*. His research interests include music history, music sociology and aesthetics in twentieth-century classical and popular music.

Carina Venter is Lecturer in Musicology at Stellenbosch University. She holds a master's degree from the same institution, a master's and doctorate from the University of Oxford, and completed a Junior Research Fellowship at Merton College (University of Oxford). Her work has appeared mostly in South African journals and she co-edited a special issue of *Journal of Musicology* on music and landscape in 2016. Her research interests include music and violence, postcolonial music studies and South African music.

Erik Vogt is Gwendolyn Miles Smith Professor of Philosophy at Trinity College (CT, USA), as well as Dozent of Philosophy at the University of Vienna. He is the author or (co-)editor of 23 books, and author of over 60 articles. His latest books include *Zwischen Sensologie und aesthetischem Dissens* (Turia + Kant, 2019) and *Jacques Rancière und die Literatur* (Turia + Kant, 2019).

Introduction

*João Pedro Cachopo, Patrick Nickleson and
Chris Stover*

What new problematics does a turn to music animate in Rancière's political-aesthetic thought? What existing problematics can be newly attended to, and what new deployments can be imagined? What musicalities are revealed *in* his thought and writings by such a turn? What, in short, is the role of music, of the musical, of musicking for Rancière, either explicitly or implicitly? And backing up slightly, what is the role of *sound*? Is sound the medium in which the art of the muses is inextricably embedded? Or can music reach beyond the sonic sphere in the course of its various metamorphoses? Music is overtly present in Rancière's writing only very rarely; indeed, it has become a truism that Rancière does not have much to say about music. But music is often tacitly – mutely – present in his thought, and we can see how it rises to the surface as a point of intersection and resonance between the arts, through or as musicality.

Rancière's multifaceted enquiry into the relationship between aesthetics and politics offers many new prospects for musical insight, research and practice, as the chapters that comprise this volume will demonstrate. Conversely, music offers a rich terrain – a rich scenographic field[1] – for continuing to develop Rancière's political/aesthetic thought. Music's essentially temporal, relational status, its modes of expressing and engendering (often non- or paralinguistic) meaning, the lines it draws between philosophical and political (in conventional usage) expression, the ontological and epistemological questions it continues to raise: all of these are fertile ground both for engagement via Rancièrean conceptual apparatuses and for developing, refining and transforming those apparatuses. Some of these themes reflect why music has been philosophically valuable for so many canonical philosophers, an abbreviated list of whom must include Rousseau, Schiller, Schopenhauer, Hegel, Nietzsche, Bergson, Husserl, Adorno, Bloch, Langer, Jankélévitch, and Deleuze and Guattari. Because music's particular mode of temporal extension does not break down into basic syntactic units in any fully agreed-upon way, it provides a valuable illustration of an irreducible temporality that extends to other modes of existence. Likewise with music's fundamental relationality: sounds acquire meaning through their interactions with other sounds, words and images, and listeners interact with those sound-constellations in ways that both express and challenge the historical and sociocultural contexts in which they find themselves. The political-aesthetic implications of music – its potential to disrupt sedimented modes of hearing and thinking – are profound here.

While we will take care not to overdetermine them – and, most important, not to overly historicise them – we should begin with Rancière's three regimes of art. As Gabriel Rockhill summarises, 'a regime of art is a mode of articulation between three things: ways of doing and making, their corresponding forms of visibility, and ways of conceptualizing both the former and the latter'.[2] In Rancière's ethical regime, art is considered directly in terms of the use to which it is put and the effects that result. Art is freed from this ethos in the representative regime and is given autonomy as art, or, more accurately, as a range of specific modes of making, perceiving and critiquing art. The aesthetic regime occurs as an interruption in this distribution of ways of doing and making: it 'strictly identifies art in the singular and frees it from any specific rule, from any hierarchy of the arts, subject matter, and genres'.[3] In doing so it calls into question the constructedness both of mimesis and hierarchies. 'The aesthetic state is a pure instance of suspension, a moment when form is experienced for itself. Moreover, it is the moment of the formation and education of a specific type of humanity'[4] – the radical implications of this last point for considerations of teaching and learning should not go underemphasised.

It is important to clarify that the three regimes are an element – a relatively recent one – of Rancière's thought, and not its culmination. Music scholars attempting to bridge the perceived gap between 'Rancière' on the one hand and 'music' on the other have often overplayed the very existence of this gap precisely *because* they overdetermine the regimes. A recent article by Jairo

Moreno and Gavin Steingo sought, in essence, to map (what they suggest are) the three regimes of the (visual) arts on to musical examples.[5] Their article proposes a pedagogico-political stance, in which a valuable theoretical lens is translated into the language of music history, but introduces more troubles than necessary in its suggestion that there might be such a thing as a Rancièrean 'equal music'. Similar concerns arise in a recent volume in which Rancière is a key touchstone. David Brackett, in his contribution 'The Social Aesthetics of Swing in the 1940s', critiques what he sees as a problematic simplicity of the three regimes because, he suggests, Rancière's focus is exclusively on French 'high culture'.[6] In instances of this sort, Rancière has been criticised for what music scholars see as a facile restatement of the ideal of modernist 'rupture' in the guise of a new theoretical framework. Rancière's regimes, according to these readings, point us back to a time when musicology focused on a prescribed Western canon ('high culture') understood through a series of epistemic ruptures articulated in a single, teleological line. This is precisely *not* how Rancière's regimes operate, though it has become a major element of how Rancière has been received among sceptical music scholars.[7]

While the three regimes of art certainly play an important role in this volume, we recognise these concepts as articulated within a broader philosophy that touches not on the historicisation, categorisation or hierarchisation of the arts, but which rather combines a concern for the relationship between aesthetics and politics, in the broad sense of their mutual interdependence as a condition of experience, and an enquiry into whether and how artistic discourses, practices and works may come to unsettle particular *distributions of the sensible*. All of this necessarily occurs alongside a well-articulated theory of politics, history and pedagogy grounded in egalitarianism. Towards that end, in this Introduction we broadly outline our approach to Rancière's work and its potential interrelations with music studies. The statement of the problem here is important. Although Rancière has not written as frequently and as profusely about music as he has about literature, cinema or the visual arts, there is, we suggest, a rich *musicality* to Rancière's thought that we will outline here. This Introduction thus focuses on two interrelated issues: first, an articulation of the role of musicality in Rancière's thought, and second, the ways in which its echoes can be deflected or prolonged beyond the scope of Rancière's work. That is, we aim to draw out some of the major places in which musicality breaches the surface of Rancière's writing as a means of pointing to the broader problem addressed by the essays in the volume: that it is not entirely clear, and certainly never fully articulated, how music as the name of a particular practice of sounding art fits into Rancière's thought, in particular how it relates to ideas about politics and aesthetics as practices of equality.

Musicality

Written as part of a catalogue for an exhibition on electronic music, the essay 'Metamorphosis of the Muses' has offered an entry point for many considerations of Rancière's engagement with music. In Rancière's conception, the muses appear already transfigured, alongside music as self-transformative: 'The screen sometimes goes black to attest to music's power to create images all on its own.'[8] The muses appear as spirits or ghosts that inhabit and animate matter; they are radicalised as 'the Dionysian roar of music which claims for itself the Apollonian shimmering of images' and 'mystical oceans of sound, blessed in the name of Bachelard, Stockhausen or Sun Ra'.[9] Music, sound and noise are thus already always flowing through one another, often as part of a larger shifting and relocation of their conception and reception: 'This roar is also the shift from an art of notes to an art of sounds, from the art of sound to the art of noises and from the latter to the boundless and anonymous murmur of life.'[10]

Much as film undercuts the *muthos* of ancient poetic principles through jump-cuts and montage, music takes the next step by locating thought non-discursively in sensibility. At first sight, it seems possible to read this as a restatement of the nineteenth-century absolute music gambit. Nevertheless, the particular kind of aesthetic eruption that music enacts takes place within the very logic of discursive thought, of language itself. Music is not the only art that does this, but very often when another medium makes this transformative move we describe it as *being musical* in some important way; hence Kandinsky's 'improvisations', Mallarmé's poems, Calder's sculptures, Chaplin's films, Flaubert's prose. That all of these examples have in turn inspired further musical activity speaks to this affinity.

We consider it productive to give a name to this element of Rancière's thought – the ways in which sound, noise and music flow into each other, the metaphorical role that music often plays in other arts and as the specific fact of music's sensible reality. With reference to his own ideas about *literarity*, we propose a persistent *musicality* in his writing. Musicality should be understood as, more within Rancière's own language, a *technē* for interrupting a given representative regime, centring affective sensation as that which engenders an event. Rancière's extensive writings on Flaubert and Mallarmé provide the most helpful evidence towards how we read his staging of musicality. Flaubert, for example, 'lets himself be lulled by the music of his own phrase in the same way that [Emma Bovary] gets lulled by the "mystical languor" of the altar'.[11] Several points can be drawn from this simple claim, which we will continue to support below. First, Rancière conflates the musicality of Flaubert's own writing with the sort of mysticism that we have already encountered in 'Metamorphosis of the Muses', music's power to create its own images. A further parallel can be drawn with Rancière's discussion of Mallarmé, who understood music as 'an art which uses a material instrument to produce an immaterial sensible milieu'.[12] In both instances, this mysticism is closely tied to a kind of para-materiality. Through the *technē* of musicality, Flaubert's staging of Emma's desire and the content of that staging fold irreducibly into one another, just as, for Mallarmé, Loïe Fuller's veil stages and transposes an *idea* of music as the production of immateriality.[13]

Similarly, a discussion of 'muteness' as essential to literature as an art form finds Rancière proclaiming that 'music is mute' in that it is able 'to claim to signify everything'.[14] Music alone 'proposes a language that is structurally pure of representation, in which representation vanishes in the fact of vibration' or 'the conversion of the mute signs of mathematics into sensuous intuitions'.[15] In these moments, Rancière seems most closely related to Romantic conceptions. Indeed, he *seems* precisely to be articulating a Romantic philosophy; Rancière's assertion here is that music becomes 'an idea of art' at precisely the time of the Romantics: 'it is the idea that comes to occupy precisely the place formerly held by poetry'.[16] While poetry had been the model of the arts at least since Aristotle, the modern ideal of art – the one that Rancière labels the aesthetic regime – appears simultaneously with, and is perhaps coexistent with, the moment when late eighteenth-century instrumental music began to take over as the purest expression of the sublime Idea. As Rancière writes,

> Instrumental music in the age of Haydn, Mozart and Beethoven freed itself from playing an auxiliary function to the language of words and being the expressive complement to feelings they described. It explored all the richness of its own harmonic language. But this autonomy only makes sense if it allows a new encounter between the power of thinking put into words and the power of the sensible fulfilment promised by the harmonic 'ocean' ... Music makes sensible what words try to make visible in vain: the ineffability of sensation, the power of unconscious life.[17]

The implication here is not only that music might be able to express a sensibility that words fail to reach, but that it does so within its own immanent space, the 'ocean' of its harmonic language. Music, then, becomes the fundamental ideal of art not in a specific (Romantic) time period, but at the precise moment when the aesthetic regime appears – that is, when *art*, in the singular, is conceived in Western thought as a category in its own right, referring specifically to the separation of the arts from their homologous function as mimetic practices owing to the propriety of their subject.

Still, Rancière is careful to warn that music – or the concept of music, its idea – is not a utopian conception that singularly solves all of our theoretical problems. He is clear that we must not overdetermine the productive power of music's representational muteness or its status as a conduit beyond representation and into a pure, Romantic, sonorous spirituality. While music is perhaps 'the idea of antirepresentation', called upon to '"sweep away" the dust of representation', it is just as quickly becomes a new law, a new order, a new *police*: 'it only frees us from the old law and the old covenant to subject us to the new covenant, to the speechless law of spirit and interiority'.[18] As we will elaborate below, every political eruption will ultimately fold back into a new logic. But even if Mallarmé or Hegel (or Rancière) are not quite willing to grant music this fully emancipatory status, we still must think seriously about the new structurings that music and musicality advance.[19] And indeed, these structurings are a major element, closely tied to the mystical and para-materialist Romantic ideal. These two aspects seem always to be in balance in music's metaphorical usage: music, despite the efficacy of its dematerialisation, seems always to carry within it its own structuring, its own logic or order that is particularly trenchant when Rancière describes shifts from noise to music. There is a particularly dimensional and affective potential in this sense:

> Flaubert ... extracts the impersonal haecceities from the personal appetites and frustrations. He hollows within the narration of [Emma's] desires and disillusions what he calls 'small apertures' through which we 'glimpse abysses'. He makes us feel the music of the impersonal, the music of true life, through the noise of her misfortunes.[20]

Across these passages, closely tied to the ideals he ascribes to Flaubert and Mallarmé especially, we can distinguish both the familiarity and the nuance of Rancière's position. We move from the proclamation of music as the very ideal of Romantic art, and therefore the operative ideal-concept at the time of the emergence of art in the singular, to the realisation that it merely proclaims a new order of things. It is in these passages that Rancière is most often misread, even by his adherents. We should briefly turn to his equally important distinction between politics and police here to make the point. At the time of the major writings of Schelling, Hegel and others (as well as the symphonies of Beethoven), systems of representation determined certain styles of painting that were appropriate for the depiction of glorious events and heroic figures, and other styles that were appropriate for the depiction of peasants and quotidian life. This division amounted to a *policing* of modes of representation. In contrast, the insistence that anything at all can be the subject of artistic expression, the confusion of art and life that heralds the arrival of the aesthetic regime, certainly stands as an instance of *politics* in that moment. Importantly, police is a largely neutral term here, despite the efforts to mobilise it in some of the more anarchist readings of Rancière; politics always and necessarily emerges from the police.[21] Still – and this is the key point – the ideal of music displacing the ideal of poetry, in all its importance, merely reinstates a new normal, a new covenant even, and pushes immediately towards a new police logic, in which interiority and 'the spirit' become the dominating constraints of artistic production.

Inseparable from Rancière's aesthetic regime is that it resists such a sedimentation into a new police count. As Rancière insists, 'the aesthetic regime allows old forms to coexist with new forms'.[22] This is a crucial point that can get lost when aesthetics is conflated with a kind of high-modernist or avant-garde eschewal of all that had been in pursuit of a putative or pure ideal of newness. Where there certainly might be musics that effect something close to complete epistemological or ontological ruptures, most don't, and don't purport to. More importantly, nothing can be permanently new, or remain inherently disruptive of the historical reality of a situation. There is still a narrative quality to the 'absolute' musicality of a late Beethoven quartet, and radical as their interventions were, those quartets have long been central to the Western art music canon. The rhythmic impetus of the dance is a vital part of a Chopin Mazurka or Corigliano Tarantella. There is still *muthos* in the *opsis* of Boulez's *Pli selon pli* or Glass's *Einstein on the Beach* or Anderson's *United States*. The aesthetic regime does not erase other modes of seeing, hearing, speaking or doing; rather, it reveals the underlying conditions for an equality of expression that *precedes* representation, which the representative regime seizes or covers over. And it is the very possibility for something new to appear in light of something old, and for the two to exist simultaneously. It is the explicit location of art in mimesis that the aesthetic regime exposes as a construct. Rancière comments on just this point in relation to music and, again, to dematerialisation: 'the specificity of music is to make both the density of things and the representative organization of words disappear'. And the clincher: 'Music alone proposes a language that is structurally pure of representation, in which representation vanishes in the face of vibration, that is, of the spiritualization of matter.'[23]

None of the Rancièrean passages we have invoked so far dive into close readings of particular works; but as he notes in the Afterword to this volume, Rancière is not exactly providing close readings of most paintings he discusses, either. More often, the staging of a scene involves turning to a particular piece of *writing* (most notably in *Aisthesis*) in which the stakes of perception and sensibility are clearly articulated in prose, rather than in the work itself. Even so, is it viable to claim that a thinker who holds music in such a reverent position is really avoiding music in his writing? In proposing the term *musicality*, we mean to articulate a latent significance that music holds, which – while not explicitly fleshed out by Rancière – perhaps contains all the more power for it.

The politics of listening

> But the whole question ... is to know who possesses speech and who merely possesses voice. For all time, the refusal to consider certain categories of people as political beings has proceeded by means of a refusal to hear the words exiting their mouths as discourse.[24]

The constellation of sounds comprising speech, music and noise plays a decisive role in Rancière's thought that can be traced all the way back to his early writings. What kind of sounds are to be heard as meaningful expression rather than as noise? What kind of discourses are to be listened to as meaningful statements rather than as senseless utterances? How are those determinations made? These questions are at the core of Rancière's seminal volume *La Mésentente*, translated into English as *Disagreement*.[25] For Rancière, a specific situation, rather than certain words, defines what disagreement is. This is why Rancière insists that 'disagreement is not the conflict between one who says white and another who says black' but rather 'between one who says white and another who also says white but does not understand [*n'entend point*] the same thing by it or does not understand that the other is saying the same thing in the name of whiteness'.[26] Crucially, the word *mésentente* evokes sound, and could be rendered in a more literal translation as 'mishearing'. While music scholarship has long highlighted that listening is never neutral – who one listens to, and how and why and in what contexts one listens to them, are politically significant questions – Rancière's close attention to mishearing and misunderstanding are novel and fundamental elements of his thought. Within a given distribution, certain expressive or communicative utterances are recognised as speech (or music), others as noise, so the ascription of noise to a given utterance amounts to a power move within a police logic that proceeds as a *refusal* to grant the status of speech to an interlocutor. For Rancière, misunderstanding and disagreement are the fundamental conditions of politics – of listening as well – precisely because there is no true, singular understanding to which one could hold firm, or which can be excavated on the level of a surface–depth metaphor of exegesis. Rancière argues this in the opening pages of *Disagreement* in a development of Aristotle's distinction between *phōnē* and *logos*, and clarifies it a few years later in his 'Ten Theses on Politics':

> If there is someone you do not wish to recognise as a political being, you begin by not seeing them as the bearers of politicalness, by not understanding what they say, by not hearing that it is an utterance coming out of their mouths.[27]

A poignant elaboration on this distinction has been articulated by Bonnie Honig: '*Phōnē* is the name for the sonorous emissions of the excluded, and *logos* is the name claimed by the included for their own sounds.'[28] All of this is brought to bear, for example, on questions about nominal boundaries between music and noise; this has been at the root of generational arguments about what counts as good or proper music, is an ongoing theme in discourses of twentieth- and twenty-first-century music, and is a framing question for the discipline of sound studies.[29] Quite tellingly, Rancière offers a negative answer to this music/noise question, which he finds crucial to the process of dissembling a given logic in the aesthetic regime. As he puts it in an interview:

> The partition of the sensible does not modify the frequency or intensity of sonorous signals. However, it places the inscription of sonorous sequences into a world of experience. A concept like music is remarkable in this regard: the concept introduced a differentiation in the sensory domain ... People of taste, Voltaire said, do not have the same sense as vulgar people. This is to say that the one lives in a world filled with music and the others in a world of noise. The aesthetic regime puts into question the sensible partition between two humanities, the partition between the world of noise and that of music. But it also emancipates the musical 'noise' from the different functions with which music is associated: religious ceremony, accompanying the text of theatrical dramas, entertainment during social functions, etc. This is the sense of the emancipation of instrumental practice at the end of the eighteenth century: a music which illustrates nothing, which serves no function.[30]

This points to a decisive aspect of Rancière's thought. In broad terms the link between aesthetics and politics leads to the notion of the 'distribution of the sensible', since the stratifications of a police logic are defined by the continuous reproduction of lines of demarcation between what can be seen and heard. Quite literally: in its first formulation, building on and critiquing the Althusserian police of the *interpeller*, Rancière pointed to the police of sensation as the one who, perhaps guiding traffic around a protest, says 'move along, nothing to see here'. Any given political disruption is therefore an aesthetic act in two senses: because it specifically refers to ways of redistributing sensoria (the purview of progressive art throughout history), and because of its declarative nature; politics proceeds by way of an announcement that one has a voice, that one ought to be listened to. This is directly opposed to the police logic that insists that one group is to be seen and taken account of, while another is quite literally no-thing. At the same time, in the narrower sense of artistic practices, this exact same link is what produces the aesthetic regime. The parallelism here is why Rancière speaks not only of an aesthetics of politics (due to the expressive redistribution of the sensible in any political utterance) but also a politics of aesthetics in the sense that aesthetics proceeds from an assertion of equality.

Here we should return to the connection between the historical origin of aesthetics in what is conventionally cast as the advent of artistic 'modernity' that emerged between the eighteenth and nineteenth centuries. This entails a radical rereading of conventional historical narratives. With the 'aesthetic revolution', new forms of practising, experiencing and thinking about art emerged – forms that challenged the centuries-long harmony between social and artistic hierarchies that characterised what Rancière calls the ethical and representative regimes. The emergence of the aesthetic regime, then, necessarily disrupts given assumptions about what art is or should be. In a certain sense, only under the aesthetic regime does the notion of a politics of art become at once operative and meaningful, since for Rancière the political moment is exactly the moment when a distribution of the sensible is recognised for what it is, and its conditions and legitimacy are challenged. As we described above, this does not mean that the aesthetic regime replaces the representative regime: the aesthetic erupts within the representational, forcing a critical engagement with the conditions that frame the experience of art (that distribute the sensible) and reconditioning experience to consider what other distributions might be possible. This is why Rancière is careful to stress that these regimes are to be taken as aesthetic-poetic-critical paradigms rather than as historical periods. It is also why this pair of regimes is so closely tied to the parallel notions of politics and police, with politics never a *pure* event or fact, but rather a force – a rare one – that disrupts a dominant order of things before becoming a new police order in its own right.

A distribution of the (sonorously) sensible is a logic within which categorisations of music, sound and noise are constituted and reiterated, and in which modes of hearing and listening are policed. The aesthetic regime emancipates the listener, freeing them to partake in new distributions and new modes of experiencing art; likewise the practitioner (the composer or performer), who is free to create within a logic of equality that was covered over by mimetic modes of making and doing.

Rancière and musicology

While musicality flows through Rancière's work, and while sound is revealed as perhaps the originary scene of politics, it remains true that Rancière has specifically engaged music only rarely. In *Aisthesis* we encounter scenes from sculpture, poetry, literature, theatre, dance, film and architecture, but not music. There is a prolonged engagement with Wagner, but as dramaturge and in the context of describing a 'theater of life', a 'theater without action' that would again eschew the plot-directedness of *muthos*.[31] Sound is key, once again: we hear the grain of the voices of Flemish peasants, we find the interiority of drama in a tone, we discover in sound a means for undoing 'the economy of visibility'.[32] As we described above, all of this is *musical* in conception, and Wagner's looming presence reinforces this point. But Rancière effects a shift from Wagner – from Wagner's 'incapacity to draw out [the] implications [of his theory of drama] for staging',[33] which Adolphe Appia takes up by refiguring the stage in terms of, or drawing out from, a musical interiority.

Rancière engages specifically with musical matters in two essays – 'Metamorphosis of the Muses' and 'Autonomy and Historicity: The False Alternative', both from the early 2000s – although in both cases we also see how an engagement with music raises issues of a fundamental heteronomy and heterogeneity among the arts. Music serves an important role in understanding how the aesthetic regime can be staged. Indeed, Rancière characterises the practice of aesthetic art as 'the constitution of a proper space which makes visible that which music says through not speaking'; thereby politicising the Romantic notion of instrumental music as the form to which art strives in its aesthetic iteration, by 'raising to the level of sensibility the speech of the mute'.[34] Music, in this account, and in the event of its aesthetic instantiation, is also the 'Dionysian roar' that speaks against or dis-identifies with the Romantic image of art's autonomy from nature. The remarkable metamorphosis that Rancière draws here brings to light a crucial aspect of the Romantic conception of instrumental music, which is the possibility that music opens a passage out of the regime of signs that for, say, Schopenhauer, traps other arts in inescapable networks of meaning-constellations. It is precisely music's inability to say anything specific at all that makes it a rich pedagogical space for understanding, not the transformation of *phōnē* into *logos*, but the valorisation of *phōnē* as a proper form of communication that nonetheless remains outside the structuring system of representational language. Rancière's point, as ever with his nuanced critique of modernity and modernism, is that music's political (which is to say, aesthetic) instantiation was already well underway in the early stirrings of the nineteenth century.

In 'Autonomy and Historicism' Rancière highlights the inherently heterogeneous relationship 'between music as the name of an art and history as the name of a form of rationality that has been asked in which sense it is or is not entitled to think that art'.[35] The essay provides a more direct exploration of the methods and problems of 'music history' as a discipline; as has often been the case in some of his most important essays, Rancière's writing is framed as an invited response to an essay of which he is fundamentally critical, in this case by the composer François Nicolas. For Nicolas, history, an instance of heteronomy in that it can capture anything in its disciplinary web, is countered by music, an instance of autonomy that operates as its own sphere or world. Rancière is concerned to overthrow this – there is no singular world of music, just as there is no singular method or concept of history, but instead always *musics* and *histories*. In contrast to the earlier 'Metamorphosis of the Muses', with its contemporary examples and para-material arguments, 'Autonomy and Historicism' is strategically methodological and even disciplinary, delivered as a response to a group of decidedly modernist French composers and musicologists.

Nevertheless, each essay suggests a conflicted and complex relationship with music on Rancière's part, particularly at the end of 'Autonomy and Historicity' where he writes of attending a Stockhausen concert at Nanterre at the end of April 1968, for at least twenty years after which he had 'not attended any concert of contemporary music'. Somewhat cryptically, he does not explain what so alienated him, claiming instead that since the concert he has 'been occupied in reflecting on what happened to history that it resisted contemporaneity'. Throughout this passage, those personae that Davide Panagia calls Rancière's typical 'writerly figures' – Flaubert, Mallarmé, Rimbaud – are replaced with musical references ranging from the Ars Nova to Rameau to Sciarrino. What emerges is an image of Rancière with his own conception of a European canon; this despite, or perhaps alongside, the fact that he introduces the essay by diminishing his own involvement with music, that he is merely 'a listener who has never learned how it was made and what makes it such a pleasure to listen to'.

A clue to Rancière's suggestion of music's resistance to contemporaneity can be found in a brief passage in *Short Voyages to the Land of the People*, in which an imaginary musician is accused of travelling 'too little or too badly to make worthwhile music';[36] one that could express the crafts, the rites and celebrations, the joys and sorrows of a people. This follows a single reference to Darmstadt, 'where they have forgotten how to sing',[37] which, in the absence of any other supporting context, is a valuable hermeneutic sign pointing to what Rancière might describe as modernist music's failure to enact the very kinds of political democratisation that would align it with the only kind of revolutionary action he deems valuable or even possible: one that erupts from within the dissensual doings of the people. Importantly, in the Büchner quote that follows, what he is not hearing are folk songs; 'the *people* don't sing'. What is Rancière suggesting about where the proper space of aesthetic music ought to be? Certainly not in the hyperkinetically controlled regime of post-serialism: it is likely that Rancière hears a parallel between the ideological prescriptions of a Boulez or Stockhausen and Althusser's insistence that only through theory and the enactment of an epistemological break can meaningful revolution occur. The revolution of May 1968 failed because its leading intellectual proponents refused to acknowledge the *part* of the student activists. As Davide Panagia succinctly puts it, 'Rancière's Althusser is committed to a specific account of authentic political work, and that account begins with telling participants that their labors don't count because they lack the necessary intellectual skills ... for political agency.'[38] We can easily envision a parallel account where we substitute the Stockhausen of 1968 for Althusser, an authentic (read: aesthetic) musical avant-garde for political work, musical sensibility for intellectual skills, and creative artistry for political agency. The implication here is that a proper musical revolution, for Rancière, can only arise from *the people* (a category Rancière always interrogates as, most simply, a construction towards political ends), and that where Boulez, Stockhausen and others went wrong was in overt or implicit prescriptions that partitioned modes of progressive music-making into right and wrong practices. From this perspective, one of the crimes of the Darmstadt composers and their high-modernist peers elsewhere was to engage in a parallel practice of constructing *a people*, what Milton Babbitt polemically characterised as an ideal audience that has done the proper homework prior to experiencing a piece of new music (and suggesting that experiencing structurally is the 'proper' mode of experience).[39]

Staging Rancière

Several excellent overviews of Rancière's thought have appeared in the secondary literature on Rancière, freeing us of the need to fully define and recount his ideas. Nevertheless, it is worth adding that in developing the concept of the 'aesthetic regime', Rancière's aim is to rewrite the history of artistic modernity, and that this rewriting implies a criticism not only of modernism but also of postmodernist discourse. Rancière explicitly seeks to criticise modernist orthodoxy while at the same time avoiding postmodernist rhetoric: for the author of *Aesthetics and Its Discontents*, many of postmodernism's alleged innovations – from the abolition of the great divide between the popular and the erudite to the entanglement of different arts and media – prolong or reformulate trends that stem from Romanticism and that have punctuated avant-garde practices. As Rancière writes frequently: 'There is no postmodern rupture.'[40] This all speaks to Rancière's redeployment of historicism: an account of measurable epistemic shifts is no longer valid; instead, we must consider the ways in which aesthetics, thought in terms of its political egalitarianism, can erupt within ongoing regimes, including postmodern ones. This forces a reconsideration of a wide array of historicising accounts of artistic and political procession.

All of these themes flow through music and discourse around music in powerful ways. Not only because the modernism/

postmodernism dualism has not yet been clarified – let alone overcome – in the field of music, but also because, as we described above, the role of music in the emergence of Rancière's historicised aesthetic regime has not been fully explored. The same applies to an understanding of the link between music and politics that eschews the assumption of music's autonomous purity – whether in its Romantic or modernist versions. Other musical matters that Rancière's thought may help explore critically include the role of listening (in relation to the notion of emancipated spectatorship), the demythologisation of silence as a manifestation of the unsayable (in parallel with Rancière's criticism of Lyotard's unpresentable,[41] and following Rancière's careful explication of what it means for something to be unsayable or what constitutes the conditions of unsayability), the plurality of music's meaningfulness (in relation not only to noise but also to senses other than hearing), and the role that sonic metaphors and what we are calling musicality play in Rancière's writing and political thought broadly.

And many other Rancièrean concepts – beyond those that specifically orbit around aesthetics, modernity, sound and noise, and regimes of sayability or sensibility – resonate through and have profound implications for music studies. These include his pedagogical interventions and his close readings of the status of workers, both of which subvert dominant accounts of sociopolitical hierarchies and should prove to be essential as certain lines of musicological research continue to enact their ongoing turn from 'great masters' and their scores to the performative and the performed, to interaction and individuation, to the musicologist's poor.[42] Furthermore, Rancière's turn to the poetics of knowledge (as well as his suspicions about epistemology as an ethical space of inquiry, given the ways it reproduces existing knowledge structures), his mappings of events, narrative and discourse, and his trenchant thoughts about the indiscernibility (and therefore mutability) of language suggests a vivid template for rethinking musicological activity – music, after all, is an art of events, and musicology has been a science of narrative imaginings. The essays in this volume develop these themes and many more.

The three essays that make up Part I, 'Music and Noise', consider the central place of noise in Rancière's writing and the productive slippages between its conceptual and literal usage. Daniel Frappier and Loïc Bertrand each consider the integration of noise into music – or the indistinction of that boundary – as central to the creation of an aesthetic regime in music. For Frappier, this musical form of the aesthetic regime is built on the identification of contraries and the blurring of lines between music and non-music. By reading several case studies alongside one another, Frappier reinforces the ahistoricity of Rancière's aesthetics, revealing how it erupts in contexts as diverse as eighteenth-century instrumental music and 1990s 'noise' rock. In contrast, Bertrand considers the inclusion of noise as an element in music by reading the development of Pierre Schaeffer's *musique concrète* as a Rancièrean aesthetic intervention. Bertrand argues that Schaeffer enacted an egalitarian conception of sound that challenged the autonomous tones of 'music itself', setting up a new distribution of sensibility that emancipates noise in much the same way that Balzac, Flaubert, Woolf and others freed the novel of *muthos*. Patrick Nickleson reads the use and thematic development of *bruit* [noise] in *Disagreement* to highlight how a sonic metaphor holds together several of the primary scenes of that text, including the Aventine Hill, Blanqui's trial and workers' strikes. Nickleson articulates the etymological relationship and 'slanted rhyme' between these forms of *bruit* and the *abrutir* of *The Ignorant Schoolmaster* – which Kristin Ross self-consciously translates as 'stultification' – to argue that it is in response to aesthetic or political 'noise' that the policing of sensation stultifies.

Part II, 'Politics of History', focuses on historical issues that permeate Rancière's account of the politics of aesthetics and some of the ways in which they relate to music. Of primary relevance in this regard are the three regimes of art – the ethical, the representational and the aesthetic – building on which Rancière proposes a counter-history of artistic modernity. Martin Kaltenecker brings this apparatus to bear on conventional historical reading of the progression of Western music, engaging Hegel and Foucault, Rimbaud and Wordsworth in the process. However, besides carefully shedding light on the various roles played by music in each of these regimes, especially after the emergence of the aesthetic regime in the transition between the eighteenth and nineteenth centuries, Kaltenecker draws attention to a recent, noteworthy development: a certain tendency of recent music to devote itself to its own medium, to the materiality of sound devoid of any structuring principle. Though equally interested in Rancière's possible contribution to rewriting the history of musical modernity, João Pedro Cachopo takes another path. Following the logic of *Aisthesis*, he imagines a musical 'scene' based on Hector Berlioz's account of a quarrel between François-Joseph Fétis and Zani de Ferranti on the legitimacy of two notes in *Harold en Italie*. This leads to a reinterpretation of programme music as a proto-cinematic experiment with sounds that eventually suggests the necessity of reappraising the affinity between Romanticism, avant-garde and contemporary trends in musical modernity. Taking as a point of departure Fénelon's *Les Aventures de Télémaque* – a text that has inspired multiple appropriations among the visual and musical arts and that plays a crucial role in Rancière's account of Joseph Jacotot's pedagogy – Katharina Clausius engages an aversion to music that Fénelon thematises in his novel, as well as a conspicuous absence of music in any substantial sense in Jacotot's treatise, and whether these have implications for how Rancière's thought might be developed on musical grounds. And finally, Carina Venter and William Fourie pursue a reading intent on reminding the reader that Rancière's entire political/aesthetic apparatus leaves invisible the fact that Western history of the last several centuries is built on a ground of imperialist/colonialist domination. By focusing on nineteenth-century political/philosophical concerns, and the role that music plays in articulating or valorising Romantic ideals, they promote music to a central position in Rancièrean discourse. They then turn to a close reading of the early history of the Eoan group, a 'coloured' opera company in apartheid South Africa, in order to demonstrate a potential didactics of dissensus that more carefully considers the actual human political ramifications of Rancière's thought.

In Part III, 'Politics of Interaction', relational politics are read in and around music in Rancièrean terms. Interaction unfolds from two perspectives in these essays: inter-ensemble interaction (the politics of relationality in ensemble music-making) and in performer–listener interactions. Kjetil Klette Bøhler considers how interlocking grooves and call–response patterns in contemporary Cuban music generate new forms of political engagement, which he analyses alongside a close reading of the context within which musician Roberto Caracassés enacted a Rancièrean 'wrong' by claiming a voice within a police logic that denied him one. In doing so, music analysis and political/social theory are brought into close dialogue with one another. Dan DiPiero interrogates the aporia between improvisation as a politically emancipatory practice and the essential impossibility of its being so. Beginning by working within music-improvisational practices, he projects outward to consider the contingent aspects of social and political interaction. Music, in this sense, becomes a ground for thinking through the social. Chris Stover, conversely, stages three moments in jazz history as dis-identificatory practices that manage to resist folding back into new police logics, in this way interrogating what happens *after* the event of the dissensual moment and theorising the ways in which new distributions of the sensible are formed and how new police actions are effected from within a community. In doing so he offers an alternative means of disrupting the speech/noise dichotomy: not the political insistence that what was heard as noise now be heard as speech, but that noise itself can carry political meaning in the aesthetic regime.

Part IV, 'Encounters and Challenges', offers a series of encounters between Rancière and other modes of philosophical thought. Sarah Collins engages what Lydia Goehr has presented as an intractable set of problems – art's ability to function as a means to 'memorialise, mourn or resist' acts of violence – by exploring the commemorative implications of (and possibilities for) art from Rancièrean perspectives. Specifically, she explores the Rancièrean paradoxical space in which the politics of aesthetics and the aesthetics of politics inflect one another without coming fully into contact. Collins offers Rancière's reading of artistic monuments as a way in, a way to begin to explore how art (and particularly music) *can* fulfil a commemorative function, and she engages iconic works by Schoenberg and Tippett from this perspective. Murray Dineen reads Adorno's essay 'Motifs' through a Rancièrean lens, finding in Rancière a possible answer to Adorno's call for a means of listening to so-called 'tragic' music from an earlier century. In doing so, he brings key Rancièrean concepts – equality, the sensible, inclusion and exclusion – into compelling dialogue with Adorno's critical apparatus. In 'On Shoemakers and Related Matters: Rancière and Badiou on Richard Wagner', Erik Vogt offers an important re-examination of Badiou's critique of Rancière, on the basis of Wagner's *Die Meistersinger von Nürnberg*. Badiou challenges Rancière's 'melancholic' reading of *Die Meistersinger* (posed on account of what Rancière perceives as an inevitably ever-widening gap between the work of the people and the art of the avant-garde) by positing a conduit between tradition and progress through the work of Wagner's lowly cobbler. Vogt's argument turns on Rancière's challenge to epistemic narratives of modernity, since for Rancière the terms that define a regime are decoupled from historical linearity; the aesthetic regime is a way of doing, a radical erupting-within that, for Vogt (and probably for Rancière) is embodied in the figure of the cobbler as conduit. And finally, as a prelude to proposing an 'equal method' for music studies, Danick Trottier engages the relationship between 'new musicology' and popular music studies to reveal some ways in which musicology, as a discipline, has opened itself to thinking about equality by challenging established hierarchies and the ways in which they have been drawn, not only of repertoires and canon-inclusions, but also of what kinds of musicking practices make valid objects of musicological study.

Notes

1. It might be argued that Rancière's illustrative method of staging a 'scene', with its implied visual bias, is productively problematised when we turn to music.
2. Jacques Rancière, *The Politics of Aesthetics: The Distribution of the Sensible*, trans. Gabriel Rockhill (London: Bloomsbury, 2013), 95.
3. Rancière, *The Politics of Aesthetics*, 18–19.
4. Rancière, *The Politics of Aesthetics*, 19.
5. Jairo Moreno and Gavin Steingo, 'Rancière's Equal Music', *Contemporary Music Review* 31.6 (2013), 487–505.
6. David Brackett, 'The Social Aesthetics of Swing in the 1940s', in Georgina Born, Eric Lewis and Will Straw (eds), *Improvisation and Social Aesthetics* (Durham, NC: Duke University Press, 2017), 119. See also Susan Kozel's chapter, 'Devices of Existence: Contact Improvisation, Mobile Performances, and Dancing Through Twitter', in the same volume, 268–87.
7. Many of the genres, composers and works drawn upon as examples throughout the current volume could, under other circumstances, have been prominent figures within musical arguments put forward by Rancière, and indeed, some of the authors seem – in following Rancière's writing about Gabriel Gauny, Joseph Jacotot and others – to step into Rancière's voice in certain passages. That said, many musics are left aside here; our concern was to prioritise theoretical approaches to Rancière by scholars who had already been engaging Rancière's work in their own writing, which seems to point towards certain interests in long histories of aesthetic and political philosophies. We note this to remind readers of a central facet of Rancière's

work that has often gone unnoticed, particularly by critics who tend to draw primarily on texts such as *The Distribution of the Sensible* to critique Rancière for, as David Brackett has astutely noted, entirely 'avoid[ing] the terrain of mass culture' ('The Social Aesthetics of Swing', 119). Within Rancière's notion of equality and egalitarianism, it is not a contest to see which art, which poetry or which music is *most* egalitarian in its practices, but rather to insist upon carving out the moments of egalitarian logic – the political moments – within the broader histories that we already know intimately. As a result, canonical figures such as Richard Wagner, Iggy Pop, Thelonious Monk and (in particular) Hector Berlioz play major roles here, and few authors take the opportunity to reflect on Rancière's thought to introduce the reader to entirely new musical figures, though the essays by Bøhler, Fourie and Venter, and Kaltenecker certainly focus on lesser-known musical actors.

8. Jacques Rancière, 'Metamorphosis of the Muses', in *Sonic Process: A New Geography of Sounds*, ed. Mela Dávila (Barcelona: Actar, 2002), 17. Rancière makes clear that the opposite is true as well: the visible also asserts itself as autonomously productive.
9. Rancière, 'Metamorphosis of the Muses', 27, 29.
10. Rancière, 'Metamorphosis of the Muses', 27.
11. Jacques Rancière, 'Why Emma Bovary Had to be Killed', *Critical Inquiry* 34.2 (2008), 239.
12. Jacques Rancière, *Aisthesis: Scenes from the Aesthetic Regime of Art*, trans. Zakir Paul (London: Verso, 2013), 97.
13. Rancière, *Aisthesis*, 96–7.
14. Jacques Rancière, *Mute Speech: Literature, Critical Theory, and Politics*, trans. James Swenson (New York: Columbia University Press, 2011), 136.
15. Rancière, *Mute Speech*, 135, 138.
16. Rancière, *Mute Speech*, 137.
17. Rancière, *Aisthesis*, 123.
18. Rancière, *Mute Speech*, 136.
19. Later in *Mute Speech* Rancière posits music as a particular mode of structuring, somewhere between 'form' and 'schizophrenic dissociation' (149). The implications of this characterisation are tantalising, and worth a detailed future investigation.
20. Rancière, 'Why Emma Bovary Had to be Killed', 243. Internal quotes from Gustave Flaubert, 'Lettre à Louise Colet, 26 août 1853', in *Correspondance*, II, ed. Jean Bruneau (Paris: Gallimard, Bibliothèque de la Pléiade, 2007), 417.

21. See, for example, Todd May, *The Political Thought of Jacques Rancière: Creating Equality* (Edinburgh: Edinburgh University Press, 2008).
22. Sudeep Dasgupta, 'Art is Going Elsewhere, and Politics Has to Catch It. An Interview with Jacques Rancière', *Krisis: Journal for Contemporary Philosophy* 9.1 (2008), 73.
23. Rancière, *Mute Speech*, 135.
24. Jacques Rancière, *Aesthetics and Its Discontents*, trans. Steven Corcoran (Malden, MA: Polity, 2009), 24.
25. Jacques Rancière, *Disagreement: Politics and Philosophy*, trans. Julie Rose (Minneapolis: University of Minnesota Press, 1999).
26. Rancière, *Disagreement*, x.
27. Jacques Rancière, 'Ten Theses on Politics', trans. Rachel Bowlby and Davide Panagia, *Theory and Event* 5.3 (2001), ¶23.
28. Bonnie Honig, 'Antigone's Two Laws: Greek Tragedy and the Politics of Humanism', *New Literary History* 41.1 (2010), 20.
29. Jacques Attali's *Noise: The Political Economy of Music*, trans. Brian Massumi (Minneapolis: University of Minnesota Press, 1985), played a seminal role in introducing noise as something to listen to in the world; Attali's book about noise as 'heralding' later changes in the economy first appeared in French in 1977.
30. Jacques Rancière, 'Politique de l'indétermination esthétique', in Jérôme Game and Aliocha Wald Lasowski (eds), *Rancière: Politique de l'esthétique* (Paris: Éditions des Archives contemporaines, 2009), 160; translation by Patrick Nickleson.
31. Rancière, *Aisthesis*, 113.
32. Rancière, *Aisthesis*, 118.
33. Rancière, *Aisthesis*, 122.
34. Rancière, 'Metamorphosis of the Muses', 26.
35. Jacques Rancière, 'Autonomy and Historicity', trans. Patrick Nickleson, *Perspectives of New Music* 57.1–2 (2019). See also Danick Trottier, 'Music, History, Autonomy and Presentness: When Composers and Philosophers Cross Swords', in Martin Kaltenecker and François Nicolas (eds), *Penser l'oeuvre musicale au XXe siècle: avec, sans ou contre l'histoire?* (Paris: Centre de documentation de la musique contemporaine, 2006), 70–85.
36. Jacques Rancière, *Short Voyages to the Land of the People*, trans. James B. Swenson (Stanford: Stanford University Press, 2003), 52.
37. Rancière, *Short Voyages*, 51.
38. Davide Panagia, *Rancière's Sentiments* (Durham, NC: Duke University Press, 2018), 27.

39. See Milton Babbitt, 'Who Cares if You Listen?', anthologised as 'The Composer as Specialist', in *The Collected Essays of Milton Babbitt*, ed. Stephen Peles (Princeton: Princeton University Press, 2003), 48–54. See also Georgina Born, *Rationalizing Culture: IRCAM, Boulez, and the Institutionalization of the Avant-Garde* (Berkeley: University of California Press): '"At the time of the *Domaine*, the only sanction worth giving to a work was not the reaction of an anonymous public but the judgment of equals; the notion of success didn't exist, only recognition by one's peers" ... Thus legitimacy came not from the positive response of the general public, which was disdained, but from the judgment of the elite circle of the *Domaine*' (80). The internal quote is from Pierre-Michel Menger, *Le Paradoxe du musicien: le compositeur, le mélomane et l'État dans la société contemporaine* (Paris: Flammarion/Harmoniques, 1983), 225.
40. Rancière, *Aesthetics and Its Discontents*, 42.
41. See Rancière's essay 'Lyotard and the Aesthetics of the Sublime: A Counter-reading of Kant', in *Aesthetics and Its Discontents*, 88–105.
42. Christopher Small's conception of 'musicking' is a fruitful parallel in this regard, as is Charles Keil's constitution of egalitarian pedagogical spaces through music and dance. See Chris Stover, 'Affect, Play and Becoming-Musicking', in Markus Bolhmann and Anna Catherine Hickey-Moody (eds), *Deleuze and Children* (Edinburgh: Edinburgh University Press, 2018), 145–61.

Part I Music and Noise

I

Musique concrète and the Aesthetic Regime of Art
Loïc Bertrand

In this essay, I propose to think about the emergence of *musique concrète* following the propositions of Jacques Rancière on the aesthetic regime of art. Starting from a text by Pierre Schaeffer on radio, I first highlight the overthrow of *muthos* (the plot or the narrative) in favour of *opsis* (the sensible) that conditions the possibility of *musique concrète*. I show how this overthrow traces a thread in the formation of *musique concrète* through different displacements that took shape in literature, radio and cinema, as well as in the field of sound composition. In doing so, I detail some aspects of a distribution of the sensible that Schaeffer articulates and I show how it belongs to the aesthetic regime of art. The very idea of sound specific to *musique concrète* or the concept of the 'sound in itself' will then appear as resulting from a singular configuration or redistribution of the sensible, where the visible and the audible interweave or oppose each other, where words can become noise and things, making sense or not of the sensible. Through this discussion, we will see that Rancière's propositions can shed new light on *musique concrète*, recapturing its possibilities, its conditions and its limits.

The background and the narrative

Let's take an example. The scene takes place in Champs-Élysées, on November 11th. By chance or by my own free will, I am physically present at the ceremony. For better or for worse, I participate in it: they elbow me, they jostle me, they walk on my feet, and moreover, I do not see much. I make a very practical use of my sonorous and visual perceptions to protect myself on the one hand, and on the other hand, to satisfy the curiosity, which is certainly vain, but almost automatically occupies me. Where are we? What is happening? This waving flag, this music, these applauses or this sudden rumor, so many signs immediately interpreted and forgotten in the expectation of the continuation ... Comfortably installed in the penumbra, I attend the same parade that presents me the Newsreel. I do not participate, I attend the event: it is banal. Without anything unforeseen, everyone holds his role. The soldiers march in step, the crowd rushes, the anchorman announces the usual solemnities. It's prose again, and the most flat one ... I'm at home. I listen to the radio, a reporter tells me what's going on. Behind this voice is a logical set: crowd noise, snoring of engines, music. I go straight to the meaning, that of the commentary, that of the rumor. As soon as it took place 'the form, that is to say the physical, the sensible' dissolves in clarity. But sometimes, because the music, the noise of the crowd, or the huge painting of the ceremony covers the reporter's voice, or because his speech, suddenly, 'the very act of (his) speech' interests me more than what he says, 'something new is declared'. I leave logic for the sensible, stop understanding [*comprendre*] to listen [*écouter*]. The words, the precise facts they bear no longer matter. What touches me, for example, is the dialogue established between a single voice and the collective rumble that sometimes submerges and sometimes supports it, the rhythm and the contexture of what was previously only a background in which the narrative was detached.[1]

These lines, extracted from *Notes sur l'expression radiophonique*, were written in 1944 by Pierre Schaeffer, a few years before the official 'birth' of *musique concrète* (1948), while the young engineer of the ORTF (Office de Radiodiffusion Télévision Française) was in search of a radio art. To grasp the properties of radio, Schaeffer evaluates the effects of broadcasting on the perception of an event. Here, we find terms that foreshadow *musique concrète*: the difference between understanding (*comprendre*) and hearing (*entendre*) is decisive. But this distinction is taken in a more general reversal, which moves from the 'logical' to the 'sensible', and which Schaeffer makes explicit by opposing the background (*toile de fond*) and the narrative (*récit*). This reversal resonates with Rancière's claim of the overthrow of the Aristotelian hierarchy between *muthos* (intelligible plot) and *opsis* (sensible effect). It makes explicit the passage between a regime where everything is given by speech, where the sensible dissolves in clarity, and another regime where the narrative sinks in the anonymous rumble of the background. According to Rancière, this overturn marks the transition from the representative regime to the aesthetic regime of art. One can thus put forward the hypothesis that Schaeffer's thwarted fable prefiguring *musique concrète* also stands out as an *aesthetic* moment.[2]

The reversal between *muthos* and *opsis* achieves a redistribution of the sensible explicit in Schaeffer's text: the reporter's voice and the background noises enter into a single sound fabric. In another part of the *Notes sur l'expression radiophonique*, Schaeffer articulates this equalisation otherwise, by discussing the broadcast of a live theatre performance:

> This broadcast from a theater, is it really that of a play? Does it not present the stage and the room together? What fascinates me more than the play – professional deformation? – is this *sound halo*, this heavy silence interspersed with parasitic noises, these scrapings, these coughs, all that which composes a reality in the nascent state which the philosophers of existence should take the trouble to bend.[3]

The radio brings to the fore a drama that is no longer that of classical theatre. It not only dilutes the plot, but abolishes the gap between the auditorium and the stage. Thus, we could say that it revokes the privilege of theatre as a separate space of representation.[4] Schaeffer expresses it simply by saying: 'The stage of radio, it is the whole world; its audience, a single man.'[5] But this redistribution of places and roles of the audience and the actors or the crossing of the narrative and the noises is not only an effect of the broadcast. Following Rancière, it first refers to an idea of art – the unity of the auditorium and the stage – which, before Schaeffer, came paradoxically from theatre and staging.[6]

In Schaeffer's text, the unity of the auditorium and the stage forms a *halo* which actualises the visual metaphor of radio as a radial or a circle that brings together the audience and the stage. In this sense, it points out a redistribution of the sensible which is also political. The image of the halo also plays a decisive role in Rancière's aesthetics: taken from the novels of Virginia Woolf and Joseph Conrad and applied to those of Gustave Flaubert, the *luminous halo* designates for Rancière the effect of a multiplicity of sensible micro-events (*opsis*) rather than the necessary sequences of the narrative (*muthos*).[7] In the same way, Schaeffer's *sound halo* makes the real appear in its nascent state. It reveals 'the naked fact that something is happening'.[8] It refers to a specific regime of the sensible that suspends the frames of representation.

The metaphor of the halo also indicates that Schaeffer's attention to sounds, silences and noises appears under a certain light that conditions the perception of sonic details.[9] What becomes audible is given in a certain relation to the visible. In other words, the sensible is always distributed, as Rancière puts it. In this case, it is mediated by words and by a visual metaphor. Sound then appears like an audio-visual complex that is always mediated by the speakable: this configuration defines what we could call, following Rancière, a distribution of the sensible that questions the dichotomy of the visible and the audible. Two relations will thus have to be clarified in the following sections: on the one hand, the entanglement of the audible and the visible, even when they seem to oppose each other; and, on the other hand, the relationship of this audio-visual complex to the words that shape and state it.

The descriptive excess

For Rancière, the overthrow of *muthos* happens in literature with descriptive proliferation.[10] Traditionally, literary description provides details, it depicts and suspends narration yet remains subsumed under it.[11] However, with the growing place of description in the realist novel of the nineteenth century, the world of stories is invaded by an excess of things. So-called insignificant details proliferate and can no longer be reduced to narrative functions.[12] For Rancière, the very rationality of fiction changed in this process. Literature, as a 'suspensive mode of speech'[13] specific to the aesthetic regime, thus became the locus of a fundamental *dissensus* that alters the places and roles of bodies and speech.

Thus, descriptive proliferation is not only the invasion of prosaic reality into the work of art. According to Rancière, it also marks the rupture of the representative regime.[14] It signals the ruin of strategic action: 'the real is no longer a space of strategic deployment for thoughts and wishes. It is the chain of perceptions and affects that weaves these thoughts and wills themselves.'[15] The descriptive excess frees sensible events from necessary sequences of the fiction.[16] It substitutes a succession of facts for the organic totality,[17] the simultaneity of sensible micro-events for the temporal chain of actions.

For Rancière, then, the 'jump' out of mimesis was not done

through abstraction, but through realism, which does not mean the valorisation of the resemblance but the destruction of the frames in which it worked.[18] This claim is one way to think about the introduction of noise in *musique concrète*. It could thus be supposed that the realist novel and *musique concrète* follow a similar aesthetic approach which breaks with the logic and the continuity of the narrative, the temporal schemas and their sequences of causes and effects (structure), and which makes room for so-called insignificant details, things or noises (singularities). Rancière warns, however, against the usual simplification in term of material and structure: 'What is at stake in this excess is not the opposition between bare singularity and structure. It is the conflict of two distributions of the sensible. This conflict disappears when the superfluous "detail" is opposed to the functionality of structure.'[19]

According to Rancière, literary realism refers to 'democracy in literature' – hence the canonical formula that regulates literature and 'the famous Flaubertian principle: there are no beautiful or ugly subjects, no reason to prefer Constantinople – the splendours of the Orient and of History – to Yvetot – the dampness and history-less dullness of the French hinterland'.[20] In other words, '[e]verything is now on the same level, the great and the small, important events and insignificant episodes, human beings and things. Everything is equal, equally representable.'[21] This aspect is essential to the founding of the aesthetic regime of art. Rancière made it especially clear with modern fiction. But we could say that a similar distribution of the sensible stands at the heart of *musique concrète*: 'For the concrete musician, there is no difference between the cut bell and the piece of train: they are fragments of sounds.'[22] Equalising the music of a bell with the noise of a train by fragmenting both, Schaeffer exemplifies a 'democracy' in sound, as Flaubert did in literature. Does this mean that there is a common politics of *music* and *literature*? It is interesting to note that Rancière uses a musical metaphor to describe the texture of the realist novel:

> This fabric was first the new music of indistinction between the ordinary and the extraordinary, which seizes within the same tonality the life of servants in the countryside and those of great ladies of the capital, the music expressing the capacity of anyone to experience any form of sensible experience.[23]

It seems that Rancière invests music with an aesthetic function. Music undoes the necessary relation between a way of doing (*poesis*) and a way of sensing (*aisthesis*) which was characteristic of the representative regime. 'The end of *mimesis* . . . is the end of the mimetic legislation whereby a productive nature and a sensible nature were to fit. With this end, the muses cede their place to music.'[24] In Rancière's aesthetic, music and literature are parallel terms: they are different names for the same idea of art, the art of the aesthetic regime, which can be said in the singular.[25] But what about *musique concrète*, which questions the material, the space and forms of music? If *musique concrète* seems at first to reflect some aspects of the aesthetic regime, does it not also complicate the idea of music and its relation to literature? If the realist novel mentions the raw noises of everyday life, can we really subscribe to Rancière's idea that it is the same 'noise' that also crosses music?[26] This thesis postulates not only the reducibility of the words of literature to the sounds of music, but also supposes the priority of the speakable over the sensible, of enunciation over visibilities, of literature over music.[27]

Language of things and mute speech

Schaeffer's sound experiments are certainly incorporated into the fabric of his thought as a writer.[28] A regime of perception is built within a discursive regime. This Foucauldian entanglement of the speakable and the sensible, which reflects in Rancière's distribution of the sensible, is articulated by Schaeffer in a singular formula, the 'language of things', which anticipates the definition of *musique concrète*.[29]

In the tripartite article 'L'élément non-visuel au cinéma', where he considers the relationships of music, speech and noise to image, Schaeffer writes: '[n]oise is the only sound perfectly adequate to the image, because the image can only show things and noise is the language of things'.[30] This idea of a 'language of things' already appeared in the *Essai sur la radio et le cinéma*: 'Silences speak; the slightest noise, a sheet of crumpled paper, the slamming of a door, and our ears seem to hear for the first time. Yes, things now have a language, even up to the similarity of words that express it: image that is the language for the eye; and noise that is the one for the ear.'[31]

Schaeffer's language of things illustrates Rancière's thesis that there is, in the centre of the aesthetic regime of art, the idea of a thought that does not think. For there to be a 'language of things', there must be thought at work in the foreign element of non-thought and non-thought that inhabits thought.[32] This identity of opposites plays a key role in Rancière's aesthetic regime: it articulates enunciation and visibility by reversing their roles, active and passive respectively. The idea of thought as the identity of opposites corresponds to Rancière's idea of writing as mute speech, a speech that speaks and is silent at the same time. That's *literature*.[33] Schaeffer's language of things thus mirrors Rancière's mute speech, in so far as it refers to this same idea of thought. It blurs the divisions between noise and voice, things and human beings, *phōnē* and *logos*. Speech is no longer opposed to noise. For Schaeffer, it becomes 'the rumor of the characters'.[34] Things begin to speak for themselves when the human being loses speech as a power of signification, as a hold on the real. Schaeffer thus discerns an area where the human is no longer distinguished from the non-human, a *no man's land* that he makes his field of research.

According to Rancière, mute speech can be understood in two ways. It is, first of all, the speech of silent things, the power of signification inscribed on their bodies: the writer is seeking to give these insignificant details of the world their power of signification. But there is another form of mute speech, of the identity of *logos* and *pathos*. It is no longer that of the hieroglyph subject to a decipherment, but the speech as soliloquy, speaking to no one, saying nothing but the impersonal and unconscious conditions of speech itself.[35]

We could say that Schaeffer oscillates between these two poles of mute speech. He first takes the language of things as a hieroglyph, a clue or a symptom (or index): 'I realised not surprisingly by recording the sound of things that we could perceive beyond the sounds, the daily metaphors they offer us.'[36] A detail, the slightest intonation, the least noise, could tell us more about a character than what is said. In this way, no detail is regarded as insignificant. As Schaeffer puts it: 'This sound datum, ordinarily so precarious, without form or intention, had become a monument, a document, a material for analysis and psychoanalysis.'[37] The language of things opens to a different reality, which cannot be fully translated into words. It reveals a fundamental alterity, a strangeness in the familiar, an estrangement. Things resist words so well that

Schaeffer opposes a *chosage* to the human *language*: an unnamed power that stands behind consciousness, that exceeds all meaning and cannot be translated into words, and that corresponds to the second aspect of mute speech.

It is this second aspect of mute speech that seems to prevail, for Schaeffer, after the *Études de bruit* (1948), the very first experiments of Schaeffer's *musique concrète*. Thus, the *Symphonie pour un homme seul* (1950), the main work following the first experiments, realised with Pierre Henry and Jacques Poullin, seeks to give an anonymous voice, a ghostly body, to this unnamed power. There are two importants reasons for this shift. The first is the very possibilities afforded by the radio medium, its capacity as a 'writing of the *opsis*' to inscribe the sounds of things without words. The second is a specific idea of music, whose function, according to Rancière, is to express the unspeakable.[38] Schaeffer's language of things indicates that if a new idea of sound takes form through words, if the sensible is woven into the speakable, it also brings language to its own limits.

Radio, literature and cinema

Radio presents specific means to record noises, and its possibilities are very different from those of literature. Schaeffer explains it clearly:

> To describe or evoke the slightest thing, language gets bogged down in interminable efforts, and the result is always disappointing. Clever at defining the nature of things, it is nevertheless very difficult for language to define its forms. Cinema and radio have precisely the opposite powers ... If language has power over the abstract, cinema and radio have real power over the concrete. If language expresses the nature of things, cinema and radio express themselves through the forms of things and in the sense that humans no longer could.[39]

Introducing the idea of the *concrete*, Schaeffer points out literature's limit, which brings back the particularity of literature, its excess. Words say too much, they are always in excess when it comes to grasping the sensible form of things.[40] The means of mechanical reproduction or broadcast available with radio and cinema open up new horizons. They do not make visible or audible things as human beings conceive or name them: the images and the noises of radio or cinema offer a specific language that is not made of signs but of signals, a concrete language recorded passively by the machine. It is this hold over the concrete which distinguishes for Schaeffer the mechanical arts or *art-relais* from the imitative arts.

Schaeffer was not the only one to dream of a direct access to things. In 'The Cinema', Virginia Woolf evoked the possibility of a secret language that would make things appear directly, a language that we can feel but not speak.[41] More than any other art, cinema has embodied this utopia of what Rancière calls a 'writing of the *opsis*'.[42] It's not a coincidence then that Schaeffer keeps coming back to cinema to develop his conception of a radiophonic art. In *Notes sur l'expression radiophonique*, he echoes Jean Epstein on the cinematograph: 'The radio reports the truth reality ... It shows people who stammer and hesitate, adventures without a subject.'[43] It is the same 'tragedy in suspense' that radio and cinema propose, a new fiction that opposes the conventions and expectations of dramatic action to reveal the intimate texture of things,[44] a writing of the *opsis* able to bring indescribable things or noises to perception.

Like *cinéma pur*, an autonomous radio art should explore the power of the machine that records things as they are, without subjecting them to the necessities of an intelligible plot. But this utopia of pure presence, this 'naked reality adorned with the new splendor of the insignificant',[45] does not refer, according to Rancière, to the nakedness of the thing opposed to the meanings of representation. Presence and representation are always two regimes of entanglement of words and forms.

The *chosage* is still a *language*. And if Schaeffer is seeking an autonomous radiophonic art, he still envisages it in relation to, even if conflictual with, literature:

> From the point of view of genres, a purely radiophonic art, which is neither information nor entertainment, is similar to the short story [*nouvelle*]. As in the short story, we can go from description to action, from dialogue to commentary, from the story of the characters to the reflections of the narrator.[46]

Schaeffer is particularly sensitive to the fact that radio can penetrate 'the inner space' and alter time and space perceptions.[47] By crossing beyond the wall of representation to enter this place where thought equals matter,[48] the radio accomplishes the metaphysics of literature.

As a writing of the *opsis*, radio reveals a matter equal to mind. Schaeffer sums it up in a pithy statement: 'Radio has the qualities of our thought.'[49] The radiophonic phenomenon establishes an intensive conjunction between two irreducible terms, 'the stream of time through all the space and the frozen duration of a motionless consciousness'.[50] This identity between an active principle and a passive one, between the interior and the exterior, between thought and things, abolishes, according to Rancière, the very foundation of *mimesis*, the opposition between deceptive appearances and substantial reality: 'Thought and things, the exterior and the interior are pulled together in the same texture indistinctly sensible and intelligible.'[51] This is specific to the aesthetic regime of art. Radio, like cinema, can overthrow the old Aristotelian hierarchy that privileged *muthos* – the coherence of the plot – and devalued *opsis* – the spectacle's sensible effect – because it settles the quarrel between thought and sensibility, it resolves the question of *mimesis* at its roots, it presents a matter equivalent to mind.[52]

Microphone and disfiguration

Radio's capacity to reveal an immaterial matter comes from the power of the microphone. But Schaeffer understands the power of the microphone,[53] comparing it to the movie camera:

> This face now fills the screen. Let the camera come closer, and the eye, isolated, begins to live a harrowing, savage life for itself. The microphone can confer the same importance and then – if it pushes the magnification further – the same dimension of strangeness, to a whisper, to a heartbeat, to the ticking of a watch. Between several shots, whether sound or visual, it becomes possible to develop arbitrary relations, to reverse proportions, to contradict everyday experience.[54]

It is the invention of the close-up that guides Schaeffer to identify the power of the microphone. The proximity to the text of Jean Epstein's *L'Intelligence d'une machine* is striking:

> The close-up is another attack on the familiar order of appearances. The image of an eye, a hand, a mouth that fills the entire screen – not

only because it is magnified three hundred times, but also because we see it isolated from the organic whole – attains a characteristic of bestial autonomy. This eye, these fingers, these lips are already beings that each possess their own boundaries, movements, life and finality. They exist by themselves.[55]

For Schaeffer, cinema plays a crucial role in the construction of a new sound sensibility: 'The microphone delivers details, contrasts, a depth that vision was masking. A close parallelism can be established in this respect between radio and the silent film.'[56] Of course, this parallel is twisted, as the mute image of the silent film opposes itself to the blind listening of the radio. But both media present a disjunction, a gap between visibilities and enunciation, between audible and visible, sensible and speakable.

Schaeffer's vision, however, does not only result from the work of a machine. The dual power of the microphone, magnifying and separating, isolates details from bodies. But these fragments are not only detached from the body of individuals, they are also separated from the body symbolising the narrative (*muthos*). The loose details of the plot, given for themselves, and the arbitrary relationships they can establish contradict both the necessary sequencing of narrative and daily experience. This process of fragmentation and defamiliarisation is what Rancière calls *disfiguration*.

Disfiguration is the activity of reconfiguration of that which is given to the sensible.[57] The microphone realises such a disfiguration because it transforms the listening without necessarily changing the nature of the sound.[58] It reveals what was already there, unheard. It separates and magnifies details, it reverses proportions: the scream wafts less than a whisper.[59] But the disfiguration finds a new accomplishment when the sound is cut from its visual source: 'The microphone makes purely sonic versions of events. Without transforming the sound, it transforms the listening.'[60]

The dissociation of sound from sight has many effects: 'Releasing us from sight, the organ of external description constantly detecting our voluntary activities, the microphone frees us from the slavery of the event. It unmasks the sonic form.'[61] The microphone does not only separate sound from sight. It frees us from a paradigm of action that focuses on external visibility. It exposes, on the contrary, an inner drama, an immobile theatre, defined by Rancière in another context: 'It consists of silent sensations through which any individual experiences the silent action of the world.'[62]

Cutting sound from the visual (*acousmatic*) represents a founding moment for *musique concrète*, as it allows focus on 'the sound itself'. Absence of sight, however, does not mean that there is no more visibility. Following Rancière's propositions, we could say that the field of the visible is redistributed. Thus Schaeffer comments on the 'blind listening' of radio: 'Blind, seeing through this new sense that are the eyes of the other and our own ears, we are possessed.'[63] The radio listener does not see but becomes 'clairvoyant'. They can see or guess what they do not see, through sounds or noises becoming index. Schaeffer may be responding here to critics of radio as a mutilated art.[64] He suggests that radio does not lack anything. It is complete, and not because the listener restores the logic of events to an invisible show. The vision of the blind listener produces something new. The main question here is one of a 'new sense' that articulates in the same sensorium the visible and the audible but in a very specific way: a sensorium that incorporates the eyes of the others (the ones who were there to record a scene and thus saw what was happening) and our own ears (the ears of the listener who only gets an acoustic experience, cut from the visual scene from which it was extracted). Thus radio is not presented as a 'voice without body'. The link established between the visible, the audible and the speakable, the distribution of the sensible on which Schaeffer relies to define a new sound sensibility, draws in fact the contours of a new body, which implies a community of bodies, giving a political dimension to this new sensorium.

Dissensus

We can now return to the beginnings of *musique concrète* to consider its 'birth' no longer as the sudden discovery of a new world, as Schaeffer likes to put it, but as the endpoint of a series of displacements and the formulation, in the sound field, of a specific regime of art that had already crossed literature, theatre and cinema. What Schaeffer first sees in radio is a medium that establishes a specific relationship between sound and image. As he recalls, *musique concrète* is born from the fact that radio is a blind art and that one tries to see with the ears, thereby reconfiguring the sensorium to dislocate sight from its predominant place.[65] Originally, the idea was to find in noises the setting (*décor*) which the eyes of the listeners were deprived of. Thus, the work on sound effects led to the creation, in 1943–44, of the radio opera *La Coquille à planètes*.[66] In this radio work, however, speech remains central and noises still hold a traditional decorative function. At this point, noises simply illustrate, anticipate or follow the action defined by the text. Now, this distribution refers to the first representative rule defined by Rancière: like the image, noise enters into a relation of subordination between a leading function, the textual function of intelligibility (*muthos*) and an imaging function put at its service (*opsis*).[67] It is this distribution, where the noise holds a representative function, that changed with the *Études de bruits* in 1948.

What became *Études de bruits* was first projected as a Symphony of Noises. Looking for material in the ORTF sound effects department, Schaeffer found objects such as clickers, coconuts, horns and trumpets. He wanted to take with him a set of bells, an alarm clock, two rattles and two turnstiles, but the service attendant was suspicious. Schaeffer comments: 'Usually, he [the attendant] is asked for a particular accessory. There is no "noise" without text, right? But what if someone wants the noise without the text, without the context?'[68] While accumulating objects, Schaeffer decided to get rid of the text. And without text, noise is no longer a 'sound effect' or a 'decor'. Free from its illustrative functions, it presents itself as a new sound material. Thus this turn breaks with the logic of representation. Schaeffer recalled it in this way:

> The findings of 1948 surprise me. I came to the studio to 'let noises talk', to get the most out of a 'dramatic sound stage', but that leads me to music. By means of accumulating sounds with index values, these indices end up canceling each other out, no longer evoking the scenery or the adventures of any action, but articulating for themselves, forming between them sound chains, of course *hybrids*. Although fragments of words or sentences may be contained (like plant inclusions in minerals), it goes without saying that they are roundabout, if not from their meaning, at least from their use. A kind of sound poetry, in absence of music, is thus created *ex abrupto*.[69]

Schaeffer confirmed the same idea later: 'It is by means of accumulating noises in the studio in search for dramatic effects that I have advised myself that they exceed the texts which they were supposed to illustrate.'[70] The birth of *musique concrète* coincides with the reversal of the *muthos*, which happens by proliferation or excess, as it did in literature according to Rancière. Because of their accumulation, the fragments of sound no longer follow narrative sequences and can therefore be taken for themselves.

As Schaeffer suggests, this moment is also supposed to mark the passage from the dramatic to the musical. But this transition is problematic. Accumulating sound objects does not make music but creates something that Schaeffer calls sound poetry, because of the discontinuity of these objects. To become music, it would be necessary, according to Schaeffer, to tear away completely from drama and to create a new continuity. In its radical version, Schaeffer's position is that only when sounds no longer refer to any anecdote, any referent or meaning (listening by reference), can they be the subject of music. Schaeffer thus opposes the musical to the dramatic and therefore seeks to define the conditions of a 'reduced' listening.[71]

After Schaeffer, studies on *musique concrète* mainly focused on issues of reduced listening, the acousmatic cut and the sound object. We could, however, displace this point of view and consider *musique concrète* in another way. Following Rancière's idea of the distribution of the sensible and the reversal of *muthos*, it appears that the most decisive moment in the emergence of *musique concrète* was Schaeffer's break with the narrative (*muthos*), rather than reduced listening, the latter being a consequence of the former. A well-known principle of *musique concrète* could illustrate this point. The locked groove enabled Schaeffer to create a loop of sound. It makes it possible to extract bits of sound from a phonograph record (before audiotape came into use) and to repeat them indefinitely. Thanks to repetition, the loop helps the passage from referential listening (where the listener focuses on the source of the sound) to reduced listening (where the listener centres on the 'sound in itself'). The locked groove is then often taken as the best example to illustrate the idea of reduced listening. But the example also shows something else: the loop is first of all a power of rupture from the narrative. It opposes 'History' [sic], writes Schaeffer, because it is isolated from any context and its repetition cancels the perception of a beginning and an end. The fragment of sound becomes then, for Schaeffer, a 'crystal of time'.[72]

Echoing Epstein and Deleuze,[73] the concept of 'crystal of time' follows an aesthetic requisite defined by Rancière as a counter-logic that stops all progression and that makes perceptible a suspended time.[74] With fragments, loops and slowdowns, the first procedures of *musique concrète* thus question the idea of time and development, as well as the traditional 'language' of music. Schaeffer opposes a 'geometry of the fragment' to the 'arithmetic of the note', a succession of sound objects to the musical phrase or development.[75] More than reduced listening, its necessity or possibility, another dilemma then arises: how can heterogeneous fragments create a coherent and continuous whole? Or as Rancière puts it in the context of the realist novel: how can the anti-representative atoms of the sensible reinsert into the mimetic circle?[76]

This conflict between the disruptive power of the sensible and a narrative logic stands at the core of *musique concrète*, defining its conditions, its possibilities and its limits. Three solutions to this conflict can be identified in the work of Schaeffer. The first relies entirely on the material. It was adopted by Schaeffer at the very beginning of his research: 'Thus, without the help of any melody, of any harmony, it would suffice to know how to detect and taste, in the most mechanical monotony, the game of some atoms of freedom, the imperceptible improvisations of chance.'[77] The composer is no longer the one who imposes an order on passive matter (representative order).[78] Rather, the composer is content to record the improvisations of chance and to hear it as a possible symphony (a position quite near that of John Cage). However, Schaeffer abandoned this posture for another, which consists of organising the sound fragments according to the principles of *montage*. Montage presents an alternative to the narrative model. It is capable of reconciling a raw material with the necessity of a form. The succession of sound objects in montage also makes it possible to consider large-scale compositions such as the *Symphonie pour un homme seul* in contrast with short forms such as the *Études de bruit*. But Schaeffer is not satisfied with what he pejoratively calls collages.[79] The montage does not build the continuity that he seeks: a perfect continuum fusing noise and speech that represents another solution to the tension between material and form. This continuity, which would signify a return to music,[80] would not be realised. As early as 1952, Schaeffer abandoned all compositional will in favour of developing a *solfège* of the sound object, which focuses on the internal structure of the objects, their morphology, and not on the global structure that would organise them in one ensemble.

Considering the idea of an overthrow of *muthos* brings us to understand the formation of *musique concrète* as an aesthetic moment undoing first of all the logic of representation. The overthrow of *muthos*, drawn in a fiction or realised in a studio, appears as a necessary condition to think, to hear or to name the 'sound in itself'. It also shows that the idea of an autonomy of sound arises in a certain configuration or redistribution of the sensible that weaves together the audible, the visible and the speakable. But the emphasis on *opsis* that I have drawn attention to in this essay is always counterbalanced with the necessity of a *muthos*. I would suggest that this tension between the disruptive power of the sensible and the continuity of a narrative reflects the tension between the conditions of *musique concrète*, as *concrete*, and its ambitions, as *music*. If this conflict remained unresolved, it does not mean the failure of *musique concrète*. It shows a conflict between *muthos* and *opsis*, or a conflict of temporalities, specific to the aesthetic regime of art, and that crosses *musique concrète*.

The distribution of the sensible then presents an apt framework for questioning the developments as well as the crisis of *musique concrète*. If they can bring useful elements to renew studies of *musique concrète* or, more generally, to open new perspectives for research on the aesthetics of sound, Rancière's propositions could also be put into question. In our discussion, one question has arisen that seems especially important. I will try to formulate it to end this essay. It concerns the idea of music as a coherent concept. Rancière's propositions helped us to see *musique concrète* as an aesthetic moment. If *musique concrète* belongs to the aesthetic regime of art, it also departs from an idea of music as a representative regime. We saw this tension at work in the project of *musique concrète*. This distinction thus questions the unity of the concept of music on the one hand, and Rancière's suggestion that music belongs to the aesthetic regime of art, on the other. It then becomes necessary to ask whether the aesthetic moment of *musique concrète* still belongs to music or whether it opens up another idea of music, the characteristics of which would still have to be defined.

Notes

1. Pierre Schaeffer, 'Notes sur l'expression radiophonique', in *Machines à communiquer 1: genèse des simulacres* (Paris: Seuil, 1970), 106–7. All translations are mine unless otherwise indicated.

2. In his text, Schaeffer comments on and quotes a text from Paul Valéry, 'Poésie et pensée abstraite', in *Variété V* (Paris: Gallimard, 1944), 151–5, where Valéry expands on the concept of regime to understand what makes a poetic moment.
3. Schaeffer, 'Notes sur l'expression radiophonique', 95–6.
4. Jacques Rancière, *Le Destin des images* (Paris: La fabrique, 2003), 138.
5. Schaeffer, 'Notes sur l'expression radiophonique', 99.
6. Jacques Rancière, *Aisthesis: scènes du régime esthétique de l'art* (Paris: Galilée, 2011), 222. Schaeffer was exposed to ideas of new theatre when he worked with Jacques Copeau for the very first experiments on radio in 1942 at the Stage de Beaune, which focuses on the radiophonic voice.
7. Jacques Rancière, *Le Fil perdu* (Paris: La fabrique, 2014), 39.
8. Schaeffer, 'Notes sur l'expression radiophonique', 195.
9. Rancière, *Le Fil perdu*, 30.
10. Rancière, *Le Fil perdu*, 17–36.
11. Gérard Genette, 'Frontières de la narration', in *L'Analyse structurale du récit* (Paris: Seuil, 1981), 158–69.
12. Rancière, *Le Fil perdu*, 30.
13. Jacques Rancière, *La Chair des mots. Politiques de l'écriture* (Paris: Galilée, 1998), 190.
14. Rancière, *Le Fil perdu*, 22–3.
15. Rancière, *Le Fil perdu*, 31.
16. Rancière, *Le Fil perdu*, 33.
17. Rancière, *Le Fil perdu*, 21.
18. Jacques Rancière, *Le Partage du sensible* (Paris: La fabrique, 2000), 34.
19. Rancière, *Le Fil perdu*, 30.
20. Rancière, *La Chair des mots*, 181.
21. Rancière, *La Chair des mots*, 136.
22. Pierre Schaeffer, *À la recherche d'une musique concrète* (Paris: Seuil, 1952), 27.
23. Rancière, *Le Fil perdu*, 29.
24. Jacques Rancière, 'La Métamorphose des muses', in *Sonic Process: une nouvelle géographie des sons* (Paris: Centre Georges Pompidou, 2002), 30.
25. Rancière, *Le Partage du sensible*, 33.
26. Rancière refers to Varèse's *Ionisation* (1929–31). See Jacques Rancière, *Aesthetics and Its Discontents*, trans. Steven Corcoran (Cambridge: Polity, 2009), 5.

27. Similar questions are addressed to Rancière regarding the relations of painting and literature. See Jérôme Game and Aliocha Wald Lasowski (eds), *Jacques Rancière. Politique de l'esthétique* (Paris: Édition des Archives Contemporaines, 2009), 137–48. On the relations between the speakable and the visible as a problematic partly inherited from Foucault, see Gilles Deleuze, *Foucault* (Paris: Minuit, 1986).
28. Marc Pierret, *Entretiens avec Pierre Schaeffer* (Paris: Pierre Belfond, 1969), 91.
29. See Loïc Bertrand, 'The Language of Things: An Archaeology of *musique concrète*', *Organised Sounds* 22.3 (2017), 254–61.
30. Pierre Schaeffer, 'L'élément non-visuel au cinéma (I): analyse de la bande "son"', *La revue du cinéma*, 1 (1946), 45.
31. Pierre Schaeffer, *Essai sur la radio et le cinéma: esthétique et technique des arts-relais, 1941–1942* (Paris: Allia, 2010), 49.
32. Jacques Rancière, *L'Inconscient esthétique* (Paris: Galilée, 2001), 33.
33. 'La littérature est le déploiement et le déchiffrement de ces signes qui sont inscrits à même les choses.' Jacques Rancière, *Politique de la littérature* (Paris: Galilée, 1998), 24.
34. Pierre Schaeffer, 'L'élément non-visuel au cinéma (II): psychologie du rapport vision-audition', *La revue du cinéma*, 2 (1946), 62.
35. Rancière, *L'Inconscient esthétique*, 39.
36. Schaeffer, 'Notes sur l'expression radiophonique', 109.
37. Schaeffer, 'Notes sur l'expression radiophonique', 105.
38. See Rancière's lecture on Béla Tarr at Centre Pompidou, Paris, 13 January 2012, <https://www.dailymotion.com/video/xnbtrd> (last accessed 15 May 2019).
39. Schaeffer, *Essai sur la radio et le cinéma*, 53.
40. In 1942 Francis Ponge wrote *Le Parti pris des choses* against the infidelity of speech.
41. Virginia Woolf, *Le Cinéma et autres essais* (Paris: Les Éditions de Paris, 2012), 16. 'The Cinema' was first published on 3 July 1926 in *The Nation and Athenaeum* in London. See also the chapter on Virginia Woolf in Bill Brown, *Other Things* (Chicago: University of Chicago Press, 2015).
42. Jacques Rancière, *La Fable cinématographique* (Paris: Seuil, 2001), 22.
43. Schaeffer, 'Notes sur l'expression radiophonique', 93.
44. Rancière, *La Fable cinématographique*, 7–40.
45. Rancière, *La Fable cinématographique*, 11.

46. Schaeffer, 'Notes sur l'expression radiophonique', 110.
47. Schaeffer, 'Notes sur l'expression radiophonique', 112.
48. Rancière, *La Chair des mots*, 184.
49. Schaeffer, 'Notes sur l'expression radiophonique', 95.
50. Schaeffer, 'Notes sur l'expression radiophonique', 93.
51. Rancière, *La Fable cinématographique*, 10.
52. Rancière, *La Fable cinématographique*, 9–10.
53. Schaeffer, 'Notes sur l'expression radiophonique', 103.
54. Schaeffer, 'Notes sur l'expression radiophonique', 104.
55. Jean Epstein, *L'Intelligence d'une machine*, in *Écrits sur le cinéma, 1921–1953*, vol. 1 (Paris: Seghers, 1974), 256.
56. Schaeffer, 'Notes sur l'expression radiophonique', 103.
57. Rancière, *Le Destin des images*, 87.
58. Schaeffer, 'Notes sur l'expression radiophonique', 102.
59. Schaeffer, 'Notes sur l'expression radiophonique', 101.
60. Schaeffer, 'Notes sur l'expression radiophonique', 103.
61. Schaeffer, 'Notes sur l'expression radiophonique', 109. See also Brian Kane, *Sound Unseen: Acousmatic Sound in Theory and Practice* (Oxford: Oxford University Press, 2014).
62. Rancière, *Aisthesis*, 141.
63. Schaeffer, 'Notes sur l'expression radiophonique', 95.
64. This question appears at the core of the work of Arnheim on radio. See the idea of 'blind hearing' in Rudolf Arnheim, *Radio*, trans. Margaret Ludwig and Herbert Read (London: Faber and Faber, 1936), ch. 7.
65. Interview with Max-Pol Fouchet in *Lectures pour tous* (Pierre Desgraupes), 17 June 1959.
66. Libretto by Pierre Schaeffer and music by Claude Arrieu.
67. Rancière, *Le Destin des images*, 49.
68. Schaeffer, *À la recherche d'une musique concrète*, 12.
69. Pierre Schaeffer, *La Musique concrète* (Paris: PUF ['Que sais-je ?'], 1967), 18.
70. Pierre Schaeffer, *De la musique concrète à la musique même*, La Revue musicale, vols 303–5 (Paris: Richard-Masse, 1977), 170.
71. Schaeffer, *À la recherche d'une musique concrète*, 20.
72. Schaeffer, *À la recherche d'une musique concrète*, 40.
73. Rancière, *La Fable cinématographique*, 18.
74. Rancière, *La Fable cinématographique*, 97.
75. Schaeffer, *À la recherche d'une musique concrète*, 115.
76. Rancière, *La Chair des mots*, 185.
77. Schaeffer, *À la recherche d'une musique concrète*, 15.

78. Rancière, *L'Inconscient esthétique*, 25.
79. Schaeffer, *À la recherche d'une musique concrète*, 90.
80. Schaeffer, *À la recherche d'une musique concrète*, 90.

2

'Rip it up and start again': Reconfigurations of the Audible under the Aesthetic Regime of the Arts
Daniel Frappier

In May 2016 Iggy Pop accompanied director Jim Jarmusch to the Cannes Film Festival.[1] The two men had been invited for the premiere of *Gimme Danger*, a passionate documentary on the chaotic history of the singer and the protopunk group that he helped co-found at the end of the 1960s, alongside brothers Ron and Scott Asheton and Dave Alexander: the Stooges. Unsurprisingly, during the press conference, the rocker was asked to give his opinion on the current state of the music industry. Sullen, he responded: 'It's different, now. You can push a button and get rich quick. And I think also that there's an argument to be made about the human races [sic] approach[ing] to the point where the technology gets to the point [sic] where it's going to grip everybody by the shoulders and shake us and then throw us down and get rid of us.'[2] Then, parodying a techno rhythm and beating on the table: 'WHOA! You know? Why don't I just die now?' This critique, fearing that a cold and dehumanising technology would come to replace the warm and authentic expression of an artist, is hardly new. At the turn of the twentieth century, the American composer and conductor John Philip Sousa could not find words strong enough to condemn the 'infernal machines' of phonography: 'The time is coming when no one will be ready to submit himself to the ennobling discipline of learning music . . . Everyone will have their ready made or ready pirated music in their cupboards.'[3] More fundamentally, perhaps, these somewhat alarmist discourses remind one of a certain reactionary press which, well before the age of mechanical reproduction, castigated the 'almost scientific precision' of the realist novel:

> Were one to forge in Birmingham or Manchester narrating and analyzing machines made of good English steel, functioning all by themselves through unknown dynamic processes, they would function exactly like M. Flaubert. One would feel in these machines just as much life, as much soul, as much human entrails as in the man of marble who wrote *Madame Bovary* with a pen of stone, like the knife of savages.[4]

If I take the time to note these resemblances, it is because I believe that they reveal – in the negative – profound mutations in the conception and practice of modern and contemporary art, where the subject more and more abandons their powers so as to let objects speak for themselves. That is to say, while wanting to denounce them, critics of mechanisation bring to light new forms of creation where the human embraces the non-human, where the intentional cedes to the non-intentional, where thought opens to non-thought. Without knowing it, they give voice to this great jamming of contraries which Jacques Rancière places at the heart of the 'aesthetic regime': a revolution in the ways of thinking and feeling which, propelled by Romanticism and still ongoing, disrupts the conceptualisations of society and culture inherited from Plato and Aristotle. This amounts to a change of paradigm in which, following the French philosopher, we go from a hierarchy to an anarchy of genres, from the organic unity of the poem to the model of the fragment, from the reign of eloquence to that of 'mute speech'.[5]

It is by relying on this last notion in particular that I propose to reflect on the reconfigurations of the audible under the new regime, to retrace some of the practices and discourses which, since the turn of the nineteenth century, have blurred music's definitions and drawn it towards noise. The essay will be articulated around three major moments. First, I will outline the emergence of the regime of mute speech and the rise of 'pure' instrumental music which, at around the same historical moment, allowed symphonic 'noise' to become not only a source of legitimate aesthetic pleasure, but also a model for all forms of creation. Next, I will follow the new sensibility into rock culture which, with its crude pop poetry and distorted ruckus, continues to displace the lines of the meaningful and to trouble the frontiers of artistic beauty. Finally I will concentrate on noise music which, if only by its name, offers a perfect example of the Romantic fusion of contraries. Taking for an example the work of Sonic Youth, I will argue that the genre prolongs and exacerbates this great blurring of everything which, if present in early rock, finds its true origin in the aesthetic revolution of the end of the eighteenth century.

Nature and life's rhythms

The Aristotelian *logos*, Rancière explains, is mastered speech: elocution led by reason,

> guided by a signification to be transmitted and a goal to be achieved. For Plato this was the speech of the master who knows how to explain his words and how to hold them in reserve, how to keep them from the profane and how to deposit them like seed in the souls of those in whom they can bear fruit. The classical representative order identified this 'living speech' with the active speech of the great orator who moves deeply and persuades, edifies and leads souls and bodies. This model likewise includes the discourse of the tragic hero who pursues his will and his passions to the limit.[6]

Under no circumstances should this *logos* be mixed up with the simple voice of ordinary people who, like animals, emit sounds only to express pleasure or pain. And yet to this exclusive speech, which sets the norm for the entire representative system from ancient Greece up until the Enlightenment, Romanticism opposes the regime of 'omni-significance' where, Rancière says, the wear of a building or the mouth of a sewer speaks as much as, if not more than, the laureate of the eloquence contest or any prince of tragedy: this is because, unlike these, they are unable to say anything and, as a result, they cannot lie.[7] This is an 'aesthetic democracy' which, for present purposes, can be thought according to two contradictory but indissociable schemas, each corresponding to one or other form of that which the philosopher names mute speech.[8] First, there is the language of the silent things themselves:

> It is the capability of signification that is inscribed upon their very body, summarised by the 'everything speaks' of Novalis, the poet-mineralogist. Everything is trace, vestige, or fossil. Every sensible form, beginning from the stone or the shell, tells a story. In their striations and ridges they all bear the traces of their history and the mark of their destination.[9]

The *logos*, formerly reserved for men of a certain quality only, is released into free circulation, inscribed in the slightest manifestations of the world. The same goes for grand art which, henceforth, can exist outside the eternal and immutable values of academicians. Gustave Courbet says this clearly when, in his 'Lettre aux jeunes artistes de Paris' (1861), he writes:

> Beauty is in nature, and is encountered in reality under the most diverse forms. As soon as it is found, it belongs to Art, or rather to the artist who knows how to see it. As soon as beauty is real and visible, it has its own artistic expression. But the artist has no right to amplify this expression. He can only touch it with the risk of denaturing it, and of thereby weakening it. The beauty given by nature is superior to all artistic conventions.[10]

Any form of existence becomes interesting, worthy of representation, and any of its manifestations is equally proper to express its hidden sense or poetry.[11] Thus, in the words of Marcel Proust, Richard Wagner can import into his music 'nature and life's rhythms, from the flow and ebb of the sea to the hammering of the cobbler, from the beating of the blacksmith to the singing of the birds'.[12] Or, as in the third act of *Tristan and Isolde* (1865), he can renounce his creative power and entrust 'the expression of the most prodigious expectation of felicity that ever filled the human soul' to the 'meagre song' of a 'poor shepherd'.[13] Music itself, furthermore, comes to know a dazzling promotion through the nineteenth century: formerly considered a 'vain noise' because of its inability, without the aid of the human voice or programme notes, to speak '[either] to the mind [or] to the soul', it becomes with the Romantic metaphysics of art the direct expression of hidden realities, inaccessible to ordinary knowledge.[14] Language, which has commanded it and provided it with meaning for centuries, is no longer able to translate or explain its effects. Worse still, tangled up as they are in the nets of human reason, words prevent the full deployment of 'the Marvels of the musical art'.[15] This is a reversal which, as will be seen, might have more to do with the second form of mute speech than the first.[16]

Aesthetic equality, Rancière tells us, is also human speech emptying itself of its meaning, lowering itself to the irrationality of ordinary things. Mute writing, here, is not the secret beauty or the message encoded within the sensible, but 'the voiceless speech of a nameless power that lurks behind any consciousness and signification, to which voice and body must be given'.[17] The artist is no longer the explorer who goes around the lowly world and who reassigns value to details without importance. Rather, he is the Orphic figure who 'plunges into the pure meaninglessness of raw life or into the encounter with the powers of darkness'.[18] The poetry of the mundane does not appeal to him as much as the elusive and senseless voice of life itself. It is the counter-movement taken by Wilhelm H. Wackenroder when, in his *Fantasies on Art* (1799), he rails against the scientists who too often, in their noble quest for truth, simply reduce existence to austere systems of ideas:

> These wise men want to create our earth anew according to a uniformity calculated by human reason and a rigid intellectual order of things. But what is the earth other than one sound audible to us from the hidden harmony of the spheres? – one fleeting flash of lighting visible to us from the concealed dark clouds of the universe? – and what are we? – – That vigorous surging up and down of earthly things … seems to me no different from the particular, mysterious pulsation, the frightful, incomprehensible respiration of the earthly creature.[19]

This path was retaken, shortly after Wackenroder, by Arthur Schopenhauer and the young Friedrich Nietzsche, who, each in his own way, turned away from the beautiful appearances of the rational world to get lost in the unfathomable profundities of the Will and the Dionysian.[20] Now, for the first as for the other two, music occupies a privileged place. Because of its immateriality and its resistance to concept, it offers immediate access to the inner being of the world. In other words, the attributes that make it a deficient language under the representative regime – its abstract quality, its semantic imprecision, its incapacity to name things properly – render music, during the Romantic era, superior to all other forms of expression. A tongue 'richer' than that of the writers, says Hector Berlioz, 'more varied, less precise and, by its very indefiniteness, incomparably more powerful'.[21] 'Veil your faces, ye poor great ancient poets, poor immortals; your conventional language, so pure, so harmonious, could not rival the art of sounds. You are some glorious vanquished, but vanquished.'[22]

Although such a reversal should have caused an outcry among writers, many of the poets and novelists of the era, and not the least among them, recognised the limits of their medium in the face of the musical mystery. Thomas Moore, for example, writes in his *Irish Melodies* (1807–34): 'Music, oh, how faint, how weak,/ Language fades before thy spell!/ Why should Feeling ever speak,/ When thou canst breathe her soul so well?'[23] Honoré de Balzac, in the course of his correspondence with the countess Ewelina Hańska, also comes to bow. In a letter from November 1837 he admits that Ludwig van Beethoven is the only man to have made him know jealousy. Barely recovered from the Fifth Symphony (1808) heard the night before at the Conservatoire de Paris, he writes: 'In that *finale*, it seems as though some enchanter raised you into a land of marvels, amid the noblest palaces filled with the treasures of all arts . . . letting you see beauties of an unknown kind.'[24] Then comes the avowal of impotence: 'No, the mind of the writer can never give such joys, because what we paint is finite, fixed, and what Beethoven flings you to is infinite.'[25]

That poets confess themselves incapable of properly translating the effects of music surely indicates a change in the dominant aesthetic conception: language is no longer, as in the time of Aristotle or the Enlightenment, the infallible model towards which all forms of creation should tend. On the contrary, at a time when many are falling for Romantic metaphysics, the narrow and earthly meanings of words become a constraint. Music, in contrast, appears as the privileged organ of the inexpressible, 'the most marvelous of . . . inventions', writes Wackenroder, 'a language which we do not know in our ordinary life, which we have learned, we do not know where and how, and which one would consider to be solely the language of angels'.[26] Thus liberated from the *logos*, from the ancestral obligation to bend to a pre-established speech, music is able to exist and can be appreciated in itself; for its 'tonally moving forms', writes aesthetician and Wagner nemesis Eduard Hanslick;[27] for its way of hitting you 'in the pit of the stomach, instead of the cerebellum', says rock criticism.[28] And it is to this that I will now turn.

Moments of inexplicable brilliance in a fog of stupidity, or vice versa

Mute speech, I noted, is first of all the power of signification given back to things of no interest. It is the particle of history or of poetry contained in the random goods of a store display or in a gesture repeated a thousand times, and that must be brought back to our conscience by a double labour of deciphering and rewriting.[29]

'It is the Romantic model of thought that goes from stone and desert to the spirit', writes Rancière, 'from thought already present within the very texture of things, inscribed in the strata of rock or shell, and rising toward even more explicit forms of manifestation.'[30] Therefore, nothing is insignificant: anything can equally carry meaning, is worthy of interest and of representation. The dreams of the peasant girl and the misery of the stone breakers, the patterns in the wallpaper and the sinuous form of the urinal, the crackling of the transistor radio and the ink smears of industrial printing. Inheriting from the blues and from country, rock is certainly not insensible to the poetry of the ordinary: it shows, as if in response to the criticism of S. I. Hayakawa, a 'considerable toughmindedness ... a willingness, often absent in popular songs, to acknowledge the facts of life'.[31] At the time of the publication of *The Greening of America* (1970), a sudden and candid tribute to the hippie movement, the lawyer and activist Charles A. Reich declared in *Rolling Stone*:

> The very first thing that began to happen when rock came in on a mass cultural level was it started to say 'we feel lonely and alienated and frightened' and music had never said that before. Blues always said it ... But white people were told how happy, how romantic, how nice, how smooth the world was. And that didn't reflect the truth. Then all of a sudden there was Elvis Presley singing about 'Heartbreak Hotel' full of lonely people, and he said no matter how full it is, when you get there you're lonely because none of those people can communicate with you and you can't communicate with them ... So the first truth of rock, the first big communication, was to say things aren't that good ... Then along comes a second kind of song that begins to acknowledge the glories of lust and sex – and that's another truth that nobody had been telling.[32]

Now, rock culture is not solely interested in the foibles and misfortunes of the human beast. Rather, it embraces reality in all its heterogeneity.[33] 'For true poetry', to use Victor Hugo's phrase, 'lies in the harmony of contraries. Furthermore, it is time to say it aloud, and it is here particularly that exceptions prove the rule, everything that exists in nature exists in art.'[34] Rock says nothing else: Little Richard sings the Sunday morning gospel as well as the Saturday night debauch, Bob Dylan draws poetry from headlines as much as from small conversations, Jim Morrison cites

Sophocles just as detergent ads.[35] This attitude is seen in the work of 'America's first rock poet', Chuck Berry who, from his debut, confounds great love with car mechanics, evokes Venus alongside Jackie Robinson, and rolls over Beethoven to the benefit of the illiterate Johnny B. Goode.[36] Often, his songs are so cluttered with daily objects that the stories that they recount almost slip into the background, seeming little more than pretexts for the enumeration of trinkets. Consider the inventory of goods that constantly interrupts the tale of the couple in 'You Never Can Tell' (1964), for instance: two youngsters get married, decorate a flat to their taste, and revisit, to mark some unspecified anniversary, the place of their union. '*C'est la vie*', the refrain says, 'it goes to show you never can tell.' Appropriate words, considering that the listener knows next to nothing of the bride and groom and their story: how they met, if they have kids, the job that provides the 'little money'. On the other hand, the listener is made well aware that they have a fridge 'crammed with TV dinner and ginger ale', a hi-fi stereo to play their '700 little discs' as well as a 'souped-up jitney, 'twas a cherry-red '53'. The accessories are given as much importance as, if not more than, the characters and their actions. The decor is dragged to the foreground, so to speak. And each object, despite bringing nothing to the narrative, is essential. As author and journalist Nik Cohn put it, in what is often considered to be the first written history of rock:

> Basically, what it boils down to is detail. Most pop writers would have written *You Never Can Tell* as a series of generalities and it would have been nothing. But Chuck was obsessive, he was hooked on cars, rock, ginger ale and he had to drag them all in. That's what makes it – the little touches like the cherry-red Jidney [*sic*] '53 or the coolerator [*sic*].[37]

Or, to use Rancière's words: 'The whole is now in the details.'[38] The essential content does not necessarily reside in the 'big picture', in some core idea or overarching principle that would hold the song together: a story to tell, a moral to convey, an emotion to trigger. It can just as well lie in the 'little touches': in the bits of ordinary reality, says Cohn, in the common words and objects that erupt in the lyrics. This levelling of hierarchies is well described by critic Greil Marcus when, in his introduction to Richard Meltzer's *Aesthetics of Rock* (1970), he writes:

> Rock is a totality: it contains, or implies that it can contain, all varieties of experience ... The most 'trivial, mediocre, banal, insipid' elements of art and life become interesting, and mysterious: a choice of one word over another, turns of phrase, LP covers (which are versions of TV commercials, billboards, of the coded social pictures to which we respond or from which we turn away), screams, silences, moments of inexplicable brilliance in a fog of stupidity, or vice versa.[39]

The last words are interesting. The rock 'totality', Marcus says, admits that there can be intelligence behind that which, at first glance, seems insignificant. Or, inversely, stupidity behind the veil of brilliance. Which brings us back, surreptitiously, to the second form of mute speech: the one that, rather than giving meaning to voiceless things, injects silence into the products of reason. The voice of the Other which, to extend the geological metaphor, 'returns the spirit to its desert'.[40]

From its very beginning, rock was perceived, by a large part of the public, as a form of insidious regression. Nothing less than a 'voodoo of frustration and defiance', says a priest,[41] a formidable 'menace to life, limb, decency, and morals', rants another, while a psychiatrist worries about this new 'communicable disease' which passes off deviant behaviours as normal.[42] The musical press is no more tender, speaking here of a 'throw-back to jungle rhythms' inciting teenagers to compromise themselves in 'orgies of sex and violence (as its model did for the savages themselves)', there of an 'acoustical pollution' contaminating both the airwaves and good moral standards: 'This is progress?'[43]

This perspective is completely overthrown by the adepts of the new music who also view it as a sort of atavism or reversion – not in a negative sense, though, but as a return to something essential, the salutary resurgence of a forgotten aspect of human nature. The folk singer Butch Hancock summed it up best when, remembering Elvis Presley's first TV appearances, he remarked: 'Yeah, that was the dance that everybody forgot. *It was the dance that was so strong it took an entire civilization to forget it.* And ten seconds on "The Ed Sullivan Show" to remember.'[44] In the early 1960s, an enthralled critic reviewing a Ray Charles concert for *Time* reported that some 'Southern spiritualists' claimed to have heard the soul man speaking the 'unknown tongue'.[45] A couple of years later, the article inspired a young Richard Meltzer to develop his own theory, which is just as confusing as it is entertaining, of rock as a form of hermetic speech. Only, the critic now recognises, certain of his reflections are

> so subarticulate (inarticulate?) that it would take a guided tour (or a supplemental voiceover cassette) to clarify, or even hint at, what I might conceivably have been trying to 'express' in the first place ... Then, likewise, there are passages, paragraphs so druggardly opaque, arcane, abstruse that no authorly assistance – I know my limits! – is at this stage even hypothetically feasible.[46]

More convincing is the thesis of the writer and film-maker Michael Ventura, according to whom rock is nothing less than the survival, on American soil, of religious and pagan cults imported from Africa and Europe through triangular trade:

> That is not to say that rock'n'roll is Voodoo. Of course it's not. But it does preserve qualities of that African metaphysic intact so strongly that it unconsciously generates the same dances, acts as a major antidote to the [Judeo-Christian] mind–body split, and uses a derivative of Voodoo's techniques of possession as a source, for performers and audiences alike, of tremendous personal energy.[47]

Just as interesting is the proposition of the conceptual artist Dan Graham who, in his fascinating video-essay *Rock My Religion* (1983–84), traces a filiation between the ecstatic dance rituals of the Shakers and punk and psychedelic concerts:

> In the ritual of the rock performance, the combination of the music's hypnotic qualities and psychedelic drugs leads performers and audiences on a 'trip', beyond the edge of the Old Consciousness into the inner psyche. Like the Shakers' deliberative evocation of the Devil in order to purify their community and communion with God, the performer tries to unleash archaic qualities.[48]

What such genealogies suggest is that rock, a bit like absolute music in the nineteenth century, can constitute a form of religious experience, or, at least, an ecstatic practice through which the subject evades ordinary existence: either in the encounter with celestial powers, by means of some sort of mystical elevation; or in the 'régrédience', by means of a return to the animal.[49] In one case as in the other, rock appears as a brutal escape from the *logos*. 'I think that language is almost obsolete anyway', Patti Smith remarked at the time of releasing *Easter* (1978): 'The language barrier will be broken not by Esperanto, not by any new neo-intellectual language, but through rock'n'roll, through sound. Something as common denominator and dirt cheap as rock'n'roll.'[50]

The debased and the sacred

The beat prophecies of the rock *poétesse* and her calls to step out of rational language found a sonorous echo in the then young post-punk generation, to whom we owe such slogans as 'Reverse Evolution' (1976?), 'Rip It Up and Start Again' (1982) and 'Stop Making Sense' (1984).[51] Or, in the words of Sonic Youth: 'Chaos is the future and beyond it is freedom. Confusion is next and next after that is the truth.' These lyrics are found on the group's first LP, *Confusion is Sex* (1983), released two years after their informal formation at 1981's Noise Fest. Flirting with the New York underground, Sonic Youth were originally close to the no wave anti-scene, 'a cacophonous, confrontational subgenre of rock', as a *New York Times* journalist explained: 'Dadaist in style and nihilistic in attitude. It began around 1976, and within four years most of the original bands had broken up.'[52] In less of a *tabula rasa* spirit than that of no wave, perhaps, the group manifested from the start a penchant for experimentation and transgression: violent performances, exacerbated noise, integration of non-conventional materials. With the years, the group honed their craft and developed a strong identity that earned them great popularity on independent circuits as well as, after ten years of underground labour, a fruitful contract with DGC Records: the young firm of David Geffen, then on the way to becoming one of the major players in the alternative scene with artists such as Nirvana, Hole and Beck. At the time of their separation, in the winter of 2011, Sonic Youth had more than thirty albums in their catalogue and were considered to be one of noise rock's main pillars. In a short essay on the subject, cultural theorist Torben Sangild writes:

> The term 'noise rock' ... denotes a part of the post-punk scene rising from the ashes of punk in the late 70s ... Post-punk ... tries to distance itself from the smoothness and cheerfulness of pop, though

mostly without discarding its melodic qualities. One of the important ways to achieve this is by using noise. Noise rock is not a coherent style, but a loose term for quite different approaches to a noise aesthetic within a post-punk idiom.[53]

Defined in these terms, the genre is reminiscent of the 'formless form' of the novelistic work which, in the nineteenth century, came to undermine the hierarchical system of *belles-lettres*.[54] But this should not make us forget that rock itself, at its base, constitutes a protean phenomenon, a 'totality', says Greil Marcus: an open form which, in its free deployment, can carry any thing and its opposite.[55] Only twenty-five years after its first scandals – Elvis's obscene gyrations on the *Ed Sullivan Show* in 1956, the Kingsmen's unintelligible rendition of Richard Berry's 'Louie Louie' (1957) placed under investigation by the FBI in 1964, John Lennon's comments about the Beatles being more popular than Jesus Christ in 1966 – rock was just as well defined as it was integrated into dominant culture, with its heroes and its repertoire, its codes and its clichés, its rituals and its institutions. What is more, its main forms of expression oscillated between diverse inward-looking and rationalising tendencies: the growing standardisation of radiophonic formats, the back-to-basics ethos of punk, the tidy sounds of synth-pop, etc. Noise, on the other hand, presents itself as a violent return of the repressed, embracing genres kept apart – from *musique concrète* to hip-hop to free jazz and hardcore – and foregrounding impurities removed by professional studios: false notes, material defects, ambient sounds, etc. It reintroduces dirt into rock's 'pollution', so to speak, a labour of 'savage' recuperation that is expressed, in noise literature, through the recurrent figure of rubbish.[56]

At the time of the eclectic *Whitey Album* (1989), on which the members of Sonic Youth plus a few collaborators allowed themselves two covers of Madonna and a karaoke version of Robert Palmer's 'Addicted to Love' (1986), bassist Kim Gordon affirmed: 'We're like the big garbage truck that goes along, scooping up the pop poop, recycling it, kind of.'[57] The formula is a caricature, of course, but it seems pretty close to reality when one observes all the *bric-à-brac* mobilised by the group over the years, from the amplified drill that opens 'The Burning Spear' (1982) to the metal file rubbing the guitar strings at the end of 'Calming the Snake' (2009), from the roaring refrigerator of 'Freezer Burn' (1983) to the distorted voicemail in 'Providence' (1988), from the piping that tinkles in 'She is Not Alone' (1982) to the indistinct metal junk of 'Teknikal Illprovisation' (2002). Although he does not directly reference these *détournements*, speaking instead of the group's fascination with mass culture and its rubbish, its disposable products and its interchangeable icons, journalist David Browne too draws on the register of garbage:

> The newfound (and sometimes aggravating) appreciation of all things tacky had some of its roots in the way Sonic Youth had long championed trash TV and movies or particularly cheesy Top 40 oldies – the way they, like Quentin Tarantino, made junk seem respectable.[58]

For his part, adopting a more general point of view, Sangild suggests that it is a dominant trait of noise rock, and of post-punk at large, to re-employ that which the broader public culture prefers to sweep aside. Borrowing from Georges Bataille, he speaks of a penchant for 'the heterogeneous'.[59] The term, dear to the author of *The Accursed Share* (1949), found its first definition in a 1933 article:

> Those are the waste products of the human body and certain analogous matter (trash, vermin, etc.); the parts of the body; persons, words, or acts having a suggestive erotic value; the various unconscious processes such as dreams or neuroses; the numerous elements or social forms that *homogeneous* society is powerless to assimilate: mobs, the warrior, aristocratic and impoverished classes, different types of violent individuals or at least those who refuse the rule (madmen, leaders, poets, etc.).[60]

In brief, the heterogeneous refers to 'everything rejected by *homogeneous* society either as waste or as superior transcendent value',[61] to the debased and the sacred. Either way, the heterogeneous element is radically other, a *'non-explainable difference'*: its reality resembles that of the unconscious, as it escapes complete rational grasp.[62] Seen from this angle, noise artists no longer so much resemble the 'poet-mineralogist' who makes speak the stones and debris of civilisation. Rather, they join the lineage of those shadow seekers who, from Wackenroder to early rockers to Patti Smith and no wave, petrify human speech and embrace the pure pathos of raw life, or engage, for the most adventurous, with the primordial forces flowing and rushing underneath the phenomenal world.

The idea of rock as a gateway to transcendent experience has been addressed already.[63] In the two main arguments offered, sound violence plays a central role. According to Michael Ventura, 'Rock's noise has been necessary to break through the crust of self-consciousness accumulated over these last three thousand years. So that a place long asleep in us would wake.'[64] For his part, Dan Graham declares: 'I always thought – particularly because I was listening to Hardcore – that rock'n'roll comes very much out of using noise and the destructiveness of noise and sound, making it into something ecstatic, where you can get in touch with God.'[65] It is not surprising, then, that the latter's video-essay relies on a deafening soundtrack, in which work songs and no wave guitars, possession dances and punk concerts, squeaky fiddles and psychedelic jams are intertwined – all blended in one continuous sound flow from which emerge, especially, the hoarse and nasal voice of Smith, the cavernous drones of Glenn Branca and those, particularly abrasive, of Sonic Youth. This is all the more interesting as the founding couple of the group, Gordon and singer-guitarist Thurston Moore, are given special mention in the end credits of the film. Alongside a certain Kirstin Lovejoy, the two are thanked for their contribution to 'important ideas',[66] a mention which, when linked with statements gleaned from the literature, suggests that the members of Sonic Youth share Graham's thesis on the transcendent powers of rock. In 1986, for example, Moore stated:

> To me, it's more sort of a personal belief. I couldn't talk about how religious [rock] is because it's just too obvious to me as something that's all-encompassing ... It's a way to communicate with myself or other people. So it's a total religious value, which to me is what religions always are, a total communication of awareness with others and yourself, physically and spirituality.[67]

In her recent memoir, Gordon recalls some of the rare performances of 'Shaking Hell' (1982) as almost 'shamanic' elevations.[68] The song, unplayed for most of the band's thirty years of activity,

> was messy and bone-chilling to sing, especially when the music dropped to a low grumble during the *'Shake, shake, shake'* ending. It

was as if the ground had dropped out from beneath me, and I was left floating, until my voice shot out and carried me. I wanted to take the audience with me, knowing, as I did, that the crowd wanted to believe in me, and us, as we created something that had never existed before.[69]

In a similar spirit, guitarist Lee Ranaldo declares:

We tend to see music as *exultational*, or something like that; as cathartic. When it's working well, whether it's just the four of us in a room, or it's in a room with a couple thousand people, on the right night when everything's aligned correctly, you're lifting off, there's a certain transcendent quality to it that everyone's involved with and there's a symbiotic thing between the audience and the performers.[70]

Communication without words, indescribable states, quasi-mystical elevations: familiar themes for anyone interested in the idea of absolute music. But it is Sangild who, undoubtedly, borrows most openly from Romantic metaphysics. Drawing upon the young Nietzsche, he speaks of a 'Dionysian aesthetics' where 'individuality is transgressed in favor of identification with the universal will – a frightening yet blissful experience'.[71] In its least conciliatory moments, that is, when it is not trying to hide or soften its more off-putting aspects under charming 'Apollonian' arrangements, noise functions as 'a direct confrontation with the terrible foundation of being, an absurd will driving us all in our meaningless lives'.[72] One can recognise, here, the second form of Rancière's mute speech, which goes from the rational and beautiful representation of the world to the incomprehensibility of raw life and to the chaos of elementary forces. Elsewhere, while trying to characterise 'the maelstrom of noise' into which many Sonic Youth songs disappear – think of the wailing midsection of 'Silver Rocket' (1988), of the magmatic second half of 'Mote' (1990), of the slowly dissolving finale of 'Small Flowers Crack Concrete' (2000) – Sangild describes a moment of disruption that is 'at the same time an explosion of energy and an *im*plosion of meaning, turning away from the distinct and semantic into the sublime and ecstatic'.[73] A whirlpool which, to conclude, could very well have its source in 'the holy, cooling wellspring' where Wackenroder and his Romantic followers loved to plunge their heads, which is nothing other than the senseless torrent of life itself: 'a rushing river' which human speech can only miserably name and describe, 'in a foreign medium', while music 'causes it to flow past ourselves'.[74]

Therefore be silent, human wit

I evoked, in the introduction, Iggy Pop's concerns about the current digital turn in the music industry and its possible effect on creation: whereas good old analogue recording is like 'throwing an amplifier into the spirit of man',[75] computer-assisted composition threatens to put a hard drive in its place. These worries are somewhat puzzling coming from a singer who, on the one hand, frequently collaborates with electronic artists – from New Order to Underworld to Norman Cook and WestBam – and who, on the other, found his prime inspiration in the mechanical hubbub of the Ford automobile assembly plants in his native Michigan: 'When I was in elementary school, we had a field trip to the Rouge industrial complex. There was a machine that would just drop a piece of sheet metal: WHOOSH!! I wanted to make music, I thought it should sound like that.'[76] Or who, during the aforementioned Cannes press conference, remembered that 'Ron Asheton's genius on his guitar was that he would plug it into the amp and turn it up and he listened to the guitar and the amplifier talk. He just let them talk!'[77] In this light, the singer seems closer to John Cage and Marcel Duchamp or to the marble author of *Madame Bovary* than to the critics of realism and the robotisation of art. In fact, he summarises quite effectively the double movement of mute speech which, to the great displeasure of these latter, freezes human expression to better give life to things without reason. He thus reaffirms the grand principle at the heart of the Romantic religion of art: 'Therefore be silent, human wit, and let yourselves be enchanted, you pious senses, by the exalted presumptuous splendor!'[78] This gives, at the same time, a new and yet quite literal meaning to 'rock' music which, by now, appears like a pop and contemporary extension of the literary 'petrification' initiated a century earlier.

Notes

1. This essay is an abridged and slightly reworked version of my master's thesis, written under the kind guidance of Michèle Garneau: '"Ici rien n'est silencieux": reconfigurations de l'audible sous le régime

esthétique des arts', Université de Montréal, 2016. I warmly thank Danick Trottier and Patrick Nickleson for the countless rounds of proofreading and translation.
2. Jim Jarmusch et al., 'Conférence de presse/Press Conference', *Site officiel du Festival de Cannes*, 19 May 2016, 24:27–24:58, <http://www.festival-cannes.com/en/films/gimme-danger#vid=1556> (last accessed 7 November 2018).
3. Quoted in Alex Ross, *Listen to This* (New York: Farrar, Straus and Giroux, 2010), 55.
4. Jules A. Barbey d'Aurevilly, *Œuvre critique*, ed. Pierre Glaudes and Catherine Mayaux (Paris: Les Belles Lettres, 2004), Book I, 1055, 1048.
5. Jacques Rancière, *Mute Speech: Literature, Critical Theory, and Politics*, trans. James Swenson (New York: Columbia University Press, 2011).
6. Jacques Rancière, *The Aesthetic Unconscious*, trans. Debra Keates and James Swenson (Cambridge: Polity, 2009), 32–3.
7. Jacques Rancière, *The Politics of Literature*, trans. Julie Rose (Cambridge: Polity, 2011), 157.
8. Quoted in Nicolas Truong, 'Il n'y a jamais eu besoin d'expliquer à un travailleur ce qu'est l'exploitation', *Philosophie Magazine* 101 (June 2007), 58. My translation.
9. Rancière, *The Aesthetic Unconscious*, 34.
10. Gustave Courbet, *Peut-on enseigner l'art?* (Caen: L'Échoppe, 1986), 5. My translation.
11. Rancière, *The Politics of Literature*, 132.
12. Marcel Proust, *À la recherche du temps perdu*, ed. Pierre Clarac and André Ferré (Paris: Gallimard, 1978), Book II, 1156. My translation.
13. Marcel Proust, *Contre Sainte-Beuve précédé de Pastiches et mélanges et suivi de Essais et articles*, ed. Pierre Clarac and Yves Sandre (Paris: Gallimard, 1978), 69. My translation. Quoted in Emile Bedriomo, *Proust, Wagner et la coïncidence des arts* (Tübingen and Paris: Gunter Narr Verlag and Jean-Michel Place, 1984), 37, 74.
14. Jean le Rond d'Alembert, *Mélanges de littérature, d'histoire et de philosophie*, ed. Martine Groult (Paris: Classiques Garnier, 2017), 926. My translation.
15. Wilhelm H. Wackenroder, *Confessions and Fantasies*, trans. Mary H. Schubert (University Park: Penn State University Press, 1971), 178–81.
16. A turnaround that is brilliantly described all through Carl Dahlhaus's *The Idea of Absolute Music* (1978). 'Now instrumental music,

previously viewed as a deficient form of vocal music, a mere shadow of the real thing, was exalted as a music-esthetic paradigm in the name of autonomy – made into the epitome of music, its essence. The lack of concept or a concrete topic, hitherto seen as a deficiency of instrumental music, was now deemed an advantage. One may without exaggeration call this a music-esthetic "paradigm shift", a reversal of esthetic premises.' Carl Dahlhaus, *The Idea of Absolute Music*, trans. Roger Lustig (Chicago: University of Chicago Press, 1991), 7. For a shorter version, see the essay on 'Emancipation of Instrumental Music', in Carl Dahlhaus, *Esthetics of Music* (Cambridge: Cambridge University Press, 1982), 24–31.
17. Rancière, *The Aesthetic Unconscious*, 41–2.
18. Rancière, *The Aesthetic Unconscious*, 31.
19. Wackenroder, *Confessions and Fantasies*, 171. Translation modified; the punctuation is Wackenroder's.
20. See Arthur Schopenhauer, *The World as Will and Representation*, trans. E. F. J. Payne (New York: Dover Publications, 1966–69), Books I and II, 255–67 and 447–57; Friedrich Nietzsche, 'The Dionysian World View', trans. Claudia Crawford, *Journal of Nietzsche Studies* 13 (spring 1997), 92–5; Friedrich Nietzsche, *The Birth of Tragedy* (Oxford: Oxford University Press, 2008), 85–90. For a general yet amazingly detailed and nuanced account of the epistemological shift that occurred during the nineteenth century, see the four penultimate books of Georges Gusdorf's massive series on *Les Sciences humaines et la pensée occidentale* (Paris: Payot, 1966–88). 'The conflict between Enlightenment and Romanticism', the philosopher writes, 'expresses the antagonism of two spiritualities in the context of a civilizational crisis. It is not a question of rejecting science, but of preventing it from occupying the whole cultural domain; the Galilean science imposes on the conscience a closure regime which dooms it to suffocation. Imagination is no longer the intelligence's inferior sister, as the positive mind asserts; it claims the role of a stimulant for a new form of knowledge, not below but beyond intellect.' Georges Gusdorf, *Le Romantisme* (Paris: Éditions Payot et Rivages, 1993), Book I, 218–19. My translation. Thus: 'A second reading of the reality overcharges and denies the first reading of scientific experiment and day-to-day positivism. Below the well-ordained chains of phenomena, another order becomes apparent, like the recurrence of a forgotten ontology.' Ibid., 194. My translation.
21. Hector Berlioz, *New Edition of the Complete Works*, gen. ed.

Hugh Macdonald (Kassel: Bärenreiter, 1990), Book XVIII, 383. Translation modified.

22. Hector Berlioz, *A Critical Study of Beethoven's Nine Symphonies with a Few Words on His Trios and Sonatas, a Criticism of 'Fidelio', and an Introductory Essay on Music*, trans. Edwin Evans (Urbana: University of Illinois Press, 2000), 78. Translation modified.
23. Quoted in *Berlioz on Music: Selected Criticism*, ed. Katherine Kolb, trans. Samuel N. Rosenberg (New York: Oxford University Press, 2015), 78.
24. Honoré de Balzac, *Letters to Madame Hańska, born Countess Rzewuska, Afterwards Madame Honoré de Balzac*, trans. Katherine P. Wormeley (London: Forgotten Books, 2016), 459.
25. Balzac, *Letters to Madame Hańska*, 459.
26. Wackenroder, *Confessions and Fantasies*, 180.
27. Eduard Hanslick, *On the Musically Beautiful: A Contribution Towards the Revision of the Aesthetics of Music*, ed. and trans. Geoffrey Pyzant (Indianapolis: Hackett Publishing, 1986), 29. Exasperated by the Romantics' high-flown sentimentality, which impedes objective analysis, the theorist advocates a scientific approach where a composition's true value is not to be found in its emotional or discursive content, but in its formal qualities. 'Of course', he writes,

    > people used to consider that a feeling wafting through a piece of music was the subject, the Idea, the intellectual content, and, on the other hand, the artistically created, well-defined tonal sequences were considered the mere form, the image, the sensuous garb of that supersensuous conception, However, precisely the 'specifically musical' part is the creation of the artistic spirit, with which the contemplating spirit unites in complete understanding. The ideal content of the composition is in these concrete tonal structures, not in the vague general impression of an abstract feeling. The form (as tonal structure), as opposed to the feeling (as would-be content), is precisely the real content of the music, is the music itself, while the feeling produced can be called neither content nor form, but actual effect. (Hanslick, *On the Musically Beautiful*, 60)

28. These are the words of critic Mark Coleman, in what is believed to be Sonic Youth's first concert review. Quoted in Alec Foege, *Confusion Is Next: The Sonic Youth Story* (New York: St. Martin's Press, 1994), 74. For similar remarks, made by or about other artists,

see Paul Williams, 'Rock Is Rock: A Discussion of a Doors Song', *Crawdaddy!* 9 (May 1967), 45–6, and Chris Salewicz, 'Oy Lemmy, Is It True You Were a Hippie??', *New Musical Express*, 25 August 1979, 18. But the most exhaustive – and sometimes quite exhausting, with all its bad faith and unnecessary ranting – account of rock music as a physical experience is provided by ex-SST Records staffer and rowdy essayist Joe Carducci. Contrary to what is commonly believed, thanks to the entertainment industry and social science-infused dominant criticism, rock is not an attitude, a lifestyle or a fashion. Nor is it a specific sound that one could simply replicate or buy at the store. Rock's true meaning, insists Carducci, is in the bodily felt efforts of a small group of musicians jamming together; in the contagious tension produced by the real-time interaction of a guitarist, a bass player and a drummer searching for communion in loud music. See Joe Carducci, *Rock and the Pop Narcotic: Testament for the Electric Church* (Centennial, CO: Redoubt Press, 2005), 13–59.

29. Rancière, *The Aesthetic Unconscious*, 41.
30. Jacques Rancière, 'Is There a Deleuzian Aesthetics?', *Qui Parle* 14.2 (2004), 10.
31. S. I. Hayakawa, 'Popular Songs vs. the Facts of Life', *ETC.: A Review of General Semantics* 12.2 (1955), 93.
32. Quoted in Alan Rinzler, 'A Conversation with Charles Reich: Blowing in the Wind', *Rolling Stone* 75 (4 February 1971), 32. See also Charles Hamm's essay on 'Rock and the Facts of Life' (1971), reprinted in *Putting Popular Music in Its Place* (Cambridge: Cambridge University Press, 1995), 41–54. It is from Hamm that I get the Hayakawa and Reich quotes. On rock's 'realist' approach to lyrics, see Simon Frith, 'Why Do Songs Have Words?', in *Music for Pleasure: Essays in the Sociology of Pop* (Cambridge: Polity, 1988), 105–28.
33. See Claude Chastagner, 'Rock: le paradoxe', in Marie-Claire Rouyer (ed.), *Le Corps dans tous ses états* (Bordeaux: Presses Universitaires de Bordeaux, 1995), 108–9, and Chastagner, *La Loi du rock: ambivalence et sacrifice dans la musique populaire anglo-américaine* (Castelnau-le-Lez: Climats, 1998), 9.
34. *The Essential Victor Hugo*, trans. E. H. and A. M. Blackmore (Oxford: Oxford University Press, 2004), 34.
35. Little Richard, who in the first version of 'Tutti Frutti' (1955) sings 'Tutti Frutti, good booty/ If it don't fit, don't force it/ You can grease it, make it easy', turns to religious songs at the end of the 1950s with

the two discs of *Pray Along* (1960) and the following *King of the Gospel Singers* (1961), before returning to rock 'n' roll and finding a compromise with the electrified 'message music' of *Lifetime Friend* (1986). Quoted in Charles White, *The Life and Times of Little Richard: The Quasar of Rock* (New York: Da Capo Press, 1994), 55, 222. Concerning Dylan, think of his anthemic 'Masters of War' (1963), written in response to the nuclear arms race of the Cold War, compared to the intimate 'On a Night Like This' (1974). As for The Doors, see 'The End' (1967) and 'Touch Me' (1969).

36. Richard Goldstein (ed.), *The Poetry of Rock* (Toronto: Bantam, 1969), 2. The songs that I am referring to are 'Maybellene' (1955), 'Brown Eyed Handsome Man' (1956), 'Roll Over Beethoven' (1956) and 'Johnny B. Goode' (1958).
37. Nik Cohn, *Awopbopaloobop Alopbamboom: The Golden Age of Rock* (New York: Grove, 2001), 41.
38. Jacques Rancière, *The Lost Thread: The Democracy of Modern Fiction*, trans. Steven Corcoran (London: Bloomsbury, 2016), 23.
39. Richard Meltzer, *The Aesthetics of Rock* (Boston: Da Capo Press, 1987), xxii–xxiii.
40. Rancière, 'Is There a Deleuzian Aesthetics?', 11.
41. William J. Shannon, 'The Presley Plague', *The Catholic Sun*, 25 October 1956, 1.
42. Both quoted in Jess Stearn, 'Rock 'n' Roll Runs into Trouble: Disgusted Adults Battling Music of Delinquents', *Daily News*, 11 April 1956, 34. This article was followed by a second one, published the next day: Jess Stearn, 'Rock 'n' Roll Runs into Trouble: More Youngsters Ignore That Primitive Beat', *Daily News*, 12 April 1956, 42.
43. Ruth W. Stevens, 'Editorially Speaking ...', *Music Journal* 16.2 (1958), 3; Howard Hanson, 'The Challenge of the Modern Role of Arts', *American String Teacher* 12.4 (1962), 2.
44. Quoted in Michael Ventura, *Shadow Dancing in the USA* (Los Angeles: J. P. Tarcher, 1986), 156.
45. 'That's All Right', *Time* 81.19 (10 May 1963), 52.
46. Meltzer, *The Aesthetics of Rock*, vii.
47. Ventura, *Shadow Dancing in the USA*, 156.
48. Dan Graham, 'My Religion', *Museumjournaal* 27.7 (1982), 328. This essay, it is worth noting, exists under a confusing variety of titles and formats, many of which are identified in Marianne Brouwer et al. (eds), *Dan Graham*, trans. Brian Holmes, Peter Ingham and Victor Joseph (Düsseldorf: Richter Verlag, 2001), 209–11. I use here what

appears to be the first printed version which, according to Anne Langlais, is itself the reworking of an unpublished 1979 lecture, presented with slides and music excerpts. Dan Graham, *Rock My Religion*, ed. Xavier Douroux, Franck Gautherot and Maryvonne Bégon, trans. Patrick Joly and Sylvie Talabardon (Villeurbanne and Dijon: Institut d'Art Contemporain and Les Presses du Réel, 1993), 279.
49. 'Régrédience', according to the sociologist Michel Maffesoli, is a 'return to archaic forms which we thought were out of date'. Quoted in Alexis Mombelet, 'La musique metal: des "éclats de religion" et une liturgie', *Sociétés: Revue des Sciences Humaines et Sociales* 88.2 (2005), 46. My translation. The latter adds: 'Régrédience is a throwback to animality and to the primitive which structures man.' My translation.
50. Quoted in Sandy Robertson, 'Behind the Wall of Sleep with the Patti Smith Group', *Sounds*, 25 March 1978, 17.
51. 'Reverse Evolution': ironic motto of the mad engineers of Devo, applied to diverse merchandise during the 1970s. 'Rip It Up' is a single by Orange Juice, which appears on the album of the same name, and was rendered doubly famous with the publication of Simon Reynolds's *Rip it Up and Start Again: Postpunk 1978–1984* (London: Faber and Faber, 2005). *Stop Making Sense* (1984) is a concert film by Talking Heads, directed by Jonathan Demme and named in reference to the lyrics of 'Girlfriend is Better' (1983).
52. Ben Sisario, 'A Brief, Noisy Moment that Still Reverberates', *The New York Times*, 12 June 2008, E1.
53. Torben Sangild, *The Aesthetics of Noise* (Datanom, 2002), 13.
54. Jacques Rancière, *Et tant pis pour les gens fatigués: entretiens* (Paris: Éditions Amsterdam, 2009), 142.
55. See Albert Goldman, 'The Emergence of Rock', *New American Review* 3 (April 1968), 127–8, and Bertrand Rouby, 'Le Rock à l'épreuve du canon', *Études britanniques contemporaines: Revue de la Société d'Études Anglaises Contemporaines* 24 (June 2003), 99.
56. Borrowing from Claude Lévi-Strauss, anthropologist Dario Rudy and literature theorist Yves Citton oppose the noise and lo-fi musics' 'bricoleur' to the professional recordings' 'engineer'. Dario Rudy and Yves Citton, 'Le lo-fi: épaissir la médiation pour intensifier la relation', *Écologie & Politique* 48.1 (2014), 110. My translation. They describe the former's approach as a '"savage" reappropriation' of both the means of production and the unwanted sound 'filth': an act of resistance against the ever-growing sanitisation of all things

material and symbolic, against the general pull towards inhuman perfection, against rapid consumption and the false idea of medium transparency (118). My translation. See also Yves Citton, 'Le Percept noise comme registre du sensible', *Multitudes* 28.1 (2007), 137–46.
57. Quoted in Foege, *Confusion Is Next*, 183.
58. David Browne, *Goodbye 20th Century: A Biography of Sonic Youth* (Boston: Da Capo Press, 2008), 389.
59. Sangild, *The Aesthetics of Noise*, 13.
60. Georges Bataille, 'The Psychological Structure of Fascism', trans. Carl R. Lovitt, *New German Critique: An Interdisciplinary Journal of German Studies* 16 (winter 1979), 69. Translation modified.
61. Bataille, 'The Psychological Structure of Fascism', 69. Translation modified.
62. Bataille, 'The Psychological Structure of Fascism', 68.
63. On the subject, see Jonathan D. Cohen, 'Rock as Religion', *Intermountain West Journal of Religious Studies* 7.1 (2016), 46–86; Mombelet (ed.), *Sociétés*; Ian W. Fowles, *A Sound Salvation: Rock 'n' Roll as a Religion* (Huntington Beach: Sonic Mystic, 2011).
64. Ventura, *Shadow Dancing in the USA*, 48.
65. Quoted in Anne Hilde Neset, 'All Shook Up', *Wire* 304 (June 2009), 32–3.
66. Dan Graham, *Rock My Religion* (Electronic Arts Intermix, 1983–84), 55:04–55:13.
67. Quoted in Stewart Sweezy, 'Sonic Youth: The Sound and the Fury', *Option* G2 (March and April 1986), 30.
68. Kim Gordon, *Girl in a Band: A Memoir* (New York: Dey Street, 2015), 133.
69. Gordon, *Girl in a Band*, 133.
70. Quoted in Matthew Stearns, *Daydream Nation* (New York: Continuum, 2007), 21.
71. Sangild, *The Aesthetics of Noise*, 25. For different takes on the Dionysian aspects of rock, see Walter Breene, 'Apollo and Dionysus', *Crawdaddy!* 18 (September 1968), 11–15; Robert Palmer, *Dancing in the Street: A Rock and Roll History* (London: BBC Books, 1996), 147–55; Ruth Padel, *I'm a Man: Sex, Gods and Rock 'n' Roll* (London: Faber and Faber, 2000), 227–44.
72. Sangild, *The Aesthetics of Noise*, 25.
73. Sangild, *The Aesthetics of Noise*, 15.
74. Wackenroder, *Confessions and Fantasies*, 179, 191.
75. Jarmusch et al., 'Conférence de presse/Press Conference', 25:27–25:31.

76. Quoted in Ben Whalley (dir.), *Motor City's Burning: Detroit from Motown to the Stooges* (BBC, 2008), 43:14–43:33.
77. Jarmusch et al., 'Conférence de presse/Press Conference', 20:56–21:17.
78. Wackenroder, *Confessions and Fantasies*, 173.

3

A Lesson in Low Music
Patrick Nickleson

In the middle of his first monograph, 1974's *Althusser's Lesson*, Rancière introduces a term that appears nowhere else in his published writing: 'the low music'. *La musique bas*. Several scholars – including many in this volume – have noted the relative absence of music in Rancière's writing. In particular, musical works have played almost no role, in comparison to how often he turns to literature, film, poetry and sculpture in making his claims about aesthetics, politics, historiography and pedagogy. Nevertheless, in this essay I would like to consider at length Rancière's use of *la musique bas* as a means of thinking about what musical and sonic terminology might mean when it appears, often metaphorically, in his published writing. To do so, I would like first to consider the appearance of *la musique bas* in its context, within a larger critique of Rancière's teacher, Louis Althusser. Next, I will expand upon the term as staging a triadic relationship between the discourses of noise and stultification in *Disagreement* and *The Ignorant Schoolmaster* respectively. Finally, I will return to low music to argue for its potential value both as a conceptual term in music studies, and for paying closer attention to the role of a metaphorical music in Rancière's broader work. My interest is in avoiding a Rancièrean 'lens' or 'frame' or even analytic, instead proposing the concept as a reflexive check on our own methods as music scholars.

The low music

On its initial appearance, Rancière uses the term as part of a long critique of Althusser's ideas about education. Throughout

Althusser's Lesson, Rancière attacks his teacher's understanding of protest and pedagogy, history and politics, often turning to the first person to reflect the reasons for his break with Althusser: 'The starting point of my commentary', Rancière writes in the original French preface, 'is ... an experience that a great many intellectuals of my generation lived through in 1968: the Marxism we had learned at Althusser's school was a philosophy of order whose every principle served to distance us from the uprisings which were then shaking the bourgeois order to its core.'[1] By 1974 Althusserianism had become a 'police' discourse:[2] one that prioritised judging which language was Marxist and which bourgeois, which words could be used as part of revolt and which could not, when the time for revolution had arrived and when it was yet to come. Althusser's 1970s works, including most prominently the essay 'Idéologie et appareils idéologiques d'État', saw 'Althusser struggling, somewhat pitifully, to reconcile his old ideas with lessons offered up by the events [of May] themselves'.[3]

Low music appears twice in an extended critique of Althusser's articulation of the school as the dominant element in the reproduction of the state ideology. 'The only way for Althusser to be able to introduce [the dominant role of the school within the ideological state apparatuses]', Rancière writes, 'was to cancel out, purely and simply, the political conditions of its production.'[4] Those political conditions were the mass protests of May 1968, during which students, alongside millions of French workers, staged their argument that the school is an apparatus of bourgeois order.[5] Instead of acknowledging this collective articulation, 'Althusser pretends to have discovered this problematic ... as he treads the arduous path of his research.'[6] Althusser is thus able to 'credit the heroic investigations of the solitary theoretician with the distinction of having discovered, amid the blindness and deafness of the population, the political role of the school'. That is, Rancière argues that Althusser insists upon the ignorance of the students to specifically credit, instead, the heroic theorist with having discovered the ideological role of the school in reproducing the dominant order. Rancière then directly quotes what Althusser, in the ideological state apparatuses (ISAs) essay, considered a 'stunning' and 'paradoxical' thesis: 'In this concert [of apparatuses], one ideological state apparatus certainly has the dominant role, although hardly anyone lends an ear to its music: it is so silent! This is the School.'[7] Rancière inhabits Althusser's voice to continue the analogy:

> Yes, the music of the dominant ideology is indeed quite 'silent' for those who do not want to hear the noises of revolt, for those whose theory depends on the theoretical suppression of that noise, for those who find – in this theoretical need – the principle for their membership in an organization [the French Communist Party, PCF] committed to putting an end to this noise in practice.[8]

Very rarely is Rancière so grounded in sonic metaphor: the concert, the silence of theory and the noise of revolt, even defining the PCF's mandate as putting an end to noise. It is of course grounded in Althusser's choice of metaphors, but he further expands upon those. Rancière reformulates Althusser's 'It is so silent' to mean 'thank heaven that it is so silent, that no noise disturbs the theoreticians of this silence'.[9]

Indeed, sonic metaphors are central to Althusser's introduction of the school as the dominant apparatus of the state's reproduction of capitalist relations of production. For Althusser – who was planning an unrealised collective publication on education to follow the ISAs essay[10] – the school had replaced the church as the dominant apparatus of reproduction of the state ideology. Why is the 'scholastic apparatus' dominant, he asks? After essentially summarising the role of the ISAs – each contributes in its own way to reproducing capitalist relations of production – Althusser continues:

> This concert [of apparatuses] is dominated by a single score, in which we hear a few 'false notes' (among others, those of the proletarians and their organizations, which are terribly discordant, and those of petty-bourgeois dissidents or revolutionaries as well): the score of the *State Ideology*, the ideology of the current dominant class, which knows very well how to integrate into its music the great themes of the humanism of the Great Ancestors, who wrought the miracle of Greece before Christianity . . .[11]

The apparatuses work 'in concert'; they are 'dominated by a single score' (in which 'false notes' appear); and in this concert, the school plays the dominant role by reproducing the relations of capitalist production – what Althusser describes as 'its music'. But the music is *silent*, inaudible even. What can this music be, then? For Althusser, the use of this musical terminology is purely metaphorical: music refers to harmonious structures, with all parts in their place, doing their own work to (re)produce together a single, complete entity. It is a convenient metaphor for a structural ideal, not an art form. Perhaps notably, there is no mention of 'harmony' or other pitch-centric metaphors that have long constituted metaphorical reliance on music as a relation of parts to whole – all of the metaphors relate instead to texture, amplitude and timbre.

In response, Rancière criticises Althusser for claiming to have discovered, alone in silence at his desk, that the school is the dominant apparatus of the ideological reproduction of the state. Indeed, comparing Althusser's 1963 essay 'Problèmes étudiantes' to the ISAs essay, originally published in 1970 in *La Pensée*, highlights a stark contrast in his thinking about education. Responding to student protests at the Sorbonne in 1963, Althusser had articulated the centrality of a 'pedagogic function', which he defines as 'the absolute condition of *an inequality between a knowledge and a lack of knowledge*',[12] signifying the gap between teacher and student, and thus necessitating the role of the teacher in the educational situation. For Althusser, the pedagogue is the person who closes this gap by the sheer foundational power of their knowledge, with the student understood on the order of an empty container; readers of *The Ignorant Schoolmaster* will recognise this formulation, and I will return to it in that context below. What is more important at this point, and in the context of Rancière's critique, is that within this ideal understanding of the pedagogic function, in 1963 Althusser displaced the line of political fracture articulated by the Sorbonne students (teacher/student) to articulate that the only location of politics in the classroom is in the *content* of the material transmitted from teacher to student. That is, there is nothing, for Althusser, political about the *form* of education or the school itself, and there is no problem in the simple fact of the pedagogic function; the only issue is whether a teacher transmits (Marxist) *science* or (bourgeois) *ideology* to the student as part of the ongoing relationship of necessary and evident inequality. In 1963 this is all that Althusser has to say about schools and schooling – and he says it explicitly in the service of order, against the students, as a reminder of their proper place within the pedagogic relationship.

In 1970, however, Althusser's essay on the ISAs raises a new set of problems. Something had changed, then, between Althusser's 1963 intervention into the comparatively small Sorbonne student protests (what Rancière calls Althusser's only explicitly political intervention) and the writing of the ISAs essay in 1970, where Althusser not only highlights the school as an apparatus in the reproduction of state ideology, but labels it the *dominant* instrument in the maintenance of those relations of production. What had changed? 'The Althusserian project of the 1960s unfolded against the *real silence of the masses*', Rancière writes. 'Now that this silence didn't exist anymore, Althusserian theory had to announce it so as to be able to claim that *only the heroes can pick out the low music, inaudible to coarse ears*, of class domination.'[13] There is thus a *real* silence, and there is a silence that must be announced by a 'theoretician of silence'. Moreover, there is a low music of class domination that is inaudible to coarse ears, but is apparently audible to 'the heroes'. Althusser makes it quite clear who he considers these heroes to be: 'I ask the pardon of those teachers who, in dreadful conditions, attempt to turn the few weapons they can find in the history and learning they "teach" against the ideology, the system and the practices in which they are trapped. They are a kind of hero.' (Perhaps most importantly, he continues, 'they are very rare'.)[14]

While I may have created some contrapuntal opacity between Rancière's and Althusser's texts here, this is perhaps part of the purpose. Much of Rancière's account is an ironic or mocking parody of Althusser's, in the free indirect style which James Swenson and others have placed so much priority on; as Katharina Clausius has written, when writing in this style, Rancière 'relishes an entangled relationship with his subject'.[15] Rancière essentially steps into the voice of Althusser, using many of the same metaphors and ideas, specifically to mock Althusser's position. Indeed, he immediately follows Althusser's quote about teachers-as-heroes with another free indirect dismissal: 'The heroes are, of course, teachers. In Althusser's "anti-historicist" history, no student has been able to pick out the low music of or turn any weapons against the system. The fundamental thesis has not changed: the masses live in illusion.'[16] This position essentially comes down to the fact that something has changed in the school system: no longer is the politics of class struggle to be found only in the content (whether ideological or scientific) transmitted to students, but in the very form of transmission and the institution of the school itself. To make this claim – without giving credit to the 'infantile leftists' of May '68[17] – Althusser must 'cancel out' those political conditions. He thus 'announces' a silence in place of the noise of revolt, marking himself as a 'theoretician of silence' and producing, in place of any practice of revolt, a 'low music' of class domination, audible only to the teachers – and which all students should rely on them to locate, as a first step towards turning weapons against the system of domination. That is, Althusser's means of articulating the role of the school as the dominant ideological state apparatus is to reposition the supremacy of the teachers, the 'coarseness' of the students' understanding, and the necessity of a 'silence' above which to articulate the heroism of research and pedagogy.

The important question for my purposes is: Why so many sonic and musical metaphors?

Silence and noise

We can perhaps best answer this question by turning to two sonic, if not musical, terms that appear frequently and explicitly in Rancière's writing, particularly in *La Mésentente*: silence and noise.[18] In the first half of that text, noise (*bruit*) is tied to Aristotelian political philosophy, with silence appearing frequently in relation: '"The people" is the name, the form of subjectification, of [the] immemorial and perennial wrong through which the social order is symbolised by dooming the majority of speaking beings to the *night of silence* or to the *animal noise* of voices expressing pleasure or pain.'[19] Rancière uses (animal) *noise* and (the night of) *silence* not as opposites, per se, but as equal designations of the opposite of *logos* from either a receptive or productive perspective: those of no account are doomed to silence, though when they do open their mouths, they emit only noise. Throughout the first half of *Disagreement*, then, noise is an Aristotelian concept deployed ironically as the sound emitted by *brutes*, as clearly articulated in the French original.

Noise returns later in relation to nineteenth-century workers' strikes, which 'consist in building a relationship between things that have none', including 'the relationship between noise (machines, shouting, suffering) and argumentative speech'.[20] Here, for the first time, Rancière moves from noise as a political concept – brutishness in opposition to reason – to an actual sonic *noise*: the noise of *machines*, in opposition to the Aristotelian *bruit* of suffering, and mediated by the both-and of *shouting*. The combination of these three terms – machines, shouting, suffering – strikes me as explicitly intended to do some conceptual knotting. Indeed, he develops the theme of the workers' strike as noisy:

> The workers' strikes of [the nineteenth century] derive their peculiar discursive structure by ... show[ing] that it is indeed as reasonable beings that workers go out on strike, that the act that causes them all to stop working together is not a *noise*, a violent reaction to a painful situation, but the expression of a *logos*.[21]

Here Rancière challenges the association between the noisy workers, with their machines and shouting, and the earlier Aristotelian *bruit* in a political sense. They are not speaking from a place of noise, but from a position of rational argumentation. The method of the strike is to stage the relation between, on the one hand, the *bruit* of the noisy strike by the noisy tool wielders who operate the noisy machines and, on the other, the rational argumentation of the *logos* which was initially defined in relation to the *bon sens*, as Davide Panagia has argued, of individuals of higher social status.[22] Those of higher status are presumably those who might be in a position to 'announce silence' in place of an existing noise. Noise is a speech situation labelled from outside that must be overcome by a clear staging of the wrong, thus enabling it to be heard as reasoned discourse. It is about making one's interlocutor hear more than only 'revolt', which Rancière defines as 'the *noise of aggravated bodies*'; it is about making the interlocutor hear this noise as reasoned speech, rather than simply 'wait[ing] for [the noise] to stop or ask[ing] the authorities to make it stop'.[23] In bringing in the authorities responding to a noise complaint, the concept comes full circle: the noise is literal sonic noise (machines, shouting), but also metaphorical political noise in opposition to reasoned speech (shouting, suffering). Perhaps most importantly, however, noise is an always dissensual term: it relates to the duplication of sense as both the sensory impact of a noise, and the *making-sense* of that sensory impact, and most importantly a disarticulation of the presumed interrelation between the two. The noisy tool wielders, even in their noisy strike, can articulate a rational argument. Acoustically loud sound does not guarantee that the subjects making those sounds are inherently associated with the opposite of *logos*, and the strike is about articulating that fact. Imagining that those who 'work' and 'do' – presumably making some noise along the way – are inherently *politically* noisy – separate from reason – is one of the core forms of mimesis that was disrupted in the modern era, most broadly, and the aesthetic regime, more specifically.

This raises a point of central importance that has not been discussed and strikes me as central to any music studies or sound studies approach to Rancière's work. In Rancière's writing, *nothing is actually noisy*. Nearly any use of the term *noise* is in the free indirect style, used to mock political philosophies that rely on this sonified and naturalised binary of inequality. While he may label particular things as noises – again, the machines and shouting – references to noise in every case, I contend, must be read as ironic references to the Aristotelian *logos/phōnē* distinction, and not as actual descriptors of individuals as noise-producing beings. That is, it is always used as a position against which Rancière is staking his own claims, rather than as a means of articulating his own position. Indeed, the passage from *Althusser's Lesson* in which Rancière first introduces the term 'noise' is specifically in relation to what Althusser and the PCF do not want to hear: 'the music of the dominant ideology is indeed quite "silent" for *those who do not want to hear the noises of revolt*, for those whose *theory depends on the theoretical suppression of that noise*, for those ... committed to putting an end to this noise in practice ...'[24] While the use of the term changed between *Althusser's Lesson* and *Disagreement*, it is nevertheless maintained as not so much a *negative* in Rancière's thought as a caricature of the position of many political theorists, Althusser included, whom Rancière represents as old writers – theoreticians of silence – hunched over their desks calling in noise complaints to the local police. In contrast, Rancière – at least in 1974 – is a veritable theoretician of noise.

I have argued that in Rancière's writing, noise and silence are not opposites. Turning to texts beyond *Disagreement*, the relation between noise and silence is perhaps clearest in a brief passage in *On the Shores of Politics*, the book written immediately before *Disagreement*. 'The advances of democracy', Rancière writes, 'have always been due to improvisation by unprogrammed actors, by surplus interlocutors: a noisy crowd occupying the street, a silent crowd crossing their arms in a factory and so forth.'[25] Here, as in the examples above, noise and silence are not opposites. A literally noisy act and a literally silent act both appear as noise: the deafening silence of the noisy tool wielders must be heard, contextually, as every bit as loud as the street occupation. Similarly, the articulation of this principle of inversion between different modalities of silence is present in his nuanced, even affectionate critique of Roland Barthes in *The Future of the Image*. There, after outlining the differences between Barthes the semiologist of *Mythologies* and Barthes the theorist of the *Camera Lucida*, Rancière outlines how they both base their arguments on the same 'principle of reversible equivalence between the silence of images and what they say'. He continues,

> the former [the semiologist of *Mythologies*] demonstrated that the image was in fact a vehicle for *a silent discourse* which he endeavoured to translate into sentences. The latter [the theoretician of *Camera Lucida*] tells us that the image speaks to us precisely when it is *silent*, when it no longer transmits any message to us.

In sum, 'both conceive the image as speech which holds its tongue. The former made its silence speak; the latter makes this silence the abolition of all chatter.'[26]

Barthes engages two forms of silence: first, images are a silent discourse that the theorist must turn into sentences; and second, photographs speak specifically in their silence. Similarly, there is perhaps no sound so deafeningly noisy as when a factory full of workers ceases their work and crosses their arms in silent protest. In both cases, Rancière places a clear priority on distinguishing between regimes of silence and noise, not as opposites of each other, or even of music, but as differing opposites of reasoned speech or action. The resonance here with the annunciation of a silence by Althusser, the theoretician of silence, in place of an existing silence is clear: Ranciere suggests that Barthes, like Althusser, makes the noisy object – the masses, the workers, the reader, the listener, the audience, the student – silent as a means of providing it instead with the theorist's choice of speech.

Articulating Rancière's method of equality as a function of this noise–silence binary perhaps helps in clarifying matters. For Rancière, the job of the scientific hero-scholar (a position he is clearly critical of) whose discourse is the central target of his critique is, first of all, to make an object silent if it is noisy, or give it a discourse if it is silent. In either case, the job of the hero-scholar is first of all to make a case as to why the object of study – a silent body suppressing noise, a noisy body made silent – cannot speak for itself. While it oversimplifies Rancière's position to treat this as a silence/noise binary – much like treating politics/police as good/bad, in an 'allegorical binary of inequality' – it is clear that Rancière's method and politics introduce noise – staged in itself rather than suppressed – onto the scene. The low music is again in effect here whenever the function of scholarship is seen as putting into effect an orderly, rational structure in place of the 'real' noise of events, speech or sound.

Stultification

'The heroes are, of course, the teachers.'[27] In this network of sonic metaphors, pedagogy plays a prominent role. It has frequently been noted in the secondary literature on Rancière that all of his thought is fundamentally about pedagogy. Samuel Chambers argues that 'the most important teaching' of Rancière's work is his 'lesson about the lesson':

> his claims about 'lessons', his arguments about teaching and pedagogy, prove fundamental to his project. Pedagogy is not something separate from theory or from politics; pedagogy is not its own subject matter. Rather, pedagogy is always contingent and yet always fundamental.[28]

While Rancière's philosophy is typically understood as reflecting on politics, historiography and aesthetics, a sympathetic understanding of his contributions must come in terms of his only fundamental axiom: that everyone is of equal intelligence. This is not to suggest that everyone is equally wise or thoughtful or correct in any given situation; rather, as James Swenson notes, 'Intellectual equality implies that people generally know perfectly well what they do and say, that the world is not – must not be – divided between those who think and those who need someone to think for them or to explain what they really think.'[29] Rancière boiled it down to a personal – perhaps even ethical – maxim in an interview:

> To caricature it a bit, the inegalitarian maxim says that it's a bit of a bore to have to go out, that it'd be better to stay at home and look at the papers or watch telly to see just how stupid people are, and tell yourself: I must be really intelligent since everyone else is so stupid. The choice of maxim is this: are you intelligent because everyone else is stupid, or are you intelligent because they are intelligent?[30]

For Rancière, pedagogy and intelligence are closely entwined. The typical ideal of pedagogy – perhaps exaggerated in Althusser's 'pedagogic function' – is premised on the encounter between two unequal intelligences. However, the central contribution of Rancière's philosophy, Davide Panagia argues, is to 'dissonate' (again with the sonic metaphors) relationships like this one.[31] Rancière articulates Althusserianism as a theory of education and expands his critiques from *Althusser's Lesson* in *The Ignorant Schoolmaster: Five Lessons in Intellectual Emancipation*. Kristin Ross has noted that both books, in 'announc[ing] themselves as "lessons"',[32] aim to displace the pedagogic function of Althusser's 'Student Problems' into the *pedagogic myth* of *The Ignorant Schoolmaster*. By turning Althusser's binary of knowledge and ignorance into a consideration of the roles of power and authority in the dynamics between the masses (a group that we can expand, especially in light of *The Emancipated Spectator*, to include the workers, the protesters, the listeners, the students, the audience . . .)[33] and those claiming to possess knowledge, Rancière shifts the terrain towards the presupposition of equality – intellectual and political. 'For Rancière', Ross writes, 'the Althusserian concept of science . . . had ultimately no other function than that of justifying the pure being of knowledge and, more important, of justifying the eminent dignity of the possessors of that knowledge.' In this introduction to *The Ignorant Schoolmaster*, Ross introduced as core context for Rancière's project these early critiques from *Althusser's Lesson*. Summarising the relationship between these two lessons, she indirectly summarises Rancière's own free indirect critique of Althusser: 'if everyone dwells in illusion (ideology), then the solution can only come from a kind of muscular theoretical heroism on the part of the lone theorist'. She similarly mocks Althusser for taking such a complex and indirect path to claiming to have discovered, along the arduous path of his research, 'what the mass student action had already revealed to everyone – the function of the school as an ideological apparatus of the state'.[34]

From the vantage point of the early 1990s, Ross clearly sees Rancière's project as a pedagogico-political one, grounded in a critique of the Althusserian pedagogic function. At its core, Althusserianism is dedicated to upholding the distinction between knowledge and ignorance, and tying it to the distinction between theory and practice, order and revolt, all via the discourse of deviation so central to Althusser's political and educational interventions.[35]

Althusserian pedagogy – and Althusserian philosophy broadly – is founded on a pedagogic myth that divides the world into two, 'the parable of a world divided into knowing minds and ignorant ones, ripe minds and immature ones, the capable and the incapable, the intelligent and the stupid'.[36] This myth operates through explication, in which the pedagogue announces 'the absolute beginning' during which the act of learning will begin; then, 'having thrown a veil of ignorance over everything that is to be learned, he appoints himself to the task of lifting it'.[37] This method of explication, Rancière argues, is rather a method of *abrutir*. Commenting on her decision to translate *abrutir* as 'stultification' in *The Ignorant Schoolmaster*, Ross highlighted that the term loses the important associations 'to render stupid, to treat like a brute'.[38]

While the parallel is unclear in English, there is a slanted rhyme in the original French between stultification (*abrutir*) and noise (*bruit*). Indeed, the French *bruit* is drawn from the English brute: brutes make noise; noise is brutish. The parallel is not particularly important in French, either, and Rancière seems never explicitly to have intended a parallel of any kind. In that sense, the parallel, if it can be considered one, only comes about in the 'in-between dialect ... guided by the idea that the activity of thinking is primarily an activity of translation', as Rancière wrote in a 1992 essay, and which Katharina Clausius has expanded upon at length.[39] This is all to say that nowhere in English translation do Rancière's ideas include the idea of brutishness that, at least in their etymological relationship to music, both 'noise' and 'stultification' carry. With all this in mind, I would like to turn at last to a consideration of what low music could mean in the context of a Rancièrean music studies. In that particular context, low music is the song that pedagogues hear that convinces them of the necessity of stultifying noisy brutes (*abrutir les brutes bruyantes*).

A lesson in low music

What, then, is low music? Before articulating why I think it is a useful idea to explore in a music studies context, it might be helpful to briefly summarise a few things we can say about this otherwise elusive term:

1. It emerges in the free indirect style that has been discussed at length by James Swenson; that is, it is not Rancière stating an

original position, but rather sees him inventing a term to caricature another position – specifically Althusser's, but perhaps more broadly that of political philosophy back to Aristotle.
2. Further, it uses the word *music* – and expands upon other musical and sonic metaphors – in response to Althusser's metaphorical usage of 'concert', 'score', 'silent', etc.
3. Following on from 1 and 2, in the 'low music' passage of *Althusser's Lesson* there is no clear demarcation between parroting Althusser and writing as Rancière. Kristin Ross discusses this narrative quality in her introduction to *The Ignorant Schoolmaster*: an 'unusual effect is created by the narrative style of the book: a particular kind of uncertainty that readers may experience concerning the identity of the book's narrator. The reader, in other words, is not quite sure where the voice of Jacotot stops and Rancière's begins.' In this case, however, we *are* aware: I contend that terms such as noise, silence and low music signal this very shift.
4. Lastly, it is intended to caricature the structural topography of the Althusserian conception of ideology: *music* is used to suggest a 'harmonious' ordering of parts to the whole, and it is 'low', not in the sense of a high/low binary, but rather in that it is only audible to those experts and heroes, the teachers (as understood by Althusser as the beneficiaries of an inherently unequal pedagogic power dynamic).

I said that I was aiming to present low music as a check on the potential danger of claims to 'applying a Rancièrean lens' that, as Samuel Chambers notes, would require scholars 'to either ignore or refute'[40] the central, egalitarian tenets of Rancière's thought, in which binaries of master and student, ignorance and knowledge, even cause and effect, are rejected. Perhaps more importantly, it is not even clear that there is a 'concept' called *the low music* present in Rancière's thought for me to draw out; instead, I am tying together a variety of sonic-metaphorical claims from his later writing to enliven a term from his first book which he uses to caricature the position of another philosopher. What's more, I am choosing that entirely contingent term for the even more contingent reason that I am a scholar of music contributing to a volume of essays called *Rancière and Music*. That is, to highlight 'low music' is not necessarily to articulate a Rancièrean term, but to grab something contingent to stage a relation between elements that do not explicitly have any – like *bruit* and *abrutir*. In this sense, my goal is not so much to expand upon Rancière as to draw a name from his writing to articulate an important point for music scholars to keep in mind.

The concept of low music involves an act of stultification: it *makes brutes* of those who cannot hear it. Nothing is literally audible to one class as a result of their intelligence that is inaudible to another as a result of ignorance. Music scholars might jump to the defence of structural and expert listening, but we should remember a core Rancièrean precept: 'our problem isn't proving that all intelligence is equal. It is seeing what can be done under that supposition.'[41] That things can be *heard through*, that one could 'lift the veil' to find something *behind* in a metaphorical sense is, as Rancière argues repeatedly, the very discursive claim that produces stultification. There is perhaps a gap though – where *stultification* is a pedagogic act that assumes the ignorance of the student, *low music* is best understood as the internalised song of order and propriety that pedagogues, convinced of their own expertise, sing themselves so as to rationalise as progressive and even benevolent the stultification of students and listeners. Low music is what heroic pedagogues and scholars are *convinced* they hear that provides them with the right and even the duty to stultify. Why would Rancière use a musical metaphor for this orderly ideal?

This is perhaps the important element of the appearance of the low music, in its relation to a volume of essays dedicated to bringing Rancière's work into dialogue with music. The novel contribution of Rancière's thought, as initially stated in *Althusser's Lesson* and carried through the rest of his career, is the contention that scholarship, disciplinarity, knowledge, power, critique – all these interrelated terms – operate through what is most often called in the Marxist literature, and most strongly in Althusser, *ideology*. This is not to say that they 'operate through ideology' in the sense of an illusion, an unconscious or repressed element in need of excavation; rather, it is that the discourse of ideology, the notion that there is a veil, that there is something under the surface in need of 'reading', is how philosophy and other forms of academic scholarship have long upheld their hierarchical position in relation to 'the masses', 'the people', 'the audience' and so on. When Rancière wants to articulate this point, for perhaps the first time in his published output, he turns to a prominent metaphor that stretches back, in music discourse, to someone who is not only the founder of this line of 'secretive' thinking, but indeed the person at least mythologically credited with having coined the term 'philosophy': Pythagoras. Rancière frames his ironic critique of Althusser by drawing on Althusser's own musical discourse: the low music of class domination is inaudible to coarse ears. *This*, for Rancière, is the place to bring in musical metaphor: the notion of an *unheard*, an *inaccessible*, a *specialist* relationship of parts to whole in which the parts are inherently, geometrically and completely subsumed to the role of the *harmonious whole*. This is the 'song' that knowing pedagogues have long sung themselves, in much the same way that 'the only song the bourgeoisie has ever sung to workers is the song of their impotence, of the impossibility for things to be different than they are'.[42]

It is constitutive not only of musical thought, but of the very terminology that music uses. We perhaps see Rancière attempting to escape this discourse – to 'dissonate' it – when, in 'Metamorphosis of the Muses', he attempts to turn to the pre-Pythagorean, the pre-mathematical discourse of music that has been largely absent since the medieval discourse of music reframed the Pythagorean mysteries into the quadrivium of academic study: 'music, of course, is the concern of the Muses before being that of the instrumentalists'.[43] This is a dissonant definition. Etymologically it is, of course, correct – but it shows a clear prioritisation of and affiliation with thinkers of music as a subdiscipline of mathematics since Pythagoras, and part of the quadrivium since the European Middle Ages. Its oddness points to the problem: for Rancière, the discourse of music is inseparable from the discourses of order, propriety and harmony that his philosophy aims at core to 'dissonate'. The language and the discourse are inseparable. How would he write of specific *songs* when the word 'song' most often signals a registral shift from an explicit claim to the free indirect style of mocking imitation? In Rancière, the use of musical terminology and metaphors invariably suggests that he is describing a police situation: an instance of the kind of 'geometric equality' that he attaches to Plato, but could perhaps consider an element of the neo-Pythagoreanism that had already begun to proliferate by the time of Plato's writing, historically if not citationally. Indeed, his discussions of arithmetical versus geometric equality in *Disagreement* are often explicitly tied to music (in terms of 'harmony'). 'For the founders of "political philosophy"', Rancière writes:

this submission of the logic of exchange to the common good is expressed in a perfectly determined way, as the submission of arithmetical equality, which presides over commercial exchanges and over juridical sentences, to that geometric equality responsible for proportion, for common harmony, submission of the shares of the common held by each party in the community to the share that party brings to the common good.[44]

Later, 'geometric equality, as the proportion of the cosmos appropriate to bringing the soul of the city into line, opposes a democratic equality reduced to arithmetical equality – that is, to the reign of the more or less'.[45] Perhaps most explicitly,

The good city is one in which the order of the *cosmos*, the geometric order that rules the movement of the divine stars, manifests itself as the temperament of a social body, in which the citizens act not according to the law but according to the spirit of the law, the vital breath that gives it life.[46]

These all relate to Rancière's summary of the Platonic ideal of archipolitics, which would later be closely tied to the ethical regime of art. But there is a very distinct sense in which, for Rancière, music – in its etymological and even in some ways artistic senses – is explicitly a part of this, and something that is perhaps difficult to extract from that logic. Music is an element of the Platonic worldview, relating back to Pythagoreanism and its association with the 'music of the spheres' and the appropriate selection of modes to organise the good city.

Noise can become music, and inarticulate speech can become comprehensible. Concentrated listening can make things once unheard clearly evident. This makes of music, in relation to noise, a far more concrete and literal metaphor than the comparable one of things 'invisible' becoming 'visible' – a practice that, at least literally, never happens. That discourses of music turn this into a specific power of the enlightened, rather than a shared capacity of the common sensorium, is at the core of our disciplinary police logic. More conceptually, this relationship is one that has a very well-known place in music studies – indeed, it is foundational to the mythology of music as a discipline, science, or field of study. Returning to the Pythagoreanism that I have already suggested is perhaps too readily present in Rancière's mobilisation of musical metaphors, it is specifically because the Pythagorean teacher (Pythagoras himself, or subsequent disciples) could *not* be invisible that he and his disciples came to rely on the dramaturgical tool of the veil; it is precisely because they used the veil that the voice, and indeed the lessons, of Pythagoras (and his disciples) took on the auratic mystery it still maintains among more gnostic scholars today. Brian Kane's work on Pythagoras and the *akousmata* is telling here. While a conclusion is an odd place to begin summarising the nuances of Kane's reading of the Pythagoras myth, two central points strike me as relevant to a discussion of Rancière and Pythagoras.[47] The first is that the *veil* is itself, perhaps, a metaphor: it seems likely that the myth of the veil appeared as a means of discussing the function and use of fables and parables – becoming important, that is, not only for the Pythagorean tradition, but to the very foundation of the idea of saying one thing and meaning another. Second, following on from this, Kane prioritises the fact that essentially what distinguished the two levels of the hierarchical Pythagorean cult is the relationship between the *akousmata* – those who only heard the lesson 'through the veil' – and the *mathematikoi* – those who were 'inside the veil' and thus able, simultaneously, to hear *and* see the master. In this sense, the veil, as Kane argues, is less likely a *literal* veil, but instead a metaphor about the idea of separating into two classes based on knowledge via an understanding of the lesson. To recall Rancière's critique of the benevolent instructors living under the *pedagogic myth* (convinced of the low music that they hear, and about which they set themselves the task of teaching their pupils): 'having thrown a veil of ignorance over everything that is to be learned, he appoints himself to the task of lifting it'.[48] This myth is really 'the parable of a world divided into knowing minds and ignorant ones, ripe minds and immature ones, the capable and the incapable, the intelligent and the stupid'.[49] The axioms of Pythagorean life were in a sense 'veiled' to those who did not know that the banishment of beans had to do with a rejection of democracy, that the articulations of various mathematical and physical theories was explicit knowledge to be retained and hidden ('veiled'), specifically so as to maintain the privilege of those who know – the heroes who can pick out the 'low music'.[50]

That Rancière is not a Pythagorean, in a spiritual or intellectual sense, is clear to any reader of his work. That he is using *la musique bas* specifically to mock Althusser's much more literal Pythagorean philosophy of education and order – in the form of a split between the knowing and the ignorant – is clear. Nevertheless, something of the triadic relationship between Rancière, Althusser and the Pythagorean worldview raises a problem in Rancière's treatment of music. In even Rancière's most recent aesthetic writings such as *Aisthesis*, where no specifically musical scene exists (as João Pedro Cachopo discusses in his contribution to this volume), but where music appears regularly, the term is most often used – like song, like concert, like silence and noise – as a metaphor for a structural ideal of parts in relation to a whole, or of parts, however contingent or however related, under a single name.[51] Would it not become difficult for Rancière, who has consistently used these terms in the free indirect style, to mock the tradition of the 'harmonious' community so central to political philosophy,[52] or the various 'songs' the bourgeoisie (and Althusser!) sing to 'the people' to keep them in their place? Would it not become difficult for Rancière to use these or similar terms to discuss, literally, the role of songs, harmony, silence, noise and music in actual concrete terms?[53] A discourse can, of course, be broken – this is one of the core lessons of Rancière's thought. But is there a certain sense in which music, as a discipline and as an art, has been painted into a corner in Rancière's metaphorical and allegorical staging of its powers?

The low music is a term that points to this discourse: of the police, of 'ideology' in the Althusserian sense, of 'illusion' to be rejected, of the veil to be lifted. It suggests the 'thing' that pedagogues and scholars recognise – or 'announce' – so as to rationalise and authorise their supremacy over their readers, listeners, students, audiences, their poor and so on. It strikes me that this is a helpful concept for musicologists turning to Rancière to keep in mind when a music or a sound relies for its power on a discourse of stultification; when it begins from suggesting the incapacity of audiences, listeners or readers. For all Rancière's rejections of an 'ethics', it strikes me that, in our efforts to dodge the too-easy notion of 'applying a Rancièrean lens', there is perhaps no better reason as music scholars to turn to Rancière than to ensure that we avoid, at all times, instantiating our own version of a 'low music' at the core or peripheries of any of our arguments. This is not a concept to apply or a lens to use, but rather a check on our own methods: a Rancièrean turn in musicology must constantly challenge and avoid reproducing the low music that only we, the heroic scholars, can pick out. The goal of maintaining low music as a reflexive critical practice is to recognise, at all turns, that listening and writing are common capacities of all – are we intelligent, is our work worthwhile, because everyone is intelligent, or because everyone is stupid and needs our guidance? Low music functions, before anything else, to remind readers, listeners and audiences of their passivity and that they need the guidance of experts, scholars, critics, historians and teachers. Attacking this discursive reflex is *the* core philosophical contribution of Rancière's project. The low music is perhaps a reverberation from Rancière's earlier career, reminding those of us hungry for his aesthetic writing of the ethical principles that have motivated his work from his very first historiographical and political writing. It is a direct response to his teacher, Althusser, for whom in the ISAs essay, the teachers are indeed the heroes. That we are not obliged to hold to Rancière's personal ethics – and that he refuses to admit that his work has an ethics – is, of course, to be assumed. But still, the ironic borrowing of terminology from our discipline such as harmony, song, silence, noise and music should remind that we are tied to a medium that necessarily relies, for its very appearance and audibility, on the suppression of noise in practice.

Notes

1. Jacques Rancière, *Althusser's Lesson*, trans. Emiliano Battista (London: Continuum, 2011), xix.
2. This usage of the police is not to read his earlier work through his later conceptual innovations. Describing the shift from what we might call 'the Young Althusser' of *For Marx* to the ideas present in *The Philosophy Course for Scientists*, where the idea of philosophy as 'class struggle in theory' appeared, Rancière writes: 'Much more than a swing to the left, the rectified Althusserianism we encounter in these texts represents the normalization of Althusser's project, the elaboration of a "partisan philosophy" conceived as a policing [*police*] of concepts.' Rancière, *Althusser's Lesson*, 58. Elsewhere in the text, outlining Althusser's distinction between ideology as bourgeois and science as Marxist, Rancière critiques this as the mechanism which 'transformed Althusserian prudence into theory's police force' (*Althusser's Lesson*, 41).

3. Rancière, *Althusser's Lesson*, xx.
4. Rancière, *Althusser's Lesson*, 74.
5. Rancière – like other French philosophers of his generation – turns often to the 'events' in his own writing, including in *Althusser's Lesson*. A reader interested in a more thorough historical account – from a decidedly Rancièrean historiographical perspective – should see Kristin Ross, *May '68 and Its Afterlives* (Chicago: University of Chicago Press, 2006).
6. Rancière, *Althusser's Lesson*, 74.
7. Rancière, *Althusser's Lesson*, 74–5; referring to Louis Althusser, *On the Reproduction of Capitalism: Ideology and the Ideological State Apparatuses*, trans. G. M. Goshgarian (London: Verso, 2014), 141–5.
8. Rancière, *Althusser's Lesson*, 75.
9. Rancière, *Althusser's Lesson*, 75.
10. See Etienne Balibar, 'Foreword: Althusser and the "Ideological State Apparatuses"', in Althusser, *On the Reproduction of Capitalism*, vii–xviii.
11. Althusser, *On the Reproduction of Capitalism*, 145.
12. Louis Althusser, 'Student Problems', *Radical Philosophy* 170 (November/December 2011), 14. The translation published in *Radical Philosophy* is a 'lightly corrected reprint' of a translation by Dick Bateman of an article that originally appeared in *La Nouvelle Critique* 152 (January 1964), 80–111. The article has not appeared in any of Althusser's collected English writings and can perhaps be considered non-canonical in the very important sense, as Rancière highlights, that it was an intervention into an ongoing dispute at the Sorbonne – his 'only political intervention, in the strict sense'. See *Althusser's Lesson*, 37.
13. Rancière, *Althusser's Lesson*, 75.
14. Althusser, *On the Reproduction of Capitalism*, 146–7.
15. Katharina Clausius, 'Translation ~ Politics', *Philosophy Today* 61.1 (2017), 251; see also James Swenson, 'Stile indirect libre', in Gabriel Rockhill and Philip Watts (eds), *Jacques Rancière: History, Politics, Aesthetics* (Durham, NC: Duke University Press, 2012), 258–72; and Davide Panagia, 'Rancière's Style', *Novel* 47.2 (2014), 284–300.
16. Rancière, *Althusser's Lesson*, 75.
17. Louis Althusser in Maria-Antonietta Macciocchi, *Letters from inside the Communist Party to Louis Althusser*, trans. Stephen M. Hellman (London: NLB, 1973), 301–20.
18. As my argument here builds from English translations of these texts,

but frequently relies on turning to the originals, I would like to acknowledge the excellent translations of *La Mésentente* by Julie Rose, *The Ignorant Schoolmaster* by Kristin Ross, and *Althusser's Lesson* by Emiliano Battiste. Further, I am heavily indebted to Katharina Clausius's conception of the role of translation in Rancière's work in her 2017 article in *Philosophy Today*.

19. Jacques Rancière, *Disagreement*, trans. Julie Rose (Minneapolis: University of Minnesota Press, 1999), 22.
20. Rancière, *Disagreement*, 41.
21. Rancière, *Disagreement*, 50.
22. Panagia, 'Rancière's Style', 290.
23. Rancière, *Disagreement*, 53.
24. Rancière, *Althusser's Lesson*, 75; my italics.
25. Jacques Rancière, *On the Shores of Politics*, trans. Liz Heron (London: Verso, 1995), 103.
26. Jacques Rancière, *The Future of the Image*, trans. Gregory Elliott (London: Verso, 2007), 11. It is notable that Rancière quotes a very similar passage from Althusser, this time from the 1972 'Reply to John Lewis'. As part of his critique of the Stalinist cult of personality, Althusser argues that 'One is even justified in supposing that, behind the talk about the different varieties of "humanism", whether restrained or not, this "line" continues to pursue an honourable career, in a peculiar kind of silence, a sometimes talkative and sometimes mute silence, which is now and again broken by the noise of an explosion or a split.' Much as in Rancière's reading of Barthes, Althusser's reading of the Twentieth Congress of the Communist Party highlights two regimes of silence in play in relation to the different kinds of 'humanism' understood by that body: a 'sometimes talkative' silence, and a 'sometimes mute' silence. Notably, Althusser introduces here what may be the only appearance of the word *bruit* in his published writing. See Louis Althusser, 'Reply to John Lewis', *Australian Left Review* (December 1972). Later published in *Essays in Self-Criticism*, trans. Grahame Lock (London: NLB, 1976).
27. Rancière, *Althusser's Lesson*, 75.
28. Samuel Chambers, 'Jacques Rancière's Lesson on the Lesson', *Educational Philosophy and Theory* 45/46 (2013), 638–9.
29. Swenson, 'Stile indirect libre', 258.
30. Jacques Rancière, *The Method of Equality: Interviews with Laurent Jeanpierre and Dork Zabunyan*, trans. Julie Rose (Cambridge: Polity, 2016), 90–1.

31. Davide Panagia, *Rancière's Sentiments* (Durham, NC: Duke University Press, 2018), 100.
32. Kristin Ross in Jacques Rancière, *The Ignorant Schoolmaster: Five Lessons in Intellectual Emancipation*, trans. Kristin Ross (Stanford: Stanford University Press, 1991), xvi.
33. See Jacques Rancière, *The Emancipated Spectator* (London: Verso, 2009).
34. Ross in *The Ignorant Schoolmaster*, xvii–xviii.
35. See Rancière, *Althusser's Lesson*, 104.
36. Rancière, *The Ignorant Schoolmaster*, 6.
37. Rancière, *The Ignorant Schoolmaster*, 6–7.
38. Rancière, *The Ignorant Schoolmaster*, 7 (translator's note).
39. Jacques Rancière, 'Politics, Identification, Subjectivization', *October* 61 (1992), 63; Clausius, 'Politics ~ Translation', 249.
40. Chambers, 'Jacques Rancierè's Lesson on the Lesson', 638.
41. Rancière, *The Ignorant Schoolmaster*, 46.
42. Rancière, *Althusser's Lesson*, 90.
43. Jacques Rancière, 'Metamorphosis of the Muses', in *Sonic Process: A New Geography of Sounds*, ed. Mela Dávila (Barcelona: Actar, 2002), 23.
44. Rancière, *Disagreement*, 6.
45. Rancière, *Disagreement*, 63.
46. Rancière, *Disagreement*, 68.
47. Brian Kane, *Sound Unseen: Acousmatic Sound in Theory and Practice* (Oxford: Oxford University Press, 2014), esp. ch. 2, 'Myth and the Origin of the Pythagorean Veil'.
48. Kane, *Sound Unseen*, 6–7.
49. Rancière, *The Ignorant Schoolmaster*, 6.
50. For more on the element of secrecy, see Kane on the Pythagorean Hippasus in *Sound Unseen*, 57.
51. Particularly useful here is the chapter on Loïe Fuller and Mallarmé's writing on her veil dances. Discussing a 'transition from sounds to fabrics', Mallarmé writes '(is there anything resembling a veil more than Music!)'; Rancière later writes, 'Mallarmé finds no better analogy than music: the body that uses a material instrument to produce a sensible milieu of feeling that does not resemble it in any way … The movement of the veil does not transpose any musical motifs, but the very idea of music. The idea is of an art which uses a material instrument to produce an immaterial sensible milieu.' Jacques Rancière, *Aisthesis: Scenes from the Aesthetic Regime of Art*, trans. Zakir Paul (London: Verso, 2013), 93, 96.

52. Or, by contrast, when he steps into a modernised voice of Plato to define 'the people' as a 'big noisy animal'. Rancière, 'Metamorphosis of the Muses', 20.
53. See Rancière, *Althusser's Lesson*, 10, 85, 87, 90, etc.

Part II Politics of History

4

Wandering with Rancière: Sound and Structure under the Aesthetic Regime
Martin Kaltenecker

The three regimes

Rancière's well-known distinction between three artistic regimes is immediately telling for the musicologist considering the evolution of Western art music since the sixteenth century. A regime is defined by Rancière as 'a specific type of link between the production of works (or artistic practice), and the forms of visibility that these forms will take, implying different modes to conceptualise both'.[1] Coming after the 'ethical regime of the images' where such a thing as 'art' is not yet identified,[2] the 'representative regime', under the overwhelming influence of Aristotle's theories, rests on hierarchies encapsulated by tragedy, installed as the ideal model for all of the 'fine arts'. Valuable forms (or, within each art, valuable strategies and techniques) are those clearly evincing, or resting on, the Aristotelian *muthos*. The central importance of the fable (defined as a logical sequence marked by a reversal, the *peripeteia*, and leading to an unforeseen end) establishes the 'representational primacy of action over character, of narration over description, the hierarchy of artistic genres following the dignity of their topics, along with the very superiority of the art expressing the act of speaking'.[3] Such artistic hierarchies imply and/or consolidate social hierarchies: the exemplary fable deals with those who encounter a destiny (not with those for whom 'time just passes'),[4] those who have a right to speak or to be spoken of, those who participate in public affairs and dominate the public space, those who are visible.

Finally, under the 'aesthetic regime of art' that emerged at the end of the eighteenth century, art is defined as the 'essence' that all arts have in common. This essence, however, is a negative force that overthrows the reign of *muthos* and dissolves its hierarchies. Art is characterised by a 'mode of presenting what is offered to the senses [*le sensible*], now exempted from its ordinary connections, as inhabited by a heterogeneous force, the power of Thought, a thought in turn alienated from itself'.[5] Hence the two fundamental procedures characteristic of the aesthetic regime: on the one hand, the continuous rereading and reworking of the past, transformed, fragmented or restaged in new artistic productions and, on the other, the integration of what is the very opposite of Thought – matter, litter, debris – and which resists its capture. From this point onward, art recombines and recycles. The art of the aesthetic regime

> comes after and dissolves the connections of the representative regime: it undoes the logic of connected actions by the becoming-passive of writing; it reconfigures the former poems or paintings. This implies that the entire art of the past is now at our disposal, so that we may reread, rewrite, rethink or repaint it; it implies moreover that every object of reality – the most banal of items, a trace of mold on a wall, an advertisement in a newspaper, or whatever – is available for art, as a double resource: it may be a hieroglyph summing up an entire world, a society, a history, or, on the contrary, a pure presence, sheer reality vested with the new splendour of what is insignificant.[6]

Essential features of advanced artistic forms in the nineteenth century stem from both operations. The ancient models are reshaped. In 1804, for instance, Count Bentheim-Steinfurt reported a rehearsal of Giovanni Paisiello's *Proserpine* at the Parisian Opera. The libretto that Quinault wrote for Lully in 1680 had been reworked, because, as the announcement said, 'nowadays, while a whole forest of laurels has filled the abyss in which France was threatened to be engulfed, followed by the whole of Europe; nowadays, while a new social order replaces universal destruction, the richest fictions of our ancient mythology cannot compete with a simple account of the modern facts'.[7] As for the novel, considered by Rancière as the form that contests, dissolves and takes the place of tragedy, it is overtaken by modern life. Balzac's famous description of the Palais Royal in *Lost Illusions* sets the tone. Here is the place where young and penniless men listen to public lectures and, standing in front of the bookshops, 'avidly' devour cheap novels. They rub shoulders with prostitutes who, at dusk, attract a huge crowd of people slowly advancing 'as though during a procession or a masquerade ball'. The impious association of the sacred and the profane corresponds to two other paradoxical statements: there is, Balzac writes, 'a poetry in this terrible bazaar' and an 'infamous poetry' in the picturesque dresses the whores were fond of in the past; but also, the whole confusion of the gallery evinces 'marvellous oppositions', thus offering the author and his reader something to *think about* (and not merely to stigmatise or to exclude). Made of 'monstrous combinations', this new theatre – a *'spectacle'* held on 'planks' that evoke an operatic stage – stirs up 'emotions ... even within the most insensitive of men'.[8] Thus the modern city increasingly produces a more intense poetry than any poet could achieve. 'The great poem of the display windows sings its stanzas', Balzac writes in his *Physiologie des Grand Boulevards*,[9] and Rimbaud in 1871 would address his colleague Théodore de Banville in the following terms: 'Let your stanzas be like commercial advertisements.'[10]

Conversely, the legacy of the past is all jumbled up. Rejecting high culture, Rimbaud seeks inspiration in yet another 'terrible bazaar':

> What I liked were: absurd paintings, pictures over doorways, stage sets, carnival backdrops, billboards, bright-coloured prints; old-fashioned literature, church Latin, erotic books full of misspellings, the kind of novels our grandmothers read, fairy tales, little children's books, old operas, silly old songs, the naïve rhythms of country rhymes.[11]

As to the reconfiguration of old histories, Rancière's analysis is already prefigured in Hegel's diagnosis of the last stage of Romantic art. Beauty, Hegel claims, becomes a 'subordinate' element; hence, everything finds a place in modern works, the prosaic and even what is 'immoral or wicked'. Irony dissolves the 'usual connections' degrading the venerable fables into a sheer 'material'. Painters enhance what is evanescent in the objects assembled in a still life, their 'scintillating' and 'changing features', to the detriment of their substantial form. The modern subject searches everywhere, and expresses 'its own reflections'. Thus every history will suit him insofar as he may rearrange it 'in the spirit of a dramatist who disposes and exposes characters that are profoundly alien to him'. The Romantic artist 'draws on a stock of images' that he or she adapts following their conformity to the present time – 'all the rest becomes bleak'.[12] Berlioz's reshaping of *Roméo et Juliette* (1839), a hybrid between opera and symphony that perfectly fits Hegel's description and comes after a long series of adaptations of Shakespeare's play during the eighteenth century, offers a most idiosyncratic example. The prologue provides listeners with an incomplete exposition of the story but tells them how it will end; in the following 'parabasis', the composer expresses his admiration for Shakespeare; in part two, the love duet is replaced by an instrumental adagio, in which the two protagonists never appear as singers, while secondary characters (Mercutio, Friar Laurence) do; the scherzo develops a rather incidental group of verses on Queen Mab, spoken by Mercutio, into an entire scintillating movement; the last part represents the funeral procession, mimicking the lover's ultimate sighs and convulsions, then giving way to the genuine finale of a Parisian *grand opéra*. Shakespeare's play is indeed considered as a material – as a set of effects and moments, to be compressed, stretched and distorted.

Two general features of Rancière's regimes seem important. First, the two basic operations of the aesthetic regime are considered as resulting in an 'equalization'. This concept allows Rancière to connect undertakings such as undoing the hierarchies of literary genres, recounting lives that make no sense, or integrating 'speechless' elements into a work, to the political distribution of what can be said, done or made visible within the public space. This distribution – resulting from the activity of what he calls in a broad sense 'the police' – can only be countered by artistic 'politics' that contest and subvert the dominant distributions and sets of hierarchies. As Rancière insists, political activity always faces 'a conflict about the existence of a common scene, and about the quality of those allowed to be present on it'.[13] Political activities deconstruct the divisions installed by the 'police' by showing that large groups or persons are absent from the political scene, ultimately stressing 'the sheer contingency of any order' that denies the 'equality of every speaking animal with every other'.[14] Thus, on the one hand, when artists choose to directly contest a given police – which is the case with *art engagé*, protest songs, propagandistic symphonies, and so forth – they may be said to slip back into counter-politics, replacing one police with another.[15] On the other hand, even such a hermetic poetry as the one chiselled by Stéphane Mallarmé may be described as the 'politics of the Siren'.[16]

Second, each of Rancière's regimes covers a *longue durée*.

Important works of the twenty-first century still subvert Aristotle and, in a Hegelian sense, 'come after' the representative regime that remains the permanent reference. Rancière's philosophical history of art constantly invites us to connect artistic practices of the nineteenth and twentieth centuries, passing over, if not undermining, such distinctions as avant-gardist, modernist or postmodernist, all of which are subordinate to the concept of the aesthetic regime. Thus, Romeo Castelluci's rendering of Shakespeare's *Julius Caesar* (1997), dispersing a handful of Shakespeare's verses throughout an extravagant post-dramatic performance,[17] would not appear, following Rancière, as *essentially* different from Berlioz's reworking of *Romeo and Juliet*. When Piet Mondrian writes in 1927 that the modern city liberates form and shows us the rhythms of a new life, no longer marked by cathedrals, palaces or towers but by complex 'relations and oppositions' contained within the noise of street cars, while church bells only knew simple repetitions,[18] we may easily link this claim to the 'marvellous oppositions' Balzac perceived in the chaotic theatre of the Palais Royal. Rancière himself detects in the remixes of certain DJs 'the two master narratives, the two great demonstrations of the metamorphic power' of art: the identification of 'the cloud of immaterial matter' and

> the sovereign artistic will seizing every material, form, or technique ... transforming into art voices broadcast on radio or TV, jingles of commercial advertisements along with every recorded music available, from Bach to Michael Jackson, from Balinese gamelan and Senegalese drums to sounds electronically produced.[19]

Towards sound

If a regime entails 'forms of visibility of artistic practices' by designating techniques and materials as belonging to art and censoring others, determining which works are 'relevant for Thought'[20] and which are not; if it is, in other words, an 'identifying regime',[21] Foucault's definition of a discourse may be helpful in understanding how such a regime works. As Foucault writes,

> between 'all that is said' and 'a discourse', I make a distinction. 'What is said' represents a set of utterances made absolutely everywhere, in the market, in the street, in a prison, in bed. The 'discourse' instead, among all that is said, comprises a series of utterances that we may

group in a systematic way, and that produces a number of regular power effects.[22]

If we turn to music, the discourse of *rhetoric* reigns during the Baroque era. Music is supposed to imitate emotions, or affects, and the model of a musical work is an oration following rhetorical rules. This issue is mainly discussed when instrumental music is at stake. Without any text, music may not have anything to narrate or to imitate, or, if it does, only in some vague and allusive way.[23] Instrumental music (when it aims at something beyond making people dance) appears as a blurred or misleading mimesis. Even if instrumental music struggles to imitate as precisely as possible (holding, for instance, to one predominating affect throughout one movement), it renders only what Aristotle considers as *second* to actions, namely depicting the changing emotions of an imaginary character or persona.[24] At the end of the eighteenth century this discourse dissolves. Riedel, quoted by Johann Gottfried Herder in 1767, already holds that music, 'through measured sounds, presents actions to our senses'.[25] In the last decades of the century Chabanon, Mirabeau and Adam Smith claim that imitation is not essential to music and that its emotional impact as such is sufficient.[26] Thus, a different model emerges. As Mark Evan Bonds writes, 'after 1800, writers gradually abandoned the metaphor of the oration, preferring instead to describe the musical work as an organism'.[27] The 'organic' work could be (though was not always) a complex object; it could be likened to a body made entirely of different and contrasting members. Music is a fable, or action, by itself, even if its secret laws may not be immediately intelligible, as the reception of Beethoven during the nineteenth century demonstrates.

When we consider the main stages of the organicist discourse, which has been itself something like the master narrative of Western music since 1800, the restructuring of harmony (Wagner) and tonality (Schoenberg) immediately come to mind. In the middle of the twentieth century this musical discourse culminates in the aesthetics of serialism, producing works that illustrate, in the terms of composer Hugues Dufourt, an 'art of splendour and contrast', though grounded on 'hidden architectonics' and 'antagonistic correlations' that elude immediate understanding.[28] From the listener's point of view, the very extreme of an overall musical organisation (resting on the exteriority of number) seems to coincide with the apex of chaos, however sublime it may be. Hence we encounter a turning point in the 1970s. What slowly emerges is the paradigm of sound.[29] Finally, a musical work is no longer (or is no longer described as) a critical structure, but a listening device allowing us to better perceive the micro-physics or mysteries of sound. Composing does not essentially mean, as it largely did prior to this point, confronting oneself with what Theodor W. Adorno called a musical *material* that bears the marks and stigmata of history. A musical work can now be legitimised, and in turn be accepted, when its essential purpose is to confront, to unfold and to zoom in on sounds, wherefrom we may deduce its formal process, as spectralism does. Material, linked to culture, is substituted by *matter*, linked to nature and understood as a complex of forces and intensities, an approach that might explain why the predominant aesthetic reference is no longer the philosophy of Adorno (the work of art as critical structure), but that of Gilles Deleuze (the work of art as 'molecular' assemblage of intensities).[30]

Rancière's description of the aesthetic regime invites us, however, to consider the opposition of structure and sound as a *confrontation* rather than a historical evolution. If the organic structure – created by a composer who, consciously or unconsciously, acts 'as' nature does – will from now on 'confront the splendour of the insignificant', the Other of structure will be sound itself, the fascinating and centripetal forces of matter. In this respect one may note the growing importance of sound in literature since the nineteenth century. Joseph Joubert, who frequently describes sounds and noises in *Carnets*, seems to dismiss the entire paradigm of oratory when he writes in 1806: 'One beautiful sound is more beautiful than a long speech.'[31] In William Wordsworth's new lyricism, sound plays an important role. From Rancière's perspective, Wordsworth achieves three transgressions: the 'lonely wandering' of the lyrical subject that encounters objects and people symbolising 'dear liberty', a new way to 'accompany' what is said, and a new use of metaphor as 'transport'.[32] The new rhythm of the poet's pace destroys, challenges or rethinks the venerable trajectory of the epic poem – and, one might add, of the *Bildungsroman*.[33] The conquest of a new space – resulting from new objects focused by the eye, from a new vision and from a new manner of expressing it – illustrates precisely what Rancière defines as 'utopian': the power, on the one hand, 'to superimpose a space for speech (*espace discursif*) and a real territory (*espace territorial*)' and, on the other hand, 'to identify a space for new perceptions, discovered by wandering through it, with the *topos* of the community'.[34]

Moreover, this 'aesthetic' utopia not only implies the rejection of the old images ('the new truth does not lie in a model, represented or misrepresented by images'),[35] but also makes the poet *listen* to the world. In Book XII of *The Prelude*, Wordsworth tells us how he freed himself from the 'intellectual eye' (as he will name it in Book XIII, line 52) that prevented him from perceiving nature. Once, he remembers, he gave way

> To a comparison of scene with scene,
> Bent overmuch on superficial things
> Pampering myself with meagre novelties
> Of colour and proportion; to the moods
> Of time and season, to the moral power,
> The affections and the spirit of the place
> Insensible. (XII, lines 114–20)

The gaze ('the bodily eye', XII, line 128) is explicitly linked to the political regime that the French Revolution had just overthrown: 'The most despotic of our senses, gained/ Such strength in me as often hold my mind/ In absolute dominion' (XII, lines 129–31). When eventually imagination is restored (the faculty that, for Kant, precisely 'dismisses *mimesis* and abolishes the distance between the *eidos* of beauty and that which is offered to our senses')[36] the poet bows

> To God, who thus corrected my desires;
> And, afterwards, the wind and sleety rain,
> And all the business of the elements,
> The single sheep, and the one blasted tree,
> And the bleak music from that old stone wall,
> The noise of wood and water . . .
> All these were kindred spectacles and sounds
> To which I often repaired, and thence would drink,
> As at a fountain (XII, lines 316–26)

To liberate oneself from the tyranny of the eye means to be aware of all that which escapes contours and surfaces suitable to be compared to each other or to be related to an ideal form. Equally important, though, are noises, sounds or bleak music. When he shifts his centre of attention to sound, or focuses upon its 'kindred' presence, the poet illustrates the new becoming-passive. He enters the opacity of things and renounces the controlling position implied by the eye: 'The republican political is not ordered by the point of view of a privileged spectator, by the spectacle of royal majesty ... Nature has dethroned the king by abolishing his place, his perspective.'[37] In literature, sound increasingly will express the non-expressible. For instance, just after being seduced by Rodolphe and first committing adultery, at the very moment when the reader expects Emma Bovary to express some feelings or the narrator to draw a moral conclusion from what has just happened, Flaubert instead makes his heroine perceive reflections of the light, sounds and the fleeting presence of animals with an incongruous intensity:

> The shades of night were falling; the horizontal sun passing between the branches dazzled the eyes. Here and there around her, in the leaves or on the ground, trembled luminous patches, as if hummingbirds flying about had scattered their feathers. Silence was everywhere; something sweet seemed to come forth from the trees; she felt her heart, whose beating had begun again, and the blood coursing through her flesh like a stream of milk. Then far away, beyond the wood, on the other hills, she heard a vague prolonged cry, a voice which lingered, and in silence she heard it mingling like music with the last pulsations of her throbbing nerves.[38]

The relation between sound and the necessary renunciation of activity reappears in Proust's *In Search of Lost Time* where the final salvation – the idea that *every life* may be written down and become a literary 'cathedral', even the life of a loser belonging to the upper classes who never did or wrote anything remarkable – does not arise, as Proust had initially planned, from the narrator's overhearing of Wagner's Good Friday Music, but when, by mere chance, he perceives the noise of a spoon hitting a plate.[39] As to the central section of Virginia Woolf's *To the Lighthouse*, the wind altogether takes over the narration: 'certain airs' explore the darkness and stillness of the house, pervaded by tiny noises and rumours, while the action outside – marriages, births, deaths, the Great War – is cut into slices and packed in brackets.

When literature distances itself from the absolute reign of the image, the soundtrack of novels and poems grows more and more dense. If, moreover, becoming-musical means becoming-passive, this may be due to the *suspensive effect* of sounds, which, for a brief moment, seem to block or to check the active progress of the narrative, evoking the potentially unstructured and haphazard space that surrounds the story. Similar effects have happened in Western music since Beethoven. Epiphanies of sound, moments when a special timbre emerges or is listened to *by music itself*, as it were, occur more and more frequently in the works of Berlioz, Wagner, Mahler, Debussy and Ives.[40] At the beginning of the 'Hostias et preces' in *Grande Messe des morts* (1838), Berlioz writes an astonishing *accord-timbre*, a chord-colour, with the flutes in the highest register playing the overtones of the F-sharp in the trombones. Separated by an abyss, the two may illustrate the distance between men and God to whom the former offer gifts and prayers. The effect, repeated eight times, punctuates but also suspends the musical progression by zooming in on what Berlioz himself calls *'l'effet matériel de la musique'*.[41] Not surprisingly, such effects were stigmatised by his conservative colleague Adolphe Adam, who had the impression 'of attending to an experiment in acoustics. He breathes into all kinds of instruments in order not to express an idea, but in order to check how they will sound.'[42]

Even Wagner's complex harmonic objects and/or orchestrations of conventional chords bear something of a cinematographic still. As Ernst Kurth has shown, the 'harmonic sensuousness' of Wagner's style affects 'not the structure of harmonies but the structure of harmonic *connections*, and there leads to destructive processes'. The chord is 'influenced by its sonic appeal as such, by its *absolute* effect'. Thus 'the harmonic colours well up from within, and so gradually engulf and destroy the unified tonal outlines'.[43] The art of infinite transitions, colours and shades prevails over the structural powers traditionally assigned to harmony and melody. Wagner perceives such a programme already in Palestrina's music – now that 'the entire art of the past is at our disposal',[44] for artists to appropriate or distort it, reading into it or drawing out of it their own concerns and fantasies. 'Here', Wagner writes,

> rhythm is only perceptible through changes in the harmonic succession of chords, whilst apart from these it does not exist at all as an asymmetrical division of time. Here the successions in time are so immediately connected with the essential nature of harmony, which is

itself out of the realms of time and space, that the aid of the laws of time cannot help us in understanding such music. The sole succession of time in music of this description is hardly otherwise apparent than in the exceedingly delicate changes of one fundamental colour. Such changes retain their connection through the most varied transitions, without our being able to perceive any distinct drawing of lines. But then, as the colour does not appear in space we get a picture almost as timeless as it is spaceless, a spiritual revelation throughout, that rouses unspeakable emotion, as it brings us nearer than everything else to a notion of the very essence of Religion, freed from all dogmatic and theoretical definitions.[45]

Most certainly, this description applies to the prelude of *Lohengrin* better than to Palestrina's *Stabat mater*, the text of which is not even mentioned by Wagner, nor the essential technical feature of Palestrina's style, counterpoint. The venerable figure of the ancient master authorises a dissolution that, in Wagner's music, equally engulfs every recognisable *melodic line*. For Johann Mattheson, in 1739, a melody is essential to music insofar as it encapsulates what is common to a group of listeners and thus may be 'recognised' by each of them.[46] Some decades later, Johann Georg Sulzer claims that a melody must allow us 'to imagine that we listen to the oration of a man who, overwhelmed by some emotion, discovers it in this way'.[47] Both descriptions still allude to tragedy as the central artistic form of a community. Wagner, however, declares a century later: 'Beautiful melodies are over!'[48] By drowning melody – rendering it 'infinite', comparing the whole of a musical drama to the melody of a forest at dusk, symbolising, with its silence, noises and bird cries, the subtle and endless texture of musical motifs[49] – Wagner already conceptualises an essentially *paratactic* music made of strokes, points, stops or loops.

Wandering

To address the question whether the history of progressive music from Beethoven onwards might be described as a conflict between structure and sound or an evolution from the former to the latter, we must turn again to the notion of discourse as defined by Foucault. A discourse never grasps *the entirety* of the elements or aspects of a given work, style or epoch. Obviously, neither structure nor sound is ever absent from music, but they may both be considered *the* fundamental aspect, or not. A discourse explains how musical forms may be understood, how a work may be declared plausible and convincing, how it may be perceived as the expression of a sensible practice, and it entails power effects such as institutions, spaces or listening attitudes. For instance, the decisions made in the second half of the eighteenth century to build concert halls dedicated exclusively to the rehearsal of music eventually led to such listening laboratories as Wagner's theatre in Bayreuth, or Arnold Schoenberg's *Verein für musikalische Privataufführungen* (1918–21), where a happy few, hearing a new work always played twice, had no right to utter any critical judgement or to applaud.[50] On the contrary, the ideal venues at the end of the twentieth century were open ones, ephemeral and preferably vast and obscure spaces. You might be lying on the floor or listening to string a quartet played in the dark. The ideal listening situation had to be exceptional, mysterious, immersive, creating the intense feeling that you belonged to an ephemeral community.

A composer does not exclusively create by means of techniques, his knowledge of the musical past or his poetic vision. He draws on discourses actually *shaping* his work. Pierre Henry's two versions of his *Dixième Symphonie* may show this interaction between discourses and actual techniques, along with its political implications. In 1974 Henry performed a kind of structural analysis of Beethoven's symphonies, highlighting typical trajectories, links or 'bridges' between the works. As Henry later recalled,

> I took only what I liked. I lined up on a sheet of paper, and then assembled on a tape 12 isolated perfect triads, 18 repeated triads, 3 isolated dominant sevenths, 8 repeated dominant sevenths ... 3 harmonic sequences, 5 fermatas, 19 tremolos, 12 trills ... I also divided into 'phrases' 41 arpeggios, 8 pedal points, 2 pizzicatos, 41 progressions, 14 thunderstorms, 2 conclusions and 33 dramas. I added to them 79 quotations, no longer than 30 seconds each. These quotations were meant to reintroduce the temporality of the original music ... The whole set of these structures was assembled in a file, a repertoire giving rise to a new work: the 10th, of which I realised a first model in 1974.[51]

The result is an avant-gardist collage full of interruptions, akin to the 'antagonistic correlations' displayed by serialism.[52] This represents an (Adornian) critical structure that assembles fragments of the past in a new way and, while doing so, challenges the traditional symphonic narration.

At the end of the 1990s Henry again turned to the work, but now seemed to rewrite history, claiming that features other than the possibility of producing a cut-up had interested him twenty years before:

> Beethoven had fascinated me because he invents melodies with only a few notes and because these are strong melodies, as strong as a thunderbolt, a wave in the sea, or the Sirens. He has invented the sculpting and dramatisation of sounds. Thus, he laid out the foundations of the music of our present ... Moreover, life itself enters his music. Simple life, with its moments of monotony, of sheer repetition, moments of exasperation, sometimes comical, but also full of suspense and surprises.[53]

The stress is now on topics typical of contemporary art music since the 1980s – the relation between music and nature (Beethoven's symphonies may be heard as a soundscape), the *topos* of sculpting sound,[54] the importance of images, the urge to recover some kind of continuity, here in the guise of melodies, and finally, as Henry explains in his presentation of the remix from 1996–98, the rhythm of the body:

> By editing and remixing I have introduced moments of resolution and frustration, prolongations and climaxes, cycles, repetitions and counterpoint by the means of canons ... The 10th remix, today, is a 10th with my own and more contemporary rhythms – more accelerated, with beats, electronic trances, sparklings out of phase, with filtering, added frequencies, doubled reverberations ... Today, the framework of the 10th remix is an imaginary film. For me, this means to pronounce a new radical sound discourse, and to engage in a new adventure expressing the new function of the composer within society.[55]

The eighth movement, *Aube*, aptly illustrates this programme. The looping of the beginning of Beethoven's Ninth Symphony (the fifth A/E symbolising a genesis, a void from which 'the sound as it were [is] welling up from nowhere')[56] is superimposed with the soft noises of a countryside pervaded by soft beats echoing modern technological culture, as though a party were to escape a techno venue and stroll around at dawn, before going to sleep. Everything in this soundtrack is fluid, homogeneous and continuous. Thus, the two versions of 1974 and 1998 illustrate what Rancière calls, on the one hand, a *dialectical editing* (as found in Jean-Luc Godard's *Pierrot le fou*) and, on the other, a *symbolic editing* (as found in Godard's *Histoire(s) du cinema*). The first technique, in order to give us the idea 'of another community imposing another measure', organises 'a shock and heightens what is uncanny in what is familiar to us, in order to make appear another order, discovered only at the expense of a violent conflict'. The second endeavours 'to establish a familiarity, an occasional analogy', emphasising 'a more profound kinship, a common world where heterogeneous elements belong to the same essential fabric'.[57]

If the model of contemporary art music is no longer that of dialectical or critical structure, but what composer Fausto Romitelli once called an 'audiodrome',[58] we might say that, in some allegorical way, the modernist persona of music, ever in conflict with the world, has been substituted by a persona walking through a soundscape, on the lookout for sounds, echoes and traces, and reacting to them.[59] Wordsworth's walking is again essential to music, as to contemporary art in general, if we believe Nicolas Bourriaud, who considers translation, transformation and wandering as its predominant features.[60] Rancière's commentary on W. G. Sebald's book *The Rings of Saturn* (1995) follows the same line. The narrator, wandering through the county of Suffolk, constantly slips from local to global history. The objects he sees or evokes, such as manors and graveyards, silent villages on the seashore or industrial buildings, constantly recall the cruel sovereigns who paraded at these resorts on ostentatious yachts or bought weapons produced in now deserted factories in order to exterminate their own people. Everywhere, memories of destruction appear. The ravages of colonialism constantly loom on the narrator's conscience and (dis)orientate his perception of the sublime desolation of idyllic landscapes.

For Rancière, this 'new kind of fiction' is 'no longer structured by the linking of causes and effects' but instead 'immerses itself in the realm of ordinary things and idleness'.[61] The prevailing model is no longer the logic of tragedy but a reverie during a journey: 'If there is anything like modern fiction, one might define it in a nutshell by saying that it suppresses the reversal, the *peripeteia*. Time has ceased to hasten towards the end.'[62] Commenting on Virginia Woolf's *To the Lighthouse*, Rancière notes that Mrs. Ramsay 'spins the great layer of coexistence, as opposed to the authority of logical connections' that is typical for her husband,[63] and, one might add, for a male-dominated society. Recent fiction, Rancière claims, simply 'establishes links between what happens at a given place and what happens at this very place at another moment, with what happens at the same moment at another place, or with what happens at another moment at another place'.[64] It illustrates 'a time of coexistence, invaded by the liberality of space'.[65]

I must add one final remark on some equivalents of such 'new kind[s] of fiction' in recent contemporary music. If, as Rancière invites us to consider, structure was the Other of sound within the new paradigm emerging during the 1980s, contemporary music has sooner or later to turn to another Other, as it were. During the 2010s wanderings were no longer sufficient. Hence, quite a number of young composers in Germany and elsewhere who advocate a new *Gehaltsästhetik* or a New Realism turn to *real images* as a more potent Other.[66] In his neo-dadaist *Charts Music* (2009), Johannes Kreidler films the graphs representing the daily quotations of big companies' stocks during the financial crisis of January 2009, accompanied by merry melodies derived from the very contours of these graphs. The opera *Kredit* (2016) for video, ensemble, pre-recorded sounds and choir by Hannes Seidl and Daniel Ott is designed as a documentary about the secret universe of the Deutsche Bundesbank in Frankfurt, inspired by journalistic investigations. Numerous recent pieces by Alexander Schubert (such as *Star me Kitten*, 2015), Michael Maierhof (in his cycle *splittings*, since 1999), Stefan Prins (*Mirror Box*, 2015) and others play with the odd and disturbing invasion of other spaces into the listening space – whether the chatter of the audience recorded while they enter the concert hall, a radio playing pop music in an adjacent room, the noises of the street outside or those of a washing machine on a tape, as in Hannes Seidl's *Zimmerrauschen – Public* (2011).

Such experiments not only attest to the growing importance of multimedia in contemporary music, they also show recent music as concerned with *connecting* places and moments in a new way – creating short circuits or rediscovering obfuscated and censored connections. Intense and innovative music, comparable in this respect to some recent fiction, 'no longer unfolds by linking different temporal moments but as a relation between two spaces'.[67] Rancière's theory as such therefore marks something like a 'spatial turn' in political philosophy. Art, he holds, never provokes a revolution but illustrates the difference between what is there and what could be there; the discrepancy, in other words, between real political spaces or communities (arranged by 'police') and possible ones (in the authentic and egalitarian sense of 'politics'). As the philosopher recently wrote, 'one does not work for the future, but one aims at creating a gap, at tracing a furrow in the present, in order to intensify the experience of another way of existing'.[68]

Notes

1. Jacques Rancière, *Le Partage du sensible: esthétique et politique* (Paris: La fabrique, 2000), 10. Thanks to Jean-Charles Beaumont and Kevin Kelly for rereading the English version of this essay. Unless otherwise specified, all translations are by the author.
2. Rancière, *Le Partage du sensible*, 27. See also Martin Kaltenecker, 'L'Hypothèse de la continuité. Variations à partir de Jacques Rancière', in Martin Kaltenecker and François Nicolas (eds), *Penser l'oeuvre musicale au XXe siècle: avec, sans ou contre l'Histoire?* (Paris: Editions du CDMC, 2006), and Jairo Moreno and Gavin Steingo, 'Rancière's Equal Music', *Contemporary Music Review* 31.5–6 (2012), 487–505.
3. Rancière, *Le Partage du sensible*, 30.
4. Jacques Rancière, *Les Bords de la fiction* (Paris: Galilée, 2017), 15.
5. Rancière, *Le Partage du sensible*, 31.
6. Jacques Rancière, *La Fable cinématographique* (Paris: Galilée, 2001), 16.
7. See Elmar Kruttge, 'Aus den Reisetagebüchern des Grafen Ludwig von Bentheim-Steinfurt (1756–1817)', *Zeitschrift für Musikwissenschaft* VI.1 (1923/24), 17.
8. Honoré de Balzac, *Illusions perdues* (Paris: Gallimard, 1977), 358–61.
9. Honoré de Balzac, *Histoire et physiologie des boulevards de Paris* (1845), <http://www.bmlisieux.com/curiosa/balzac02.htm> (last accessed 20 March 2018).
10. Arthur Rimbaud, *Œuvres complètes*, ed. Pierre Brunel (Paris: Le Livre de Poche, 1999), 264.
11. Arthur Rimbaud, 'L'Alchimie du verbe', trans. Paul Schmidt, <http://www.mag4.net/Rimbaud/poesies/Alchemy.html> (last accessed 20 March 2018).

12. Georg Friedrich Wilhelm Hegel, *Vorlesungen über Ästhetik*, vol. 2 (Frankfurt am Main: Suhrkamp, 1986), 221–3, 229, 235–6.
13. Jacques Rancière, *La Chair des mots* (Paris: Galilée, 1998), 49.
14. Rancière, *La Chair des mots*, 53.
15. Matthew Lampert, 'Beyond the Politics of Reception: Jacques Rancière and the Politics of Art', *Contemporary Philosophical Review* 50 (2017), 184.
16. Jacques Rancière, *Mallarmé. La politique de la sirène* (Paris: Hachette, 1996).
17. Hans Thies Lehmann, *Postdramatic Theatre* (London: Routledge, 2006).
18. Piet Mondrian, *The New Art – The New Life: The Collected Writings of Piet Mondrian* (Boston: G. K. Hall, 1986), 144.
19. Jacques Rancière 'La Métamorphose des muses', in *Sonic Process: une nouvelle géographie des sons* (Paris: Centre Pompidou, 2002), 26.
20. Jacques Rancière, *L'Inconscient esthétique* (Paris: Galilée, 2001), 12.
21. Rancière, *La Fable cinématographique*, 11.
22. Michel Foucault, 'L'Inquiétude de l'actualité', *Le Monde*, 19–20 September 1975.
23. Charles du Bos, *Réflexions critiques sur la poésie et la peinture* (Paris: Mariette, 1719), 634–59.
24. Aristotle, *Poétique*, trans. Barbara Gernez (Paris: Les Belles Lettres, 2001), 27.
25. Johann Georg Herder, *Viertes Kritisches Wäldchen* (Erlangen: Bläsing, 1846), 426.
26. See Michel Pierre Guy de Chabanon, *De la musique considérée en elle-même et dans ses rapports avec la parole, les langues, la poésie et le theatre* (Paris: Pissot, 1785), 34; Belinda Cannone, 'Le Lecteur y mettra le titre: un pamphlet de Mirabeau en faveur de la musique instrumentale', *Dix-huitième siècle* 20.1 (1988), 403–14; Adam Smith, 'Of the Nature of Imitation', in *Essays on Philosophical Subjects*, vol. 3 (Oxford: Clarendon Press, 1980).
27. See Mark E. Bonds, *Wordless Rhetoric. Musical Form and the Metaphor of the Oration* (Cambridge, MA: Harvard University Press, 1991), 4; M. H. Abrams, *The Mirror and the Lamp. Romantic Theory and the Critical Tradition* (Oxford: Oxford University Press, 1971); Ruth Solie, 'Living Work: Organicism and Musical Analysis', *Nineteenth-Century Music* 4.2 (1980), 147–56; and Lothar Schmidt, *Organische Form in der Musik. Stationen eines Begriffs 1795–1850* (Kassel: Bärenreiter, 1990).

28. Hugues Dufourt, *Musique, pouvoir, écriture* (Paris: Bourgois, 1991), 292.
29. Martin Kaltenecker, 'The Discourse of Sound', *Tempo* 70 (2016), 1–10.
30. Kaltenecker, 'The Discourse of Sound'. John Cage, Iannis Xenakis and Pierre Schaeffer are now considered to be the most important figures, replacing the founding fathers of organicist aesthetics, from Beethoven to Boulez, via Brahms and Wagner. Likewise, such composers as Giacinto Scelsi and Savatore Sciarrino, still marginal figures during the 1980s, are little by little inserted in the new configuration. The whole evolution exemplifies the 'power effect' of the *discourse of sound*, which doesn't imply that structures, forms, numerical calculations, Fibonacci series and so forth disappear: however, all these are included in the search for sound that legitimises the work, used as a tool rather than as a *telos*. Or, to put it in perhaps more Rancièrean terms, sound is allowed to undo structure, while it was considered before to enhance, to clarify or to clothe structure.
31. Joseph Joubert, *Pensées* (Paris: Christian Bourgois, 1966), 218.
32. Rancière, *La Chair des mots*, 18–30; see also D. F. Bell, 'Writing, Movement/Space, Democracy: On Jacques Rancière's Literary History', *SubStance* 33.1 (2004), 127–30.
33. Rancière, *La Chair des mots*, 23.
34. Rancière, *La Chair des mots*, 27–8.
35. Rancière, *La Chair des mots*, 26.
36. Rancière, *La Chair des mots*, 27.
37. Rancière, *La Chair des mots*, 27.
38. Gustave Flaubert, *Madame Bovary*, trans. Eleanor Marx-Aveling, <https://www.gutenberg.org/files/2413/2413-h/2413-h.htm> (last accessed 20 March 2018).
39. Martin Kaltenecker, *L'Oreille divisée. Les discours sur l'écoute aux XVIIIe et XIXe siècles* (Paris: Musica falsa, 2010), 416.
40. Kaltenecker, *L'Oreille divisée*, 406–22.
41. Hector Berlioz, *Critique musicale*, vol. 3 (Paris: Buchet-Chastel, 2001), 387.
42. Quoted in Paul Scudo, *Critique et littérature musicales*, vol. 2 (Paris: Hachette, 1859), 118.
43. Ernst Kurth, *Selected Writings*, ed. and trans. Lee A. Rothfarb (Cambridge: Cambridge University Press, 1991), 119–221.
44. Rancière, *Le Partage du sensible*, 16.
45. Richard Wagner, *Beethoven*, trans. Edward Dannreuther (London: Reeves, 1903), 32–3.

46. Johann Mattheson, *Der Vollkommene Kapellmeister* (Hamburg: Christian Herold, 1739), 142.
47. Johann Georg Sulzer, *Allgemeine Theorie der Schönen Künste* (Berlin: Directmedia, Digitale Bibliothek, 2004), article 'Melodie'.
48. Richard Wagner, *Über das Operndichten und Komponieren im besonderen*, in *Sämtliche Schriften und Dichtungen*, vol. 10 (Leipzig: Breitkopf & Härtel/Siegel, n.d.), 173.
49. Richard Wagner, *Zukunftsmusik*, in *Sämtliche Schriften und Dichtungen*, vol. 7 (Leipzig: Breitkopf & Härtel/Siegel, n.d.), 121.
50. See Arnold Schoenberg, *Schönbergs Verein für musikalische Privataufführungen, Musik-Konzepte 36*, ed. Heinz-Klaus Metzger and Rainer Riehn (Munich: text+kritik, 1984), 4–5.
51. Pierre Henry, liner notes of the CD *Pierre Henry remixe sa dixième Symphonie* (Philips 462821-2, 1998).
52. Dufourt, *Musique, pouvoir, écriture*, 292.
53. Henry, liner notes of the CD *Pierre Henry remixe sa dixième Symphonie*.
54. Tristan Murail, *Modèles et artifices* (Strasbourg: Presses universitaires de Strasbourg, 2004), 82; Wolfgang Rihm, *Ausgesprochen, Schriften und Gespräche*, vol. 1 (Winterthur: Amadeus, 1997), 94; Ramon Lazkano, 'Entretien avec Lionel Esparza', in *La Ligne de craie* (Champigny-sur-Marne: 2e2M, 2009), 97; James Saunders, interview with Rebecca Saunders, <http://www.james-saunders.com/interview-with-rebecca-saunders/> (last accessed 20 March 2018).
55. Henry, liner notes of the CD *Pierre Henry remixe sa dixième Symphonie*.
56. Nicholas Cook, *Beethoven: Symphony No. 9* (Cambridge: Cambridge University Press, 1993), 27.
57. Jacques Rancière, *Le Destin des images* (Paris: La fabrique, 2003), 66–8.
58. See his orchestral piece *Audiodrome – Dead City Radio* (2003).
59. See, for instance, Luigi Nono, *Prometeo* (1981–85), Helmut Lachenmann, *Nun* (1999), Fausto Romitelli, *Audiodrome – Dead City Radio* (2003), Ramon Lazkano, *Ortzi Isilak* (2005), Mark Andre, *auf...* (2007), Rebecca Saunders, *chroma IX* (2008), Heiner Goebbels, *Stifters Dinge* (2008), Hugues Dufourt, *Voyage par-delà les fleuves et les monts* (2010), Jérôme Combier, *Austerlitz* (2011), Yann Robin, *Inferno* (2014), Wolfgang Mitterer, *Crush* (2012), Olga Neuwirth, *Le* Encantadas *o le avventure nel mare delle meraviglie* (2015).
60. Nicolas Bourriaud, *The Radicant* (Berlin/New York: Sternberg/

Merve Verlag, 2009). See also Tim Rutherford-Johnson, *Music after the Fall* (Berkeley: University of California Press, 2017), 93–119.
61. Rancière, *Les Bords de la fiction*, 120.
62. Rancière, *Les Bords de la fiction*, 131.
63. Rancière, *Le Fil perdu. Essais sur la fiction moderne* (Paris: Galilée, 2014), 56–7.
64. Rancière, *Les Bords de la fiction*, 131.
65. Rancière, *Les Bords de la fiction*, 127.
66. See Johannes Kreidler, Harry Lehmann and Claus Steffen Mahnkopff (eds), *Musik, Ästhetik, Digitalisierung. Eine Kontroverse* (Hofheim: Wolke, 2010), and Harry Lehmann, *Die digitale Revolution in der Musik. Eine Musikphilosophie* (Mainz: Schott, 2012). For a presentation of the recent German 'Gehaltsästhetik' in French, see Martin Kaltenecker, 'De l'effrangement à la connexion', in Wilfried Laforge and Jacinto Lageira (eds), *À la frontiere des arts: Lectures contemporaines de l'esthétique adornienne* (Paris: Minerve, 2019), 125–54.
67. Rancière, *Les Bords de la fiction*, 133.
68. Jacques Rancière, *En quel temps vivons-nous? Conversation avec Eric Hazan* (Paris: La fabrique, 2017), 32.

5

Staging Music in the Aesthetic Regime of Art: Rancière, Berlioz and the Bells of *Harold en Italie*
João Pedro Cachopo

> Art is art insofar as it is also non-art, or something other than art.
> Rancière, *Aesthetics and Its Discontents*[1]

A scene is missing

This essay explores the hypothesis that bringing Rancière's political-aesthetic ideas to bear on matters of music may productively unsettle and enrich our understanding of musical modernity. Such an exploration is both timely and risky. It is timely because Rancière has consistently reflected on the politics of art in the context of a reappraisal of artistic modernity that pays particular attention to the erosion of the arts and their connection to life – a debate in which the role of music should not be underestimated. Still, it is risky, albeit worthwhile, because Rancière's references to music have been somewhat sporadic and elusive.[2] The above-mentioned hypothesis thus takes on the form of a double challenge: to venture into a less explored area in Rancière's thought while also – indeed, with the main goal of – developing new insights into the history and politics of music.

In order to tackle this challenge, my approach will be neither philological nor systematic. That is to say, I will neither delve into the texts in which Rancière deals more specifically with musical issues, nor attempt to apply aspects of his theorisation – say, the three regimes of art or the politics/police binary – to the history and practice of music. Instead, turning to what I consider to be a pivotal element of his undisciplined thought, I will draw on the 'method of the scene'. If, for Walter Benjamin, method is 'detour' [*Umweg*], it might be fair to say that method is 'staging' [*mise en scène*] for Rancière. As he explains, the setting of a scene involves a number of theoretical operations, all of which are found at work in each of the fourteen chapters of *Aisthesis: Scènes du régime esthétique de l'art* (2011):

> Each one of these scenes thus presents a singular event, and explores the interpretive network that gives it meaning around an emblematic text. The event can be a performance [*représentation théâtrale*], a lecture, an exhibition, a visit to a museum or to a studio, a book, or a film release. The network built around it shows how a performance or an object is felt and thought not only as art, but also as a singular artistic proposition and a source of artistic emotion, as novelty and revolution in art – even as a means for art to find a way out of itself. Thus it inscribes them into a moving constellation in which modes of perception and affect, and forms of interpretation defining a paradigm of art, take shape. The scene is not the illustration of an idea. It is a little optical machine that shows us thought busy weaving together perceptions, affects, names and ideas, constituting the sensible community that these links create, and the intellectual community that makes such weaving thinkable.[3]

After describing this *modus operandi*, Rancière goes on to clarify in what sense its specificity influences and resonates in his thematic choices:

> The fourteen episodes that follow are so many microcosms in which we see the logic of this regime being formed, transformed, incorporating unexplored territories and forming new patterns in order to do so. Their selection might give rise to some surprise; the reader will seek in vain for landmarks that have become unavoidable in the history of artistic modernity: no *Olympia*, no *Suprematist Composition: White on White*, no *Fountain*, nor *Igitur* or *The Painter of Modern Life*. Instead there are reviews of Funambules and the Folies Bergère written by poets who have fallen into the purgatory of literary anthologies, talks by thinkers or critics who have fallen from grace, sketchbooks for stagings rarely performed . . . Influential histories and philosophies of artistic modernity identify it with the conquest of autonomy by each art, which is expressed in exemplary works that break with the course of history, separating themselves both from the art of the past and the 'aesthetic' forms of prosaic life. Fifteen years of work have brought me to the exact opposite conclusions: the movement belonging to the

aesthetic regime, which supported the dream of artistic novelty and fusion between art and life subsumed under the idea of modernity, tends to erase the specificities of the arts and to blur the boundaries that separate them from each other and from ordinary experience ... One could thus consider these episodes, if so inclined, as a counter-history of 'artistic modernity'.[4]

It is not by chance that Rancière's argument evolves from explaining his method to formulating his overarching goal in this book (paradigmatic as it is of his political-aesthetic endeavour as a whole): namely, to put forward a 'counter-history of "artistic modernity"'. It is as though each scene, as a microcosm or a monad, contained the entire project in itself. For the sake of clarity, and taking into consideration not only *Aisthesis* but also other works such as *Le Partage du sensible* (2000), *L'Inconscient esthétique* (2001), *Malaise dans l'esthétique* (2004) or *Le Spectateur emancipé* (2008), I would summarise the theoretical twists that embody such a rewriting of the history of 'artistic modernity' through the following key points:

- The 'revolution' associated with the emergence of the aesthetic regime of art, which replaced the representative and the ethical regimes, harks back to the late eighteenth century and consists of a set of transformations in the ways of making, experiencing and interpreting art that put it at odds with the hierarchical order of the world (or, in Rancière's terms, the 'police distribution of the sensible').
- In a way, only within the aesthetic regime did it become possible to imagine a 'politics of art' in the sense of a valorisation of its egalitarian and emancipatory dimensions (yet without conflating the latter with the formulation of explicit ideological messages or the search for immediate social effects).
- These transformations, despite the fact that their onset can be traced to a certain moment in history, occurred in a slow manner, which is to say that the regimes of art cannot be mistaken for historical periods, as they continue to coexist, as different ways of putting art practice and aesthetic experience in perspective, in the present day.
- The aesthetic regime of art blurs the boundary between production and reception: at stake are not only ways of creating, but also of perceiving, critiquing and appropriating art (in which

artists, critics, theorists, spectators, amateurs and detractors play an equally decisive role), and it is crucial to acknowledge their reciprocal influence.
- Comprehending the 'aesthetic revolution' in its full consequences leads to a critical reappraisal of the ways in which modernist discourse, with its characteristic emphasis on the autonomy of the arts and the boundary between art and life, has interpreted artistic modernity in retrospect.
- Finally, this leads to a re-evaluation of how Romantic, avant-garde and contemporary trends reverberate in one another in ways that the traditional understanding of artistic modernity, conditioned as it is by the postmodern debate, fails to do justice to.

In light of the above, the question arises as to how these ideas apply to music and what their consequences are for musicological research. To begin with: is it possible to unfold a musical scene along the lines of *Aisthesis*? Rancière himself considered the possibility of dedicating a chapter of *Aisthesis* to Edgard Varèse's *Déserts* (1950–54), but later gave up on the idea because he could not find a critical text that would open and set the tone for the discussion.[5] The fact thus remains that a scene accounting for the entry of music into the aesthetic regime of art is missing. In this essay, in order to suggest that several of Rancière's insights may help us hone a critical reflection on musical modernity – which, it goes without saying, should not be mistaken for an attempt to add a chapter to Rancière's book – I will attempt to imagine an unheard scene around Hector Berlioz's *Harold en Italie* (1834).

Two wrong notes

A curious debate ensued, I was told, between Fétis, who was still hostile to me, and another critic, M. Zani de Ferranti, an artist and writer of note who set up as my champion. When the latter singled out, among the items that I had performed, the Pilgrims' March in *Harold* as one of the most interesting things he had ever heard, Fétis answered, 'How can I be expected to approve of a piece in which one is constantly hearing two notes that are not part of the harmony?' (He was referring to the C and B which recur at the end of each stanza, like a slow tolling of bells.)

'Indeed?' de Ferranti replied. 'Well, I don't believe in this anomaly of yours. Or rather, if a composer has managed to write a piece which delights me from the beginning to end as this has done, with two notes that are not part of the harmony, then I can only say he must be a god, not a man.'[6]

This passage taken from Berlioz's *Mémoires* focuses on the second movement of *Harold en Italie*. The composition, a symphony with a viola solo, was the result of a commission by Niccolò Paganini, who was eager to show off his new Stradivarius and wished for a concerto in which the role of the soloist would be emphasised to the extreme. Despite his admiration for Berlioz, Paganini would not play the piece: it was not difficult enough. The composer had only sketched the first movement when they met and the violinist realised, somewhat disappointed, that there was not enough for him to do.[7] After Paganini's withdrawal, the role of the viola, despite not being treated in a traditionally virtuosic manner, lost none of its relevance. The episode that interests me occurred almost one decade later, after one of the composer's performances in Brussels in the autumn of 1842. According to Berlioz, a 'curious debate' occurred between the critic and musicologist François-Joseph Fétis (1784–1871), one of the most prominent musical figures of that time in France, and the guitarist Marco Aurelio Zani de Ferranti (1800–78). The reason for their disagreement was simple: it concerned the merits and faults of the compositions performed that evening, which included the *Symphonie fantastique*, the *Grande Symphonie funèbre et triomphale* and the 'marche de pèlerins chantant la prière du soir' (the second movement of *Harold en Italie*). The third had deeply impressed Zani de Ferranti. Fétis, by contrast, reproached this piece for including two wrong notes: a C and a B heard repeatedly throughout.

The two notes occur at the end of each of the ten-measure melodies of 'canto' – which Berlioz refers to as 'stanzas' – and are meant to evoke, as the composer puts it, the sound of a 'slow tolling of bells'. *Harold en Italie*, inspired by Lord Byron's *Childe Harold's Pilgrimage* (1812–18), seeks to give musical shape to the wanderings of the Romantic character in the land of the Abruzzi (a region that the composer had visited during the year he spent in Italy as a winner of the Rome prize). The second movement focuses on one specific episode in Harold's excursion when he encounters a religious procession, over the course of which the bells of a church – those that the controversial notes are meant to depict – are heard in the distance. Berlioz, in any case, seems less eager to delve into the details of the programme than to invest in a purely musical account of those two notes. He might be 'an ordinary man' but he is also a proud musician:

> Alas, I would have replied to my Italian enthusiast [Zani de Ferranti], I am but an ordinary man and M. Fétis a poor musician, for those famous notes are part of the harmony. Fétis had not observed that it is precisely through their addition to the chord that the various keys in which the stanzas end are resolved into the main key, as no real musician should or could for a moment fail to see. In fact from a technical point of view that is precisely the curious and novel thing about the March. When I heard of this strange misapprehension I was tempted to publish an open letter to Zani de Ferranti in one of the papers, pointing out Fétis' error.[8]

From the perspective of musical analysis, Berlioz's claim that the notes belong to the harmony is sound. Indeed, the C invariably belongs to a pivot-chord allowing for modulations to E major (the 'main key' referred to by Berlioz) coming from various, sometimes quite distant keys: D-sharp minor (measures 22–6, 110–14), F-sharp minor (mm. 42–6, 130–4), G-sharp minor (mm. 140–4), A major (mm. 150–4). In its first occurrence, the C irrupts in the context of D-sharp minor (the key into which the first iteration of the *canto* melody modulates), but can certainly be interpreted, from the point of view of E major (the key in which each iteration of the *canto* melody begins), as belonging to a diminished seventh chord on the seventh degree (D♯, F♯, A, C). So viewed, as always when a diminished seventh chord is built on the seventh degree of a key, this chord functions as a dominant ninth chord from which the root is omitted (in this case, [B] D♯, F♯, A, C). The typical resolution of this chord involves both diminished fifths resolving inward into thirds, causing the dominant-functioning chord on the seventh degree to resolve to the tonic. This is exactly what happens in measures 24–6 (see Example 5.1), where D♯ and A turn into E and G♯, and F♯ and C turn into G♯ and B, thus forming an E major chord (E, G♯, B). So not only the presence but also the juxtaposition of C and B would find a quite straightforward justification.[9]

Although Berlioz's claim is technically accurate – if 'error' there is, it is the critic's, not the composer's – things are not as simple

Example 5.1: Hector Berlioz, *Harold en Italie*, second movement ('Marche de pèlerins chantant la prière du soir'), mm. 16–27.

as a harmonic analysis suggests. The strange feeling caused by the two notes (especially the first) is undeniable, and is one to which neither Fétis nor Zani de Ferranti remained indifferent, their diametrically opposed reactions notwithstanding. The reasons for their wonder, oscillating between hyperbolic admiration and narrow-minded rejection, are worth investigating further.

To begin with, it is worth pointing out that the very repetition of the two pitches is odd in itself. Fétis's reported characterisation of the 'marche de pèlerins' as a piece in which the listener is 'constantly hearing two notes that are not part [or, at least, sound as if they were not part] of the harmony' is not completely far-fetched. In fact, no matter where the harmony goes – and it goes quite far, and quite quickly, in various directions – those Cs and Bs are heard, as stubborn as the sound of a bell, at every turn of the procession. After the piece is over, even the untrained listener will easily recall the precise sound of the two notes. Indeed, the *precise sound* of those two notes – by which I mean not only their pitch but also their timbre – is the crux of the matter. From the standpoint of orchestration, the strangeness of their iterations is due to various factors (all of which are apparent in Example 5.1). The most obvious one consists of the assignment of the C to the horns, which break through with their characteristic metallic sound the hustle that animates the slightly agitated strings and woodwinds each time the *canto* melody ends. Furthermore, the C of the horns does not resolve. That is to say, both the harp and the III and IV horns play the C. However, whereas the harp subsequently resolves to B (joined by the strings and the woodwinds), the horns remain silent until the next stanza comes to an end. Finally, regarding the resolution of the C into the B in the harps, it is also noteworthy that the C and the B are juxtaposed in different octaves: thinking in terms of pitch rather than pitch-class, the B is at the distance of a major seventh (rather than a semitone) from the C. All this makes the C sound not only thoroughly unexpected, but also, despite its harmonic justification, defiantly unresolved.

These technical observations are critical to clarify the stakes of the quarrel between the two listener-critics, and will hopefully prove helpful as a background for the unfolding of my argument. It should nonetheless be made clear that I am much less interested in discussing the technical complexities of the piece than in drawing attention to what I think is the ambivalence of Berlioz's observations when it comes to justifying these two notes. The composer asserts that they are 'part of the harmony'. However, he also observes that they evoke a 'slow tolling of bells'. In a sense, they can be justified *either* because they respect the rules of harmony *or* because they follow the programme. From the standpoint of the latter, the dissonance – or, for that matter, even the alleged mistake – turns out to be *necessary*: the passage is meant to express the spatial distance between the procession and the church. Now, it was the *necessity* of a 'sonic dissensus' that gave rise to the *possibility* of a 'critical disagreement' in which the question of what sounds are legitimate in a musical composition is debated with musical *and* non-musical arguments. It is this disagreement – this tension between two conflicting views of what counts as music – that I find intriguing and illuminating in this passage of Berlioz's *Mémoires*.

Having said that, the fact that I associate the entry of music into the aesthetic regime of art with a 'programmatic composition' might seem perplexing. After all, the idea behind programme music is that it is possible to evoke objects, events or ideas by means of music alone. Is this idea not closer to the representative regime of art? Does it not betray an allegiance to the principle of *mimesis* – in which case turning to *Harold en Italie* would be, at best, counterproductive and, at worst, absurd? The short answer is no. In spite of being a programmatic composition – in fact, as I venture to demonstrate, for reasons that are inextricably linked to its being one – *Harold en Italie* is in no way closer to the principles of *mimesis* than to the logic of *aisthesis*. The perplexity, however, is legitimate and needs to be clarified.

From the barometer of Flaubert to the bells of Berlioz

For starters, it is of the utmost importance to recall a decisive aspect of Rancière's theorisation of the aesthetic regime. The principle of *aisthesis*, with all the crossovers and blurrings it entails, stands in opposition to, confuses and dissolves the rules of *mimesis*. The latter, however, cannot be simply equated with figuration. As Rancière puts it in *Les Temps modernes*, 'the destruction of the representative order has nothing to do with the abandonment of figuration in the visual arts. It is the destruction of a hierarchical order inscribed in the very forms of the perceptible and the thinkable.'[10] Rancière refers to the visual arts in this passage, yet it should be noted that the same applies to literature.[11] Take an author like Flaubert, for instance. If the mere prevalence of description over narration were enough to indicate a relapse into the representative regime, it would be unviable to claim him – or Dostoevsky, or Proust, or Woolf – for the aesthetic regime. According to Rancière, however, 'Flaubert made all words equal just as he suppressed any hierarchy between worthy [*nobles*] subjects and unworthy [*vils*] subjects, between narration and description, foreground and background, and ultimately, between men and things.'[12] This is precisely what the aesthetic revolution amounts to: a radical upheaval of the norms that structure the representative regime of art in keeping with a police distribution of the sensible. As we shall see, pointing out that the aesthetic revolution does not entail a figurative taboo will also have crucial consequences when it comes to debating music.

Here, I would like to draw a parallel between literary and musical practices. Indeed, it seems to me that Berlioz's 'dramatic symphonies' and Liszt's 'symphonic poems' occupy a position in the history of music that resembles the one attributed to Balzac's or James's novels in the history of literature. From this perspective, programme music may be envisaged as a kind of 'musical realism'. Needless to say, this is not to ignore the gap that exists between the efforts of music to 'evoke' the adventures of Harold or Mazeppa, on the one hand, and literature's or painting's capacity to actually narrate or depict them, on the other – a fact that neither Berlioz nor Liszt would counter – but simply to stress that the non-musical references inherent in their programmatic compositions are inalienable aspects of the listening experience they propose. My point, in any case, is not to initiate a conversation about music's arguable capacity to represent non-musical entities: a literary character, a pictorial motif, a philosophical notion. Instead, what I want to stress is that the allusion to such a capacity cannot be seen as a symptom of an 'inclination' to the representative regime, insofar as the divergence between the representative and the aesthetic regimes does not lie in *whether* figuration is promoted or banned, but in *how* it is imagined and employed.

To come back to my example – and if I may linger on this musical-literary analogy a little longer – I want to venture that the two bell-like sounds that punctuate the pilgrims' march represent what some literary theorists might call a 'useless detail'. Roland Barthes introduced this notion in his famous essay 'The Reality Effect' (1968), in order to account for the proliferation of descriptive details in realist literature. Despite their apparent irrelevance, and the fact that their presence increases 'the cost of narrative information',[13] the description of anodyne and vulgar objects would find a justification in the fact that they connote the real in its contingent and arbitrary nature. Those useless details 'say nothing but this: *we are the real*'.[14] In a sense, as Rancière sums up Barthes's position in *Le Fil perdu*, 'the usefulness [of the useless detail] lies precisely in its being useless'.[15] A paradigmatic example of such 'useless details', one that is at the centre of both Barthes's and Rancière's essays, is Madame Aubain's barometer in Flaubert's *Un Coeur simple* (1877). Curiously enough, it also bears similarities with the bells of Berlioz's *Harold en Italie*. Both the barometer and the bells 'connote' the real; both, by the same token, are secondary to the literary and musical 'narrative'. I am interested in the tension between Barthes's and Rancière's readings of the barometer, as it may suggest two different ways of listening to the bells.

If one follows Barthes's line of interpretation, one may argue as follows: just as the (literary) 'useless detail', while and insofar as it causes a 'reality effect', is ultimately to be accounted for at the level of narrative form, so too its sonic counterpart would find justification in terms of musical structure alone. In other words, as long as what can be listened to is what really matters, that (musical) 'useless detail', once recognised as an allusion to the real, would play no other function than the one assigned to it within musical discourse. True, the composer made a point of naming the movements of *Harold en Italie* according to a literary source. Nevertheless, it would be the task of the musicologist to reappraise the work as music and nothing else. This is exactly what Jacques Barzun did in *Berlioz and the Romantic Century* (1950). In fact, he did it quite literally when he proposed to 'translate' the four poetic subtitles of the piece into purely musical terms: 'Harold aux montagnes' is thus presented as an 'Adagio and Allegro', the 'Marche de pèlerins' as an 'Allegretto', the 'Sérénade' as a 'Scherzo', and the 'Orgie de brigands' as a 'Finale'.[16]

Barzun is not alone in his urge to erase, or at least to relativise, the importance of literary references in Berlioz's programmatic compositions. In fact, his attitude is typical of a broader trend in musicology in which the very idea of programme music is approached with a blend of irony, embarrassment and exasperation – Donald Francis Tovey and Wolfgang Dömling are worth mentioning in this regard.[17] 'As a genre', Barzun claims, 'program music is more dinned against than dinning; as an intellectual monster, it's a unicorn.'[18] Bluntly put, people talk about it, yet they do not realise that such a thing does not exist. Paradoxical as it may sound, this dismissive account of programme music is anything but a symptom of disregard for Berlioz. Quite the contrary, it is a consequence of Barzun's attempt to make the praise of the composer fit into a modernist framework. That is to say, seen as a dubious flirtation with non-musical realities – and therefore as a threat to the autonomy of music – the principles of 'programme music' would be unworthy of a 'genius' like Berlioz, whose contribution to the future of music Barzun is particularly keen to emphasise. It is not surprising, in this context, that Barzun characterises *Harold en Italie* as a 'step towards the fulfilment of Berlioz's persistent aim: the dramatic symphony'.[19] The emphasis on the attempt to bring drama and music together is crucial because it substantiates the analogy with Wagner, thus sealing Berlioz's place in the 'grand narrative' of modern music that goes from Beethoven to Wagner to Schoenberg.[20]

In its distance from Barthes's interpretation, Rancière's reading of Flaubert's novel allows me to suggest that a different path can be followed when it comes to appraising a composition such as *Harold en Italie*. According to Rancière, the description of the barometer is anything but useless. Yet the secret of its 'usefulness' is a far cry from the connotative function summoned up by Barthes. The question, when all is said and done, is not to know 'if the real is real' but rather is about 'the texture of this real'.[21] Both the literal and symbolic features of the object, along with how it is perceived by the characters themselves, must be taken into account: 'the [barometer's] needle that indicates variations in atmospheric pressure also symbolises the immobile existence of those whose horizon is limited to knowing each morning the favourable or unfavourable conditions that the weather will lend to the day's activities'.[22] Something, however, seems to change as the narrative unfolds: the needle comes to mark something more, namely, 'the relation these obscure existences have with the power of atmospheric elements, the intensities of sun and wind, and the multiplicity of sensible events whose circles expand to infinity'.[23]

> *Un coeur simple* testifies to the revolution that occurs when a life commonly doomed to endure the rhythm of days and variations of climate and temperature, assumes the temporality and intensity of an exceptional chain of sensible events. The needle of the useless barometer marks an upheaval in the distribution of capacities of sensible experience in which life doomed to utility is separated from existences

destined for the grandeurs of action and passion ... The purported 'reality effect' is much rather an equality effect.[24]

Read in this way, as implying an 'equality effect' rather than a 'reality effect', the barometer of *Un Coeur simple* may come to inflect the way in which we hear the bells of *Harold en Italie*. The bells, too, mark time and space. What is more, they stand for the regularity of life in a quiet village, and the monotony of their tolling is what strikes the listener in the first place. However, as the piece develops, their resonance comes to manifest itself in its mesmerising and hypnotic quality: the bell-like sound blends with the song of the pilgrims and ends up triggering the delightful daydreaming of the protagonist (I have in mind the middle section of the piece with the *sul ponticello* arpeggios in the viola solo). Juxtaposing one another, the enjoyment of the local peasants and the reverie of the foreign traveller come to mingle as equals in the musical fabric. It seems to me that this intersection of programmatic and musical elements leads to an insight that is not without aesthetic and political consequences: not only in literature but also in music, the question is not that 'the real is real' but about 'the texture of the real'.

This insight is what justifies the analogy between Berlioz and Flaubert. Just as in *Un Coeur simple* the boundaries between high and low, popular and erudite, objects and people dissolve, so too in *Harold en Italie* the lines that separate music and non-music, sonic and visual, metaphorical and literal, near and distant, materiality and spirituality, outer and inner, singing and chatting, sublime and anodyne would become blurred. It is crucial to begin with the dissolution of the pair of 'music' and 'non-music'. Only when one starts listening to, meditating on, or writing about music in impure, non-musical terms is one able to imagine that one *sees* what one *hears*: the procession slowly appearing and vanishing in the landscape. In other words, the ensuing dissolutions – between near and distant, materiality and spirituality and so on – are triggered by the hypothesis behind the idea of programme music: that the 'audible' is inextricably linked to the 'visible', the 'imaginable', the 'conceivable'.

In claiming that those two notes do not belong to the harmony, Fétis implicitly relegates them to the status of noise. Berlioz's reply is intriguing because, in his considerations, he oscillates between taking the rules of harmony and the prescriptions of the programme into account. From the perspective of the latter, as I mention above, even a 'wrong' note – one that aptly expresses displacement – would be 'right'. This is of the utmost importance for reasons that must be clearly grasped. In fact, it is when Berlioz, driven by his synesthetic imagination, writes those two notes with the goal of having them sound 'wrong' despite being 'right' that he goes farthest from the perspectives of harmony and orchestration. In other words, Berlioz's musical audacities are inextricably bound up with his consideration of the programme. The 'anomalies' that delighted Zani de Ferranti and continue to seduce musicians and non-musicians today are inseparable from the composer's attempt to suggest the mixture of voices and bells, pilgrims and travellers, prayer and daydreaming or song and chatter. (Can we not hear in this way – as an attempt to suggest the intermingling of voices chatting and singing – the contrast between the linear melodies of canto and the cacophony that follows with superimposed semiquavers and triplets in the second violins and woodwinds? Am I – as a listener who writes and as a writer who listens – hallucinating? I will return to this question below.)

The noise and grain of music

In addressing a nineteenth-century controversy in the spirit of *Aisthesis*, my primary goal is to highlight the possible contribution of Rancière's political-aesthetic ideas to the debate on music and modernity. It is therefore high time to contemplate that such a contribution, if taken to its full potential, would develop as a 'counter-history of musical modernity'. The latter, it should be added, would require a critique of modernist and postmodernist discourses as they operate in musicology. In order to clarify this point, I will briefly consider one of the most challenging and misunderstood aspects of Rancière's thought: his critique of the postmodern debate.

In very simple terms, the singularity of Rancière's take on the quarrel between modernism and postmodernism consists of embracing a neither–nor stance. Crucial, on the one hand, is his rejection both of the emphasis on artistic purity and the dialectic of continuity and rupture that characterise modernism. As he puts it in *Le Partage du sensible*, 'the teleological model of modernity became untenable at the same time as its divisions between the "distinctive features" of the different arts, or the separation of a pure domain of art'.²⁵ Rancière has in mind authors such as Clement Greenberg, for whom the concentration of each art in its own medium is not only necessary for an account of their autonomy but also vital to the appreciation of their political relevance.²⁶ Rancière considers this view both flawed, in its disregard for intermediality, and detrimental to an understanding of the emancipatory dimensions of artistic practice and experience. According to him, the autonomy and heteronomy of art are in tension but inseparable, and the politics of art goes hand in hand with the intermingling of genres and the utopian promise inherent in the blurring of art and life. At first sight, this seems in keeping with the postmodern critique of the 'great divide' between high art and popular culture.²⁷ Yet things are not so simple, as Rancière is very straightforward in his rejection of the postmodernist model. 'There is no postmodern rupture', he claims in *Malaise dans l'esthétique*.²⁸ Postmodernism 'was simply the name under whose guise certain artists and thinkers realised what modernism had been: a desperate attempt to establish a "distinctive feature of art" by linking it to a simple teleology of historical evolution and rupture'.²⁹ Therefore, '[t]here is no need to imagine that a "postmodern" rupture emerged blurring the boundaries between great art and the forms of popular culture, [because] [t]his blurring of boundaries is as old as "modernity" itself'.³⁰ In fact, in its insistence on the logic of rupture, postmodernism is closer to modernism than its theorists are willing to admit. Both paradigms would make comparable mistakes, failing to grasp the political stakes of art under the aesthetic regime.

I would like to bring this neither–nor stance, which has proven liberating in debates on literature and the visual arts, to bear on musical matters. As I suggest above, the disdain for programme music was strategic in securing Berlioz a position in the tradition that runs from Beethoven to Wagner, and binds the latter – as the main protagonist of the 'inevitable' crisis of tonality – to the 'necessary' advent of dodecaphony. In this context, the point of the analogy between Berlioz and Wagner is that both composers would have sought to bring music and drama together so as to dissolve the latter in the former. Yet Berlioz's music, I want to reiterate, turns out to be rougher, drier, earthier – there is more noise and grain in it – than such an ideal of an art increasingly concentrated in the purity of its own medium lets us hear. In order to account for how this impurity manifests itself in his music – and to do justice to its political implications – an approach is required that deviates from both modernist and postmodernist playbooks.

Although the emphasis on autonomy that characterises modernism is not devoid of political intentions – the collapse of tonality and the advent of serialism have been interpreted both as a liberation from reified expression and as a democratisation of musical composition – its consequences were often detrimental to its purpose. The 'aging of new music', as Adorno put it, entails more than an increasing 'totalisation' of compositional procedures.[31] It also exacerbates the allergy to the 'erosion of the arts' – that is, the blurring of lines that separate the arts from one another.[32] In this context, it would be impossible to perceive and value the political undertones inherent in the intermingling of conscious and unconscious, spiritual and material, sublime and anodyne that accompany – if only in metaphorical terms – the confusion of sight and sound implied by programme music. On the other hand, it is not clear that much has been gained in this regard with the postmodernist stance that claims that a 'paradigmatic shift' in music practice and musicological research took place around the 1980s.[33] The way in which the modern history of Western art music is envisaged has definitely changed since then, a process that favoured critical approaches in which notions of 'media purity' and 'historical linearity' are viewed through critical lenses. Yet the challenge goes beyond the question of whether one glorifies or disavows 'grand narratives'. A counter-history of musical modernity – one inspired by Rancière's notion of the aesthetic regime of art – would also involve questions of how the objects and practices that fell under such a 'grand narrative' were and are perceived, whether they can be experienced, appropriated or assembled otherwise, and to what extent the framework that determines their tradition-laden consideration should be revised.

My discussion of *Harold en Italie* emerges from precisely these preoccupations. In this context, my aim is first and foremost to draw attention to the affinity between programme music and later trends in a constellation of modern musical practices and discourses in which the entanglements between forms, genres and arts continually grow in importance. I am well aware that the image of Berlioz is more complex today than it was a few decades ago when Barzun portrayed him as an inheritor of Beethoven and a precursor of Wagner. Thomas Adès – to quote a composer rather than a musicologist – recently compared Berlioz's music with Lewis

Carroll's prose: 'his harmony functions, but irrationally', he ventured.[34] What he had in mind, however, was in no way the parallel to Wagner but rather the connection to twentieth- and twenty-first-century composers, himself included. Indeed, what is remarkable about *Harold en Italie* is that it paves the way for several shifts that would come of age many decades later: from experiments in sound spatialisation,[35] to the renegotiation of the high/low divide,[36] to the blurry relation between written and improvised music,[37] and, last but not least, to the acknowledgement of music as 'organised noises'.[38] Yet there is more to it than just the noise. There is also the grain: the fragments of reality that the listener may 'hallucinate' – as I suggest above – at their own risk. Put otherwise, the creative force that unsettles the boundary between music and noise is also that which opens up a breach through which the 'audible' and 'visible' can intersect in the imagination of the listener.

The requirements of a counter-history of musical modernity would thus include a subtler listening practice; a sharper awareness of how practices and discourses influence each other; a deeper appreciation of the affinities that bind together the bells of Berlioz's *Harold*, the sirens of Varèse's *Ionisation* (1931), the car horns of Ligeti's *Le Grand Macabre* (1977), or even the actual bells and pieces of metal that Augusta Read Thomas brought together in her *Sonorous Earth* (2017). In addition, it would also involve a keener investigation of the synesthetic associations induced by programme music. There seems to be a proto-cinematic quality to Berlioz, which would explain the resurfacing of his music in contemporary cinema – two recent examples would be Terrence Malick's *To the Wonder* (2012) and Alfonso Cuarón's *Roma* (2018), where the daydreaming episode of *Harold en Italie*, the Hungarian March of *La Damnation de Faust* and the waltz of the *Symphonie fantastique* reappear and acquire new functions and meanings.

As I conclude, I would like to underscore what this essay is *not*. It is not an attempt to 'complete' Rancière's thought, which, it goes without saying, would be both pedantic and futile.[39] Nor is it a belated encomium to Berlioz. To present the Romantic composer as a 'hero' of the aesthetic regime of art would make little, if any, sense – as little sense as to portray him as a modernist or a postmodernist *avant la lettre*, or to reduce him, as was common in the nineteenth century, to the caricature of a disheveled composer directing an orchestra of brass and cannons.[40] What should nonetheless be stressed, and warrants the prominence of Berlioz in this essay, is that several of his compositions lend themselves to the insight that *music is music insofar as it is also non-music, or something other than music*. This alone explains why his ambivalent account of those two controversial notes deserves our attention. Although the justification of the C and B is of little importance as such, Berlioz's indecision between harmony and programme – along with the blurring of lines between music and non-music that such an indecision both manifests and promotes – emblematises the entry of music into the aesthetic regime of art. When all is said and done, those two bell-like sounds still matter to us because they carry the impurity of the real in the midst – and as a source of the noise and grain – of music.

Notes

1. Jacques Rancière, *Aesthetics and Its Discontents*, trans. Steven Corcoran (London: Polity, 2009), 36; *Malaise dans l'esthétique* (Paris: Galilée, 2004), 53. I want to thank Michael Gallope for his comments and suggestions on an earlier version of this essay. His insights were invaluable and sincerely appreciated.
2. It would be unfair and inaccurate to suggest that music is absent from Rancière's work. Not only does the constellation of sound, noise and speech play a crucial role in his writings on politics and emancipation, music, too, as an art form and as an idea of art, takes centre stage in some of his essays such as 'Autonomy and Historicity' and 'Metamorphosis of the Muses'. What is more, as Rancière explains in the afterword to this volume, music resurfaces as well, not only as an 'art of sounds' but also as an 'art of the muses', both in essays dealing with other arts, especially cinema, and throughout his entire output as a metaphor for the 'distribution of the sensible'.
3. Jacques Rancière, *Aisthesis: Scenes from the Aesthetic Regime of Art*, trans. Zakir Paul (London: Verso, 2013), xi; *Aisthesis: scènes du régime esthétique de l'art* (Paris: Galilée, 2011), 11–12.
4. Rancière, *Aisthesis*, xii–xiii; 12–13.
5. Personal conversation (2 October 2017). Rancière comes back to this topic in his Afterword to this volume.
6. Hector Berlioz, *The Memoir of Hector Berlioz* (1870), trans. and ed. David Cairns (New York: Alfred A. Knopf, 2002), 251; *Mémoires*, vol. II (Paris: Garnier-Flammarion, 1969), 44.
7. The events, however, seem to have occurred in the most courteous

way, and there is no reason to doubt that the mutual admiration of the two composers was sincere. Paganini's willingness to help Berlioz financially bears witness in this regard. See Berlioz, *Memoir*, 240–6. Conversely, the reader of Berlioz's *Mémoires* can hardly mistake his relief when he realises, after Paganini's withdrawal, that the way is now free for him to 'carry [the project] out with a different emphasis and without troubling myself any more about how to show off the viola in a brilliant light'. Berlioz, *Memoir*, 216. On the circumstances of Paganini's commission and withdrawal, see Maiko Kawabata, 'The Concerto That Wasn't: Paganini, Urhan and *Harold in Italy*', *Nineteenth-Century Music Review* 1.1 (2004), 67–114.

8. Berlioz, *Memoir*, 251–2; *Mémoires*, 44–5.
9. For a thorough analysis of the pilgrims' march, see Stephen Rodgers, '*Marche des pèlerins* from *Harold en Italie*', in *Form, Program, and Metaphor in the Music of Berlioz* (Cambridge: Cambridge University Press, 2009), 32–8.
10. Jacques Rancière, *Les Temps modernes: art, temps, politique* (Paris: La fabrique, 2018), 52; my translation.
11. On the political and historical implications of Rancière's approach to literature, see Grace Hellyer and Julian Murphet (eds), *Rancière and Literature* (Edinburgh: Edinburgh University Press, 2016).
12. Jacques Rancière, *The Politics of Literature*, trans. Julie Rose (Cambridge: Polity, 2011), 8; *Politique de la littérature* (Paris: Galilée, 2007), 17.
13. Roland Barthes, 'The Reality Effect' (1968), in *The Rustle of Language*, trans. Richard Howard (Berkeley: University of California Press, 1986), 141.
14. Barthes, 'The Reality Effect', 148 (italics in original).
15. Jacques Rancière, *The Lost Thread. The Democracy of Modern Fiction*, trans. Steven Corcoran (London: Bloomsbury, 2017), 5; *Le Fil perdu. Essais sur la fiction moderne* (Paris: La fabrique, 2014), 19.
16. Jacques Barzun, *Berlioz and the Romantic Century*, vol. 1 (Boston: Little, Brown and Company, 1950), 252.
17. See Donald Francis Tovey, '*Harold in Italy*, symphony with viola obbligato, Op. 16' (1937), in *Symphonies and Other Orchestral Works: Selections from Essays in Musical Analysis* (Mineola, NY: Dover, 2015), 171–8, and Wolfgang Dömling, *Hector Berlioz und seine Zeit* (Laaber: Laaber-Verlag, 1986). While Tovey claims that 'there is no trace in Berlioz's music of any of the famous passages of Childe Harold' (171), Dömling goes so far as to suggest that

Harold en Italie 'is definitely not literature set to music [ist ... keine Literaturvertonung]' (122).
18. Barzun, *Berlioz and the Romantic Century*, 197.
19. Barzun, *Berlioz and the Romantic Century*, 247.
20. For an account of *Harold en Italie* particularly concerned with Beethoven's influence, see Mark Evan Bonds, '*Sinfonia anti-eroica*: Berlioz's *Harold en Italie*', in *After Beethoven: Imperatives of Originality in the Symphony* (Cambridge, MA: Harvard University Press, 1996), 28–72.
21. Rancière, *The Lost Thread*, 12; *Le Fil perdu*, 25.
22. Rancière, *The Lost Thread*, 13; *Le Fil perdu*, 25.
23. Rancière, *The Lost Thread*, 13; *Le Fil perdu*, 25.
24. Rancière, *The Lost Thread*, 13–14; *Le Fil perdu*, 26.
25. Jacques Rancière, *The Politics of Aesthetics: The Distribution of the Sensible*, trans. Gabriel Rockhill (New York: Continuum, 2004), 23; *Le Partage du sensible* (Paris: La fabrique, 2000), 42.
26. See, for instance, Clement Greenberg, 'Towards a Newer Laocoon', *Partisan Review* 7 (fall 1940), 296–310.
27. See Andreas Huyssen, *After the Great Divide: Modernism, Mass Culture, Postmodernism* (Bloomington: Indiana University Press, 1986).
28. Rancière, *Aesthetics and Its Discontents*, 42; *Malaise dans l'esthétique*, 60.
29. Rancière, *The Politics of Aesthetics*, 23; *Le Partage du sensible*, 42.
30. Rancière, *Aesthetics and Its Discontents*, 49; *Malaise dans l'esthétique*, 93.
31. See Theodor W. Adorno, 'The Aging of the New Music', trans. Robert Hullot-Kentor and Frederic Will, in *Essays on Music*, ed. Richard Leppert (Berkeley: University of California Press, 2002), 181–202.
32. Theodor W. Adorno, 'Art and the Arts' (1967), trans. Rodney Livingstone, in *Can One Live After Auschwitz? A Philosophical Reader* (Stanford: Stanford University Press, 2003), 368–87.
33. Derek B. Scott, 'Postmodernism and Music', in Stuart Sim (ed.), *Companion to Postmodernism* (London: Routledge, 2005), 122. For an attempt to account for a postmodernist paradigm in the domain of music, from the perspectives of analysis, practice and listening, see Jonathan D. Kramer, *Postmodern Music, Postmodern Listening* (London: Bloomsbury, 2016).
34. Thomas Adès and Tom Service, *Thomas Adès: Full of Noises.*

Conversations with Tom Service (New York: Farrar, Straus and Giroux, 2012), 144.

35. Berlioz designed the form of the pilgrims' march as a long *crescendo-diminuendo*. The listener is invited to hear in the exact same way as Harold, as he gets closer to, and then drifts away from, the procession. Listening thereby emerges as an experience of both temporal and spatial nature. Without changing the position of any musician vis-à-vis the audience or within the orchestra, Berlioz fosters a new 'way of listening' that suggests a new 'way of composing' in which time and space coalesce.
36. It can be said that Berlioz's willingness to superimpose categories such as the sublime and the anodyne, the spiritual and the material, or the conscious and the unconscious paved the way for various musical trends, which later defied the high/low divide.
37. One observation made by musicologist Stephen Rodgers seems exemplary in this regard: 'There is a strangely improvisatory quality to the *Marche des pèlerins*, an impression that the tunes are being invented on the spot, each a lazy, varied riff upon the others.' Rodgers, *Form, Program, and Metaphor in the Music of Berlioz*, 35.
38. Due to the 'noise' they make or intimate, the 'bells' of *Harold en Italie* can be said to anticipate Russolo and Cage. As Varèse would put it: 'to stubbornly conditioned ears, anything new in music has always been called noise. But after all what is music but organised noises?' Edgard Varèse and Chou Wen-chung, 'The Liberation of Sound' (1936), *Perspectives of New Music* 5.1 (1966), 18.
39. At first sight, this might seem in contradiction with my suggestion that a scene is missing in *Aisthesis*. My purpose, however, is not to 'fill the gaps' of the book – which would presuppose an ideal of completion that is at odds with Rancière's thought – but simply to test his approach on a musical case with a view to addressing the broader debate on musical modernity.
40. See Jean Ignace Isidore Gérard's cartoon, published in *L'Illustration* on 15 November 1845, with the title 'Un concert à mitraille et Berlioz' [A concert of cannons and Berlioz]. This, among many other cartoons of the composer conducting seemingly chaotic orchestras, is available at <http://www.hberlioz.com/Cartoons/> (last accessed 11 June 2018).

6

Rancière on Music, Rancière's Non-music
Katharina Clausius

Rancière is the first to admit that he is 'neither a musician nor a music historian',[1] and indeed, the subject I propose here – 'Rancière on music' – risks curtailing itself through a relative absence of materials. A seminar paper from 2003 on contemporary music and history remains Rancière's only sustained discussion of music, and even here he does not so much tackle a music-specific history as unpack a more general historiography through approximate musical contexts. The unobtrusive conjunction of our volume's title, *Rancière and Music*, thus forecasts a productive convergence between the philosopher and his most evaded art form with an optimism that in some ways contradicts Rancière's own confessed reticence. By his own account, this small word 'and' paradoxically includes a very specific exclusion, a silent but palpable disjunctive conjunction: *Rancière or Music*. Precisely because the applications of Rancière's political aesthetics are so demonstrably varied – and even, as my colleagues have shown here, musical – the need to hear Rancière speak on the art of music is all the more urgent, as is the suspicion that Rancière's relationship to music is not only diffident but perhaps also deeply uneasy. The fact that Rancière says little about music is a statement in and of itself, and it is this statement that I will pursue here.

Directing Rancière's words to speak more directly to music in some respects seems more of an exercise in ventriloquism than textual interpretation. However, this strategy might in fact prove enlightening; after all, the philosopher's own indirect discourse practises a type of ventriloquism that invites exactly this approach. Indeed, Rancière's ambivalent relationship to music is not entirely his own but rather one that he inherits from his source materials. For example, the project of intellectual emancipation that Rancière adopts from his nineteenth-century counterpart Joseph Jacotot relies on a source that is vehemently opposed to music: François Fenélon's epic novel *Les Aventures de Télémaque*, which already at the time of its first publication in 1699 defined itself as a manual for emancipation through an explicitly anti-music moral.[2] Fenélon's controversial novel endorses a strict political-aesthetic order in which music represents a corrupting influence. Thanks to its symbolic authority in Rancière's foundational text *The Ignorant Schoolmaster*, the novel inevitably transfers its antipathy towards music to the Jacotot–Rancière adventure. In other words, the novel that is 'the thing in common'[3] between Jacotot and his Flemish students might serve a similar function here and make Rancière's silence on music sound (even faintly) like a philosophical strategy rather than a professional disclaimer.

I therefore propose to take up Rancière's invitation to think alongside and inside his source texts and scrutinise Fenélon's novel for its insight into Rancière's quiet – or perhaps disquieted – relationship to music. This insight is unlikely fully to account for the philosopher's relative lack of interest in music or to consolidate a comprehensive role for music in his political-aesthetic framework, but will instead force a productive collision – a *mésentente* ('disagreement' or 'mishearing'), even – that will open up a juxtaposition rather than foreclose comparison. In this sense, my point of departure is that our volume's premise to conjoin Rancière and music echoes the radical 'arrangement of a space of the conjunction of contradictories' that Rancière attributes to the continuing revolution in historical thinking. In this revolution, 'non-history and history' are posited as compatible opposites in a functional poetics of knowledge.[4] By analogy, within the 'space of conjunction' that we are curating with this book, I propose to scrutinise one of Rancière's historical sources in order to posit 'music and non-music' as reciprocal agents in his ever-resonating theory of intellectual emancipation. In this comparative source study, 'music' indeed 'rises to the surface as a point of intersection and resonance between the arts, through or as musicality'.[5]

The charm and the difficulty of *The Ignorant Schoolmaster* lies in the complicated narrative triad that sees Rancière's voice thoroughly entangled with both Fénelon and Jacotot, who become his interlocutors, his spokesmen, his proxies and even his antagonists. This overlapping discourse more or less compels the reader to accept a fluid interchange of concepts across these three constitutive voices. One problem with this type of synthetic reading is that it obscures points of friction among the three voices as well as the relative prominence of each voice, which – to put it in musical terms – harmonise so seamlessly in Rancière's narrative that the contribution of each individual voice can get lost in the acoustic of the combined effort. If the prospect of isolating one speaker risks violating the tangled chorus that Rancière so carefully contrives, the advantage of disentangling *The Ignorant Schoolmaster*'s constituent texts is to expose the boundaries of overlap among them. In Rancièrean terms, extricating the individual sources makes it possible to redistribute what is 'sensible' of each and render music's role more audible. The most immediate consequence of this redistribution is that Fénelon's voice becomes much more audible; in the trio that Rancière orchestrates throughout *The Ignorant Schoolmaster*, Jacotot emerges as the louder, more active participant who subsumes Fénelon's voice, and with it the vexed points of dissonance between the Fénelonian and the Rancièrean adventures. Jacotot's treatise on the universal teaching of music might seem like the most obvious influence on *The Ignorant Schoolmaster*. After all, Rancière cites extensively from Jacotot's volume on 'Music, Drawing and Painting',[6] and yet he scrupulously avoids the sections on music, focusing instead on passages related to the universal method in relation to the visual arts. In some ways, however, Rancière's selective appropriation of the treatise does justice to the spirit of Jacotot's discussion, which constantly insists on the universality of his teaching method at the expense of music's particularity. Aside from generic instructions to his hypothetical student at the keyboard, Jacotot's lengthy explanations staunchly defend his innovative method without really discussing music at all.[7] Learning music, he claims, is exactly the same as learning a language or painting or economics, and so there is little need for specific instruction. As a universal language, music lends itself easily to the principles of universal teaching. In other words, its title aside, the promotional angle of Jacotot's treatise more or less effaces music by equating it with all the other arts and sciences.

In stark contrast to Jacotot's catchy mantra that 'everything is in everything',[8] a music that sits easily alongside emancipatory learning is certainly not in Fénelon's *Télémaque*, where music is relentlessly vilified in the foreground of the narrative. This confrontational stance towards music underpins the novel's entire pedagogy. Unlike Jacotot's treatise, in which music is incidental to the text's main mandate, Fénelon's book structures itself around the musical encounters of its protagonist. Moreover, where Jacotot casually broaches music as a universal language, *Télémaque*'s sustained preoccupation with music is far more specific and isolates the persuasive power of song as a carnal sensuality at odds with political sense. Surprisingly, then, although the title of Jacotot's treatise promises a direct engagement with music, Fénelon's novel harbours much more outspoken claims regarding music's part in pedagogy, claims that by extension resonate in Rancière's 'Lessons in Intellectual Emancipation'. In what follows, I will first extricate Fénelon from the synthetic texture of *The Ignorant Schoolmaster* in order to probe the distinctive political aesthetics of *Télémaque* and then reaffirm the novel – and its hostility towards music – as an integral premise for Jacotot's universal teaching and, subsequently, for Rancière's philosophical narrative.

~

For a novel bent on silencing music, Fénelon's *Télémaque* was an exceptionally noisy publication. In his capacity as tutor to King Louis XIV's grandson, Fénelon had undertaken to write an allegorical adventure by means of which his young pupil would learn the principles and duties of an enlightened monarch. The Homeric epic follows a young prince – Telemachus – as he travels the world under the guidance of a tutor, who supervises from afar as the future monarch confronts perilous tests of his virtue and works to escape natural disasters, cruel despots, irresistible sirens and innumerable wild beasts on his way to an understanding of benevolent and merciful kingship. Fénelon neatly narrativises this search for political wisdom: the young Telemachus sets out on his journey to find his missing father, Ulysses, and in the process undertakes a symbolic quest to fulfil his patriotic duty as his successor. Throughout his adventure, music – especially singing – reappears as his most persistent and menacing foe. Neither the book's modest conception nor this anti-music agenda would seem to have predicted *Télémaque*'s enormous success, and yet few Enlightenment texts were as widely known, as readily available or as frequently translated and adapted.

With its first appearance in 1699, the book immediately won fame and notoriety. In its first year alone, it appeared in sixteen editions; by 1912, 550 different editions had been printed along with 170 translations (including, as Jacques Le Brun has documented, Hungarian, Polish, Armenian and Greek).[9] This instant mass popularity far exceeded the scope of the pedagogical novel that Fénelon intended to teach privately to his royal pupil. More ironic still given its suspicion of music and of song in particular, *Télémaque* became a favourite among opera librettists for more than a century; Fénelon inadvertently inspired an entire operatic tradition, quite against his deep ambivalence towards singing.[10] Before documenting the novel's insistent denunciation of music, it is worth briefly considering why Jacotot secures *Télémaque* over other texts as the prototypical textbook for his innovative system of learning.

In her translator's notes to *The Ignorant Schoolmaster*, Kristin Ross asserts that 'in terms of Jacotot's adventure, the book could have been *Télémaque* or any other'.[11] Thanks to its pattern of dissemination, its politics and its literary style, however, I would counter emphatically that the book could have been none other – both in terms of Jacotot's universal learning and Rancière's intellectual emancipation. The book's astonishing popularity, its international reach and its contradictory operatic afterlife makes it the perfect tool for a pedagogy with explicit ambitions to universality and egalitarian politics. According to Jacotot, 'anything can be used'[12] for intellectual emancipation – but it is certainly opportune, even strategic, that that 'anything' was *Télémaque*.

Pragmatically, the novel's unparalleled commercial availability (in countless foreign translations, no less) lends itself to exactly the universal pedagogy that Jacotot is determined to promote. Even beyond this practical consideration, the book carries a potent symbolic clout that could not have been lost on Jacotot's followers. This symbolic value has to do with the strange circumstances of the novel's writing as well as its hotly controversial reception. On the face of it, *Télémaque* is a straightforward didactic text in the style of a typical Homeric epic. The story's classical setting, however, belies a stinging political critique that enraged some of its eighteenth-century readers, most dangerously Louis XIV himself, who saw his likeness in one of the novel's most prominent characters, King Idomeneus, whose immoderate rule leads to his disgraceful downfall and exile by his own subjects. Certainly, Fénelon ensures that there is nothing subtle in the cautionary example that the pathetic figure of Idomeneus sets for the young

Telemachus. By way of introduction on the occasion of their first meeting, Idomeneus offers Telemachus a harsh but eloquent expression of self-contempt:

> What a terrible example am I made to all those who exercise the sovereign power! I ought to be held up as a lesson to all who reign in the world, that they may take warning by my fate. They imagine they have nothing to fear, being exalted so high above the rest of mankind. Alas! it is on that very account they ought to fear ... Pride ... and the flattery to which I listened, have overturned my throne. And thus will all kings fall, who give themselves over to their desires, and listen to the voice of adulation.[13]

Small wonder, then, that Louis XIV took exception to the bluntly anti-autocratic message: the novel penned at court for a young prince barely conceals its vehement critique of France's absolutist monarchy and its hope for the liberation of Europe from corrupt rule. If Fénelon's book represents a practical tool for learning in Jacotot's system, its radical political ideology also suits *The Ignorant Schoolmaster*'s message of egalitarian emancipation from the oppressive influence of 'masters'. Far from a random text that might have been any other, *Télémaque* is uniquely primed to perform the crucial emancipatory function that Jacotot and Rancière lay out.

We might say that Fénelon himself was the original 'ignorant schoolmaster' as he set about teaching a profession that he himself had no direct experience of via a 'book in common', and letting his pedagogy unfold regardless of the risks involved. And the risks were very real: shortly after *Télémaque*'s unauthorised publication, Fénelon was dismissed from his post and banished from court.[14] Fénelon's persecution was only the start of the turmoil that surrounded the novel, whose stylistic eccentricities quickly overshadowed the political implications of the narrative. Within a year of its appearance, a veritable paper war erupted over the book's supposed degeneracy. Writer Pierre Valentin Faydit published an enormous tome denouncing Fénelon's epic as inaccurate, decadent and un-Christian: 'I would love to know what use such reading can possibly serve other than to corrupt the spirit of youthful readers and excite in them visions that Religion in contrast dictates we discard and stifle.'[15] Faydit's critique is at once utterly absurd and savagely astute. Hilariously, he only managed to rush his damning review to press by neglecting to read most of the novel; as he confesses to the reader, 'my patience was not up to the painful test I anticipated suffering were I to undertake to read all four volumes'.[16] Indeed, Faydit's hysterical protestations initially turn on tedious trivia and petty orthographic corrections; his impatience is palpable but not too convincing. Eventually, however, Faydit alights on a more meaningful complaint that addresses the crux of Fénelon's text, namely that 'this book inspires images of vice and of promiscuity'.[17] The accusation that Fénelon indulges so much in evocative description that the sensuous imagery on the pages risks corrupting the rational reader into hedonism was echoed by other prominent critics at the time, including Nicolas Gueudeville.[18] The charge is a bizarre one given that the novel's main lesson is one of abstemiousness; Telemachus spends most of his adventure bravely resisting the stream of nubile goddesses, nymphs and princesses who try to seduce him with their incomparable beauty and their ravishing singing voices. His tutor, meanwhile, looks on disapprovingly until the epic's final episode, when Telemachus proves conclusively that his modesty and reason are steadfastly beyond the reach of vanity and carnal temptation. According to Faydit and Gueudeville, *Télémaque*'s message of temperance is actively undercut by Fénelon's chosen literary style, which conjures up images of temptation with a vividness that smacks of the very type of indulgence it pretends to banish. For his critics, then, Fénelon failed to strike the balance between the evocation and the suppression of the senses that would drive home his pedagogical message.

Although neither Faydit nor Gueudeville preoccupies himself with music's prominent role in the book's narrative, Fénelon repeatedly insists on the terms of this balance from an explicitly musical perspective – or rather, from a vehemently anti-music position. Both in its moral content and its literary style, *Télémaque* engages directly with music as a kind of limit case for pedagogy and for political enlightenment. Music, morality and personal sovereignty are firmly entwined throughout the novel, and so the success (or failure) of *Télémaque* as a harbinger of Enlightenment discourse, as a pedagogical tool for Jacotot's method and as a symbol of Rancièrean political emancipation hinges not on images (Christian or otherwise) but on music's authority to sway its listener.[19] As much as Louis XIV might have had cause to censure Fénelon's politics and Faydit and Gueudeville found reason to lament the author's provocative writing, *Télémaque* succeeds as the quintessential novel for emancipatory learning precisely because of its moral stance towards music. As we will see, tracing the novel's engagement with music over the course of Telemachus's adventures neither substantiates nor contradicts Fénelon's critics; instead, it clarifies the stakes of the debate and the value of the novel as a site of moral and political contest.

~

Fénelon's portrait of King Idomeneus is remarkably blunt, and yet if anything his position regarding music is even less forgiving. Even the lexicon associated with the performance of music over the course of the novel establishes a confrontational relationship between the protagonist and the musical arts. The adjectives Fénelon pairs with music are overwhelmingly negative. Words such as 'effeminate', 'intoxicating', 'corruptive', 'soft', 'entrapping', 'distracting', 'imprisoning', 'seductive' and 'deceitful' permeate the narrative and leave the reader in no doubt that the most immediate threat to Telemachus is music's sensual power, while his epic journey is in pursuit of the wisdom to withstand its temptation. This trajectory to disempower music is immediately evident if we set the novel's first and final episodes alongside one another.

Fénelon firmly asserts his indictment of music in the novel's opening chapter. The nymph Calypso – a musical siren whose very name means 'to deceive' – tries to entrap the young Telemachus (recent survivor of a shipwreck, who washes up on the shore of her island) by tempting his senses. Calypso and her nymphs flaunt their beauty, their hospitality and their songs until Telemachus loses himself in their charms:

> A wine more delicious than nectar was poured from large silver flagons into cups of gold adorned with flowers. Baskets were brought loaded with all the fruits that spring had promised and autumn spread upon the face of the earth. At the same time four young nymphs began to tune their voices ... The chief of the nymphs ... accompanied with her lyre the charming voices of all the rest ... The tears ran down [Telemachus's] cheeks.[20]

His senses overwhelmed, Telemachus capitulates to the easy pleasures of Calypso's realm for six long chapters (far beyond the point at which Faydit's patience failed him). Only when Telemachus's tutor finally intercedes does the young prince manage to extricate himself from Calypso's sensual paradise and remember his filial mission to find his father. By this point, however, it is clear to Fénelon's readers that Calypso embodies all the fickle enticements that would contort a future wise king into a selfish pleasure-seeker, and that her beautiful voice nearly makes a prisoner of Telemachus.

In the concluding scenes of the epic, Fénelon brings his protagonist full circle, but reverses this outcome in a satisfying demonstration of his pedagogy's success. Faced with the ultimate temptress – the ravishingly beautiful singing of Idomeneus's own daughter, Antiope – Telemachus proves conclusively that his reason is untempered by sensual pleasure. This time, however, he finds liberation not in fleeing helplessly at his tutor's side but in steadfastly withstanding the siren's performance. Fénelon explicitly sets the two episodes up as parallel trials so that Telemachus's transformation from ill-prepared, skittish youth to seasoned hero capable of retaining sovereignty over his desires is obvious:

> Antiope's gentle and touching voice produced great rapture and emotion in the heart of the young son of Ulysses. But Telemachus maintained a superiority over his passion; he was not now the same Telemachus who had been such a slave to a tyrannical passion in the island of Calypso. While Antiope was singing, he listened in profound silence; but she no sooner finished, than he immediately began to talk of some other subject.[21]

It is no coincidence that Telemachus proves his mettle against Idomeneus's own daughter, the feminine heir to a kingdom forfeited by an imprudent and narcissistic ruler. For the fictional Telemachus, as for Fénelon's august pupil, humility and discipline are not simply spiritual values for a righteous life but practical policies for enlightened kingship. Sovereignty over self and over realm are synonymous for a would-be ruler.

Throughout the novel, Fénelon constantly emphasises that the stakes of Telemachus's journey are both personal and political. The characters encounter numerous kingdoms driven to ruin by monarchs and populations bent on indulging their appetite for pleasure. The remedy that Telemachus's tutor often prescribes is the banishment of all music other than explicitly religious rituals:

> In the next place, [the tutor] suppressed that soft and effeminate music that tended to corrupt the manners of the youth. Nor was he more

favorable to that bacchanalian music which intoxicates almost as much as wine, and is productive of impudence and violent passions. He proscribed all music except on festivals in temples, there to celebrate the praises of the gods and heroes who have set an example of extraordinary virtue.[22]

This ruthless censure of music in its secular contexts emphatically demonstrates to Telemachus that his struggle to master his personal desires translates directly to his public duties. The premise of the entire Telemachus story consolidates these two spheres: the young man in search of his father is also a prince in search of his kingship, and their reunion at the end is made irrelevant by the journey of maturation that makes his succession to the throne possible. In the attempt to recuperate the absent older generation, the heir learns the art of governance and renders his father and regent obsolete. Politics, Fénelon argues, begins with the individual learning to exercise sovereignty over himself.

As Telemachus gradually realises the inextricability of his private and official personae and accepts both the practical and the symbolic import of his education, music emerges as a metonym for all the arts, for sensuality, for desire and for human excess; the suppression of music therefore becomes paramount. In other words, Telemachus's emancipation (from human desire, from corruption, from tyranny) hinges on his triumphing over music. Reason, enlightenment and a productive monarchy are bought at the expense of the musical arts. Logically, the resulting ethical regime would be one of silence: the song of the sirens muted, the prince's authoritative voice can sound uninhibited.

Strangely, though, this triumph over sensual pleasure is not accomplished by the total imposition of silence – in every episode of musical temptation and suppression, some vestige of music remains active. In each of the various kingdoms they visit together, Telemachus's tutor admits religious songs capable of 'elevating minds and civilizing manners'.[23] He even evokes a musical metaphor to describe the principle of governance: 'Do not doubt, my dear Telemachus, that the government of a kingdom requires a certain harmony, like music, and proportions as exact as those of architecture.'[24] On a couple of occasions, the tutor even delights Telemachus with a musical performance in praise of the gods. (Significantly, this is no ordinary pedagogue but the goddess Minerva in disguise, and so by implication the performance of music can only be safely undertaken by a deity with superhuman resilience.) Even Telemachus's final encounter with Antiope is oddly ambivalent rather than unreservedly antagonistic towards music. After all, he does not jump to his feet and put an end to her sumptuous performance. Instead, he listens 'in profound silence' to the song's end.[25] Remarkably, then, the endpoint of Telemachus's journey is not to disempower music but rather to empower himself through exposure; Antiope's song produces 'great rapture and emotion' in the young prince's heart, and in spite of this he maintains 'superiority over his passion'.[26] If Telemachus is not rendered immune to the rapture and emotion stirred by music – but on the contrary is content to let the performance continue in his presence – then Fénelon's lesson is not that moral fortitude is impervious to the sensual arts. (Such a moral would constitute a banal promise for an unstimulating existence.) Rather, Telemachus's triumph is to be able to *listen* with the utmost attention, to feel the profundity of his passion, and to be able to talk of something else.

The future king has been held at the mercy of music's beguiling sensuality over and over throughout his travels, and he finally learns to withstand its influence without silencing it. Indeed, he does well to listen carefully: the bombardment of passion that music provokes above all other arts is the catalyst for his emancipation. Telemachus's struggle against Antiope's song is quiet because the antagonism is not an external one between an impressionable traveller and a siren but an internal conflict between the vulnerable prince and his own aspirations to become a benevolent monarch. In other words, in *Télémaque* the collision of silence and music represents the ideal conditions for personal emancipation first and for political sovereignty second. Music's provocation, then, is the choice between corrupt absolutism and enlightened (self-) governance. In a peculiar way, Fénelon furnishes Jacotot and Rancière with a paradox, that is, music as an agitating vehicle for oppression and for emancipation. Somehow, *Télémaque*'s pedagogy fulfils its moral-political agenda by actively evoking and denying music – the novel shakes music off but does not want to be completely rid of it. As much as Faydit and Gueudeville decried the contradictions of Fénelon's text as symptoms of a failed pedagogy, the novel's unresolved ambivalence towards musical sensuality is in fact the crucial mechanism that underlies the whole lesson.

By extension, the aesthetic-political philosophy that Rancière develops in *The Ignorant Schoolmaster* absorbs a similarly vexed relationship to music. Rancière not only shares with Fénelon a preoccupation with the emancipation of the individual as the ground zero for politics but also the Fénelonian instinct to ostracise music for the sake of political progress. If, as Rancière claims in his lecture on music historiography, he knows little about music, his ignorance may be better informed than he credits; Fénelon's influence makes itself felt in *The Ignorant Schoolmaster*, along with his complicated reliance on music as an antagonist for his protagonist. Indeed, upon closer examination, Rancière's absorption of *Télémaque* seems to include Fénelon's ambivalent relationship to a music that, at its *quietest*, plays a crucial (if unobtrusive) role in resisting aesthetic, political and intellectual oppression.

~

The 'intellectual adventure' in *The Ignorant Schoolmaster* does not involve the stream of mythical beasts, storms and episodes of divine wrath that poor Telemachus weathers over the course of his journey. Rancière jettisons this epic framework in favour of a much more restrained narrative. The resulting text is no less vibrant,[27] however, and Rancière explicitly picks up the pedagogical method where Fénelon concludes: Telemachus's silence at the end of the epic becomes the starting point for the universal learning that Jacotot and his students stumble across. In place of the heroic throngs and expansive geographies that make up *Télémaque*'s Homeric topography, Rancière's cast of characters is extremely restrained – a small group of Flemish students and their French schoolmaster. The plot likewise is far from epic: the Flemish students speak no French and their teacher speaks no Flemish, and so they sit staring at one another in silence. Breaking this silence becomes an urgent pedagogical aim, and the fact that the students succeed with the help of an edition of *Télémaque* is far from irrelevant to the lesson they absorb.

Nowhere in *The Ignorant Schoolmaster* does music make a prominent appearance (unlike the visual arts, which at least appear in a chapter subheading, 'Me Too, I'm a Painter!'). Certainly, the Flemish students' lesson in a foreign language does not initially seem to have anything to do with music. And yet Rancière's memorable description of the process of universal learning is oddly musical – it begins with recitation and ends with a type of composition: 'the student will begin to repeat, "Calypso", "Calypso could", "Calypso could not" and so on . . . He will be asked to write compositions and perform improvisations.'[28] Reciting without fully understanding, the student practises a kind of sonic pattern in which words and sentences have contours and cadences that are indifferent to the semantic meaning of the text. The book itself becomes, like a musical performance, an inescapable event that unfolds and carries with it its unwitting spectators: 'The book prevents escape. The route the student will take is unknown. But we know what he cannot escape: the exercise of his liberty.'[29] It is difficult not to imagine Jacotot's students reciting and repeating *Télémaque*'s words in cadenced tones, declaiming the phrases over and over, performing first one sentence and then the next, committed to following the process through to the book's final chapter. In some ways, their pedagogical activity actuates the musico-poetic side of the oral epic tradition that Fénelon's text does its best to suppress. From this perspective, Jacotot's adventure is a reversal of Télémaque's lesson in abstemiousness; where the future king demonstrates sovereignty by asserting his silence in the face of the most exquisite music, pedagogical success for the Flemish students is measured by a virtuosically oral engagement with Fénelon's text. To the same degree that Télémaque's contemplative silence represents a blunt indictment of Louis XIV's authoritarian regime, by the same token Jacotot's students loudly proclaim their intellectual (and political) equality with their quasi-musical recitations.

If *Télémaque* and *The Ignorant Schoolmaster* seem to spin their narrative endpoints from opposite directions – the one condemning the human voice as corruptive, the other applauding it as liberating – this apparent divergence is as illusory as Fénelon's anti-music campaign. In keeping with *Télémaque*'s productive entanglement between music and non-music, Rancière capitalises on a parallel contradiction in his recounting of the Jacotot narrative. *The Ignorant Schoolmaster* in some ways seems to prescribe a distinctly un-Fénelonian pedagogy that celebrates rather than silences the student's voice, but here again Rancière's formula for emancipation takes its legacy from *Télémaque* rather than positing itself as a corrective to the novel's original layout. In other words, *The Ignorant Schoolmaster* inhabits a familiar conflicted stance between voice and silence, between music and non-music that underpins Fénelon's whole pedagogical strategy.

All throughout Rancière's Jacotot story, the acts of voicing and silencing emerge alternately as opposites and as synonyms, simultaneously symbolising stultification and enlightenment, repression and liberation. To begin with, Rancière offers the reader of *The Ignorant Schoolmaster* evocative glimpses of Jacotot's pupils busy declaiming their revolutionary lesson, but compounds these fragmentary images with vehement statements against the primacy of speech over written discourse:

> This privileged status of speech . . . [institutes] a paradoxical hierarchy. In the explicative order, in fact, an oral explication is usually necessary to explicate the written explication . . . How can we understand this paradoxical privilege of speech over writing, of hearing over sight? What relationship thus exists between the power of speech and the power of the master?[30]

On no account does Rancière prescribe speech as the key to emancipatory learning; perhaps the Flemish students' recitation is only tolerable because it is profoundly repetitious – an automatic mnemonic device rather than a conscious effort to initiate and direct communication aloud. Speaking the words of another, enunciating written words verbatim, emerges as a compromise between dogmatic speech and acquiescent silence.

Indeed, the model for emancipation that Jacotot and Rancière champion directs its energy towards protecting the 'silence of the taught material' and validating the silence of ignorance. In such a model, muteness in the face of the incomprehensible speech of an instructor is not a symptom of the student's impoverished state of illiteracy but rather an important impetus to reconfigure the parameters of communication entirely. And this reconfiguration should not compel the student to learn French in order to listen obediently to the schoolmaster's authoritative voice, which always threatens to dominate the pedagogical interaction, or even in order to be able to declare sovereignty over the material. On the contrary, this silent impasse between tutor and pupil most usefully resolves itself through the celebration of this silence. Emancipation is not loquacious. It must not '[speak] in order to silence'.[31] Rather, it denies the presumed incompatibility of knowledge and ignorance, between speaking and listening, between music and silence, which remain complementary opposites. Jacotot's circular logic asserts the equality of all voices (ignorant and learned) so that nobody is rendered silent; at the same time, this logic legitimises silence as an activity of intelligence, of learning and of politics so that nobody need speak at all: 'The circle forbids cheating, and above all, that great cheat: incapacity. I can't. I don't understand. There is nothing to understand.'[32] 'Listening in profound silence' and then 'talking of some other subject' make the very same anti-authoritarian statement as transforming the written word into an aural performance. Both activities constitute a type of 'mute speech' that is inescapably musical in its cultivation of a type of speech that evades traditional syntax, is uninterested in linear discursive logic and renounces communicative directionality. For all their overt suppression of music, both Fénelon and Rancière uphold a politics that makes itself heard against music, in music and alongside music with relentless indifference to these contradictions.

Fénelon's legacy within the Jacotot–Rancière adventure is the politicisation of the pedagogical process, but more than this, it is also the convolution of the terms underlying this politicisation. Certainly only *Télémaque* – the epic novel written at court for a prince that preaches a treasonous and radically egalitarian moral – can act as the 'minimal link of a *thing in common*'[33] that knits together the Jacotot–Rancière mandate of intellectual emancipation. Moreover, if we take seriously for an instant that 'everything is in everything ... and everything is in *Télémaque*',[34] then we might venture that regardless of Rancière's own professed ignorance, music inevitably makes itself heard in the 'Five Lessons' and far beyond. As much as Jacotot 'remained a man of the [Age of Enlightenment]',[35] so too does Rancière remain thoroughly entrenched in the eighteenth century's moral-political paradox: the disjunctive conjunction of aesthetic sensuality and rational emancipation.

While this Enlightenment inheritance makes a productive strategy out of a frustrating antipathy to music, it leaves a troubling deficit. If music – the epitome of sensuality in Telemachus's world – needs to operate as a latent obstacle in the pedagogical process, then emancipatory politics is a costly endeavour. Indeed, at the intersection of politics and art, sensual influence is conspicuously absent. The students in *The Ignorant Schoolmaster* translate, recite and verify, but their enjoyment in the book, their pleasure in the performance goes unmentioned. Rancière appears reluctant to prioritise aesthetic pleasure as a legitimate – indeed, the most legitimate – political activity, in spite of his frequent protestations that the regimes of art are not confined to discrete historical periods but rather represent, in the words of this volume's Introduction, overlapping 'aesthetic-poetic-critical paradigms'.

Fénelon's wariness of art's sensual power seems to carry over into the Rancièrean politics of aesthetics. Like his Enlightenment predecessor, Rancière on some level arrives at a politics of emancipation through art but is content to forgo artistic pleasure. It is as though our political equality is bought at the cost of asserting its separation from aesthetic sensibility. Surely this type of emancipation is neither desirable nor viable in that it silences the irrational, instinctive, even corruptive power of art to jolt us into a new disposition towards ourselves as sovereign intellects. Fénelon's legacy leaves unresolved an urgent conundrum: does redistributing the sensible entail suppressing the impact that the sensible has on us? Or is Rancière's silence on the subjects of music and the catalysing (if risky) pleasure of the arts his way of practising Télémaque's triumph, of 'listening in profound silence' without compelling 'great rapture and emotion' into a stultifying discourse?

Notes

1. All translations are my own unless noted otherwise. Jacques Rancière, 'Autonomie et historicisme: la fausse alternative (Sur les régimes de l'historicité de l'art)', presented for the seminar 'Penser la musique contemporaine avec/sans/contre l'histoire?' at the École normale supérieure, December 2003. An English translation by Patrick Nickleson appears in *Perspectives of New Music* 57.1–2 (2019).
2. François Fénelon, *Telemachus, Son of Ulysses*, ed. and trans. Patrick Riley (Cambridge: Cambridge University Press, 1994).
3. Jacques Rancière, *The Ignorant Schoolmaster: Five Lessons in Intellectual Emancipation*, trans. Kristin Ross (Stanford: Stanford University Press, 1991), 2.
4. Jacques Rancière, *The Names of History: On the Poetics of Knowledge*, trans. Hassan Melehy (Minneapolis: University of Minnesota Press, 1994), 7.
5. See the Introduction to this volume.
6. Rancière cites from the 1830 edition, although the treatise was initially published in 1824. See Joseph Jacotot, *Enseignement universel: musique, dessin, peinture*, 2nd edn (Paris: Bureau du Journal de l'émancipation intellectuelle, 1830).
7. The lessons outlined in the treatise progress from 'Lesson 1: Have the child sit facing the piano' to 'Lesson 6: After the first piece, we learn the second piece by repeating it without fail' to the final 'Lesson 13: We do whatever we want provided we don't forget

what we learned.' The context is explicitly musical and yet conveys almost nothing in terms of specific musical knowledge. See Jacotot, *Enseignement universel: musique*, 285–7.
8. Fénelon, *Telemachus*, 26.
9. Jacques Le Brun, '*Les Aventures de Télémaque*: destins d'un best-seller', *Littératures classiques* 70.3 (2009), 133.
10. Many of the eighteenth century's most prominent French and Italian composers set versions of the epic, including the very first *Télémaque* opera by Antoine Danchet and André Campra (1712), and subsequent adaptations by Destouches (1714), Scarlatti (1718), Gluck (1765), Gazzaniga (1776), Le Sueur (1796), Mayr (1797) and Mozart (1781).
11. Kristin Ross, translator's note in *The Ignorant Schoolmaster: Five Lessons in Intellectual Emancipation* (Stanford: Stanford University Press, 1991), 2.
12. Rancière, *The Ignorant Schoolmaster*, 28.
13. Fénelon, *Telemachus*, 126–7.
14. Fénelon had already incited the monarch's ire through his involvement with the Quietist movement and the publication of *Télémaque* proved to be the last straw. See Patrick Riley, 'Introduction', in Fénelon, *Telemachus, Son of Ulysses*, xv.
15. Pierre Valentin Faydit, *La Télémacomanie, ou La Censure et critique du roman intitulé, Les Aventures de Télémaque Fils d'Ulysse, ou suite du quatrième Livre de l'Odyssée d'Homère* (Paris: Pierre Philalethe, 1700), 20.
16. Faydit, *La Télémacomanie*, 66.
17. Faydit, *La Télémacomanie*, 21.
18. Nicolas Gueudeville, *Critique générale des aventures de Télémaque* (Cologne: Heretiers de Pierre Marteau, 1700).
19. The way that Fénelon thematises music thus mimics the disruptive activity of writing that Rancière describes as 'the regime for the utterance of speech that undoes the [hierarchical] order ... among the "logical capacities of beings"'. While it is tempting to hear Fénelon's profound ambivalence towards music as the echo of a Platonic republicanism, in fact the ethical sway that Fénelon attributes to the musical arts carries with it writing's potential to '[introduce] a radical dissonance in the communal symphony as Plato understands it, namely, as a harmony between the modes of *doing, being*, and *saying*'. Jacques Rancière, *Mute Speech: Literature, Critical Theory, and Politics*, trans. James Swenson (New York: Columbia University Press, 2011), 95.

20. Fénelon, *Telemachus*, 7.
21. Fénelon, *Telemachus*, 308–9.
22. Fénelon, *Telemachus*, 164.
23. Fénelon, *Telemachus*, 195.
24. Fénelon, *Telemachus*, 300.
25. Fénelon, *Telemachus*, 309.
26. Fénelon, *Telemachus*, 309.
27. Many of the criticisms levelled against *Télémaque* turn on Fénelon's casual repudiation of classical epic style. Jettisoning the epic's usual verse form, Fénelon crafts his epic characters and Mediterranean scenography in vivid – but unmetered – prose. This hybrid style inspired a whole movement championing the value of prose poetry, but it also infuriated traditionalists who found Fénelon's descriptive prose too undisciplined. Not coincidentally, scholars have also commented, albeit much less critically, on the generic ambiguity of *The Ignorant Schoolmaster*, a book that borrows features from numerous different genres: fable, history, parable, manifesto, fictional novel. Kristin Ross, contemplating the reception of Rancière's unusual style, describes *The Ignorant Schoolmaster* as a 'fragment of anecdotal history, a curiosity piece, an archival oddity . . . a kind of suicidal pedagogical how-to . . . essay, or perhaps a fable or parable' (Ross, translator's note, *The Ignorant Schoolmaster*, viii–ix). The literary qualities of Rancière's writing have also been discussed more broadly by Davide Panagia in 'Rancière's Style', *Novel* 47.2 (2014), 284–300. Rancière himself even cultivates a definition of poetry that encompasses unversified writing, speech, and indeed any communication that takes as its starting point the presumption that 'thought [is] communicable [and] emotions sharable' (Rancière, *The Ignorant Schoolmaster*, 65).
28. Rancière, *The Ignorant Schoolmaster*, 23.
29. Rancière, *The Ignorant Schoolmaster*, 23.
30. Rancière, *The Ignorant Schoolmaster*, 5.
31. Rancière, *The Ignorant Schoolmaster*, 85.
32. Rancière, *The Ignorant Schoolmaster*, 23.
33. Rancière, *The Ignorant Schoolmaster*, 2.
34. Rancière, *The Ignorant Schoolmaster*, 19.
35. Rancière, *The Ignorant Schoolmaster*, 2.

7

Coloured Opera and the Violence of Dis-identification
William Fourie and Carina Venter

> In the day [Jimmy Momberg] polishes the floors of the City Hall. Night time he sings the leading role ... And we always used to joke among ourselves and say to him: 'Jimmy, you really polish up that front part nicely, not so, [sic] because you're standing there tonight!'[1]

Jimmy Momberg's story defies the neat categorisations of apartheid classification. Marked by the state as a so-called coloured body, Momberg was employed as a cleaner at the Cape Town City Hall, the kind of vocation deemed too lowly for a white man in apartheid South Africa.[2] At night, he stepped on to the very same stage, not as a cleaner, but as one of the stellar soloists of the Eoan group, South Africa's first grassroots company to perform full-scale operas.[3] This chapter draws on the work of Jacques Rancière to understand better the suturing of aesthetics and dissensual politics acted out by the Eoan group. More importantly, it will set scenes from the Eoan archive to work on Rancièrean thought to render visible the limits and omissions that his avowedly Eurocentric premises are at risk of normalising.

Commenting on the Eurocentric underpinnings of Rancière's work, decolonial theorist Walter Mignolo writes that '[Rancière's] examples never cross the Mediterranean toward the south of Italy, neither does he go toward the east of Greece, and never to the north of Germany'.[4] Mignolo's observation is not entirely accurate. In *The Emancipated Spectator*, Rancière traverses the destitute geographies of Rwanda, Sudan, Cambodia and Palestine.[5] Yet these examples often serve only a demonstrative purpose in Rancière's conception of politics and aesthetics, formulations that

Coloured Opera and the Violence of Dis-identification

have theoretical origins in his earlier writings, notably his research on nineteenth-century French worker archives.[6]

Despite this demonstrative presence, there is little in Rancière's published writings that could act as a postcolonial antidote to his largely Eurocentric focus. This is not surprising if one considers his reluctance to state the problem of politics in terms of postcolonial identity. Rancière concedes that his interest has not been in formulating a theory of the subject (postcolonial or otherwise), but in the 'process of subjectification' as a form of dis-identification.[7] Rather than dismissing Rancière's thought in its totality (as indeed Mignolo seems to do), we locate in Rancière's reading of Plato's *Republic* theoretical corollaries of the very problem that Mignolo finds in his work, corollaries that reside in Rancière's rhetorical treatment of the figure of the slave. Tracing the figure of the slave in *The Philosopher and His Poor*, we show how Rancière's 'polemical interventions' concerning the politics of equality fail as a discursive tactic in relation to the position of the slave.[8] As is well known, when Rancière speaks about politics, it is not in any conventional sense of the word; politics constitutes the active 'affirmation of the equal capacity of anybody'.[9] This assertion of equality as the basis for action is closely bound up with the processes of dis-identification or subjectification. These processes, as Holloway Sparks summarises, bring 'into existence those who should not count, those "who have no right to be counted"'.[10] The question then arises as to whether, discursively and as a critical-interpretative tactic, the process of subjectification is extended equally to the slave and the artisan-labourer in Rancière's reading of Plato's *Republic*. In answering this question, we show how Rancière's own reading of Plato refuses subjectification to the figure of the slave, even as he faults Plato for instituting an unequal political order in which the labourer is kept as the lesser of those who think and philosophise.

Turning to the Eoan group in the third section of this chapter, we move from subjectification as a critical-interpretative tactic to subjectification as an exemplary instance of the staging of politics. In seeking to draw instruction from voices formerly written out of history, our approach is decidedly Rancièrean. The reason for this approach is twofold. We wish to show that Rancière's notion of a politics of aesthetics can provide a powerful vocabulary for articulating a form of struggle unreliant upon conventional mechanisms of emancipatory politics, specifically with reference to the ways in which the Eoan group reconfigured what was deemed appropriate from within the confines of apartheid policy. Conversely, it is from the recollections of Eoan members that there emerges a fault line in Rancière's notion of dis-identification. If dis-identification marks a process that renders visible those who are not counted, then it cannot be thought responsibly without acknowledging the potentially violent consequences stemming from the legal-racial matrix of apartheid South Africa. Our critique ultimately recognises that Rancière's reluctance to theorise the raced and enslaved body in postcolonial or decolonial terms is not without consequences. This reluctance renders dis-identification uncritically Eurocentric; it becomes analogous to – and in a way prefigured by – Rancière's failure in his early work to afford the figure of the slave the emancipatory force of what he calls subjectification.

Rancière, slavery and subjectification

Before turning to *The Philosopher and His Poor*, it is necessary to clarify what Rancière means by the notions of subjectification and dis-identification. With these terms he designates an ongoing process rather than any fixed entity, one that is open rather than impermeable. For Rancière, this process occurs when an individual, subjected to asymmetric power relations or structures of discrimination, stages an assertion of equality: the assertion, say, that the worker is a citizen or the black person a human being.[11] As Rancière puts it in *Disagreement*, '[b]y subjectification I mean the production through a series of actions of a body and a capacity for enunciation not previously identifiable within a given field of experience, whose identification is thus part of the reconfiguration of the field of experience'.[12] That reconfiguration works in two directions: those already recognised by the police order as having a part are afforded an opportunity to see for themselves the sinister principles instituted by an order that denies the oppressed the fundamental right of equality; whereas for the oppressed, experience is reconfigured is such a way as to contest the inequality produced by an asymmetrical ordering in which they are not counted.

How might the notion of subjectification be set to work as a critical-interpretative tactic in Rancière's own work? In *Proletarian Nights*, the answer is relatively straightforward. What Rancière uncovers in this volume is a process of subjectification embarked upon by the labourers, who, through the micro-subversions they practised, were able to disrupt – albeit momentarily – the presumed socio-aesthetic strata of society. In *The Philosopher and His Poor*, a work that takes a more overt theoretical turn, the answer hinges on locating the intellectual underpinnings that foreclose the conditions of possibility of subjectification for some and not others. In this work, Rancière brilliantly unmasks the double lie of philosophy, the first of which holds that, as Adeimantus puts it, 'we aren't all born alike, but each of us differs somewhat in nature from the others, one being suited to one task, the other to another'.[13] Thus, the distinction between manual labourer and philosopher-ruler is so divined by nature, a distinction given rather than man-made. This first lie is the functional corollary of the second, the single most important guiding principle of Plato's idealised city. To maintain excellence and high standards in the production of goods, Plato suggests that each inhabitant will be permitted one vocation only. The farmer will only farm, the cobbler make and mend shoes, the philosopher philosophise, and so on. This double lie is what ultimately sustains belief in the fundamental equality that Plato alleges between the respective logics of the philosopher and the artisan.

Rancière's critique of Plato hinges on unmasking this double lie in a move that discloses Plato's primary interest: laying down the rule of the Republic. To advance his argument, Rancière draws on the figure of the slave to illustrate how Plato's view of manual labour contradicts the notion that all vocations, regardless of kind, are deemed equal. As Rancière points out, the idea that multiple vocations or roles should not be performed by any one person ultimately exists to safeguard against artisans who are in actual fact aspirant philosophers. Plato reserves harsh judgement for such philosophical pretensions: '[t]he artisan who presumes to meddle in philosophy is more than a newly rich worker; he is a fugitive slave akin to those who take refuge in the temples'.[14] This statement, for Rancière, reveals as much about the discriminatory criteria implemented under the spurious guise of nature as it does about Plato's true sentiments in relation to the artisan: 'Here Plato broadcasts what he does not allow himself to say elsewhere: manual labor is a servile labor.'[15]

The slave and the artisan masquerading as a philosopher emerge in Rancière's reading as mutually reducible, a case of equivalence through which Plato's true position on the question of manual labour slips to the surface of a specious argument. The fugitive slave doubles in the role of artisan, and through that doubling discloses in Plato an arbitrary discrimination. However, one does wonder what actual slaves become for Rancière here, even within the confines of a figurative argument based on abstract types. Within the parameters of his critique of Plato, the slave seems to be scripted merely as a rhetorical prop whose sole purpose is to drive home Plato's disparaging of the artisan. In this process of unmasking the systemic complicity of Plato, and by extension philosophy in general, Rancière himself performs a masking of the very conditions of possibility on which Athenian democracy relies. In the context of Athenian democracy, the role of the slave far exceeds that of an accidental prop to be smuggled in and out of an argument according to rhetorical demand. As Andrés Fabián Henao Castro has evocatively argued, in Plato's allegory of the cave there emerges a dramatisation of 'the material dependency of "freedom" in the polis upon slavery in the mines of Greek antiquity'.[16] The cave thus moves beyond its allegorical nature into the material zone of mining, and, by extension, the slave gains an identity beyond the argumentative prop that simply has no part in the democratic order. The extent of democratic Athens's dependence on slavery has been debated among scholars, with some maintaining that not only the illustrious advances in philosophy and literature, but also – and crucially – the invention of democracy occurred against the paradoxical backdrop of slavery.[17] Others have qualified this dependence, noting that agricultural slavery was not particularly widespread, and that the wealth generated from the silver mines worked by slaves benefited a small albeit very wealthy elite.[18] The crucial point for our argument is not one that rests on degree (the extent to which slavery powered Athenian democracy), but that the slave occupied a fundamentally different position to that of the artisan, a difference smoothed over in Rancière's critique of the Platonic order.

Later on in *The Philosopher and His Poor*, Rancière finds in the sociological work of Pierre Bourdieu an extreme manifestation of Plato's unwillingness to recognise the fundamental equality of artisans. For Rancière, both Bourdieu and Plato necessarily share the relegation of the oppressed to a position of inequality. As Rancière shows, Bourdieu does this by means of a reversed ordering: 'the sociologist reaches necessity starting from the illusion of freedom. He proclaims that it is the illusion of their freedom that binds artisans to their places. The declared arbitrariness thus becomes a scientific necessity, and the redistribution of cards an absolute illusion.'[19] In this reversal, Bourdieu does not cement the position of the poor by recourse to a 'natural' (that is, arbitrary) order, but rationalises their position as an outcome of their immanent inequality.

The recognition of the way in which both Plato and Bourdieu refuse fundamental equality to the oppressed through the assignation of roles and identities intended to keep them in their place points towards the supposition of equality on which Rancière will insist throughout. It is this same supposition that leaves him forever distrustful of identity politics, a version of politics which, like that espoused by Plato and Bourdieu, assigns to the subject an identity or subjectivity that ultimately amounts to the foreclosure of equality. Indeed, when equality is acted out, says Rancière, the embodiment of identification becomes an impossibility for the subject who utters that identification.[20] If this is correct, then perhaps it is because, as with the example of slave miners in Plato's cave allegory, there is another identity that is passed over unnoticed, silenced by the slowly crystallising contours of a new sensory reality. To consider more closely what goes unnoticed here, we turn now to the Eoan group and their operatic productions in apartheid South Africa.

Eoan: staging the (coloured) worker

Founded in 1933 by British immigrant Helen Southern-Holt, the Eoan group was established in District Six, Cape Town, as a cultural and welfare organisation for the so-called 'coloured' community, providing at first elocution classes, before expanding to include lessons in literature, drama and ballet.[21] In 1940 the group added a choir to their offering and appointed to the position of conductor a second-generation Italian immigrant and amateur musician, Joseph Salvatore Manca. Under Manca, the choir, now almost a fully fledged opera company, would stage a series of operettas between 1949 and 1954. The first mounting of a full-scale opera came two years later, in 1956, when Eoan staged Verdi's *La Traviata*, sung in Italian and performed 'in traditional Italian style'.[22] The group would go on to perform this work during each of their following eleven seasons, and it would also be their last opera in 1975.

Though the company would continue to produce operas for

almost twenty years, its eventual demise was already prefigured in its very first production in 1956. It was in this year (and again from 1965 onward) that the group, which was in dire need of financial support for its elaborate productions, accepted funding from the apartheid government's Department of Coloured Affairs.[23] Coloured Affairs (for short) was tasked with the supervision of the coloured community's participation in social and civil life in apartheid South Africa. If the Eoan group wanted to perform in a theatre reserved for whites only, such as Cape Town City Hall, which they had to do in order to attract further financial support, it was necessary first to obtain a permit from Coloured Affairs. Moreover, by accepting grants from the department, the opera company bound itself to upholding the regime's policies of separate development along racial lines by performing to segregated audiences.[24] This trade-off would lead in 1980 to the group at large (not only the opera section, which performed its last opera five years before) being declared a 'banned organisation' by the South African Council of Sport, the resistance body concerned with recreational activities.[25] Though it came late, the ban consolidated smaller charges of complicity levelled against Eoan members by individuals and groups from within the coloured community, often to devastating effect. Singer Ruth Goodwin, for instance, recalls the domestic tension that arose from these charges when she says, 'it's a wonder my husband didn't divorce me, because he was very much against' the group singing for segregated audiences, while Peter Voges remembers the ultimatum he was given by his colleagues at the school where he taught:

> So they very kindly . . . came to me and spoke their minds. '[I]f you go there [to sing with the Eoan group] you are not here [teaching].' And this is where I was earning my bread and butter, teaching. [S]o at the end of 1980 I had to resign from there.[26]

'Here' and 'there': two incommensurable worlds that the Eoan members had to straddle in defiance of their own community.

Despite the charges of complicity, we argue that the history of Eoan, when read through a Rancièrean lens, is a story about various forms of dissensus in opposition to the police (understood as that which partitions the sensible world in a way that grants a part to some and not others).[27] Despite the charges of complicity, the Eoan group could be understood as a disruptive presence

Coloured Opera and the Violence of Dis-identification 163

within apartheid's distribution of the sensible, thus enacting a Rancièrean form of politics.[28]

Politics, as Rancière puts it elsewhere, is that which 'breaks with the tangible configuration whereby parties and parts or lack of them are defined by a presupposition that, by definition, has no place in that configuration'.[29] As it is defined here, politics can be understood as constitutive of deliberate incitements of equality undertaken by those said to have no part in the dominant order. The language of parts and partitioning resonates with the ways in which apartheid went about its business of gridding and categorisation. 'A Coloured person is a person who is not a white person nor a native', reads the Population Registration Act 1950.[30] Quite literally, then, to be coloured in apartheid South Africa was to be defined by law as the part with no part; it was to be defined as having no part in whiteness, nor in blackness, thus signalling an ambiguous category defined negatively.[31] In Rancièrean phraseology, colouredness was a racial classification rendered invisible by 'a distribution of the sensible whose principle is the absence of void and supplement'.[32] In the case of coloured identity, the void represents all non-white subjects in apartheid South Africa; bodies that are stripped of freedom and equal representation. The supplement is specific to coloured identity. Being neither white enough, nor black enough, the coloured body, the offspring of what apartheid ideologues condemned as 'bastardy', provided the supplement that furnished one of the lies at the core of apartheid politics, namely that apartheid was merely the realisation of a natural state of things.

Yet it was these street sweepers, teachers, factory workers and domestic servants who took to the stage when Eoan performed Italian opera, and in so doing it was the coloured body that took the place of the Western operatic subject endowed with all the trappings of civilisation, thereby asserting itself as equal in the face of continued disenfranchisement. Virginia Davids, a soprano of the Eoan group, recalls the following:

> There came a time that Jimmy [Momberg] was without work and I asked my dad, 'don't you have a job for Jimmy,' because everybody had to have a day job. Now just imagine, having a day job and singing *La Traviata* in the evening or something like that. Having a family to feed and you were working the whole day, whether you are a bricklayer or a street sweeper or what. At the end of the day, at night, you

put on your tails. It was also a very levelling factor, nobody cared the hell whether you're the school principal and whether you are a street sweeper or whatever. At night, you go on the stage, dressed up and you're all even.[33]

Davids's recollection is of a group of disparate people, some with better employment than others, some without any employment, and the vertical collapse of social and racial hierarchies set to work upon the operatic stage where 'all are even'. Yet it is also an acknowledgement of the site and hour of this supposition. In this sense, Davids's observation points towards another definition of politics offered by Rancière. 'Politics', he writes, 'revolves around what is seen and what can be said about it, around who has the ability to see and the talent to speak, *around the properties of spaces and the possibilities of time.*'[34] That is, among other things, politics is concerned with a spatial-temporal structure maintained by the police.

The Eoan group enacted a disruption of the police order at the level of both space and time. Like the subjects of Rancière's research in the workers' archives, many members of the Eoan group defied the division of time predicated on the assumption that the worker is too exhausted by their daytime labour to partake in artistic pursuits at night. Such a defiance is particularly evident in the following recollection of Sophia Andrews.

I worked in a factory called the African Clothing Factory in [Zonebloem]. And [my husband] knew after work I never used to come home. I had to go stage [sic] at City Hall. And from there we used to do our operas and so on and come home quarter to twelve. And tomorrow night is the same procedure.[35]

Hers was a claim upon the night as a time when she could step into the part of soloist or chorister, slipping out of the part of coloured factory worker. Yet it is also an appropriation that stands in stark contrast to the way in which the state attempted to restrict the night-time movement of non-whites by imposing curfews.

As much as Eoan members appropriated a time that was not theirs, they also appropriated a space to which, according to the mangled logic of apartheid, the coloured body had no claim: the operatic stage. Opera, along with other forms of 'high culture' imported from Western Europe, was inextricably linked to whiteness.[36] This link was largely forged by institutions such as the South African Broadcasting Corporation, which considered Western European art music as the 'bounteous heritage' of the white population.[37] In 1961 these policies became formalised through the establishment of four provincial arts councils tasked with supporting the performing arts, including those of Western European origin. These state-funded councils and the financial and infrastructural support they offered were intended for the white population only, effectively declaring the performative arts – and especially those bearing the cultural imprint of Europe – off limits for South Africans classified as non-white.

The operatic productions of the Eoan group, however, cut across this administered logic of apartheid. Not only was it the coloured body that came to occupy the operatic stage in place of the white body, it was also the coloured worker who stepped into the space of the Western operatic subject. The switch from worker to operatic soloist in many ways signals the duality of the spaces occupied by the Eoan group. On the one hand, Eoan members functioned as an invisible and inaudible labour force, relegated to the confines of factories and non-white schools. On the other, as Juliana M. Pistorius has argued, 'the coloured singers, stepping into the spotlight, moved from the periphery into a position of visibility and audibility, thus assuming the authority of those who have the right to be heard and seen'.[38] And it is exactly in the shuttling back and forth between these positions that a Rancièrean politics emerges. It is a movement predicated on a supposition of equality, which holds that the coloured body, once it occupies the space of the Western operatic subject, stages the capacity of its equality. Yet it is a movement in which divisions of time and space allocated to colouredness are fundamentally undermined: the coloured factory worker, the police order of the apartheid state maintained, does not have time to perform opera, nor does she belong on the operatic stage since that is the space of whiteness. Thus, by performing Italian opera, the Eoan members effectively enacted a redistribution of the sensible in which there emerged a dissensus in the racial sensorium parcelled out by the police.

The darker side of dis-identification

Moving from the periphery into a zone of visibility and audibility, however, is also to step out of the community of the oppressed.

For Rancière, politics is marked by this rupture, which he calls dis-identification. That is, politics is possible in 'the interval or gap between two identities'.[39] Rancière illustrates this poignantly in *Disagreement* by drawing on the case of Auguste Blanqui.[40] Blanqui was put on trial in France in 1832 for his role as a leader in the revolution. When asked by the magistrate to state his profession, Blanqui replied defiantly, 'proletarian', which at that time was not the name of a profession nor of a social group. For Rancière, this proclamation is an exemplary instance of dis-identification. It is a moment in which 'proletarian' as a designator of a profession is repartitioned.

> Blanqui gives [profession] a different meaning: a profession is a profession of faith, a declaration of membership of a collective. Only, this collective is of a particular kind. The proletarian class in which Blanqui professes to line himself up is in no way identifiable with a social group ... They are the uncounted that only exists in the very declaration in which they are counted as those of no account ... What is subjectified is neither work nor destitution, but the simple counting of the uncounted, the difference between the inegalitarian distribution of social bodies and the equality of speaking beings.[41]

This difference, the interval between the oppressed and the insistence of the oppressed as equal beings, is the gap in which dis-identification emerges. An identical condition of in-betweenness is manifest in the history of the Eoan group: while they would occupy the space of the Western operatic subject, Eoan members remained, in the eyes of apartheid law, lesser citizens. However, by accepting financial support from Coloured Affairs for the very purpose – unwittingly or otherwise – of staging equality, members of Eoan became ostracised from the coloured community. This can be seen clearly at the end of an interview conducted by Ruth Fourie[42] and film-maker Aryan Kaganof with Alethea Jansen, who was involved in Eoan's management during the 1940s.

> Ruth Fourie: Anyway, I think that's it for today.
> Aryan Kaganof: I am just interested in one question that I don't understand what the politics were of the time: the issue of how the community felt about what they called Coloured Affairs. What was the position within the community about participating with or not participating with Coloured Affairs, what they called Coloured Affairs?

Coloured Opera and the Violence of Dis-identification 167

Alethea Jansen: Now listen, you have all your fancy things off?
AK: Yes.
AJ: You are not recording anything?
AK: Yes.
AJ: You are asking me something in conversation . . . Put your question again.
RF: Let me put this [the audio recorder] off.
AK: Yes. How did people feel about this term Coloured Affairs?
AJ: They hated the term! Now you have it; it's a direct answer.
AK: Now what about the people who worked with Coloured Affairs, worked in Coloured Affairs?
AJ: Hated them more! They can rather do another job than to work with Coloured Affairs. That was the attitude at the time. And I used to think to myself, 'But what's wrong? If I worked for that factory or I worked for that business enterprise, I am working for them. What's wrong with that?' So, I didn't care. I went on. And I went to work for Coloured Affairs eventually. They sent me to the United Nations. I went to the United Nations, to represent South Africa there.
AK: Did that stigmatise you within the community? Did people not like you for that reason?
AJ: Oh, no. They never liked me. Be quite sure, they never liked me. Because I am a collaborator, for want of an adjective. They talked about people like me as a collaborator. Collaborating with the Boere . . . and with the whites. How stupid, man. Absolutely stupid . . . I am one of them, I am one of the coloured community.[43]

The moment when the film-maker ostensibly grants Jansen's request to stop recording is highly suggestive.[44] When she thinks the recording device has been turned off, Jansen effectively exits the framed space of politics. When she exits the stage, what we hear and see is how the Eoan members were disowned by the coloured community, and forced to assume the identity of the collaborator. But, says Jansen, she is one of them: she is one of the part with no part in apartheid South Africa, she is one of the coloured community. Jansen's statement that she is part of the coloured community bears a striking resemblance to Blanqui's own declaration that he is a proletarian. Despite this resemblance, the consequences of each utterance differs remarkably: Jansen is marked within her community as collaborating with the police order, whereas Blanqui's statement amounts to a proper form of politics in the strictly Rancièrean sense.

Why, then, do the consequences of dis-identification differ for the Eoan members in apartheid South Africa from those of Blanqui's trial? When and how, if at all, does Rancière's aesthetics of politics account for the devastating tension between alienation and belonging felt within the community of the oppressed? Is this tension omitted altogether from the stage of politics from which figures such as Blanqui speak? What the aesthetics of politics leaves untold, it would seem, is the subjects and bodies buried underneath the wreckage of framed emancipation, a framed emancipation that Jansen has to exit in order to articulate the way in which she was rejected by her own community. It is at this juncture that a reading attentive to the structures of identity could become productive, a reading that Rancière, as we suggested at the start of this chapter, is reluctant to undertake.

Such a reading would have to take into account the precariousness of the liminal space that Rancière calls the in-between. In apartheid South Africa this in-between space was encoded into the racial categories ordered and legalised by the apartheid regime. Recall the definition of colouredness set out in the Population Registration Act cited above. 'A Coloured person is a person who is not a white person nor a native.' That is, colouredness is defined as a category in between whiteness and blackness. It is an in-between space coded by the racial stratification enforced by the apartheid police order. What is revealed here is the unavailability of an in-between space, a space of dis-identification, which is merely assumed in the Blanqui example. Whereas Blanqui's occupation of the position of the proletarian initiated a moment of politics for Rancière, Jansen's occupation of a similar position also meant entry into a pre-inscribed category of in-betweenness. That is, for Jansen to be in-between was also to partake in the partitioning of colouredness ordered by the police.

What we have called the violence of dis-identification in the context of apartheid South Africa occurs on two distinct levels. The first is structural: the violence that is enacted on racialised bodies already classified as in-between, a violence stemming from the unavailability of a space unmarked by racial stratification. The second is psychological: it is the form of violence that emerges in the incommensurability between Jansen's desire to belong to the coloured community and her rejection by that very same community. These forms of violence only emerge clearly in Jansen's account once the tidy frame of staged dis-identification falls away, to be replaced by a far more complicated nexus of identities and dis-identities than Rancière's examples – overwhelmingly white and class-based – allow for.

Read alongside the example of Blanqui's act of dis-identification, another crucial differentiation is necessary. The violence experienced by Jansen emerges at the point where racial stratification cannot merely be subsumed into a politics of class, without leaving behind residual traces on bodies marked by colonial (racial) difference.[45] Perhaps this is what goes unnoticed in Rancière's writings on white workers who can slip in between social strata, unencumbered by a racialised identity politics.[46] The logical conclusion of such an argument would suggest that Rancière's refusal of identity politics, when placed in contexts such as apartheid South Africa where race cannot be subsumed into class without leaving a residue, is not so much a refusal to disentangle race and class, as a subtle neutralisation of whiteness, which, through the dismissal of identity politics, becomes invisible. Blanqui, after all, is not only a revolutionary who speaks as a 'proletarian', but also a white European body.

The lessons offered by the group of coloured workers who by night sang Italian opera despite having no part under the apartheid regime renew the question of subjectification. On the one hand, their recollections show us that Rancière's aesthetics of politics is a powerful tool for articulating forms of protest in the margins, forms of protest that, while not seen as such in conventional readings of struggle, serve to disrupt a sensory reality parcelled out by the police. On the other hand, it shows us that the suggestion of an impossible identification cannot be thought so neatly within a discussion of subjectification. What the recollections of Ruth Goodwin, Peter Voges and Alethea Jansen seem to suggest is that there is indeed a necessary identification in the process of subjectification. That they are part of the coloured community, whether accepted as such or not, is bound up with the very conditions of possibility of disruption. The danger inherent in a reading of the group's activities strictly through the lens of an aesthetics of politics is one of passing over or leaving unnoticed this condition. To set the Eoan archive to work on Rancière's thought, then, is to bring into sharp relief the violence of dis-identification where the staged frame of politics gives way to the structural violence experienced by bodies marked and counted according to race.

Notes

1. Gerald Samaai, quoted in Eoan History Project, *Eoan: Our Story*, ed. Wayne Muller and Hilda Roos (Johannesburg: Fourth Wall Books, 2013), 42.
2. 'Coloured' has acquired a specific – and not uncontested – meaning in South Africa. As a racial designation, 'coloured' was one of four classifications enforced by the apartheid government, the other three being white, African and Indian. 'Coloured', as apartheid nomenclature, referred to individuals of mixed race. As a specific identity, 'coloured' has a longer history, stemming from the days of early colonisation and the importation of slave labour in the Cape. See Richard van der Ross, *In Our Own Skins: A Political History of the Coloured People of South Africa* (Cape Town: Jonathan Ball, 2015).
3. Juliana M. Pistorius, 'Coloured Opera as Subversive Forgetting', *Social Dynamics* 43.2 (2017), 231. Though the Eoan group is credited as the first company to stage regular, full-scale operatic productions, opera performances in South Africa date back to 1802, with a history of small-scale and fragmented performances and short-lived companies which followed. See Hilde Roos, 'Remembering to Forget the Eoan Group – The Legacy of an Opera Company from the Apartheid Era', *South African Theatre Journal* 27.1 (2014), 2–3.
4. Quoted in Rubén Gaztambide-Fernández, 'Decolonial options and artistic/aestheSic entanglements: An interview with Walter Mignolo', *Decolonization: Indigeneity, Education & Society* 3.1 (2014), 201.
5. Jacques Rancière, *The Emancipated Spectator*, trans. Gregory Elliott (London: Verso, 2009), 95–105.
6. We are specifically referring to Jacques Rancière, *Proletarian Nights: The Workers' Dream in Nineteenth-Century France*, trans. John Drury (London: Verso, 2012). For a discussion of Rancière's early writings and their theoretical gains, see Joseph Tanke, *Jacques Rancière: An Introduction* (London: Continuum, 2011), 7–42.
7. Quoted in Sudeep Dasgupta, 'Art is Going Elsewhere, and Politics Has to Catch It. An Interview with Jacques Rancière', *Krisis: Journal of Contemporary Philosophy* 1 (2008), 75.
8. This formulation belongs to Rancière, who insists that his work on politics does not amount to an overarching theory – neither a theory of politics, nor of the subject as inherently political. See Jacques Rancière, 'A Few Remarks on the Method of Jacques Rancière', *Parallax* 15.3 (2009), 116.
9. Rancière, 'A Few Remarks', 120.

10. Holloway Sparks, 'Quarrelling with Rancière: Race, Gender and the Politics of Democratic Disruption', *Philosophy and Rhetoric* 49.4 (2016), 424.
11. Jacques Rancière, 'Politics, Identification and Subjectivization', *October* 61 (1992), 60.
12. Jacques Rancière, *Disagreement: Politics and Philosophy*, trans. Julie Rose (Minneapolis: University of Minnesota Press, 1999), 35.
13. Plato, *Republic*, trans. G. M. A. Grube, rev. C. D. C Reeve (Indianapolis: Hackett Publishing, 1992), 45 (370A).
14. Jacques Rancière, *The Philosopher and His Poor*, trans. John Drury, Corinne Oster and Andrew Parker (Durham, NC: Duke University Press, 2003), 32.
15. Rancière, *The Philosopher and His Poor*, 32.
16. Andrés Fabián Henao Castro, 'Slavery in Plato's Allegory of the Cave: Alain Badiou, Jacques Rancière and the Militant Intellectual from the Global South', *Theatre Survey* 58.1 (2017), 87.
17. Tina Chanter, *Whose Antigone? The Tragic Marginalization of Slavery* (Albany: State University of New York Press, 2011), 2. Chanter cites the work of Yvon Garlan, who went so far as to claim that 'chattel slavery in classical Athens and communal servitude of one type or another elsewhere did constitute the "basis" of Greek society or – to put it another way – the necessary element for it to affirm its identity'. Quoted in Chanter, *Whose Antigone?*, 2.
18. Ellen Meiksins Wood, *Peasant-Citizen and Slave: The Foundations of Athenian Democracy* (London: Verso, 2015), 42–64.
19. Rancière, *The Philosopher and His Poor*, 179.
20. Rancière, 'Politics, Identification, and Subjectivization', 61.
21. Eoan History Project, *Eoan*, 4.
22. Roos, 'Remembering to Forget', 3.
23. Pistorius, 'Coloured Opera', 231.
24. Pistorius, 'Coloured Opera', 231.
25. The South African Council of Sport was recognised by the anti-apartheid movement as its section tasked with resisting racial segregation within sports by organising boycotts against whites-only sporting events. However, the organisation took a hardline anti-collaboration approach which effectively rejected any form of compromise between non-white and white entities. It is along these lines that the Council vehemently rejected Eoan's activities, which they saw as a form of collaboration with the white government. For a comprehensive discussion of the South African Council of Sport's

politics, see Douglas Booth, *The Race Game: Sport and Politics in South Africa* (London: Frank Cass, 1998).
26. Quoted respectively in Eoan History Project, *Eoan*, 26, 36.
27. Rancière, *Disagreement*, 28.
28. Juliana M. Pistorius has similarly argued that the Eoan group represents a form of struggle against the apartheid regime, but one that has to do with a postcolonial form of forgetting. See Pistorius, 'Coloured Opera', 231.
29. Rancière, *Disagreement*, 29–30.
30. Union of South Africa, 'Population Registration Act (Act No. 30 of 1950)', *Statutes of the Union of South Africa 1950*, 277.
31. See Mohamed Adhikari, *Not White Enough, Not Black Enough: Racial Identity in the South African Coloured Community* (Athens: Ohio University Press, 2005). This ambiguous racial classification was felt by Eoan members. Ruth Goodwin, one of the Eoan soloists, recalls being invited to tea by some of the 'European' (read white) members of the Eoan orchestra: '"Ruth, can I take you out for tea?" I said, "No, you can't because I am black." They would say, "But you're not black." I said, "But I am not white."' Quoted in Eoan History Project, *Eoan*, 20.
32. Jacques Rancière, 'Ten Theses on Politics', in *Dissensus: On Politics and Aesthetics*, trans. Steven Corcoran (London: Continuum, 2010), 36.
33. Quoted in Eoan History Project, *Eoan*, 170.
34. Jacques Rancière, *The Politics of Aesthetics: The Distribution of the Sensible*, trans. Gabriel Rockhill (London: Continuum, 2011), 13 (our emphasis).
35. Quoted in Eoan History Project, *Eoan*, 116.
36. There emerges an interesting distinction between the sociopolitical histories of opera and, for that matter, theatre. Whereas theatre was frequently utilised as a platform for political dissent in which critiques of the regime were acted out, opera remained a site of consensus that seldom challenged the status quo. The difference becomes evident when one considers the emergence of a strong tradition of so-called Struggle Theatre, where no similar tradition emerged in opera in South Africa. Indeed, new compositions in opera during this time, when they infrequently appeared, were beholden to the state. See Hilde Roos, 'Opera Production in the Western Cape: Strategies in Search of Indigenization', PhD dissertation, Stellenbosch University, 2010, 20–71.
37. Quoted in John Hinch, 'Stravinsky in Africa', *Muziki* 1.1 (2004), 73.

38. Pistorius, 'Coloured Opera', 237.
39. Rancière, 'Politics, Identification, and Subjectivization', 61.
40. Rancière, *Disagreement*, 37.
41. Rancière, *Disagreement*, 38.
42. No relation to the co-author.
43. *An Inconsolable Memory*, film, directed by Aryan Kaganof, DOMUS: Documentation Centre for Music, 2013.
44. Whether or not this moment constitutes an ethical breach on the part of the film-maker is not our concern here. However, it is worth stating that Kaganof showed this scene to Jansen prior to the film's release. An amused Jansen raised no objection to its inclusion in the final version. Stephanus Muller, '*An Inconsolable Memory*: Ethical and Methodological Challenges for Music Historiography in Traumatic and Post-Totalitarian Contexts', paper presented at Royal Holloway, University of London, 25 November 2014.
45. For the inextricability of race and class in South Africa, see Nicoli Nattrass and Jeremy Seekings, *Class, Race, and Inequality in South Africa* (New Haven, CT: Yale University Press, 2005). Already on the second page, they note that apartheid South Africa, more than any other capitalist nation, has instituted racial laws as, among other things, a means of systematically structuring income inequality. For a historical account of the connection between colonialism and the race–class matrix, see Shula Marks and Stanley Trapido, 'The Politics of Race, Class and Nationalism', in Shula Marks and Stanley Trapido (eds), *The Politics of Race, Class and Nationalism in Twentieth-Century South Africa* (London: Routledge, 2014), 1–70.
46. This point is also made by Tina Chanter when she argues that Rancière 'blindly acquiesce[s]' to the invidious mechanics of race and gender around his theoretical exemplars. Tina Chanter, *Art, Politics and Rancière: Broken Perceptions* (London: Bloomsbury, 2017), 12. What this chapter contributes to Chanter's work is a further problematisation of the position of the in-between, especially in the way that it is rendered unavailable to the coloured community.

Part III Politics of Interaction

8

Musical Politics in the Cuban Police Order

Kjetil Klette Bøhler

This chapter explores how Cuban popular dance music nurtures and contests revolutionary values in today's Cuba.[1] I focus on the performance and discursive construction of the song 'Cubanos por el mundo' by Interactivo, one of Cuba's most popular bands in the last decade, using a combination of textual and musical analysis framed by Jacques Rancière's notion of 'police' and 'politics'.[2] From this perspective I analyse the formation of a 'Cuban police order' structured around a shared notion of the revolutionary and discuss how the experience of the song dialogues musically with that order by associating it with pleasure and critique. Empirically, I focus on the recording and an improvisation by Roberto Carcassés, the director of the band and composer of the song, during a live performance at a massive concert held to celebrate revolutionary unity at Plaza Anti-Imperialista in Havana. The second part of the chapter discusses how the song nurtured new articulations of 'politics' and 'police' discursively by studying blogs and newspaper articles written in response to the improvisation.

Listening to the pleasures and politics of Cuban grooves through Rancière's two concepts call for a relational understanding of the politics of music that examines both the broader police orders within which music makes sense *and*, through in-depth listening, how music disputes and amplifies such orders. It suggests that the multidimensional meanings of music in experience allow sounds to both pleasurise and criticise police orders as rhythms, melodies and sung statements interlock in time. More importantly, the study shows how these relationships create pleasurable ways of being together that both reproduce and change 'what is common to the community'.[3] It resonates with John Street's emphasis on 'the political possibilities inherent in [musical] pleasure'[4] and calls into question studies that focus exclusively on lyrics and music's circulation to capture the politics of music.[5] A relational understanding of the politics of music grants more political agency to musical sounds than most existing studies while still considering music's discursive context.[6]

'Police' and 'politics' in Cuban grooves

Rancière's 'police' has nothing to do with common understandings of police officers. Instead, it refers to a way of making sense of sense perceptions that shape what is common in a community by delegating different subjects to specific positions in a hierarchy.[7] While a police order may seem universal for the subjects that live in its context, it is only one among many different ways of 'making sense of sense' that situates subjects in relation to each other.[8] It should be understood as a description of how society is organised because '[t]he essence of the police is not repression but distribution – the distribution, or partitioning, of the sensible, of what is made available to the senses and what is made to make sense'.[9] The police underscores the impossibility of instituted orders of equality, such as that claimed to be operative in post-revolutionary Cuba, because any such order creates the illusion that the problem of democracy is resolved and prevents productive ruptures in the future.

It is on this basis that Rancière defines politics as an expression of dissensus against the police that claims the emergence of a new subject and new forms of community to be imagined and acted upon. Rancière describes it as the 'declaration of a wrong' by a subject that was not there prior to that declaration and that constitutes itself through this very act.[10] Expressions of politics are always relative to a given police order and they frequently use, or signify upon, the places, words and symbols defined by this order.[11] Here is one way Rancière describes the relationship between the two concepts:

> The police says that there is nothing to see on a road, that there is nothing to do but move along. It asserts that the space of circulating is nothing other than the space of circulation. Politics, in contrast, consists in transforming this space of 'moving-along' into a space for the appearance of a subject: i.e., the people, the workers, the citizens.

Musical Politics in the Cuban Police Order   179

> It consists in refiguring the space, of what there is to do there, what is to be seen or named therein.[12]

The defining feature of 'politics' is a gap in perception where 'a police order' is no longer reproduced and a new subject appears. This gap may operate in different sensible domains (e.g. sounds, images or words), which in each case works in practice by restructuring our affects, perceptions and senses of meaning, thus contributing to views that a different world is possible. It is in this way that Rancière understands politics as an expression of aesthetics because aesthetic experiences may change what is common to the community (the police order) and contribute to what he terms political subjectivisation:

> Aesthetic experience ... is a common experience that changes the cartography of the perceptible, the thinkable and the feasible. As such, it allows for new modes of political construction of common objects and new possibilities of collective enunciation ... Film, video art, photography, installation, etc. rework the frame of our perceptions and the dynamism of our affects. As such they may open new passages toward new forms of political subjectivization.[13]

We should of course add music to Rancière's list of artistic media.

This quote illustrates how Rancière grants a potential political agency to aesthetic experiences that is fruitful for studying the politics of Cuban popular dance music. However, this also forces us to operationalise Rancière's two key terms in the context of Cuban culture and music. While many different 'police orders' can be identified in Cuba, I will draw attention to how shared understandings of the 1959 Cuban revolution have divided subjects and organised 'a totality comprised of groups performing specific functions and occupying determined spaces', which I will term the 'Cuban police order'.[14] However, as this order is defined by the rupture of the revolution, it allows us to examine the temporal interplay between 'the police' and 'politics' in practice. Furthermore, by applying the two concepts to a study of musical sound by listening to Interactivo's 'Cubanos por el mundo', we can examine how musical grooves both nurture and contest the Cuban police order. This calls for in-depth qualitative research on how specific organisations of sounds create affective communities through which embodied pleasures strengthen the Cuban police order while also criticising it. However, before we get into the groove it is important to outline what is meant by a Cuban police order.

From politics to police: a Cuban police order?

The 'Cuban police order' is structured around contradictory definitions of the Cuban revolution that emphasise both rupture and order. On the one hand it is understood as a revolutionary moment that made an end to the neo-colonialist and racist Batista government by calling for social equality and freedom of expression. One of Fidel Castro's descriptions of that moment may illustrate this:

> [1] Revolution is feeling the historical moment, [2] it is changing everything that needs to be changed, [3] it is full equality and freedom, [4] it is being treated and treating others as human beings, [5] it is emancipating ourselves for ourselves and by our own efforts.[15]

In one sense this definition of the revolution becomes an expression of 'politics' because it gives voice to those Cubans who were 'without a name [and] deprived of *logos*' prior to 1959.[16] However, Castro's words also exemplify a specific 'police order': they were the opening of a speech to Cuban workers on 1 May 2000 that became part of a propaganda campaign aimed at convincing Cubans of the importance of continuing the revolutionary struggle forty-one years after it began.[17] This 'Cuban police order' can be understood as an interpretative framework that separates individuals in a hierarchical system where the revolutionary government is given full authority. It operates through an implied distinction between the revolutionary and the counter-revolutionary that undermines Castro's emphasis on 'full equality' and 'makes some more equal than others', to borrow a phrase from George Orwell. An example is Castro's famous statement concerning the freedom of artistic expression in Cuba: 'Within the revolution, complete freedom; against the revolution, none.'[18]

The Cuban police order works through a dichotomous discourse that equates the US government with American imperialism and defines it as an eternal threat to the revolutionary project and Cuba as an independent country. This declared enemy legitimises the Cuban police order as such. It is on the basis of these arguments that a footnote at the end of the Cuban constitution states that all constitutional rights (e.g. freedom of expression) may be subject to change based upon the priorities of the Cuban communist party, as revolutionary needs matter more than liberal rights such as freedom of expression.[19] In short, the Cuban police order should be understood as an interpretative lens through which certain perceptions, actions, ideas and subjects are defined as 'revolutionary'. Within the field of music this rationale was used to ban certain structures of musical sound as counter-revolutionary, although the exact definition of what was revolutionary and what was not has changed over time.[20] This distinction has structured ways of listening through shared concepts such as *música patriótica*, which refers to music that reminds listeners of the beauty of Cuban culture and society[21] as well as its antithesis, *música contestária*, which refers to songs that question this beauty.[22] In short, the Cuban police order works as an interpretative principle through which any homage to *or* critique of Cuban culture can be viewed as a political act (in the conventional sense of the term).

People who have been excluded in this police order have been expelled and punished in different ways because of their disagreement with the revolution.[23] These exclusions, as well as people's dissatisfaction (economic or political) with this police order, have led millions of Cubans to emigrate and have disrupted families. At the same time, it is important to mention that those who position themselves within a revolutionary community in Cuba have been entitled to a welfare state unique in Latin America, which gives people access to music, arts, healthcare and education. This has led to support for the revolution, both in Cuba and abroad. However, as much as Cubans appreciate these 'beautiful' sides, the realities of disrupted families, fear of the secret police and a poor economy has led to an ambivalent 'love and hate' relationship for many. My informant 'Juan' elaborates on this point through a description of Cuba as a Janus face that is beautiful and ugly at the same time:

> Look, you have to understand the difference between the beautiful Cuba and the ugly Cuba. Cuba has two faces, you understand? Like one of these Janus faces you know. In the face of the Beautiful Cuba we have *la música*, the dance, the education, public health, *la cultura*, all the good and beautiful things about Cuba that everybody loves, you know. But, the other face, the Ugly Cuba, is *los militares, el partido, la policía, la política, la corrupción, la burocracia*, the legislation and laws, you know, all the bad things. But these two faces are

not connected, and in the end the Ugly Cuba is the leader. They only use the Beautiful Cuba to look nice. But the Ugly Cuba is dangerous, don't get yourself into *la política*, it is very dangerous. That's why we like the music, because we don't like *la política*, here nobody likes *la política* besides the people in the party.[24]

Following Juan, we may conceive of music as something that the Cuban government uses to show its beauty and hide its ugliness. Cuban grooves may add 'flesh and bone' to positive perceptions of the Cuban police order as 'beautiful'. Shared joys in Cuban music may even shake the hearts and souls of those Cubans who have an ambivalent relationship with the revolution because, as my informants said, Cuban music is *arte* not *política*, it belongs to a different sphere. In fact, it is this very distinction that provides Cuban music with a unique political potential as its ways of moving people may provide common pleasures that both challenge and reproduce 'who can have a share in what is common to the [revolutionary] community',[25] while simultaneously claiming that it is *arte* and not part of *política*. Hence in order to understand how Cuban music contests and strengthens the Cuban police order we have to listen carefully to how music moves us.

Listening to 'Cubanos por el mundo'

'Cubanos por el mundo' opens with a soft, airy, male voice that sings the words 'Cuba, la tierra de sublime tradición, música de corazón, e cuando bailas tu, te lo digo yo' (Cuba, the soil of sublime tradition, music from the hearth, and when you dance, you feel it) over jazzy piano chords (0:00–0:20). The sung words invoke Cuba as a beautiful sensory experience defined by music. Immediately afterwards a rich Afro-Cuban groove invites the listener to dance. Its rhythmic impetus shapes, and is shaped by, Francis del Rio's off-beat singing. He sings about strong family relations and the shared embodied experiences of partaking in the musical groove. The family becomes a concrete example of the togetherness celebrated in the introduction. However, by also singing that these family relations contain 'los de aquí e de allá' (those here and there, 1:14–1:15) he hints at a Rancièrean 'wrong' by creating associations with the split families that have resulted from Cubans leaving the country because of the struggle of everyday life. In terms of Juan's argument, he uses the beautiful Cuba to direct attention to Cuba's ugliness; however, as the Cuban police order controls the cultural industries on the island, the critique is not explicit. A similar message is expressed when the chorus enters through a mixture of speaking and rapping by calling out 'Cubanos por el mundo' (Cubans around the world, 1:25–1:26). In one sense the words may refer to the above-mentioned migration. However, listening to the words from the viewpoint of the Cuban police order they may also refer to the global spread of 'the revolution', manifested, for example, through Cuban doctors' *haciendo misión* as revolutionary workers who develop welfare capacities in Third World countries.[26] The sung words may also be heard as a celebration of the growing popularity of Cuban music that is evidenced by how the sounds of Cuban salsa and reggaetón remind dancing listeners around the world that Cuba is beautiful and pleasurable.

These words are followed by new voices that repeat the lyrics from the introduction; however, this time the voices are harmonised in minor sixths and phrased in the fashion of R'n'B singing (1:37–1:52). Through this a sense of pleasure is amplified while the message from the introduction is restated; namely that what makes Cuba Cuba is the very act of dancing to Cuban rhythms. Vocalist Telmary Díaz's subsequent rap (1:51–2:08) elaborates on how a unique Cuban community is structured around shared pleasures, even though she also hints at a critique by rapping; 'Cuba bella todos temores, repartiendo amores' (beautiful Cuba, all the fears and broken hearts, 1:52–1:53). Singing about 'all the fears' (*todos temores*) brings associations of shared feelings of anxiety in Cuba as many are afraid of expressing criticism because of the secret police. However, the fast delivery of the words (with fifteen syllables expressed in less than two seconds) and the ways in which they interact with the groove draw more attention to their musicality than their literal meaning. These musical meanings consist in increased intensities through the words' delivery as a series of sixteenth notes articulated slightly out of time but still within the rhythmic fabric.

The return of Francis del Rio's voice elaborates on how this uniquely pleasurable Cuban community is the product of Afro-Cuban religion and culture (2:08–2:25). The break and the following *montuno* (a repeating open-ended refrain organised in catchy call-and-response singing) increase these sensations through specific musical sounds as the interplay between an energetic piano *tumbao* (a repeated syncopated ostinato), a forward-moving rhythm played on the *güiro* and multiple 'breaks' invites us into a more powerful *timba* groove (2:25–2:33). By responding to and interacting with the groove in the Yoruba language, vocalist Oscar Valdez adds further sentiment to the *montuno* rhythms. The very act of singing in Yoruba is a signifier of intensification as it brings reference to the role of spirit possession and musical intensities in Afro-Cuban religions. It is further amplified by singing mainly in a pressed high register of the male voice and by articulating sounds that mimic the possessed (e.g. 'grrrrrr', 'eeeeee'). After singing about the musical pleasures that make the Cuban community valuable, Valdez articulates a hint of critique against the Cuban police order while bringing del Rio's prior evocation of Cubans 'here and there' into a new musical context, singing: 'Que los de aquí se siente mas de allí, que los de allá se echa mas pa' acá' (So that those here can feel more at home there, and that they over there can come closer to us, 2:53–2:57). The 'here' and 'there' refer to the boundary that separates Cubans on the island from those outside Cuba. Listened to in the light of Juan's above-cited comments, Valdez's singing aims to bring down the division between the ugly Cuba and the beautiful Cuba and create a new Cuba Libre that includes those in Miami and elsewhere, as well as those on the island. However, due to hegemony of the Cuban police order the critique is not explicit but is hidden through associations and metaphors. More importantly, as with Telmary's critique (1:52–1:53), musical meanings derive from pleasurable syncopations from the vocalist that interlock in an intensifying groove and constitute the forefront of the sensory experience, rather than the words themselves.

The real musical climax is reached by the last *coro* (chorus) 'Quiero, recuérdate que siempre quiero' (I want, remember that I always wanted, 4:14–5:37). The *coro* is catchier than what has transpired thus far because of its repetition, vocal delivery and musical organisation – the ways in which it interlocks with the underlying *clave* rhythm – and the fact that it is easy to sing along with. Julio Padrón engages in a dialogue with the *coro* by singing improvisatory calls in dialogue with its steady repetition. These call-and-response interactions add syncopated energies to the groove and interlock with funky *mambos* in the horn section and multiple 'breaks' in the percussion parts. These sounds take the listener towards musical states of euphoria. However, the catchiness of the *coro* makes these impressions even stronger than Valdez's earlier singing, and make the *coro* the focal point of the song. Listening to the song from the viewpoint of the contagious *coro*, the prior celebration of Cuban culture and music is revealed as what the Cuban people 'wants, and always wanted'. In one sense it situates everybody as participants in the 'Cuban police order' as they demonstrate their love for cultural traditions that the revolution has supported by dancing to Cuban grooves. However, heard another way, Cubans also want to break down the boundaries that have split Cuban families and separated Cubans from the rest of the world. Still, these acts of musical dissensus were only hinted at, making the celebration of Cuba as a unique sensory experience the main message of the song.

As the recorded version of 'Cubanos por el mundo' – as with most other music productions in Cuba – is controlled by the Cuban government in multiple ways, it is understandable that the song reads overtly as a celebration of Cuban culture while only hinting at critique. If it this were not the case, it would probably not have been played frequently on Cuban radio and TV, nor circulated freely in the system of music distribution on the island. After all, it is a risky business to run against an omnipresent Cuban police order; as 'Jorge', a rapper in Santiago de Cuba, explained to me during an interview: 'Like all musicians, we want to get our voice out there, to be heard, to become popular, and if you voice strong critique your music will not go anywhere. Your sounds won't leave your doorstep. It is all very well controlled.'[27] However, in an earlier interview about Interactivo's music, Roberto Carcassés suggested that musicians have a political duty to address what Juan describes as both the beautiful *and* the ugly sides of Cuba, and that they should partake in political debates musically:

> We want to describe the good as well as the bad things about Cuba. We want to participate in the bigger debates about Cuba in our time. And we express this with our music, which is a very strong medium of communication. In our music we want to define the big questions like the concept of being *revolucionário, la revolución, socialista, capitalista*, as well as criticising stupid laws ... As artists we both have the possibility and the duty to shape the meanings for the young Cubans. We have to constantly define *cubania* and our idiosyncrasy.[28]

While the ubiquitous presence of the Cuban police order makes it difficult to translate Carcassés's visions into practice through recorded music,²⁹ a dimension of Cuban music itself – namely improvisation during live performance – may create such spaces. Close listening to how Carcassés transformed 'Cubanos por el mundo' from an expression of the police order into a statement of Rancièrean politics through improvisation during a big concert at Plaza Anti-Imperialista in 2013 demonstrates how a musician can go about enacting such a political disruption musically. However, as this particular improvised utterance took place during the energetic and rhythmically propulsive *montuno* section of the song, it requires a specific attention to how sung words groove and interact with other musical layers. In analysing the improvisation I will pay attention to how political statements come to the listener through the prosody of improvised singing and how they interact with other musical layers in a pleasurable groove experience. It is on this level that the political and the musical interact.³⁰ In particular I will focus on how the lead singer employs the style of *guia*-singing, a form of vocal improvisation during call-and-response parts in much *son*-based Cuban music that is marked by syncopated and melodic elaboration of existing musical material. Translated back into Rancière's conceptual terms, the following analysis aims to describe how Carcassés expressed 'politics' by changing the structure of 'who can have a share in what is common to the [revolutionary] community based on what they [can] do and on the time and place in which this activity is performed' through specific musical means.³¹

Improvising pleasurable dissensus

On 13 September 2013 Interactivo performed alongside some of the most popular bands in Cuba at the biggest concert venue in the country, Plaza Anti-Imperialista, strategically located in front of what was then the American interest section in Havana. It was a political celebration of the *Five Cuban Heroes*, a political campaign that called for the liberation of Cuban intelligence officers who according to the Cuban government were illegally imprisoned in the US.³² More than thirty bands performed in addition to Interactivo, including Los Van Van, Qva Libre, Baby Llores, Amaury Pérez, Sílvio Rodríguez, Tony Ávila, Elito Revé and NG La Banda. Thousands of Cubans attended the concert and many more people followed it live on national television. In different ways the music added hearts and souls to a larger message that called for national unity in the continuation of the revolutionary struggle against an American imperialism evidenced by the illegal imprisonment of the Cuban heroes.

On stage Interactivo began vamping over the *montuno* of 'Cubanos por el mundo', one of their biggest hits. The *montuno* consists of a piano *tumbao* that interlocks with a forward-moving pattern played on the *güiro*, a laid-back but energetic *songo* groove played on congas and drumset, a funky bassline, sparse interjections by the electric guitar, and the voice of Roberto Carcassés. The catchiness of the piano *tumbao* makes it the audible centre of the groove as it interlocks with the played *güiro* pattern and an implied 2-3 rumba *clave* while contextualising the rhythms harmonically in G major (measures 1–2) and A minor (3–4). All of this is shown in Example 8.1.

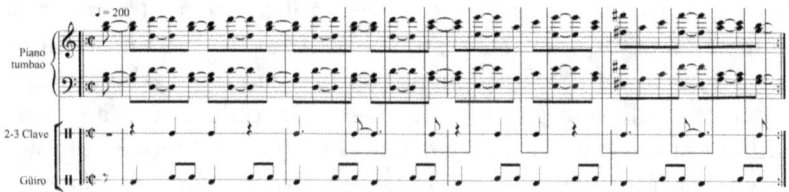

Example 8.1: 2-3 rumba *clave*, piano *tumbao* and *güiro* rhythm (0:00–0:14).

The music grooves thanks to the constant displacement of downbeats in the piano *tumbao*. These syncopated structures – see, for example, the relationship between tripled octaves and doubled thirds – make sense musically in that they produce pleasure in a listener who feels the beat through the ways in which they suspend it. The pulse becomes a source of participatory engagement thanks to the friction between multiple structures of syncopation that draws the listener deeper into the groove. It is in this musical context that Carcassés engages with the audience. However, the groove contextualises Carcassés's utterances musically by separating them into syllables, which are grouped into words and statements, and which interlock with the syncopated rhythms. These musical sounds affect the way the words are felt by dancing participants and group them in structures of on-beats (see underlined words in statements 2 and 3), and freely styled off-beats (see italics in statements 1, 4, 5, 6, 7):

1. '*Es-se co-ro es fac-il-it-o*' (this chorus is easy [to sing]) (0:00–0:02)

2. *'e to-dos lo pue-den ha-cer'* (and everybody can do it) (0:03–0:04)
3. *'por que som-os Cu-ban-os'* (because we are Cubans) (0:05–0:07)
4. *'e quer-em-os much-as caus-as'* (and we want a lot of stuff) (0:07–0:08)
5. *'quer-em-os que regr-es-en nuestr-os her-ma-nos'* (we want our brothers to come back) (0:09–0:10)
6. *'e much-as cos-as mas'* (and a lot of other things) (0:11–0:12)
7. *'y el co-ro di-ce as-i'* (and the chorus sounds like this) (0:12–0:13)

By calling for musical participation (statements 1 and 2) and defining this as what defines Cubans and their way of being together (statement 3), Carcassés paraphrases common perceptions of unity and togetherness in the Cuban police order. The next two statements (4 and 5) strengthen this message through a call for the liberation of the Five Cuban Heroes. However, the following statement (6) suggests that the Cuban people also want more, without specifying exactly what that might be. On the following downbeat, the *coristas* Tammy Lopez Moreno, Brenda Navarette and Haydee Lopez sing the *coro* 'Quiero, recuérdate que siempre quiero' (I want, remember that I always want) (0:15–0:18) in harmony while preserving its rhythmic flavour by articulating the consonants as forward-moving syncopations. Accompanied only by the piano *tumbao*, the *güiro* and a *songo* pattern played on the hi-hat, it catches the listener's attention as the signature hook of the hit that people remember. Example 8.2 shows the repeating *coro* along with the implied 2-3 rumba *clave*.

Example 8.2: The repeating *coro* and implied 2-3 rumba *clave* (0:15–0:18).

Musically, the sung words are expressed in two related phrases (see numbered phrasing lines, Example 8.2). They are catchy and easy to sing along with thanks to their percussive delivery and the structural development of a melodic motif organised around a third, which is aligned rhythmically with the groove and the underlying rumba *clave*. One beat after the *coro* finishes, Carcassés starts to improvise in the fashion of *guia* singing (0:19–0:23). His improvisation is composed of two short phrases, shown in Example 8.3.

Example 8.3: Carcassés's first *guia*, with implied 2-3 rumba *clave* (0:19–0:23).

The combination of syncopations on the three-side of the *clave* (see Example 8.3, measures 4 and 6) and downbeats on the two-side (measures 5 and 7) make the sung words perfectly 'in *clave*' as they interlock with the syncopated piano *tumbao*.[33] Melodically, Carcassés elaborates on the melodic third interval while adding diatonic elaborations (see measure 4 and the transition from measures 6 to 7). Rhythmically, he adds new syncopations that provide energy to the rolling groove. It is through this musical context that twenty-one sung syllables become audible and pleasurable through the words: 'Yo quie-ro que li-be-ren a los cin-co he-roes e li-be-ren a Ma-ri-a' (I want them to free the five heroes and to free Maria). Maria, a code name for marijuana, takes the audience by surprise but is, in fact, simply the first of the 'other things' that Cubans want, in addition to freeing the Five Heroes, according to Carcassés. The sung word 'Maria' changes what had been until then a patriotic revolutionary statement into a musical act of dissensus criticising the legal regulations on drugs within the Cuban police order. Carcassés's semantic swerve plays upon political discourses linked to the recent legalisation of marijuana in countries such as Colombia, Uruguay and several states in the US, as well as discourses from marijuana consumers in Cuba (particularly young adults and those in artistic circles) who argue for its legalisation.

Carcassés starts his second *guia* improvisation a little earlier than the first, by beginning on the last beat of the *coro*'s last measure, and it consists of three, short, connected phrases. These musical features are shown in Example 8.4. These three phrases introduce new melodic material that is not related to the interval of a third. Instead, a sense of lyricism is expressed by the legato articulation of an arpeggiated G major triad (measure 5) through the word '(la) información' (information) that also stands out thanks to an increase in ambitus (e.g. the dropping interval of a fifth in the fifth measure). Temporally, a change in rhythmic structure makes the word 'in-<u>for</u>-ma-<u>ción</u>' (downbeat syllables underlined) seize our musical attention, as Carcassés disrupts the prior flow of syncopation by articulating two on-beats (beats 1 and 3 in measure 5). The *guia*'s lyricism is then dispelled in the next measure by a percussive stream of eighths in the second phrase (see measure 6) that starts with off-beats and moves diatonically from the seventh to the tonic to set the words 'para tener yo' (so that I can have) (0:30–0:31). The third phrase (Example 8.4) add a new layer of rhythmic tension by introducing a triplet figure that ends on the following downbeat, giving further emotional presence to the words 'mi propia opinión' (my own opinion) (0:31).

Example 8.4: Carcassés's second *guia*, with implied 2-3 rumba *clave* (0:27–0:31).

Taken together, the words that make up the second *guia* improvisation – '[quiero] libre acceso a la información, para tener yo, mi propia opinión' ([I want] free access to information so that I can make up my own opinion) – intensify the dissensus introduced in the first *guia*. They represent a sharp critique of the common Cuban experience of a lack of free speech, and of uncensored information and even internet access being rigorously controlled by the government. In doing so, Carcassés turns Juan's argument on its head by using the beauty of Cuban music to declare 'a wrong' and show the ugliness of the Cuban police order. He breaks the silence musically by not perceiving *la política* as a dangerous and restricted place that belongs exclusively to the Cuban government and the military, as Juan argued, but as a space of musical dissensus and engaged subjects. He transforms the musical pleasures produced at Plaza Anti-Imperialista in celebration of the Five Cuban Heroes, which until this point had strengthened patriotism and revolutionary unity, into pleasurable dissensus by claiming 'the appearance of a subject' through groovy singing among dancing listeners.[34]

The third *guia* elaborates on this musical dissensus via the two connected phrases shown in Example 8.5. The first phrase is rhythmically rich, as Carcassés alternates between binary and ternary subdivisions with an emphasis on syncopation (see, for example, the transformation of a triplet figure into a syncopated one from measures 4 to 5 in the example), while singing the words 'Yo quiero elegir al presidente' (I want to elect the president, 0:35–0:38). Rhythmic friction and intensity increase as Carcassés starts the second part of the third *guia* with two *triplet cubano* figures (see measure 7) that add a stirring affective sense to the words 'por vo-to dir-ect-o' (through direct voting, 0:39). He then concludes the last part of the third *guia* by returning to the binary subdivisions in a downward diatonic movement ending with two on-beats, singing 'e no por otra via' (and not any other way; see measure 8). These structures of rhythmic complexity add sensibility to the political statement: 'Yo quiero elegir al presidente por voto directo e no por outra via' (I want to elect the president through direct voting, and not any other way). Again political critique is intensified as Carcassés reminds the audience that the island has not seen a democratic election since the 1950s and that even these earlier elections were corrupt affairs. It is also a critique of the practice of indirect democracy in Cuba, in which

Cubans vote on representatives for the national assembly, which then decides who will become the president.

Example 8.5: Carcassés's third *guia*, with implied 2-3 rumba *clave* (0:35–0:41).

In the fourth *guia* Carcassés broadens his critique by singing the phrase shown in Example 8.6. The first six syllables, 'Ni mi-li-tan-tes ni' (0:45; see measure 4), sustain what has now become an established pattern of off-beat phrasing before Carcassés disrupts this rhythm by singing 'dis-si-dent-es' as triplets on the following

Example 8.6: Carcassés's fourth *guia*, with implied 2-3 rumba *clave* (0:44–0:49).

four syllables. The words that follow, 'Cu-ba-nos to-dos, con los mis-mos der-e-chos' (all Cubans with the same rights, 0:46–0:49, see measures 6–8), are delivered as a mixture of off-beats and on-beats as Carcassés starts speaking rather than singing. By singing 'all Cubans with the same rights', the sung words contest the Cuban police order and call the participating listener to engage in politics.

By emphasising 'Cubanos, todos' (all Cubans), Carcassés broadens his critique to encompass both the political authorities in Cuba (*ni militantes*) *and* the dissidents (*ni dissidentes*), who are often accused of being financed by right-wing capitalist expatriates in Miami. In so doing, Carcassés calls for the equality of all Cubans, independent of revolutionary opinion and geographical location, and argues that Cubans should be united and enjoy the same rights. In that sense the sung words function as a critique of Castro's speech to the Cuban workers that takes Castro's third statement at face value by underscoring the importance of 'full equality and freedom' for all Cubans. Carcassés therefore revisits a key message from the name of the recording and the album *Cubanos por el mundo* that advocates for unity and the reintegration of the Cuban diaspora with the Cubans still on the island.

While it is important to specify the musical structures through which Carcassés's political expressions gained affective valence, it is also crucial to examine the responses that these improvised statements generated in Cuba after the concert. However, before I move on to this analysis it is important to have in mind that these seemingly disconnected discursive domains (groovy singing, in the moment of its public utterance, versus later critical responses) are related through their very difference. It is the sung melody's ability to produce affect in a shared groove experience that enabled the words to be felt as pleasurable sounds, reconfiguring 'what is common to the Cuban community' and providing the conditions for the debate that followed.[35] If Carcassés's sung statements were written on a piece of paper or uttered in common speech, no public debate would have happened. Hence, the production of musical pleasure should be understood as a precondition for the debate that followed the performance.

From dissensus to censorship

Immediately after the concert, the state-run Instituto Cubano de la Música suspended Roberto Carcassés from engaging in any musical or artistic activities in Cuba. As Interactivo wrote on its Facebook page:

> They invited us all to a reunion at Instituto Cubano de la Música, where we were informed that Roberto [Carcassés] would be 'separated from the sector'. In other words, he cannot play, alone or with Interactivo or any other state-affiliated group.[36]

The Cuban cultural ministry argued that Carcassés had dishonoured the revolution by expressing his harsh critique on live Cuban television at an event in honour of the brave Cuban Five. The performance also sparked a massive debate on Cuban social media and in the newspapers. While some Cuban artists and intellectuals defended parts of Carcassés's critique, most of the commentators on state-controlled websites and social media platforms condemned the improvisation. The overarching indictment was that Carcassés had been *oportunista* by choosing such a public time and place to address these matters. An excerpt from an article written by musician Conrad Monier, who also performed at the concert, illustrates this:

> I also wanted our message to reach the hearts of the North American people, but you, Robertico [Carcassés], damaged what, with so much effort, thousands of artists aimed to express [...] What you said is not exactly the most serious thing, although it denotes a lack of political culture (*incultura política*) that I would encourage you to overcome. What is unforgivable is who you told it to, where, and at what time. Then I ask myself: Why, Robertico? What did you want to achieve with that act? From my glorious Guantánamo, only millimetres from the Yankees, this humble Cuban musician tells you something: 'WE DON'T DO THAT!' [...] There are values, Robertico, that are deeply Cuban and that we don't play with![37]

Monier criticises Carcassés's improvisation and defends a revolutionary consensus that strengthens the Cuban police order by drawing on paternalistic arguments, as evidenced by 'WE DON'T DO THAT' written in capital letters. Monier's critique further puts into question Carcassés's Cuban identity by calling him 'politically uncultured' because 'there are values that are deeply Cuban and that we don't play with'. With this last statement, Monier evokes a broader dichotomous argument by playing with José Martí's famous statement, 'Being cultured is the only way of being free' (*Ser culto es la única forma de ser libre*), to dignify the revolutionary project aesthetically and criticise Carcassés's performative gesture as *incultura política*.

Other commentators elaborated on this critique by drawing on more emotional and subjective language, as illustrated through a commentary written by Digna Guerra, a highly renowned Cuban choral conductor, who also performed at the concert and holds an important political position as a member of the national assembly:

> Compatriots: I am writing to you to express my outrage concerning the attitude of the musician Robertico Carcassés during the concert for the Five Cubans on September 13 at the Anti-Imperialist Tribune 'José Martí'. It is not that we cannot have diverse opinions. It is about having ethics and responsibility, and raising our voice and concerns at the right place and time. To use that scenario, in which numerous artists were representing the people in a sacred battle for the nation, is an absolutely reprehensible act, which reveals at least selfishness and lack of collective feeling. As a Cuban, as a musician and as a mother I consider this act unacceptable and I feel more committed now than ever to the cause of the Five, the Revolution and the young people that I strive every day to educate through cultura for *la Patria*.[38]

Guerra refines Monier's critique by speaking frankly and emotionally ('outrage', 'an absolutely reprehensible act', 'unacceptable'), and by referring to dichotomies linked to personal ethics and national independence (implying that Carcassés lacks a sense of 'ethics and responsibility' and is not among the 'numerous artists representing the people in a sacred battle for the nation'). She even appears to question whether Carcassés really is 'Cuban' in the revolutionary sense, as opposed to herself, describing herself as 'a musician, music educator and mother' and 'as someone who is committed to the Cuban Five, the Revolution and Patria'. In a Rancièrean sense both Guerra and Monier reproduce the Cuban police order by separating 'those who take part [in the revolutionary society] from those who are excluded'.[39]

Carcassés stuck to his guns when confronted by acts of censorship and government critiques, writing three days after the event:

> As much as I see the video and reread what I said, I do not see why my ideas do not conform to the line of the Cuban revolution, if we are trying to improve our system and if it takes courage to harm yourself by saying what you think ... Perhaps I was wrong to expect that my words would provide an image of tolerance and evolution in the current Cuban government ... I don't think that electing the president through voting would affect our system much – instead, it could give the people the chance to feel represented by the state on a higher level.[40]

Carcassés draws implicitly on Castro's aforementioned speech to the workers to legitimise his improvisation within a revolutionary Cuban society, suggesting that he was only singing about 'what needs to be changed' and arguing for 'full equality and freedom'. A closer look at political developments in Cuba from 2006 to the concert in 2013 further suggests that many political reforms occurred thanks to dialogues between the Cuban communist party and other, more progressive voices that have pushed to change 'what needs to be changed', giving further weight to Carcassés's argument. Raul Castro, who was president during this period, said several times that the Cuban government had to learn from 'errors and insufficiencies'[41] in the past in the context of the instigation of market reforms and reconciliation between Cuba and the United States during Barack Obama's tenure as US president. Still, despite Carcassés's arguments, the Cuban cultural ministry sustained his ban, and multiple actors expressed critiques of Carcassés that were similar to those of Monier and Guerra, reproducing the hierarchical division of the Cuban police order.

Four days after the event, one of Cuba's most famous musicians, Silvio Rodríguez, a deputy member of the national assembly for fifteen years and an important spokesperson within Cuban culture and politics, openly criticised the way in which the Cuban government had banned Carcassés from all cultural activities. He also criticised Carcassés's use of a patriotic event as an opportunity to offer a political critique:[42]

> I believe that Robertico committed a great stupidity in choosing the act for the release of the Five Cubans to launch his claims. I would have

preferred if he would have done so in another concert, on a record, or in another area, because I believe that the struggle for the freedom of the Five Cubans is a sacred flag of the people of Cuba, well above other considerations.

Regrettably, my partner's clumsiness was followed by another one from the institution that governs the work of music professionals in Cuba.

As a critique of practices of this type in the past [that is, the practice of censorship against artists who criticise the Cuban state], and as an attempt to avoid that such things happening again, I made the decision to invite the sanctioned musician to my next concerts, because one error should not lead to another, but mainly because I think it is frightening that the cause of the Cuban Five can be used as a pretext for an act of repression.

As a Cuban citizen, Robertico has the right to express what he thinks in his own country. But I think it is regrettable that he did what he did during an act for the Cuban Five, people who have sacrificed their lives for the safety of the [Cuban] people. I also don't agree with the excessive sanction of forbidding a musician to perform his function.[43]

Via a double critique of both Carcassés's use of a sacred political space and the sanctions against him by the cultural ministry, Rodríguez assumes the role of a mediator. Under these auspices, he invited Carcassés to play with him during his upcoming concerts on the outskirts of Havana, which was both an implicit critique of the government's withdrawal of Carcassés's music licence *and* an offer to Carcassés to practise his revolutionary musicianship by playing at a government venue. In the same paragraph, Rodríguez uses vague language and allusions to criticise earlier acts of artistic censorship in Cuba by suggesting that it is 'frightening' that 'the cause of the Cuban Five can be used as a pretext for an act of repression'. The last paragraph supports Carcassés's right to express politics musically as a Cuban citizen because he has 'the right to express what he thinks in his own country', again echoing the second and third statement in Castro's speech to the workers.

On 18 September, one day after Rodríguez's statement was published, Cuban cultural ministry officials and Rodríguez met with Carcassés to discuss the issue, and the government decided to lift the ban. In the words of Rodríguez: 'Authorities from the Cultural Ministry had a reunion today with Roberto Carcassés and the conversations were so positive that they decided to lift the sanction.'[44] Interactivo and Carcassés promptly returned to giving concerts in Havana and abroad.

Conclusion: three Rancièrean lessons

The aim of this chapter was to examine the politics of Cuban popular dance music through a study of Interactivo's song 'Cubanos por el mundo' by drawing on Rancière's concepts of 'politics' and 'the police'. Three lessons can be learned.

First, in order to understand the politics of music we have to conduct a twofold analysis that both identifies the broader 'police order' through which music make sense *and* studies the specific ways in which musical sounds challenge and nurture that order, for example, through pleasurable grooves. This insight elaborates on Rancière's emphasis on the role of affect and aesthetics in the expression of politics and calls for a musical operationalisation of Rancière's argument that aesthetics is prior to politics because it conditions what 'presents itself to sense experience' (in the case of music, specific structures of musical sounds with particular affordances).[45] To specify how music amplifies and alters such spaces of politics, we should pay attention to how temporal structures of musical sound enable the production of new affective communities in specific contexts that change the framework of 'who can have a share in what is common to the community based on what they [can] do and on the time and place in which this activity is performed'.[46]

The second lesson is that in order to understand the political power of music, we should not only focus on musical ways of enacting 'a wrong' but also on the complex ways in which musical sounds amplify existing 'police orders' by modifying political communities (whether international, national or local) through affect. It is this double play of both beautifying and criticising Cuban culture that provided 'Cubanos por el mundo' with a unique political potential. By shaking the hearts and souls of dancing Cubans through particular musical means, the song constructed spaces of simultaneous identification (with the groove) and disidentification (with the revolutionary police order) that together created a new imagined community of equality. Music gains a particular political force in countries such as Cuba where many have lost faith in political representation, as the emic perception of music as non-political makes it political, as grooves move people and instigate new forms of political subjectivisation. This is why Carcassés believed that music was a particularly powerful tool for communication that gave him the 'possibility and the duty to shape the meanings for young Cubans [and to constantly redefine] the concept of being revolutionary ... as well as criticising stupid laws'. It is also the reason why Carcassés believed musical expressions were key in the making of a new Cuba when he gave the following response to my question about why he constantly returned to the issue of creating a new fatherland:

> Probably because it is still not done. Three million Cubans are living in all sorts of different countries. They also belong to our idiosyncrasy. And we have big social problems. Still, *cubanía*, *la patria* and our nation are yet to be defined. And now we are living in a crucial time, trying to find our own identity. We have to define what is Cuba, who we are, and mark the future. So, in our music we communicate messages to shape the meanings of the people.[47]

As the imaginary Cuban community that Carcassés aimed to construct both implied a recognition of the merits of 'the revolution', and the expression of multiple Rancièrean 'wrongs' to improve it, the political power of Interactivo's music was intrinsically linked to existing police orders as well as critiques of these orders.

The third lesson forces us to rethink temporally the relationship between 'politics' and 'the police' within the internal logic of existing police orders. In the same sense that 'politics' is always related to a given 'police order', we should understand the formation of a 'police order' as the product of earlier 'politics' through which that police order finds its legitimacy. The ways in which the 'Cuban police order' understands itself through the 'politics' of the 1959 revolution underscore the temporal interplay between Rancière's two concepts in historical practice. Most, if not all, 'police orders' – including those of contemporary welfare states, institutional democracies, political parties and movements, NGOs and human rights organisations – define their existence in terms of a rupture at a certain point in time. This temporal perspective may also illuminate how expressions of 'politics' are linked together historically. Read along these lines, Carcassés's improvised critique at Plaza Anti-Imperialista in Havana 2013 was not something new but part of a broader critical 'police order' that brings associations to other

Cubans who have argued for a more transparent, independent and pluralistic democracy in Cuba. Examples include the work of bloggers such as Yoani Sánchez, the critical hip-hop group Los Aldeanos and civil society networks such as Cuba Posible.[48]

In short, while 'the police' and 'politics' play out in practice as mutually defined dichotomies, they also interact temporally in that expressions of 'politics' invariably have a history and 'police orders' invariably have beginnings. To identify these connections and disconnections it is crucial to add a temporal dimension to further research on how music expresses Rancièrean 'politics' and 'police orders' that points towards both its causes and effects.[49]

Notes

1. Jacques Rancière, *The Politics of Aesthetics: The Distribution of the Sensible*, trans. Gabriel Rockhill (London: Continuum, 2004), and *Disagreement: Politics and Philosophy*, trans. Julia Rose (Minneapolis: University of Minnesota Press, 1999).
2. The song was released on the CD *Cubanos por el mundo* in 2010 and was played numerous times on Cuban radio between 2010 and 2013 (personal conversations with 'Maria', 'Alberto', 'David' and 'Alejandro'; in accordance with the research ethics stipulated by the Norwegian Center for Research Data, I refer to all informants in this study through pseudonyms).
3. Rancière, *The Politics of Aesthetics*, 19.
4. See John Street, '"Fight the Power": The Politics of Music and the Music of Politics', *Government and Opposition* 38.1 (2003), 126; see also Barry Shank, *The Political Force of Musical Beauty* (Durham, NC: Duke University Press, 2014).
5. This is in contrast to dominant approaches to studies on the politics of music that focus on lyrics and broader social and discursive constructions rather than on musical sounds, such as Keith Negus, *Popular Music in Theory* (Malden, MA: Polity, 1996), 193, and Simon Frith, *Performing Rights: On the Value of Popular Music* (Cambridge, MA: Harvard University Press, 1998), 22–6.
6. By bringing the affordances of specific musical structures into the examination of music's political meanings, the present study echoes recent scholarship such as Chris Stover's 'Politicking Musical Time', in *The Oxford Handbook of Time in Music* (Oxford: Oxford University Press, forthcoming 2020), and Kjetil Klette Bøhler, 'Theorizing Musical Politics through Case Studies: Feminist Grooves

against the Temer Government in Today's Brazil', *International Journal of Gender, Science and Technology* 9.2 (2017), 118–40.
7. Rancière, *The Politics of Aesthetics*, 22.
8. Joseph J. Tanke, *Jacques Rancière: An Introduction* (New York: A&C Black, 2011), 28.
9. Mustafa Dikeç, 'Beginners and Equals: Political Subjectivity in Arendt and Rancière', *Transactions of the Institute of British Geographers* 38.1 (2013), 78–90.
10. Rancière, *Disagreement*, 39.
11. Rancière, *Disagreement*, 33.
12. Jacques Rancière, 'Ten Theses on Politics', trans. Rachel Bowlby and Davide Panagia, *Theory & Event* 5.3 (2001), §22.
13. Jacques Rancière, 'Aesthetic Separation, Aesthetic Community: Scenes from the Aesthetic Regime of Art', *Art & Research* 2.1 (2008), 4–14.
14. Jacques Rancière, 'Dissenting Words: A Conversation with Jacques Rancière' (with Davide Panagia), *Diacritics* 30.2 (2000), 124.
15. 'Nuevo Lineamientos VI Congreso del Partido Comunista de Cuba', political manifesto agreed upon by the Cuban Communist Party (2010), <http://www.granma.cu/granmad/secciones/6to-congreso-pcc/Folleto%20Lineamientos%20VI%20Cong.pdf> (last accessed 3 May 2019).
16. Rancière, *Disagreement*, 23.
17. See Maria Gropas, 'The Repatriotization of Revolutionary Ideology and Mnemonic Landscape in Present-Day Havana', *Current Anthropology* 48.4 (2007), 536, and Kjetil Klette Bøhler, 'Grooves, Pleasures, and Politics in Salsa Cubana: The Musicality of Cuban Politics and the Politics of Salsa Cubana', PhD dissertation, University of Oslo, 2013, 115–54.
18. Oscar Quiros, 'Critical Mass of Cuban Cinema: Art as the Vanguard of Society', *Screen* 37.3 (1996), 283.
19. *Constitución de la Republica de Cuba* (Havana, 1976), <http://www.cuba.cu/gobierno/cuba.htm> (last accessed 17 May 2019). The constitution was updated in 2019.
20. Examples here include the censorship of Anglo-American popular music (e.g. the Beatles and the Rolling Stones), as well as salsa music in general in the 1970s and 1980s; see Vincenzo Perna, *Timba: The Sound of the Cuban Crisis* (New York: Routledge, 2017).
21. This is most commonly found in Nueva Trova; see Rina Benmayor, 'La "Nueva Trova": New Cuban Song', *Latin American Music Review/Revista de Música Latinoamericana* 2.1 (1981), 11–44.

However, Yvonne Daniel shows how a sense of revolutionary patriotism is also expressed musically in rumba in *Rumba: Dance and Social Change in Contemporary Cuba* (Bloomington: Indiana University Press, 1995), while I show how this is expressed in salsa cubana in Kjetil Klette Bøhler, '"Somos la mezcla perfecta, la combinación más pura, cubanos, la más grande creación": Grooves, Pleasures, and Politics in Today's Cuba', *Latin American Music Review* 37.2 (2016), 184–200.

22. For studies on *música contestaria*, see Geoffrey Baker, 'Cuba Rebelión: Underground Music in Havana', *Latin American Music Review* 32.1 (2011), 3–32, and Nora Gámez Torres, '"Rap is war": Los Aldeanos and the Politics of Music Subversion in Contemporary Cuba', *Trans. Revista Transcultural de Música* 17 (2013), 2–11.

23. The consequences of these actions have varied dramatically, as some have been sent to so-called UMAP concentration camps to learn about truly revolutionary values, while others have been harassed, tortured and imprisoned because of their disagreement with the Cuban state. For studies on the UMAP camps, see Lillian Guerra, 'Gender Policing, Homosexuality and the New Patriarchy of the Cuban Revolution, 1965–70', *Social History* 35.3 (2010), 268–74; Joseph Tahbaz, 'Demystifying las UMAP: The Politics of Sugar, Gender, and Religion in 1960s Cuba', *Delaware Review of Latin American Studies* 14.2 (2013), 1–7, <http://www.udel.edu/LAS/Vol14-2Tahbaz.html#_ednref19> (last accessed 22 November 2019); and Rebecca San Juan, 'Cuba's Unresolved UMAP History: Survivors' Struggles to Counter the Official Story', PhD dissertation, Mount Holyoke College, 2017. For reports on illegal imprisonment and torture in Cuba, see Amnesty International, <https://www.amnesty.org/en/countries/americas/cuba/> (last accessed 3 May 2019).

24. Interview with 'Juan' in Vedado, Havana, 14 July 2010.

25. Rancière, *The Politics of Aesthetics*, 12.

26. *Haciendo misión* refers to Cubans who work abroad for the Cuban government on temporary contracts, often in order to strengthen welfare services in developing countries (for example, doctors and nurses working in remote areas in Venezuela and Brazil).

27. Interview with 'Jorge' in Santiago de Cuba, 23 July 2018.

28. Interview with Roberto Carcassés in Havana, 15 November 2010.

29. The recording and distribution of music is controlled by the Cuban state through a complex network including institutions such as Casa del Autor, which is supposed to protect the copyrights of Cuban musicians, but which in practice also censors controversial songs.

Musical Politics in the Cuban Police Order   203

See Kjetil Klette Bøhler, 'How Live Cuban Popular Dance Music Expresses Political Values in Today's Cuba', *Danish Musicology Online* (2015), 64. <http://www.danishmusicologyonline.dk/arkiv/arkiv_dmo/dmo_saernummer_2015/dmo_saernummer_2015_musikcensur_03.pdf> (last accessed 3 May 2019). However, the distribution of music in Cuba is also controlled by the state and the state may censor controversial songs that express strong critiques of revolutionary values.

30. This perspective echoes Chris Stover's understanding of politicking musical time, which underscores the importance of considering the multiple agencies that are articulated as sounds and subjects meet in experience.
31. Rancière, *The Politics of Aesthetics*, 12.
32. However, at the time of the concert only four of the five intelligence officers, Gerardo Hernández, Antonio Guerrero, Ramón Labañino and Fernando González, were still in prison, as René González had returned to Cuba in April 2013, five months prior to the concert. While the Cuban state argued that the five intelligence officers worked to prevent terrorist attacks on Cuban soil and were illegally imprisoned in the US, government officials from the United States argued that the Cuban Five were engaging in espionage.
33. This is in line with existing research which points out that phrases played or sung in *clave* tend to have more syncopation and higher degrees of rhythmic density on the 3-side of the clave and more on-beats on the 2-side. See Ives Chor, 'Microtiming and Rhythmic Structure in Clave-Based Music: A Quantitative Study', in Anne Danielsen (ed.), *Musical Rhythm in the Age of Digital Reproduction* (Farnham: Ashgate, 2010), 42–9, and Bøhler, 'Grooves, Pleasures, and Politics'.
34. Rancière, 'Ten Theses on Politics', §22.
35. Rancière, *The Politics of Aesthetics*, 12.
36. Translated by the author, original in Spanish: 'Nos citaron ayer a todos a una reunión al Instituto Cubano de la Música, donde se nos informó que Roberto queda 'separado del sector' por tiempo indefinido. Quiere decir que no se puede presentar solo, ni con Interactivo, en ningun lugar estatal.' In 'El régimen sanciona "indefinidamente" a Robertico Carcassés', *Diario de Cuba* (2013), <http://www.diariodecuba.com/derechos-humanos/1379201826_5071.html> (last accessed 3 May 2019).
37. Translated by the author, original in Spanish: 'Yo también quise que nuestro mensaje llegara al corazón del pueblo norteamericano, pero

tú, Robertico, dañaste lo que con tanto esfuerzo miles de artistas habíamos gestado. Lo que dijiste no es exactamente lo más grave, aunque denota una incultura política que si yo fuera tú, me esforzaría un poco por superar. Lo imperdonable es a quién se lo dijiste, donde y en qué momento. Entonces me pregunto: ¿Para qué, Robertico? ¿Qué querías? Desde mi glorioso Guantánamo, a solo milímetros de los yanquis, este humilde músico cubano te dice algo: ESO NO SE HACE . . . Hay valores, esos que habitan en lo más profundo de un cubano verdadero, con los que, Robertico, no se juega.' Conrad Monier, 'Carta del músico guantanamero Conrado Monier', *La Jiribilla* (2013), <http://laplumaquecuenta.bloguea.cu/2013/09/18/blogs-y-medios-digitales-cubanos-opinan-sobre-la-actuacion-de-robertico-carcasses/> (last accessed 3 May 2019).

38. Translated by the author, original in Spanish: 'Compañeros: Me dirijo a ustedes para manifestar mi indignación por la actitud del músico Robertico Carcassés durante el concierto por los cinco el pasado 12 de Septiembre en la Tribuna Antiimperialista "José Martí". No se trata de que no podamos tener opiniones diversas. Se trata de tener ética y responsabilidad para plantear nuestros criterios en su justo lugar y momento. Utilizar ese escenario, en que numerosos artistas estábamos representando a todo un pueblo en una batalla sagrada para la nación, es un acto absolutamente reprochable, que cuando menos revela egoísmo y falta de sentimiento colectivo. Como cubana, como músico y como madre considero inaceptable este hecho y me siento ahora más comprometida que nunca con la causa de Los Cinco, con la Revolución y con los jóvenes que cada día me esfuerzo en formar para la cultura y para la Patria.' Digna Guerra, 'Carta de Digna Guerra, Directora del Coro Nacional de Cuba', *La Jiribilla* (2013), <http://laplumaquecuenta.bloguea.cu/2013/09/18/blogs-y-medios-digitales-cubanos-opinan-sobre-la-actuacion-de-robertico-carcasses/> (last accessed 3 May 2019).

39. Rancière, *The Politics of Aesthetics*, 3.

40. See 'Roberto Carcassés Responds to Banning from Cuban Stages', *Havana Times*, 16 September 2013, <https://havanatimes.org/?p=98832> (last accessed 3 May 2019).

41. Raul Castro, quoted in 'Raúl Castro admite "errores e insuficiencias" en las reformas económicas impulsadas por su Gobierno', *Europapress*, 27 March 2018, <http://www.europapress.es/internacional/noticia-raul-castro-admite-errores-insuficiencias-reformas-economicas-impulsadas-gobierno-20180327184555.html> (last accessed 3 May 2019).

42. See 'Sílvio Rodríguez considera "torpezas" la crítica de Carcassés y la sanción en su contra', *Diario de Cuba*, 17 September 2013, <http://www.diariodecuba.com/derechos-humanos/1379424616_5110.html?page=1> (last accessed 3 May 2019).
43. Translated by the author, original in Spanish: 'Creo que Robertico cometió una gran torpeza al escoger el acto por la liberación de Los Cinco para lanzar su pliego de reclamaciones. Hubiera preferido que lo hiciera en otro concierto, en un disco, en otro ámbito, porque considero que la lucha por la libertad de Los Cinco es una bandera sagrada del pueblo de Cuba, muy por encima de otras consideraciones. Lamentablemente, a la torpeza de mi compañero siguió otra por parte de la institución que rige el trabajo de los profesionales de la música en Cuba. Por repudio a prácticas de este tipo en otros tiempos, por rechazo a la idea de que volvieran a instaurarse, tomé la decisión de invitar a mis próximos conciertos al músico sancionado, porque un error no debe conducir a otro, pero sobre todo porque me parece espantoso que la causa de Los Cinco pueda usarse como pretexto para un acto de represión. Como ciudadano cubano, Robertico tiene derecho a manifestar en su país lo que piensa. Me parece un error lamentable que lo haya hecho en el acto por nuestros héroes atiterroristas, que han sacrificado sus vidas por la seguridad del pueblo. Asimismo tampoco estoy de acuerdo con la sanción desmedida de prohibirle a un músico realizar su función.' In 'Puntualizando', published at 'Silvio Rodriguez Blog *Segunda Cita*, 17 September 2013, <http://segundacita.blogspot.no/search?updated-max=2013-09-19T09:44:00-04:00> (last accessed 3 May 2019).
44. Translated by the author, original in Spanish: 'Autoridades del Ministerio de Cultura se reunieron hoy (martes) con Robertico Carcassés y las conversaciones fueron tan positivas que han decidido dejar sin efecto la sanción'. In *Cubadebate*, <http://www.cubadebate.cu/etiqueta/robertico-Carcassés/> (last accessed 3 May 2019).
45. Rancière, *The Politics of Aesthetics*, 13.
46. Rancière, *The Politics of Aesthetics*, 12.
47. Translated by the author, original in Spanish: 'Probablemente porque todavía no esta hecho. Tres millones de Cubanos están viviendo en cualquier tipo de países. Ellos también pertenecen a nuestra idiosincrasia. Y tenemos grandes problemas sociales. Todavía, Cubanía, la Patria y nuestro país no están definido. Y ahora estamos viviendo en una época importante, tratando de buscar nuestra identidad. Tenemos que definir lo que es Cuba, quienes somos, y marcar el

futuro. Entonces, en nuestra música comunicamos mensajes para fomentar los conceptos del pueblo.'
48. Yoani Sánchez's blog *Generation Y*, <https://generacionyen.wordpress.com/> (last accessed 3 May 2019), and Gámez Torres '"Rap is war"'. For more information on Cuba Posible, see their web page: <https://cubaposible.com/> (last accessed 3 May 2019).
49. I here refer to Rancière's emphasis on cause and effect in *The Politics of Aesthetics*, 20, as multiple and moving in different directions, and often unintended, and not in the strict sense of cause and effect understood in the natural sciences and economics.

9

Rancière and Improvisation: Reading Contingency in Music and Politics
Dan DiPiero

In this essay, I want to attempt a kind of Rancièrean double movement: to reflect on the politics of improvisation as well as the improvisation of politics. The impetus behind this approach originates in what appears to me a correspondingly double lack. On the one hand, while political interpretations of improvised music are appearing with more frequency, Rancière's interventions into the notion of politics have not appeared in these conversations.[1] On the other hand, while one of Rancière's central concerns involves showing the 'contingency of any order', his precise focus on the contingency of the police tends to obscure 'smaller' contingencies such as improvisation. The moments in history that rupture the sensible appear in Rancière as quasi-transcendental events, or, as Giuseppina Mecchia puts it, they occur 'between historicity and event'.[2] How these ruptures come into being has always been less of a concern for Rancière, and it is here that I think improvisation can raise productive questions. My goal is not so much to arrive at a better reading of Rancière (the notion of a 'proper' reading being anyway anti-egalitarian) as it is to better reflect on the relationships between agency, subjectivity and contingency within a police order.

The politics of improvisation

Rancière's interventions into the notion of politics challenge us to consider the efficacy of actions that take place as a function of an already established or given way of doing. Rancière's politics is opposed to the police, which is any pre-existing order of doing and being.[3] In a given police order, people are organised into their 'proper' places according to the 'logic' of the system, and as such, controverting actions that take place as a function of that system do not constitute politics so much as they remain paths of dissent that are 'appropriate' to those dissenting. In their appropriateness, such methods can always be managed, mitigated or redirected. Politics, by contrast, occurs in the moments that 'rupture the sensible', redistributing not only the sense of what is and is not appropriate, but also the presupposition of the existence of appropriate positions.[4] Locating politics in improvisation would thus involve locating a situation in which a given improvisation produced a redistribution of sense, through which new ways of doing or being would be allowed to emerge.

However, the effort to locate a politics of improvisation must already be qualified, since there can actually be no politics of improvisation as such; there can only be politics in improvisatory *practices*, each of which is specific and, despite some common generalities, properly singular. As Ingrid Monson and Scott Currie have argued,[5] speaking of improvisation as an unmarked category tends to privilege one particular understanding of improvisation (what Currie describes as 'the cluster of North American and European traditions – variously glossed as free or avant-garde jazz and creative, free, or improvised music')[6] as a universal notion, masking its own particular ideological commitments while at the same time discounting cross-cultural understandings of improvisation, the specificities of which might interrupt scholarly and artistic approaches to improvisation that are invested in Western conventions. In other words, improvisation means different things to different people in different times, places and situations.

Following these arguments, improvisation can be seen as an empty or a contingent universal insofar as human beings improvise – whether in musical or social situations – in every cultural context, but also insofar as the practice and significance of such improvisations vary greatly depending on the specificities involved in a given articulation. But pushing further, it is not only that improvisation varies across cultural contexts or media iterations; rather, I and others have argued that improvisation is properly singular each and every time it is enacted, even *within* the same generic or discursive paradigm.[7] Rather than unfolding according to certain cultural archetypes (e.g. 'bebop soloing' or 'batá drumming'), improvisation consists in what I characterise as a *contingent encounter*, an active and co-constituting interaction between subjects, objects and different kinds of environments.[8] Each and every improvisatory situation is brought about through interdependent interactions in time and space, and produces affective forces that are singular to that moment. Insofar as every musical performance navigates and is composed of such contingencies, *all* musical performance can be understood as improvisatory.[9] Considered in this way, models of musical practice rooted in the composition/improvisation binary only get us so far. Rather than viewing improvisation on a sliding scale, as an opening of greater or lesser freedom depending on the musical tradition or context, improvisation as contingent encounter is always non-trivially *different* – a singular constellation of possibilities and impossibilities, virtualities and actualisations that is incommensurate with every other improvisation. Following this argument, it is not enough to examine formal musical elements when discussing performance, because improvisation is not strictly a musical phenomenon that unfolds according to constraints such as the presence or absence of a chord progression. Rather, improvisation emerges in and through contingent social relations and material mediations, of which (for example) a chord progression is only one. On this view, understanding anything about the politics of an improvisation would involve tracing such interactions as constitutive elements of how the music emerges.

If there can only be politics of specific improvised practices, then I have still chosen to interrogate one such instance of 'transatlantic improvised music' in order to question the political valence with which it is typically endowed, or to bring that valence into conversation with Rancière's politics. Before addressing that specific example, however, a Rancièrean reading of improvised music in general might begin with an attempt to understand the paradigm of 'transatlantic improvised music' vis-à-vis Rancière's three regimes of art. The track in question here is 'Waves, Linens, and White Light', a freely improvised recording from the Norwegian band Mr. K's 2015 release, *Left Exit*.[10] Mr. K is a group that emerged from the freely improvised and avant-garde musical scene in Norway, a scene that I propose is allowed to emerge as such through the aural inauguration of an aesthetic regime of art.[11]

In this interpretation, and in the same manner as abstract painting, improvised music emerges when the link between form and content is severed. The aesthetic regime permits a kind of equality by opening the possibility for any sounds to be deployed, not only the 'appropriate sounds' in the 'appropriate arrangements'. While not all improvised music corresponds to the aesthetic regime, and while the logics of the representative and poetic regimes are still in play, it nevertheless appears that the avant-garde improvised musics that emerged between the free jazz movement in the United States, the Association for the Advancement of Creative Musicians (AACM) and other activist collectives that emerged in the US in the 1960s and 1970s, and the European Improvised Music scene have always existed as forms of art in the singular.[12] This singularity that designates art as a realm apart is also made possible through the paradox of the aesthetic regime, in which any sound whatsoever becomes potentially legitimate, just as toasters, radios or even 'silence' become artistic experiences in the music of John Cage.

If this understanding of avant-garde improvised music holds, then the first point to be drawn from Rancière is that the politics of the aesthetic regime is always posited in a specific way, as a certain kind of meta-politics. That is, the aesthetic regime inaugurates an equality that is nevertheless limited to the realm of aesthetics: 'Aesthetics has its *own* politics', or, put differently, 'literary equality is not the same thing as democratic equality' because 'there is no criterion for establishing a correspondence between aesthetic virtue and political virtue ... [T]here is no formula for an appropriate correlation.'[13] With improvised music, it is perhaps even more tempting to extrapolate from the equality of formal content, as there are also other kinds of equalities involved in the production of improvised music that are not present in other art forms, such as the musical principles that allow each musician to 'have their say' in the course of performance. Nevertheless, as I will show, Rancière's work is particularly helpful in pointing to some of the problems with conflating aesthetic equality and political equality. If there are any politics to be found here that hold up outside the realm of metaphor, these moments will have to be located not only in the aesthetic realm but between aesthetics and some other social space. Indeed, that would bring us well within Rancière's established thoughts on the 'dream' of political art.

In this dream, political art is art that holds in tension, undermines or fully subverts the distribution of the sensible that is common to the police. It is a dream for Rancière insofar as it follows from the understanding of politics as 'rare', as a rupture that cannot be willed into being.[14] Neither art that presents a political message nor art that directly intervenes in the sociopolitical realm necessarily produce a break with the regime of sense in which they operate. Thus for Rancière,

> [t]he dream of a suitable political work of art is in fact the dream of disrupting the relationship between the visible, the sayable, and the thinkable without having to use the terms of a message as a vehicle. It is the dream of an art that would transmit meanings in the form of a rupture with the very logic of meaningful situations.[15]

Rancière's understanding of political art seems to straddle, in some way, the methodologies employed throughout his *oeuvre*. While his work in *Aisthesis*, for example, corresponds to his career-long concern with historical singularities, with those moments of aesthetic disruption that produced a break with the sensible, the notion of political art offered in *The Politics of Aesthetics*, *Dissensus* and elsewhere is not limited to historical sites. In *Dissensus*, for instance, Rancière writes that 'Practices of art ... contribute to the constitution of a form of common sense that is "polemical", to a new landscape of the visible, the sayable, and the doable. They may thus contribute to constituting a new idea of what "critical" art could mean *today*.'[16] He then offers three examples that 'seem ... particularly significant in this respect': two films (Chantal Akerman's *De l'autre côté* and Anri Sala's *Give me the Colours*) and a video installation (Pedro Costa's *No Quarto da Vanda*). In doing so, Rancière dislocates the 'dream of political art' from its mooring in history, and identifies it in the present. As such, this is the closest that we come in Rancière's work to a method or a frame of understanding through which we could interpret works of art. No doubt this is a difficult space to inhabit, given Rancière's reticence around questions of method. Still, I hope to prove that thinking in this space is worthwhile.

This discussion must be grounded in an example. However, in turning attention to 'Waves' specifically, there are yet again difficulties that delay interpretation. When I want to analyse this piece of music, what is it exactly that I propose to discuss? Returning to the argument that all music consists in and through contingent encounters, the picture is quickly complicated: such encounters are not only in play among the musicians themselves (in their environments, with their objects, and so on), but also between the musicians and listeners, whether the latter are present in performance or are listening to a recording. The recording of this performance is certainly one 'object' I am capable of thinking about (and is indeed all I have access to); but the experience of listening is different each time I encounter it. As many scholars have shown from a variety of perspectives, the listening experience is not a passive relation whereby listeners decode and consume the sounds that are contained in a recording; rather, listening is an active process in which the listener partially constructs the music in question, and as such, by virtue of being a multiple and changing human being, the listening experience is not the same today as it was two weeks ago, two years ago.[17] How can I then speak about a collection of sounds that seem, in some non-trivial way, to continue changing, even as they remain the same? This inescapable difficulty is one that must be dealt with in thinking the politics of any music. But it is not the only one.

If the world and I are changed each time I encounter the recording, then the recording itself changes over time – music only exists through relationality.[18] Moreover, the recording differs not only from itself but also from the performance that the recording purports to have captured – and yet both are a part of the 'object' we call 'music'. A performance sets up and emerges through a series of social relations, each of which contributes to the development of the music. We can hear the results of such an encounter, but the encounter itself is not contained in the recording. The inter-group interaction is different from the performers/audience interaction, is different from the recording/listener interaction. Before the recording/listener interaction, the recording is itself already the result of an interaction between the performance and its technological mediation. This mediation does not reproduce an original but represents it, changes it, and in so doing contributes to the quality and character of what we now hear. In other words, recordings do not transparently transfer, contain or copy the original sounds of performance; rather, recordings *represent* the performance, meaning (as with all representation) that they are always alterations or new productions. As with the performance and the space in which it occurred, the 'sounds themselves' are always already audible as such because of the contingent media through which they flow – they do not exist but through.[19]

Adding to this constellation is the score: even if that score, in the case of improvised music, consists only of a set of indeterminate instructions, it is also a part of what constitutes a musical 'object'.

Indeed, in the Western Romantic musical paradigm, the score constituted the musical object *par excellence*.[20] One of the key utilities in examining improvised music is the extent to which it foregrounds the fact that music is not reducible to the score, that the score in itself refracts forces, conditioning social interactions to come. But on the other hand, insofar as it affects certain possibilities and impossibilities, the score, when present, clearly matters. As a script or virtuality, the score – like the recording – exists beyond the ephemeral live performance. But like the recording, it contains only partial information (and of a different kind).

Furthermore, what becomes of the music if it is disseminated in certain contexts, to a mass audience, or through academic scholarship? The discourses that attach themselves to a piece of music as it circulates through various ecosystems come to affect the meaning and interpretation of the music. In other words, these interpretations do not exist outside of or in addition to the original music, but come to constitute it. A piece of music, if it has a politics, does not have the same politics at the time of its recording that it does, for example, if it is taken up by millions of people, if it comes to signify a certain articulation in the public sphere. From this perspective, the question would be less *whether* a song is political and more *when* is it political, and by extension, how, why, and to what extent?[21]

The difficulties I have pointed out here are also raised by Georgina Born. She writes:

> More obviously than visual and literary media, music has no material essence but a plural and distributed material being... music's multiple simultaneous forms of existence – as sound, score, discourse, site, performance, social relations, technological media – indicate the necessity of conceiving of the musical object as a constellation.[22]

Moreover, each of the 'moments' that compose such a constellation come into being through their own social relations. In the same way that music (collectively performed) foregrounds this sociality more so than literature (individually composed), improvised music in particular emphasises what is true of all musical and artistic production: what we think of as 'works' are the result of contingent interactions between subjects, objects and multiple environments, each dependent on the other. 'All of these connections – all of these relations – are irreducible in the sense that none takes priority over any other; performing bodies, historical contexts, sonic materialities, and affective forces exist in an ongoing flux of mutually constitutive relations.'[23]

Given such complexities, Born proposes that musical 'objects' can be analysed according to four 'planes of social mediation', which are 'irreducible to one another' at the same time that they are 'articulated in contingent and nonlinear ways through relations of conditioning, affordance or causality'.[24] These planes include not only the relations between the musicians on stage, but also between band and audience, as well as the sociopolitical/discursive and material frameworks within which these relations are situated and constituted. Taking this premise seriously, the task of locating politics in the track I propose here would have to proceed sequentially, from one plane to another. I will attempt such a reading below, before turning the question back to Rancière.

'Waves'

In Mr. K's 'Waves, Linens, and White Light', a series of relatively static notes roll over one another at regular but unfixed tempi.[25] Some of these notes move up or down, stepwise and briefly; but any reference to a fixed tonality is eschewed throughout. Instead, what musical developments emerge seem less developments than extensions of the initial gestures, the originally sounding pitches that, once sounded, only fade at the conclusion of the piece. In short, relatively little happens. And yet, unlike much minimalist music – in which long sounds or repeated patterns reveal their innermost workings and subtle evolutions as the listener becomes increasingly attuned to them – both the track and the sounds that compose it are quite short. 'Waves', at two minutes and 47 seconds, is simply not long enough to produce the meditative quality the music seems to establish as an expectation. As for the sounds themselves, they are played on reeds, drums and double bass, with no echo effect or other editing that would elongate their tones. We hear in each rearticulation the physicality of the instrument and the body of the performer. Every note is the same, with differences that are foregrounded through repetition.

The first plane of social interaction on which to think this piece of music has to do with the immediate, micro-social scene that consists of these four musicians improvising in a Trondheim studio. This is the plane on which to investigate the claim that free improvisation creates a space of egalitarian participation, a claim that has, as Born suggests, overdetermined many political readings of improvised music. Born urges us to consider other planes of social mediation in order to nuance the quasi-utopian readings that emerge from the first plane. But do those readings hold up, even in the first plane itself? A Rancièrean perspective undermines such claims by reminding us that even in freely improvised music there are police orders in operation, both within the micro-social scene and in the larger structures in which the micro-social sits. In terms of the micro-social, the musicians in this group are playing a game according to rules they have established in pursuit of the delight of contingency, of the unexpected moment when one sound encounters another, when four subjectivities collide with their instruments in a particular time and place, producing an unexpected result. These rules include not only such factors as musical proficiency, stylistic familiarity, depth of experience and common vocabulary, but also unspoken agreements about style and approach. From a Rancièrean perspective, then, the utopian microcosm of musical interaction is such because it contains not a radical politics but *no politics at all*; it is the place of consensus or parapolitics, an isolated community of equals operating 'freely' within a police order. Those playing together in this order are *already* those equals who recognise or are in a position to recognise the sounds of the others as speech, rather than noise. It is certainly possible for dissensus to emerge here, as a constitutive element of any political 'count', for Rancière, is the double wrong that produces a *sans-part*.[26] But dissensus is not guaranteed simply by the appearance of ostensibly egalitarian musical dialogue; on the contrary, dissensus would disrupt this dialogue itself.

If the space of free improvisation is still the space of a police, it may well be that this police is one of comparative equality. As Rancière writes, there can be forms of police that make room for greater or fewer freedoms.[27] But while this form of consensus may seem to operate with a higher degree of openness than other orders, the question with improvisation must always be: open to what – and for whom? The notion that openness is somehow opposed to closedness returns to the age-old binary that improvisation and composition represent freedom and restriction. But improvisation and composition are not opposites locked in a dialectical relation; they are already contaminated within one another. What we are dealing with in both composed and improvised music is a particular arrangement of possibilities and impossibilities within which subjects, objects and environments act. It is those very particularities that produce an encounter that is equally contingent no matter what the given rules happen to be.

The second plane of social mediation that Born identifies is that which engages a listening public, whether they are present at the performance or are listening to a recording (although that distinction is yet another that matters). On this plane, music 'has the power to animate imagined communities'[28] by concentrating and grouping together listeners around certain sounds. This social relation, as with the previous plane, carries the potential for dissensus. As Barry Shank argues,

> The political agency of music works by distributing the sensible in such a way that it transforms the experience of the common ... The experience of musical beauty, when it emerges from unfamiliar sounds or surprising combinations of sounds quite common, has the capacity to redistribute an auditory sensible and to change, thereby, the sonic *sens* of the political.[29]

In contrast to the ways in which ethnomusicology (along with popular music studies, and, we might add in the context of Rancière, Bourdieu's sociology) often relies 'on a static concept of identity and a relatively firmly bounded notion of the group',[30] Shank shows how music is capable of reorganising a community of difference, constituting, in some meaningful way, a new group in the process. In other words, the way in which music becomes political is not through a process in which pre-constituted social groups gravitate towards the musical sounds with which they identify, whether through overt political messaging or through connotative semiotic expressions. That is indeed an important political process, as 'the musical confirmation of already existing political [or social] groups helps to consolidate them as self-aware communities'.[31] However, Shank is interested in showing how group formation becomes political in the Rancièrean sense, and this occurs when a pre-existing sense of what is 'beautiful' shifts so as to bring into being a *new* group formation; this rupture constitutes a new community of sense, composed of difference, and gathered around a newly perceptible form of music's 'right sonic relations'.[32] Music, when it ruptures the police order of acceptable sounds, configures and prefigures sociocultural identities to come. This happens when traditional notions of beauty are disrupted.

One consequence of the way such disruptions occur is that this kind of politics cannot be located except retroactively – we can never identify in advance what music will rupture the sensible, but we can try (as Rancière does) to locate moments that make such a rupture thinkable. This is what brings politics into the realm of the event. Because 'Waves' was recorded in 2015, it is perhaps too early to conclude whether or not this kind of rupture has occurred among a listening community. It is *always* possible that sense will be disrupted in the double relation between musicians and listeners; but insofar as 'Waves' has not produced, in musical discourse, a new sense of what 'counts' as beautiful, the best we can say for now is that it *will have occurred* if this relation produces consequences that are upheld and can be later traced to this piece of music. At the moment it still appears that 'Waves' operates squarely within an accepted paradigm of musical sense, and that a new community of difference is not coalescing around newly beautiful sounds. The audience for European improvised music operates based on a consensus that establishes a particular sense of musical beauty, and 'Waves' appears to operate firmly within that sense. At what point do we judge that a given recording has produced a redistribution of the sensible?[33]

Born's third plane addresses the larger sociopolitical structures I referenced earlier, those 'wider social relations, from the most concrete to the most abstract of collectivities' such as 'social relations of class, race, religion, ethnicity, gender, or sexuality'.[34] Here again, it is difficult to conclude that the homogeneous make-up of the band – white, male, university-educated Norwegian citizens – engages with or heralds anything but a police order. As many scholars have noted, the history of jazz and improvised music, both in the US and abroad, is a history from which women have been excluded. Whatever else we may say about Mr. K's music, the make-up of the band does not disrupt this police order. Beyond the sociocultural identities of the band members themselves, there is no space here to attend to all of the factors that Born lists as potentially in play in the third plane. However, to the extent that we know who is in the band, and to the extent that we understand the overarching social hierarchy in European patriarchal society, we can hypothesise that 'Waves' operates according to the established paradigm, rather than in between it. But before leaving this plane entirely, the social positioning of the band vis-à-vis broader sociocultural structures functions as a reminder of the ultimate inseparability of these planes of interaction, a fact well emphasised by the ways in which this third plane intersects with Born's fourth and final plane.

According to Born, the fourth plane is that in which music is 'bound up in broader institutional forces' or the material and ideological means of production through which music is produced.[35] Here too, there are many relationships on which one could focus attention. But where the means of production are concerned, I am interested in the ways in which improvised music is institutionally supported by various agencies with funding from the Norwegian government. Through such programmes, a certain national conception of improvisation both conditions access to funding and distributes a certain sense of who this music is *for*. In the US context, we have seen a division between jazz and improvised music, whereby the former has adopted a Western European musical model (institutionalising itself, in universities and concert halls, as 'America's classical music'), while the latter has been institutionally marginalised (as with other avant-garde practices) such that it is diffuse and esoteric. From an international perspective, then, Norway is in some senses quite exceptional insofar as jazz and improvised music enjoy comparatively robust levels of funding (although still less than 'classical' music), and insofar as this music, having taken on a certain kind of national character as a 'distinctly Norwegian art form',[36] is distributed as a normalised and quotidian aspect of life in Norway. This is not to say that experiences with improvised music are ubiquitous or are ubiquitously favoured; it is only to say that in networks of circulation and distribution, the music is characterised as specific to Norway, and as such, as part of life in that country. Thus, as opposed to the situation in the US, in which the logic of the police regulates jazz and improvised music by attributing to them certain places and correspondingly certain people who are 'proper' to them, Norway's institutional infrastructure promotes this music in a more egalitarian manner, attributing to it a character that discursively casts it as 'for anyone and everyone'.[37] This is, indeed, part and parcel of the police order that classifies and constitutes improvised music in Norway; but insofar as it disturbs international social relations and conversations around the significance and meaning of this music, a certain kind of politics can here be found.

The improvisation of politics

In many ways, trying to force a Rancièrean perspective on a given piece of music is a difficult, counter-intuitive proposition. Rancière does not formulate a method of analysis which can then be applied uniformly to given instances of artistic production; rather, he researches historical singularities, trying to understand the conditions through which an event was able to occur. The answer to the question of where or whether 'Waves' has any politics should have been clear from the beginning, insofar as we cannot discern (as yet) a break whereby the relations of what counts as music in this particular generic and discursive space have been redistributed, questioned or suspended. This is not to say that there are not political questions circulating around this piece of music; it is only to say that these are taking place within already established modes of doing.

And yet there is value, it seems to me, in thinking about this track, this once-performance, which surely fails to rise to the level of a Rancièrean politics. As I remarked above, Rancière's focus on contingency has traditionally been in the service of highlighting the contingency of a given police order, always drawing attention to the ways in which established 'facts' of 'common sense' could have been otherwise, or will be otherwise, or are. But what is the role, in Rancièrean thought, of action, of human behaviour? If there is a value in examining 'Waves', it derives, in my view, from its very position inside its police, in its very identity with a 'normal' way of doing, and from what this helps to uncover about improvisation as a human capacity to act.

To move beyond metaphorical analogies between the musical and the social, we have to ask: What is improvisation *doing* in this piece of music? In its different repetitions, this improvisation foregrounds not an open, boundless capacity for musical innovation, but rather a world closed unto itself, a collision of contingent forces in a moment. We return here to the crucial point about contingency, which is that it is singularising: to think improvisation as a contingent encounter is to take seriously the singularity of *this* moment, with *this* constellation of virtualities and actualisations, possibilities and impossibilities, the sounds that produce and tie a situation together in a perceptible and imperceptible tapestry of *now*. Following outward from performance, the consequence of thinking each improvisation as singular is that – as a concept

– improvisation cannot be considered inherently democratic or egalitarian. Nor does it necessarily privilege variation over repetition, nor does it necessarily function by way of listening, empathy, cooperation or consensus, nor is it opposed to composition, fixity or restriction. Rather, improvisation, seen as a series of contingent encounters, shows itself as something more akin to everyday experience. As an everyday experience, necessarily engendered through and as a part of contingent circumstances, improvisation must be considered 'flagrantly ambivalent: the same *mode* of operating can be both expansively inclusive and oppressively exclusive'.[38]

And yet to leave the argument there would be to miss something critical, for it is not just the 'ordinariness' of this improvisation that is of interest; it is also what the musicians do with it. In other words, we must also consider what it is that distinguishes improvised music from those contingent encounters in our everyday lives. For all of the ways in which improvisation itself references an identical process of contingently encountering, there *is* still a characteristic of musical performance that distinguishes musical improvisation from everyday life. This characteristic is what I call *liveness*, which not only refers to the fact that something is taking place in the moment, but also to a musician's awareness of the live situation itself.[39] In short, the musicians in an improvised performance know that they are improvising, or are critically attuned to the fact that they are engaging with contingency. The musicians in Mr. K knew what they were doing, or knew what they were *trying* to do when they set out to play together. They cultivated an awareness of the contingencies inherent to the rules of the musical 'game' by choosing to play it, in order to actively engage the plurality and contingency involved in the performance. They pursued these potentialities, exploring them, dancing with them purposefully, such that it is not the case that there *happened to be* plurality and contingency, which after all are always present in music and in everyday life; rather, plurality and contingency were intentionally foregrounded in performance. Liveness here is an active, aware, embodied engagement whereby those participating, even though and especially because they cannot see what is coming, do nevertheless know that improvisation is occurring. Thus, although contingency invites us to consider musical improvisation and quotidian improvisation as coextensive, liveness is still a performative capacity that makes a difference in the playing and listening-to of music, or in any contingent encounter.

Although every musician improvises insofar as they navigate contingencies, a musician performing improvised music is actively attending to that fact, is plumbing its depths. This kind of live and aware improvisation is one that may or may not be operative in music and/or in everyday life. But insofar as contingencies are always already present, and insofar as we can attune ourselves to those contingencies in a given situation, liveness reveals what we might call 'musical' improvisation not as rarefied behaviour but as a potentiality hidden inside every situation. This potentiality does not simply snap into place due to an activated state of awareness; rather, liveness must be cultivated over time as we turn towards what we want. In my view, this brings liveness into the realm of *affective attunement* inasmuch as Brian Massumi's use of this notion is less about a certain political practice and more about the cultivation of certain tendencies. Massumi writes:

> If a simple encounter between two bodies like a blow involves resistance, and as such can be modulated as it occurs ... that means that there are affect modulation techniques accessible in the event. They become accessible to the event through reflex, habit, training and the inculcation of skills ... These automaticities cannot be reduced to slavish repetition, a lack of freedom to manoeuvre. In fact, as any musician will tell you, they are the necessary foundation for improvisation ... What I am suggesting is that affect can be modulated by improvisational techniques that are thought-felt into action, flush with the event.[40]

Although this kind of attunement comes from a bodily predisposition, it is still multiply mutable: one can change one's own capacities (over time, through repetition) and one can also use those capacities to change event factors as they unfold in real time, as we modulate and improvise through a situation. Such potential contingencies carry political implications for Massumi, and although I want to stay grounded in Rancière's notion of politics, Massumi's formulation is useful for understanding how attunement can cultivate contingency. He continues:

> Politically, this changes the whole framework. Affective techniques of thinking-feeling improvisationally are relational techniques that apply to situations more directly than to persons. They are directly collective. They are fundamentally participatory, since they are activated

in situation, couched singularly in the occurrence of that encounter. They are event-factors, not intentions ... Tendencies are oriented, but open-ended.[41]

Tendencies are *oriented*, but open-ended.[42] If improvisation is the contingent encounter that is always already engendering experience, 'musical' improvisation as I have described it is simply a willingness to acknowledge the contingencies of that encounter according to our necessarily incomplete understanding/experience of its parameters, a willfulness that can be practised at any time. In such an encounter, we interact with others, with objects and with environments, conditioned as we are, but still straining towards something new. This straining or turning towards contingency is only ever partial, because we cannot fully apprehend the affective resonances of a situation. Moreover, improvisational responses to contingent situations are never fully within our control or even perception – as with sound itself, there is always an excess in the situation beyond what is knowable by the performer. Furthermore, if musical improvisation is a form of attending to the improvisation that is always already happening – this attention does not guarantee anything; it is perhaps more likely to fail than not, or to become refracted through the encounter, because intentionality and agency are hopelessly compromised by (even as they are engendered through) the field of the situation.[43] And yet my argument here is that this attempt, this straining, this attunement, is at one and the same time the only way that politics gets done.

To return finally to Rancière, this view of musical improvisation reorients the improvisation of politics by describing a specific set of relations: the improvisation of politics as developed here resembles neither the indiscriminately reactionary behaviour that politicians perform when they are making things up as they go along, nor the obligatory adaptations that precarious subjects perform without recourse to stable social structures, nor does it have to do with the performative aspect of all political *appearance*, in Arendt's sense. Rather, it has to do precisely with the active cultivation of the unknown inside the known, towards the contingency of being-with that resists sedimented orders and established ways of doing. The improvisation of politics consists in trying to activate musical improvisation in everyday life, necessarily without knowing the result.

The essential point here is that these actions are *small* and that they matter *anyway*. While politics may be rare in Rancière's thought, he also reminds us that politics does not erupt *ex nihilo*; rather, politics emerges from the police itself, which is to say from everyday life.[44] In this limited sense, then, I want to suggest that improvisation is analogous to Arendt's notion of *action*, in which 'processes are started whose outcome is unpredictable, so that uncertainty . . . becomes the decisive character of human affairs'.[45] Although Arendt's notion remains fixated on the sovereign acting subject, rather than on the subject's contingent interactions, her argument shows something crucial by directly linking contingent human action such as improvisation to the contingency of Rancière's police; the outcomes of everyday behaviours are so unpredictable that, in sum, every order is built on unstable ground. Things could change at any moment.

If Arendt is right in asserting the transformative potential of *action*, and if the contingency that musical improvisation searches for is also the space in which politics – as opposed to the predetermined, the pre-established order of the police – can emerge, then those actions that are willfully attentive to contingency are those that at the very least reach for the political.[46] This is not a will towards any end-goal but towards contingency itself. The police consists in knowing – indeed, in knowing all too well – what will happen, what this means, who this is for and not for, where we do and do not belong, what we should and should not do. But musical improvisation (as outlined here) shares with both Rancière's universal teaching and with politics the conviction that '[k]nowing is nothing, *doing* is everything'.[47] Or put another way, '[t]urning answers into questions is a political act'.[48] This, in the end, is how Rancière's politics happens: through improvisatory actions in everyday life, which, while they may not qualify as properly political, and whether or not they achieve anything recognisable, nevertheless try. It is through this trying that we leave a trace, and through this trace that 'the smallest act in the most limited circumstances bears the seed of [the same] boundlessness, because one deed, and sometimes one word, suffices to change every constellation'.[49]

Notes

1. For notable exceptions, see Joshua Mousie, 'Rancière, Resistance, and Improvisation', *Improvisation, Community and Social Practice*

(Online Research Collection, 2010), <http://www.improvcommunity.ca/research/ranciere-resistance-and-musical-improvisation> (last accessed 22 November 2019); Federico Reuben, 'Imaginary Musical Radicalism and the Entanglement of Music and Emancipatory Politics', *Contemporary Music Review* 34.2–3 (2015), 232–46; and Chris Stover's chapter in this collection.

2. Giuseppina Mecchia, 'Mute Speech: The Silence of Literature in Rancière's Aesthetic Paradigm', in Patrick M. Bray (ed.), *Understanding Rancière, Understanding Modernism* (London: Bloomsbury, 2017), 97–110.

3. The opposition between politics and the police is not a rigid binary, nor are the concepts themselves a priori forms; rather, they are tools aimed at diagnosing complex and entangled situations. See Jacques Rancière, 'Afterword/The Method of Equality: An Answer to Some Questions', in Gabriel Rockhill and Philip Watts (eds), *Jacques Rancière: History, Politics, Aesthetics* (Durham, NC: Duke University Press, 2009), 273–88.

4. Jacques Rancière, *Disagreement: Politics and Philosophy*, trans. Julie Rose (Minneapolis: University of Minnesota Press, 2004); Jacques Rancière, 'Ten Theses on Politics', in *Dissensus: On Politics and Aesthetics*, trans. Steven Corcoran (London: Continuum, 2010), 27–44.

5. See Ingrid Monson, 'From the American Civil Rights Movement to Mali: Reflections on Social Aesthetics and Improvisation', in Georgina Born, Eric Lewis and Will Straw (eds), *Improvisation and Social Aesthetics* (Durham, NC: Duke University Press, 2017), 78–90; Scott Currie, 'The Other Side of Here and Now: Cross-Cultural Reflections on the Politics of Improvisation Studies', *Critical Studies in Improvisation/Études critiques en improvisation* 11.1–2 (2016), <https://www.criticalimprov.com/index.php/csieci/article/download/3750/3980> (last accessed 22 November 2019).

6. Currie, 'The Other Side of Here and Now', 1.

7. Marcel Cobussen, for example, has argued this point from the perspective of complex systems and Actor Network Theory; see Cobussen, *The Field of Musical Improvisation* (Leiden: Leiden University Press, 2017). Alternatively, I use the language of contingency in order to reference both the interdependent 'bodies' that engender improvisations (instruments, acoustic spaces, recording technologies and so on) as well as the unquantifiable affects that defy capture and are irreducible to the questions of musical 'outcomes' implicit in complex systems analyses. For more on how I understand

the relationship between contingency, singularity and improvisation, see Dan DiPiero, 'Improvisation as Contingent Encounter, Or: The Song of My Toothbrush', *Critical Studies in Improvisation/Études critiques en improvisation* 12.2 (2018), <https://www.criticalimprov.com/index.php/csieci/article/view/4261/4863> (last accessed 22 November 2019).

8. Environments here include everything from physical to discursive contexts, as well as both larger sociocultural structures and immediate sounding environments in which the music takes place, each of which has an effect on the performance.
9. This is true both because there are always 'compositional' elements present in improvisation (and vice versa) but also because 'when considered from the perspective of its temporal, embodied enactment', all music responds to and emerges from contingencies of a specific time/space/context. 'In other words, the temporally unfolding, performing/performed subject is in dialogue with the historically and textually bounded nature of the musical material, and the acting out of this dialogue is what defines the context of some specific performed utterance. Each performance, in this sense, unfolds as a singularity, a double selection of active and passive syntheses that Deleuze would describe as the becoming-actual of the virtual space of the performance.' Chris Stover, 'Affect and Improvising Bodies', *Perspectives of New Music* 55.2 (2017), 5, 6.
10. Mr. K, *Left Exit* (Clean-Feed Records, 2015).
11. 'The scene is not the illustration of an idea. It is a little optical machine that shows us thought busy weaving together perceptions, affects, names and ideas, constituting the sensible community that these links create, and the intellectual community that makes such weaving thinkable. The scene captures concepts at work, in their relation to the new objects they seek to appropriate, old objects that they try to reconsider, and the patterns they build or transform to this end.' Jacques Rancière, *Aisthesis: Scenes from the Aesthetic Regime of Art* (London: Verso, 2013), xi.
12. While there has never been just one improvised music scene in Europe, the capitalisation here is meant to reference the specific effort – discursive, stylistic and otherwise – that emerged in the 1960s European context to reify a genre/practice of improvised music that would be distinct from American jazz, and as such would be seen as a unique contribution, rather than a derivative practice (as European jazz was initially viewed, even or especially internally).
13. Jacques Rancière, *The Politics of Aesthetics: The Distribution of the*

Sensible, trans. Gabriel Rockhill (London: Bloomsbury, 2013), 56, 50, 57.
14. '[N]o direct cause–effect relationship is determinable between the intention realised in an art performance and a capacity for political subjectivation ... [The politics of aesthetics] produces effects, but it does so on the basis of an original effect that implies the suspension of any direct cause–effect relationship.' Jacques Rancière, 'The Paradoxes of Political Art', in *Dissensus: On Politics and Aesthetics*, trans. Steven Corcoran (London: Continuum, 2010), 134–51.
15. Rancière, *The Politics of Aesthetics*, 59.
16. Rancière, 'The Paradoxes of Political Art', 149 (my emphasis).
17. See, for instance, Vijay Iyer, 'Improvisation, Temporality and Embodied Experience', *Journal of Consciousness Studies* 11.3–4 (2004), 159–73.
18. For more on sound and relationality, see Georgina Born, 'On Nonhuman Sound – Sound as Relation', in James A. Steintrager and Rey Chow (eds), *Sound Objects* (Durham, NC: Duke University Press, 2019), 185–210.
19. 'Since music is always materially and relationally contingent, it is never the same external force that both restores and destroys. Rather, since music is vibration, there are multitudes of material circumstances that contribute to each of its particular articulations, each unrepeatable and hence unique, and each with a potential to affect us that can be revealed only in the particular articulation that takes place within and among each material situation and unique listener.' Nina Sun Eidsheim, *Sensing Sound: Singing and Listening as Vibrational Practice* (Durham, NC: Duke University Press, 2015), 55.
20. See Georgina Born, Eric Lewis and Will Straw, 'Introduction', in Born et al. (eds), *Improvisation and Social Aesthetics*; Lydia Goehr, *The Imaginary Museum of Musical Works: An Essay in the Philosophy of Music* (Oxford: Oxford University Press, 2007).
21. Rockhill makes a similar argument when he writes that 'works of art are never fixed objects that can be judged once and for all from the privileged position of the philosopher of art. Artistic production is a dynamic process that is part of a sociohistorical world. This means that there is no permanent politics of art; there are only various modes of politicisation. And these take place in different dimensions: not only at the level of historical regimes (Rancière) but also at the level of production, circulation, and reception.' Gabriel Rockhill, 'The Politics of Aesthetics: Political History and the Hermeneutics

of Art', in Rockhill and Watts (eds), *Jacques Rancière: History, Politics, Aesthetics*, 215.
22. Georgina Born, 'After Relational Aesthetics: Improvised Music, the Social, and (Re)Theorizing the Aesthetic', in Born et al. (eds), *Improvisation and Social Aesthetics*, 33–58 (44).
23. Stover, 'Affect and Improvising Bodies', 6.
24. Born, 'After Relational Aesthetics', 43.
25. Mr. K is Karl Hjalmar Nyberg (sax) and Andreas Skår Winther (drums). On this album, they are joined by Michael Francis Duch on bass and Klaus Ellerhusen Holm on reeds.
26. Think about, for instance, the unspoken rules that have excluded women from fully participating in this jazz sensible: the police consists not only in musical conventions, but – because they are interdependent – social ones as well.
27. 'There is a worse and a better police . . . The police can procure all sorts of good, and one kind of police may be infinitely preferable to another.' Rancière, *Disagreement*, 31.
28. Born, 'After Relational Aesthetics', 43.
29. Barry Shank, *The Political Force of Musical Beauty* (Durham, NC: Duke University Press, 2014), 28, 17.
30. Shank, *The Political Force of Musical Beauty*, 14.
31. Shank, *The Political Force of Musical Beauty*, 15.
32. However, this political function is of a specific kind: it does not 'form a newly unified political community' but rather 'establishes the shared feelings required for an intimate public to form'. Shank, *The Political Force of Musical Beauty*, 260.
33. Moreover, we have to keep in mind that this kind of political redistribution cannot ground itself in an order of politics; as soon as the rupture occurs, it reorganises a new police, a new community of sense, which, in order to change anything about the world around it, must take its moment of politics as only a precondition to action. This returns us to Rancière's point about different kinds of equality. Shank, following Rancière's formulation, puts it this way: 'there is no necessary political trajectory that results from musical listening. At best, the experience of musical beauty does redistribute the sensible, and in so doing, it does demand a deeper interrogative listening to any political claims made. But the political force of music stops at that point.' Shank, *The Political Force of Musical Beauty*, 260.
34. Born, 'After Relational Aesthetics', 43.
35. Born, 'After Relational Aesthetics', 43.
36. Within the framework in Norway, 'A lot of people say that you can

forget about getting funding if you're not doing something crazy ... You know, if you do something experimental and you live up north, you're sort of home free for life, because you're so "correct". Whereas standard repertoire played in the traditional way – the sort of thing you can see all over America all the time – if we try to do that in Norway, it's like, "Why should we do that? There's enough of that."' Kristin Danielsen, quoted in Michelle Mercer, 'How Norway Funds a Thriving Jazz Scene', *A Blog Supreme*, NPR online, 6 April 2013, <https://www.npr.org/sections/ablogsupreme/2013/03/26/175415645/how-norway-funds-a-thriving-jazz-scene> (last accessed 22 November 2019).

37. This egalitarianism and quotidianism are advanced in other ways as well, including the robust tradition of amateurism in Norwegian approaches to improvised music. While this amateurism sometimes inflames the insecurities of Norwegian musicians and/or critics looking to assert Norwegian distinction on the world stage (see Luca Vitali, *The Sound of the North: The Norwegian Jazz Scene* (Milan: Mimesis International, 2016)), it nevertheless taps into what I believe to be a fundamental character of the avant-garde (or the aesthetic regime) in the first place: the radical questioning of notions of excellence, the equal possibility of including any and all subject matter as 'appropriate', and the long-established link between the avant-garde and the everyday.

38. Ben Highmore, *Michel de Certeau: Analysing Culture* (London: Continuum, 2006), 114. This is Highmore's characterisation of de Certeau's notion of 'everyday practices', practices that I argue are inherently improvisatory. The quote continues, 'This is why Certeau insists on the *singularity* of operations within the everyday.'

39. See DiPiero, 'Improvisation as Contingent Encounter'.

40. Brian Massumi, *Politics of Affect* (Cambridge: Polity, 2015), 96.

41. Massumi, *Politics of Affect*, 97.

42. Here, attunement links with Sara Ahmed's notion of *orientation*. There is, in the end, no state of consciousness that would totally apprehend a situation in its event-ness, in its unfolding in and through various bodies, nor is there any form of intention that can translate – in linear fashion – into a given outcome. But at the same time, I would argue that there is still something *willful* about the improvising musician's responses that differs from other possible reactions. This difference, in my view, comes down to the improviser's openness to the fact that a contingent situation is currently occurring all around them. Such an openness is not 'consciousness'

with its implications of capture, nor is it 'attention' with its implications of focus; again, this awareness, foreknowledge or willfulness is, first, only ever partial, and second, indeterminate, in that all kinds of things can happen. This is what makes liveness into an orientation: if everyday life consists in practices, and if practices can sink into or reorient 'habit spaces', then, as Ahmed reminds us, there are other ways of orienting our practices, other paths or 'desire lines' that point in a direction while keeping open the possibility of change. Both Ahmed and Massumi are careful to emphasise the lack of prescription in these practices, insisting instead on the full presence of contingency. See Sara Ahmed, *Queer Phenomenology* (Durham, NC: Duke University Press, 2006).

43. 'The subject . . . is the way in which the performer and performed act are constituted through their interaction in the singular ongoingness of the event. There is a human body, there is perspective, there is agency (often), but those are conceived around the orbit of the event. The same is true of the listening body. The listener exists in an affective relationship with the experienced sonic data, and has a capacity to affect and be affected that increases or decreases according to the eventful terms of the relationship.' Stover, 'Affect and Improvising Bodies', 22–3.
44. 'We should not forget either that if politics implements a logic entirely heterogeneous to that of the police, it is always bound up with the latter.' Rancière, *Disagreement*, 31.
45. Hannah Arendt, *The Human Condition* (1958) (Chicago: University of Chicago Press, 1998), 232.
46. 'The method of equality was above all a method of the will. One could learn by oneself and without a master explicator when one wanted to, propelled by one's own desire or by the constraint of the situation.' Jacques Rancière, *The Ignorant Schoolmaster: Five Lessons in Intellectual Emancipation*, trans. Kristin Ross (Stanford: Stanford University Press, 1991), 12. For more on will and willfulness, see Sara Ahmed, *Willful Subjects* (Durham, NC: Duke University Press, 2014).
47. Joseph Jacotot, *Enseignement universel: musique, dessin et peinture*, 2nd edn (Paris: Bureau du Journal de l'émancipation intellectuelle, 1830), in *The Ignorant Schoolmaster*, 65.
48. Lauren Berlant, in a talk delivered at the 'New Universalisms: Aesthetics, Media, Politics' Graduate Student Conference, University of Minnesota, 7–8 October 2016.
49. Arendt, *The Human Condition*, 190.

10

Rancière's Affective Impropriety
Chris Stover

The foundation of politics ... is the lack of foundation, the sheer contingency of any social order. Politics exists simply because no social order is based on nature, no divine law regulates human society.[1]

In the Dionysian state ... the whole affective system is excited and enhanced: so that it discharges all its means of expression at once and drives forth simultaneously the power of representation, imitation, transfiguration, transformation ... The Dionysian ... enters into any skin, into any affect: he constantly transforms himself. Music, as we understand it today, is also a total excitement and a total discharge of the affects ...[2]

I always thought I was shaking people up, but now I want to go at it *more*, and I want to go at it more *deliberately*, and I want to go at it *coldly* – I want to shake people up so bad that when they leave a nightclub where I performed I just want them to be in pieces.[3]

'Politics for Rancière ... begins with an act of aesthetic impropriety.'[4] Such an act proceeds as a partaking of sensibilities and modes of participation by an individual or group that has not been given the right to do so within a given temporal, spatial and relational distribution. Politics, then, as the aesthetic practice of dissensus that reveals how the conditions of existing configurations determine what is sensible and how, is in every event an action or constellation of actions that exists *only* in the staging of a singular scene. This is what makes politics aesthetic. While its singularity disallows a fully transferable or generalisable 'Rancièrean theory' of political action, it also brings into relief the affective relationality of any given event in terms of the movements of affective forces that reconfigure and newly constitute bodies (human and otherwise) in new relational dispositions. It is *only* in the enactment of an individual act, the staging of a singular scene, that politics unfolds.

Rancière insists, therefore, that politics occurs only rarely.[5] Similarly, the constitution of a political subject (for Rancière the only kind of subject that matters) is a rare and contingent process that must be carefully tended through an iterative practice of willfully and disruptively *announcing* one's dis-identificatory status, which proceeds via 'the production through a series of actions of a body and a capacity for enunciation not previously identifiable within a given field of experience, whose identification is thus part of the reconfiguration of the field of experience'.[6] This does not amount simply to an assertion that what was unsayable is now suddenly sayable, but unfolds as an ongoing practice through which the conditions of its unsayability are revealed and interrupted. While this continuous series of operations animates new connections, configurations and distributions and calls into question assumptions about who can or cannot speak, and who can or cannot be heard, within the hierarchical arrangements of a police logic, it turns out to be a cripplingly challenging action to continue to enact, since the tendency of a police logic is to refold itself around a political eruption, refiguring it in its own name and in the terms of a now-new dominant distribution in order to continue to reproduce the ideologically bound configurations that the police logic exists to enact. In this way, for example (as Luciano Berio puts it), 'formation becomes Form; an instrument, Gadget; a social ideal, Party; Schoenberg's and Webern's poetics, The Twelve-Tone System'.[7] So to be politically effective, a dis-identificatory practice must be nimble, creative, insistent and tireless, ever aware of the ways in which newly enacted distributions allow or foreclose different ways of saying and doing, and ever directed towards new utterances and affective improprieties that shake up what is considered to be possible within a given distribution (as well, of course, as who is able to make that utterance).

This essay locates certain kinds of dis-identificatory practices in the affective spacetime that flows between bodies in relations, and suggests that certain kinds of musical practices do this dissensual work well, or at least in ways that offer compelling case studies. Rancière is obviously not an affect theorist, so some explanation of this claim is necessary. As Davide Panagia states, a key concern of Rancière's lies in

> that inattentive moment that precedes judgment – a presubjective, but also preobjective, moment when the distensions of sensation have yet to assign value to specific persons, things and events. This is the aesthetic moment of indistinction, which is also the political moment of equality, when anything whatsoever and anyone whosoever can count.[8]

Several crucial themes emerge from Panagia's analysis. First is the important point – sometimes lost in scholarship that aims to deploy Rancière's conceptual apparatus in the activist sense of *creating* the conditions for equality – that equality *precedes* any given representational logic. Equality is always already there, but is covered over by the hierarchical distributions of a police logic or epistemological mode that normalises or naturalises certain sensible arrangements; the task of a political act therefore is to recover the equality that has been hidden or suppressed by a given distribution. Second, Panagia's characterisation locates in that affective gap an inattentive instant where we (can) forget the structurings of sensations, thus opening the world to creative ranges of relational connectivities. In affective terms, there is a 'form of *shock* (the sudden interruption of functions of actual connection)' within which the virtual forces that underpin and constitute signifying or structuring strata are revealed.[9] Third, stemming from this, is an affinity with similar key concepts from affect-oriented theorists: Bergson's 'zone of indeterminacy', Deleuze's 'dark precursor'.[10] Both Bergson and Deleuze describe the brief interval within which perception precedes cognition. For the former, this is the gap where free will is activated; for the latter, the event of the continuous production of difference: both of these concepts are entirely analogous to what Panagia describes as the 'interval in judgment's urge to direct perception and attention, thereby enabling a transformation of the possible'.[11] Affect is *productive* – constitutive of bodies and relations in proliferating double movements – and *liminal*, always in between. Its continual movement of productive, liminal flows is, however, constantly impinged upon by ideological forces that reproduce what Panagia calls 'the centripetal tendencies of social isomorphism'[12] that constrain *how* a body can affect and be affected: this is the fourth way that Rancière's conception of the distribution of the sensible resonates with affect theory (and reinforces why Rancière's politics is aesthetic), since both involve turns from causal logics towards the constitutive force of sensations, feelings and transversal relations.[13]

My contention is that music – or, more specifically, certain singular *stagings* of musical utterances – provides illustrative, dis-identificatory political-aesthetic moments that refigure, at least locally and contingently, dominant codes that determine right and wrong practices. In describing these scenes I will bring Rancière into dialogue not only with theorists of affect and relationality, but also with the political thought of Jacques Attali, whose theory of the disruptive role that noise plays in a given communicative regime and the political implications of what it means to ascribe noise status to a given utterance resonate in powerful ways with Rancière's conceptual apparatus, not least the latter's careful explication in *Disagreement* of what it means to hear one's interlocutor *as noise*, thereby denying them a fundamental humanity.[14] The specific space of my inquiry is a series of utterances made in and around jazz improvisation, which will proceed from big to small (or general-conceptual to local): the relationship between jazz theory and the practice of jazz improvisation, the putative relationship between jazz's improvised utterances and some political claims made on jazz's behalf, and how the ruptures of specific, well-known dissensual acts in jazz – recorded performances by Thelonious Monk ('I Should Care', rec. 1957), Pharoah Sanders (on John Coltrane's *Live at the Village Vanguard Again*, 1966) and more recently the sextet Mostly Other People Do the Killing (*Blue*, 2014) – have or have not resisted folding into the reconfigurations of new police logics. In each of these scenes a wrongness is enacted – which Samuel Chambers emphasises is also a wrungness, a 'twisting or torsion of the police order and its logic of inequality'[15] – an improper playing technique or gesture that in each case calls into question how proper modes of doing and relating ought to proceed and why. Each of these scenes will develop an affective pragmatics in the sense that each illustrates a singular constellation of affective relationalities that operate both transversally (as co-constitutive flows between proximal bodies that define a context in the moment of its unfolding) and temporally (as the traces left on a body that partially condition it for a next encounter).[16]

Jazz theory and its object

The constitutive role of dis-identification looms large in considerations of the relationship between jazz theory as a pedagogical practice and the embodied, active doing of jazz improvisation. Elsewhere I suggest that the most important, perhaps singular distinction between contemporary music theory as it pertains to the Western art music tradition versus that of jazz can be expressed as a distinction between what I call hermeneutic versus pragmatic perspectives.[17] In its hermeneutic orientation, contemporary music theory produces a range of analytic frameworks for continued inquiry into the codes and structures of some existing piece (or corpus) of music, on which it is brought to bear in order to better understand that music, perhaps in order to perform it in a way that expresses what the analytic act reveals as an epistemologically valuable bundle of meaning constellations. This is a continuous process: there is always another perspective to consider, another layer to uncover. In its pragmatic orientation, on the other hand, music theory is frankly and unapologetically *useful* – it exists primarily, and perhaps even exclusively, for the purpose of enabling a performing musician to engage the materials of her practice, providing a set of tools to be used in 'real-life' scenarios. Theory in this case is a conduit between an object and its subjective engagement, and the subject–object relation is creatively mimetic: the performing subject engages in the process of creating a *new* object that takes on certain characteristics of the existing one. The simulacrum becomes the space where meaning is generated, the object upon which the simulacrum is derived (never very clearly defined in the first place)[18] recedes into the background, and theory informs the way in which the simulacrum is drawn. Put another way: the subject is emergent and performative, and the object is sublated into the subject, which is defined through this relationship, legislated by theory. It is important to note that as a conduit, this sort of pragmatic theory allows certain lines to be drawn between subject and object in simulacrum-formation, but that it forecloses other lines – I will return to this point below.

This all manifests in two ways, which together express the complexly entangled relationship between police and politics in Rancière's thought. A purely pragmatic music theory methodology, oriented towards successful expression within a given melodic, harmonic and rhythmic syntax, necessarily involves faithfully reproducing that syntax. Thus we find in jazz theory chord-scale isomorphisms, voice-leading schemata, canonical repertoires, iconic solos and firmly entrenched ideas about proper roles and best practices in collective improvisational contexts. This, of course, represents the police-logic side, the mimetic reproduction of a social order, and from this perspective its alignment alongside and in accord with hermeneutic theoretical orientations – to which it was originally opposed – starts to become clear. This is less a dialectical opposition than the peeling away of an obfuscating layer in order to reveal a hidden representational affinity, reproduced in difference.

But there is another side of this equation, which has to do with the ways in which jazz theory is continually (re)invented and disseminated by practitioners: by those who within a given distribution of roles are not given permission for such invention and dissemination. Like Rancière's worker-poets, they invent, refine and share in the margins. They write and self-publish books, create web resources and online teaching demos, produce manifesto-like recordings.[19] They plunge with impassioned, solitary fervour into myriad technical and expressive spaces, developing new ways of thinking through harmonic or rhythmic concepts, for example, while simultaneously developing the proficiencies needed to actualise these concepts in played musical expressions. This ongoing process is the driving force that animates at least one way of reading jazz's history, as a series of dissensual acts – the radical temporal fluidity of Louis Armstrong's 'West End Blues' cadenza; the timbral distensions of Duke Ellington's 'Daybreak Express'; Kenny Clarke's transformation of the jazz drummer's role into one of improvisatory 'comping'; Charlie Parker's blistering tempos and baroque gestural contours; Miles Davis's chord-scales; Ornette Coleman's redeployment of blues as a new avant-garde. Each of these scenes has been described in overtly political terms, as expressions of contemporaneous black American political actions, or, as Attali would suggest, as harbingers of political actions to come.[20]

If jazz theory has a primarily pragmatic function grounded in an ongoing series of dis-identificatory acts that call into question regimes of doing and knowing, then we should think carefully about the relationship between what theory aims to do for practice and the political aspirations of jazz as expressed by its practitioners and advocates. Here are three political claims that have been made on jazz's behalf:

> The esthetics of jazz demand that a musician play with complete originality, with an assertion of his own musical individuality ... At the same time jazz requires that musicians be able to merge their unique voices in the totalizing, collective improvisations of polyphony and heterophony. The implications of this esthetic are profound and more than vaguely threatening, for no political system has yet been devised with social principles which reward maximal individualism within the framework of spontaneous egalitarian interaction.[21]

> Its entire history has been the freeing of time, pitch, and harmony from fixed, regulated, predictable standards. Every major innovation in the history of the music has been from the struggle of musicians to attain greater and greater levels of expressive freedom through liberating the two basic fundamentals of music: time ... and sound ...[22]

> That's what brought us right back home: we were forced to deal with very basic issues, like being in exile; children dying of hunger. In what way can you assist? You become like the voice of the voiceless who have been forced into silence. In some sense we're blessed, because the struggle kept us oriented at the same time as pursuing personal aspirations.[23]

The sentiments expressed in these passages resonate with the kinds of questions that concern Rancière: profound aesthetic implications that threaten establishment logics, maximal individual freedom as the announcement of equality, spontaneous egalitarian interaction, struggle as a force that foments innovation, expressive freedom (and freedom as something that must be expressed or announced), giving voice to the voiceless within a normative regime that has stifled them into silence. Indeed, the first quote could almost have been uttered by Rancière himself: note the parallel to the latter's evocation of the Gothic artist who, 'while subordinating himself to the collective work, to the function of the building and the constraints of the material ... expresses his own will, and his singular manner within this framework'.[24] Aesthetic ideas are transformative inventions; 'the ontology of art under the aesthetic regime is what is weaved by the inventions of art by instituting their dissensuses, by placing one sensible world in another'.[25] This aesthetic art, of which I argue jazz and other improvised musics strive to be exemplary, is an 'invention [that constructs] the effectiveness of the ontological difference that [it presupposes]'.[26]

This, then, leads to a constellation of questions. What *are* the (Rancièrean) political aspirations of jazz? How do they manifest in practice, *as* practised? What is the relationship between what we might call a purely musical politics (for example, inter-ensemble politics), the police logic of sensible distributions within which the music is being made (and the ways in which it is policed by the very community of jazz musicians and associated figures such as listeners, promoters and critics; see below), and politics expressed *through* music? And most important: *How do the police counts of jazz-as-practised, as-theorised and as-policed support or conflict with narratives of jazz's liberatory politics?* There is a double critique that underlies all of these questions: that perhaps jazz fails to live up to its political claims, and that perhaps it does so *because* its repeated attempts to rupture established police counts, like all such acts of dissensus, tend to fold back into the enactment of new counts. Jazz's counts – its distributions of who can be heard and how, its declarations of certain utterances as music and others as noise, its histories and biographies, its precarious place within complex market forces – are policed from within its communities. This fact brings to the foreground many of Rancière's nuanced points about who exactly it is that does the counting, how consensuses are (mostly tacitly) propagated, and how truly difficult it is not only to stage a political act but, more importantly, to continue to do so.

What this means is that if jazz improvisation is going to be read as political or aesthetic in Rancière's technical usage, it must first engage its own hierarchising structures or police logics – its own internal ways of distributing the sensible. This includes not only its various structural or syntactic a priori and its logics of inclusion and exclusion (viz. internecine arguments about what does or does not get to count as jazz), but also, and especially, interrogating its own 'freedom' narratives (*Free how? Free for whom (and from what)? Free in the name of what? Free with what kinds of implications?*) If improvised music is to be read as a model of liberatory politics, that is the first step – its own narrative of freedom must be carefully excavated, held up to scrutiny, deconstructed – *why* is improvisation valorised as free or liberatory or emancipatory, and what is at stake in such a claim?

Second, jazz's own police must be acknowledged. This includes carefully understanding the sources of its consensuses, including its histories, its mythic narratives, its theories, its assumptions, its values, its modes of representation – who is or has been making these determinations, and for what reasons? Who stands to gain by continuing to propagate a police logic that allows some voices to be heard (as jazz) and censors others?

Third, to enact a move into an active equality that exceeds existing counts, counts the uncounted and redistributes the sensible, the conditions of its nominal equality must be examined, as well as the ways in which a given consensus might be productively shaken up without simply folding back into a new consensus. This gets into crucial questions about music and noise, about understanding and being understood, and about mimesis and aesthetic expression. Before continuing to develop all of these themes, it will be valuable to engage another theorist of communication and noise in order to explore some productive affinities with Rancière's thought.

Attali's meaningful music

Jacques Attali describes music as 'a channeler of violence, a creator of differences, a sublimation of noise, an attribute of power'.[27] Music expresses 'a social meaning ... in a code relating to the sound matter music fashions and the systems of power it serves'.[28] And in a more utopian vein, 'music appears in myth as an affirmation that society is possible'.[29] What society? Attali suggests that music's relational structurings prophesy new forms of social order and new ways of functioning, connecting and communicating within those orders. But not *only* that, since the codes of a given musical utterance, according to Attali, are not simply expressed within and through the sound structures (the 'sound matter') themselves but operate within and, importantly, reflect and – in the eventful reconfigurations that announce the move from one regime to the next – subvert the systems of power that constitute the contexts within which a given utterance is made. If we believe Attali's claim, then we should take seriously the possibility that inquiry into music's structure (the purview of music theory) is exactly inquiry into the social/political formulations towards which it points.[30]

The underlying assertion that drives Attali's four developmental stages is that the social or political (or economic) models that they describe are prefigured in certain kinds of musical formulations. Attali's account begins with the *sacrificial* or *ritual* (as pre-artistic concepts), through *representation* as the simulation of ritual and the beginning of art, through *repetition* as its co-option by capitalist forces, to a culmination in a *compositional* stage where art transcends itself, as a purely creative expression. Attali expresses the conditions of his compositional stage in terms of a politically utopian ontology of continuous autochthonous generation that transcends syntax and value ascriptions: 'in the absence of any a priori code music creates an order', which is to say its own order, free of the ideological constraints of representational logics.[31]

Rancière's account begins, similarly, with a pre-artistic *ethical* regime. In Rancière's *representative* regime, a gap opens between depiction and depicted, locating the origin of art in mimesis. The logic of representation manifests as value judgements based on agreed-upon conventions about how one ought or ought not make, perceive or interpret art. Art breaks its reliance on the mimetic in the *aesthetic* regime, where the limitations of representational discourse are revealed through art's overspilling beyond representational discourses. While Rancière generally describes these as actual historical regimes, largely in pursuit of a project that rewrites conventional accounts of the advent, progression and conditions of modernity, it is important in drawing connections between aesthetics and politics to be able to locate moments of aesthetic eruption within any number of different representative regimes, under any historical conditions.[32] Aesthetics is less an epistemic change, then, than the singular staging of an action that temporarily disrupts accepted modes of doing and perceiving. I read Attali's compositional stage likewise: less a future utopian epoch than a practice by which representation or repetitive constraints are revealed and loosened or evaded.

Returning to the relationship between music and social formation, Attali writes of his fourth stage: 'Thus composition proposes a radical social model, one in which the body is treated as capable not only of production and consumption, and even of entering into relations with others, but also of autonomous pleasure.'[33] From a Rancièrean perspective, this suggests that bodies are capable of inventing their own ways of experiencing the aesthetic; indeed, that it is in the compositional stage that the aesthetic can even *be* experienced. This signifies a break with established codes in Attali's representation and repetition networks, or the police counts of Rancière's representative regime. In both cases, a voice is given to the individual (who, according to both accounts, was previously not allowed a voice other than that accorded by the prevailing codes/count). For Rancière, this effects a transformation from noise to speech, challenging the distinction between the two and problematising the hierarchical system that determines who gets a voice and who doesn't, who is heard and understood and who is not. For Attali, this is a radical act: noise attacks and transforms a network, carrying new information, substituting 'new differences for the old differences', serving as a 'source of [mutation] in the structuring codes'.[34] Noise, for Attali, carries meaning: it interrupts the existing message, and by doing so frees the listener's imagination. Noise is productive; it produces new modes of bodily relationality, which is to say new affective modes. The result is the (potential) presence of all possible meanings, or even 'a construction outside meaning'[35] – in Rancièrean terms an egalitarianism of potential meaning-trajectories. It is interesting to compare the ways in which Rancière and Attali are using the concept of noise differently, but with a similar aim: both the Rancièrean insistence that one's noise be heard as speech (or music) and the Attalian tenet that noise is in itself a form of communication locate noise as the very space of disruptive, and therefore transformative, politics.

For a mutation to transform a code, or for a dominant network to undergo a change, a shock must occur. For Attali, 'catastrophe is inscribed in order'; that is, a network of codes is already inscribed with the potential for its own overcoming.[36] Another way to say this is that there is no order that does not contain the seeds of disorder within it, and conversely there is no disorder incapable of creating a new order. For this reason Eric Drott characterises noise as a 'generative force' that proceeds via the normalisation of elements that were alien to the code within which noise was erupting. Thus, 'initially resistant to interpretation, a noise may with time lose its radical alterity and become just another sign within a system of signification'.[37] This should again remind us of Rancière's warning about the ease with which a political or aesthetic rupture can sediment into a new count. But at the same time I wish to entertain the possibility that some kinds of noise continue to resist folding back into regimes of signs or into new sedimentations, that they continue to express a radical alterity that resists seizure by a (new) representational logic. In order to work through the political implications of this double movement, I will turn to three scenes from jazz's history, each of which enacts a political interruption through the insistence that what the artist is doing, while considered a form of noise by the terms of an existing logic, be heard as music. Importantly, in each case the reception history of the aesthetic event included, paradoxically, a valorisation of the 'genius' of the artist in practically the same breath as an insistence that utterances of this sort are outside the bounds of accepted jazz expression.

Monk's micro(political)timing

Pianist Thelonious Monk included several jazz standards – repertoire pieces with which insiders are expected to be intimately familiar, and knowledge of which is necessary for inclusion in the community of a certain subset of jazz practitioners – on his 1957 recording *Thelonious Himself*.[38] His recording of Sammy Cahn and Axel Stordahl's 1945 composition 'I Should Care' is well known in the extended jazz community: it is frequently anthologised, and is the object of at least one article-length scholarly study.[39] It is also a song with a rich history in popular music, with hit interpretations by the Tommy Dorsey Orchestra, Frank Sinatra, Julie London, Nat 'King' Cole and others.

Monk's staging of 'I Should Care' brings to light the affective and political–aesthetic questions I have been posing so far. Monk's performance exaggerates a representational engagement with his object to the point of ironic caricature: in the opening moments of the performance we experience a wildly varied timbral palette enacted through diverse modes of pianistic articulation, from a jarring, heavy-handed way of 'attacking' the piano keys to crystalline flourishes that recall Monk's stride predecessors. We experience stilted, stuttering melodic phrasing, broken up by pregnant pauses that disrupt any sense of continuous temporal flow. We hear in this an idiosyncratic lyricism that always recalls the original even in its sometimes severe distortions (I never have trouble 'hearing' the lyrics in a Monk performance). And we witness the song's harmonic progression doubly displaced, via chord substitutions and 'extra' notes that introduce an element of noise to what would otherwise be a syntactically clear signal. These notes have been characterised as (deliberately) 'wrong' in journalistic writings about Monk; I might suggest that Monk's is precisely a Rancièrean wrongness (or wrungness) in the sense described above: a twisting or torsion of the logic of tonal harmonic syntax. From this perspective, we get a glimpse in Monk's performance of what a harmonic object *can* do that radically transcends what it *ought* to do according to the prescriptions of the prevailing count. Hence Rancière's affective pragmatics: as Deleuze is fond of saying, 'we do not even know what a body is capable of',[40] but through the double movement of affective impingements (here, between Monk and the 'body' of 'I Should Care') possibilities are revealed through performative enactments, possibilities that were already part of the equal substrate that precedes stratification.[41]

Importantly, all of this occurs in the space of the simulacrum, which utterly displaces the striated original (such as one might be identified), transforming its codes by revealing and refiguring latent possibilities that were always there to begin with. Another (Deleuze-Guattarian) way to make this last point is to suggest that Monk territorialises the song through the very deterritorialising acts staged by his unconventional rhythmic and textural approach, each of which redistributes immanent, virtual forces. Let us return to each of these dis-identificatory themes in slightly more detail. The way that Monk's pianistic touch disrupts agreed-upon notions of 'correct' or 'good' piano playing amounts to a practice that *transforms the representational into the aesthetic*. This is an aesthetic act precisely because Monk insists, through his performative actions, that his is a viable way to play the piano, and that it should never be in doubt that he has a right to such an insistence. Indeed, it is a Rancièrean aesthetic question to ask what it is that draws listeners to Monk's music when it seems to reconfigure so many consensual notions about beauty or technical proficiency; when it seems to cut against so much of what we say we like or value about good music-making – Monk's engagement with this latter concern was patently to dismiss it.[42] Likewise his halting, unpredictable rhythmic approach, with its long pauses and abrupt self-interruptions, which prefigure what Robin James describes as a 'corporeal disagreement' that 'interrupts [a] body's habitual distributions of sensibility'.[43] The lingering silences of 'I Should Care' are unpredictable and somewhat awkward; we can practically hear Monk thinking about what he is going to play next, which Amiri Baraka once described as 'looking for a chord to shake somebody . . . up'.[44] This is the apotheosis of improvised music's most important conceit: that the act of creation is done right out in the open, and therefore is an essentially *social* practice. We, as listeners, participate in the constitution of the way the affective space opens on to an immanent range of possible futures; in this sense, Monk's prolonged pauses draw our attention to the opening-on-to-future that affect's temporal modality animates, and very often in Monk's performances our expectations are thoroughly shaken up by whatever it is that comes next. That this is problematised by the fact that we are engaging a recording and can return to any given future opening again and again does not change the impropriety of any given performative utterance; if anything, its repetition (in Attali's sense) continually reaffirms the shock of the original iteration in that it never becomes normalised or naturalised: Monk's dissensual gesture remains fully in the realm of the production of the aesthetic.

And we can go on. Monk's harmonic conception similarly dislocates the original song, introducing striking dissonances that cut against the consensus of what is harmonically allowable within the police count of jazz syntax. All of these themes are irreducibly connected, of course – jarring dissonances interrupting pregnant pauses articulating the boundaries of rhythmically disjointed melodic utterances and always slightly orthogonal harmonic realisations. Monk's improvisational approach dissembles pretty much all contemporaneous consensus – it is crucial to know that Monk is considered a central figure in the advent of bebop in the late 1940s, but that his music does almost none of things that dominant narratives claim to be fundamental to the genre.[45]

There is no overt line in Monk's performance to a politics outside of music – what is political are the *musical formations themselves*, in the dis-identificatory process of their being performed. Part of the mythology around Monk is that he had astonishing technique from a conventional perspective, and chose to play the way he did.[46] Whether Monk's music formations are prophetic of social formations to come (as Attali would suggest) or expressive of Rancièrean political reconfigurations does not seem to be Monk's point, and we should probably resist making it ours. Rather, Monk's expressive enactment of the redistribution of multiple strata of sensoria (timbral, microrhythmic, harmonic, etc.) amounts to an aesthetic act precisely through his insistence that this is a viable way to play the piano, to interpret a popular song, to 'voice' chords. Following Rancière, we might describe this last characterisation as transforming the noise of chromatic pitch clusters into the meaningful utterances of semantic chords, thereby insisting that those previously 'noisy' sounds have voices that carry meaning.[47] I do, however, wish to draw lines between these specifically musical phenomena and a micropolitics of musical contexts, to which I will now turn.

A politics of jazz improvisation can be expressed in three ways, which map loosely on to the three quotes cited above, from John Szwed, Fred Ho and Abdullah Ibrahim respectively. The first is the fluid internal politics that emerges from the shifting and ever-proliferating roles of the participants involved, including their affective capacities, the temporal unfoldings of their collective musical utterances and the ways those utterances impinge affectively on one another. This account of ensemble interaction is a relational politics in Rancière's terms, in the sense that the way it unfolds in any given instance is constrained by interwoven nexuses of police logics, but at the same time the equality that precedes these distributions is expressible through any number of potential political/aesthetic instantiations. Another way to say this is that a collective improvisational space is a formulation within which the forces that determine the character of a particular action are selected by that action according to their appropriateness. (To suggest that the action selects its character is a strategic affective turn; one implication is that more-than-human agents are equal participants in the constitution of the musical context.)[48] The truly radical, consensus-shaking act is to decouple those forces and replace them with others. Important questions thus emerge: what other kinds of relationalities – roles, lines, linkages, gestures, affect attunements – can be imagined? What kinds of actions can be invented to enact them?

Second is the utopian claim of improvised music, or rather, the utopian ideals that improvised music has occasionally been pressed to fulfil. Attali expressed disappointment over improvised music's failure to actually foment social change.[49] I suggest – and by doing so support and extend Attali's position – that the compositional stage is best expressed by collective improvisation, and that the collective forms put forth by artists such as Sun Ra and the Art Ensemble of Chicago were intended as and remain *conduits* to radical thinking; expressions of possibilities of redistributions, repartitions and repartakings; lessons, parables and aphorisms.[50]

The third modality involves the overt use of improvised music as didactic practice or to foment social awareness or change. Fred Ho considers jazz's actual musical structures to *be* a form of revolutionary action.[51] While acknowledging admiration for, and the influence of, Sun Ra, Ho nonetheless criticises the latter for working within abstract discursive frames rather than direct activist movement. Ho, a self-identified radical Marxist (Maoist/Leninist), aligns more with an artist/activist such as Cal Massey:

> Since [Cal Massey's] death, there's a real gap concerning all aspects of music reflecting social, political things ... Sun Ra gets rather deep, talking about space, putting things on a different plane ... But Cal made direct statements ... Cal dealt with what was happening at that minute from his perspective. Sun Ra is looking at the whole thing, Cal was talking about that day.[52]

In Rancièrean terms, Massey's (and Ho's and Monk's) actions expressed an aesthetic plane largely because of their quotidian everyday-ness.[53]

In what ways, then, are the distributions of the sensible interrupted? If there are sedimented or institutionalised or reified codes of 'proper behaviour' for jazz practice, it is precisely because the sensoria of jazz as a minoritarian language have themselves been partitioned and distributed according to the actions of a police logic, actions that inscribe correct ways of 'doing' jazz improvisation and that foreclose the possibility of a void or supplemental count. A politics that emerges on this ground must 'disturb this arrangement by supplementing it with a part of the no-part identified with the community as a whole'.[54] A Rancièrean politics would do this by redistributing the sensible, by *taking over the distribution of communal 'musical' sensoria* – it would, as Katherine Wolfe puts it, 'not replace the partitions of the sensible, but ... erupt within them'[55] – hence the way I am framing Monk's music.

Stripped to the marrow of being

> My favourite things are playing again and again
> but it's by Julie Andrews and not by John Coltrane[56]

Allow me briefly to stage a personal scene. John Coltrane's 1960 studio version of Rogers and Hammerstein's 'My Favorite Things' is an iconic recording in the jazz community and a crucial conduit between the American Popular Songbook and the extended modal expressions through which Coltrane was enacting the transformations that would soon take him into the last, radically exploratory period of his life. How surprised was my 16-year-old self, then, to have my first experience of Coltrane's distended interpretation of this famous song from the 1966 live recording released as *Live at the Village Vanguard Again!*, featuring tenor saxophonist Pharoah Sanders, pianist Alice Coltrane, and Jimmy Garrison and Rashied Ali on bass and drums respectively. After a lengthy bass introduction an ostinato begins, and Coltrane enters on soprano saxophone, eschewing the song's melody for several minutes (relying on the audience's insider knowledge?), developing and layering intricate melodic ideas in conjunctive dialogue with drums, piano and bass. A remarkable, intense, beautiful moment in progressive jazz, and a landmark event in my own inchoate progression towards being a jazz musician.

Then Pharoah Sanders enters. Concepts of pitch, melody and rhythm are sublated into gesture and intensity. The sound of the saxophone is utterly transformed – into what? A cry, a scream, the expression of *phōnē*, unfettered from the constraint of *logos*. My 16-year-old self did not know what to make of Sanders's approach to the instrument. Neither did contemporaneous critics; hence a comparison to 'elephant shrieks, which went on and on and on [and] appeared to have little in common with music'.[57] More recent assessments have done little to temper these dehumanising barbs: 'passionate, almost feral style of playing', 'avant-squawks'.[58] This line of critical response to Sanders's improvisational language has been the very embodiment of the *partage* that refuses to hear an utterance as *logos*, thereby denying its utterer human status. Contrast this with Nat Hentoff's liner notes for *Live at the Village Vanguard Again!*: 'What we're hearing – if we allow ourselves to hear – is a man trying to strip himself to the marrow of being.' Hentoff goes on to quote John Coltrane: 'Pharoah is a man of large spiritual reservoir. He's always trying to reach out to truth. He's trying to allow his spiritual self to be his guide. He's dealing, among other things, in energy, in integrity, in essences.'[59] In affect, in a word. This is what my 16-year-old self was hearing, although I had no such words to describe it (but *had* read Hentoff's album notes): not animal, not less than human, not outside of expression and certainly not not-music. I first heard Albert Ayler right around this same time, who was more recently described in similar terms:

> Ayler's music was a barbaric yawp, a sound beyond the self, a resonance of tradition and memory. Breathy and ululating ... equal parts holy shout and Ben Webster flutter, submitting to and subjugating

simple folkish lines – like melodies from some other culture's pageantry – suspended in a wondrous oscillating group sound ... Ayler ... once said 'Trane [John Coltrane] was the Father ... Pharoah was the Son ... I am the Holy Ghost'. Despite the shock and rugged fervor of the soft-spoken man's sound, Ayler believed that he 'soared with the spirits' because his music was contributing to a larger propagation of truth that would lead humanity to a new age.[60]

Sanders, Ayler and other early exemplars of what has sometimes been called 'energy music'[61] remain firmly outside the count of contemporary jazz's distribution of what is utterable and hearable. To adopt Sanders's mode of engagement with a jazz standard like 'My Favorite Things' at a jam session would be to be booted off the stage and not invited back. Or at least to invite jazz's foundational police question: *have you paid your dues?* Meaning, *maybe* you can get away with that kind of expression *after* you've demonstrated that you can work fluently within the syntactic structures decreed by the jazz police. This leads to a remarkable paradox. Pharoah Sanders, the man, is in the canon – not least because of his association with John Coltrane. But his musical language is 1) utterly misunderstood in the sense that little scrutiny has been given to its internal structurings, to the precise ways that Sanders crafts the long arc of an improvisatory 'story', and 2) unacceptable, according to jazz's counts, as an exemplar that one might copy when developing one's own sound and approach.

Whereas Monk's aesthetic–political procedure is to continually introduce elements of noise into established codes, dislocating them by pushing, with varying degrees of firmness, against their sonorous, rhythmic and semantic boundaries, Sanders's dissensual mode is to reclaim the expressive potential of pure *phōnē*, to resist the idea that only through the syntactic–semantic structures of *logos* can communication and expression occur. My last scene turns to the status of improvisatory newness; what it means both to improvise and to announce a new way of doing so.

Blue

The principle regulating the external delimitation of a well-founded domain of imitations is thus at the same time a normative principle of inclusion. It develops into forms of normativity that define the conditions according to which imitations can be recognised as exclusively belonging to an art and assessed, within this framework, as good or bad, adequate or inadequate, partitions between the representable and the unrepresentable; the distinction between genres according to what is represented; principles for adapting forms of expression to genres and thus to the subject matter represented; the distribution of resemblances according to principles of verisimilitude, appropriateness, or correspondence; criteria for distinguishing between and comparing the arts; etc.[62]

Many forces impose forms of consensus on jazz, including what we might call the 'gig economy' and the 'gotta be busy' police counts. The first of these involves a double movement between 1) the challenging economic conditions of being (especially) an early-career jazz musician, playing shows for a percentage of the door, with an expectation of bringing one's own audience, which 2) stretches that audience's ability to continue to attend and support the more success (in terms of procuring more door gigs) one achieves. The 'gotta be busy' police count says that one must be working all the time, that free time equates to some sort of pseudo-Calvinist moral failing. A corollary, however, is that there are right and wrong ways to be busy – right and wrong kinds of gigs that allow one to raise one's status in and according to the police logic of the community. But those wrong kinds of gigs – the weddings and corporate Christmas parties – tend to be the very gigs that pay the bills and subsidise the door gigs. Furthermore, wrong gigs beget wrong gigs, leading to a centripetal spiral from which many musicians find it impossible to escape. A third count underlies both of these, which stems from the market conditions in which jazz musicians, like all artists, live and work – between art and mass culture, creativity and conformity, search and survival. Rancière lays out the issue perfectly, speaking not of jazz but about visual art's parallel relationship with the marketplace:

> For artists as for everyone else, there's the problem of knowing where to plant one's feet, of knowing what one is doing in ... a particular system of exchange. One must find ways to create other places, or other uses for places. But one must extricate this project from the dramatic alternatives expressed in questions like, How do we escape the market, subvert it, etc.? If anyone knows how to overthrow capitalism, why don't they just start doing it? But critics of the market are content to rest their own authority on the endless demonstration that

everyone else is naïve or a profiteer; in short, they capitalise on the declaration of our powerlessness.[63]

That partaker of the wrong kind of gigs is not only failing from an artistic perspective (according to the 'gotta be busy' police), but is a profiteer. And in the very same breath that the profiteer is denounced as a political failure, the aesthetic-oriented jazzer announces their powerlessness, decrying the unfair conditions of the marketplace where creativity for its own sake is seldom rewarded financially.[64]

The most relevant counts for this essay, however, orbit around the conditions of the inutterability of a liberatory politics for jazz that is internally self-policed by the very community within which potentially liberatory expressions can and ought to be made. This manifests as boundaries of inclusion or exclusion ('that's not jazz' or 'that's not the kind of jazz that's *in* now'), the extension of these boundaries into various kinds of music-syntactic foreclosures that emphasise notation and inscribability (thereby privileging, again, certain types of structures – the 'easily notatable', with concomitant right and wrong ways of doing so), valorisations of certain kinds of technical precision (and suspicion about any kind of dissensus that disturbs their count – Thelonious Monk again stands out as a remarkable but historically complex exception), the ubiquitous trope of 'paying your dues' (and tightly prescribed ways of doing so), 'right' ways to negotiate chord progressions, the complex etiquette of the jam session (which expresses most of these issues), and right and wrong ways of attending to jazz's history (which also involves the erasure of aspects of that history by those who have been (self-?) charged with telling it). A case study that touches on many of these points is the 2014 record *Blue* by the jazz sextet Mostly Other People Do the Killing (MOPDtK). The band's name is a sardonic reference to the shockingly metaphorically violent language used within the jazz community: a particularly satisfying solo is often described as *killin'*, and an ensemble might be said to have *killed it* after a dynamic set. Even a recent jazz theory textbook recounted a story of an older jazz musician admonishing a younger colleague by suggesting 'you're killin' and killin' and ain't nobody dyin'': a rather disturbing pedagogical moment.[65]

Blue is a highly unusual record: a note-for-note, nuance-for-nuance recreation of Miles Davis's iconic 1959 recording *Kind of Blue*, certainly one of the best-known and best-regarded recordings in the history of jazz.[66] As leader and bassist Moppa Elliott describes, MOPDtK worked for three years to capture every gesture, every timbral nuance, every microrhythmic inflection. Tracy McMullen notes the irony of this intensive labour, since Davis's original recording was famously accomplished with very little preparation, in spite of the various ways that it broke with the conventional practice of its time.[67]

When it was released, *Blue* sounded many of the most predictable alarmist calls within the jazz community: 'Is this jazz?', 'Have these guys *paid their dues*?'[68] Are MOPDtK serious, treating the original recording with the white gloves of a museum curator? Or are they having a go at the scene? Of particular interest here might be a real or implicit response to Jazz at Lincoln Center's Essentially Ellington programme, in which high school bands from across the United States and Canada compete to demonstrate that they can reproduce the sound and spirit of a Duke Ellington Orchestra recording (an ensemble famous for the radically idiosyncratic playing styles of its members) more accurately than the next band. Such is the paradoxical state of jazz education today . . .[69]

While MOPDtK's stance is indebted to Baudrillard and Borges – they explicitly reference the latter's 'Pierre Menard' in their liner notes – we might also read it as a response to Adorno's famous critique of jazz, which has been maligned (unfairly, as Gary Peters has demonstrated)[70] by the improvising music community, which insists that Adorno is utterly disconnected from the reality of what jazz is claimed to be trying to do.[71] But if, as Adorno suggests, improvisation really is a kind of pseudo-improvisation, then MOPDtK's ironic repetition radically amplifies the degree to which nominally spontaneous improvisatory acts actually rehearse gestures that have been learned and internalised through an individual participant's repetition and careful practice. That the original *Kind of Blue* marked an aesthetic moment that broke with the police logic's determination of correct ways of 'doing jazz improvisation' (for example, by largely eschewing goal-oriented chord sequences), thereby mitigating the degree to which the performers could rely on rehearsed gestures and 'pseudo-improvisation', only further reinforces *Blue*'s ironic relationship with jazz's distributions and configurations.

The degree to which *Kind of Blue* broke with established norms, refiguring what was by 1959 well on its way to becoming the sedimentation of a consensus of performance practice within the jazz community, is one of the foundational stories in the history of jazz as it is repeatedly told. It is important to recognise the degree to which that consensus was constructed *by* the community. This is one reason jazz serves as such fecund ground for working through Rancière's thoughts on aesthetics and politics: there is no police count imposed by an identifiable *them* mandating this or that way of doing jazz, but there are distributions of the hearable and sayable – ways of hearing, ways of creating – that, as they become reified, draw increasingly firm borders around what is included in the count. In this telling, *Kind of Blue* (the original Davis recording) marks a perfect dissensus moment, for all of the reasons that musicians have celebrated: ushering in a focus on sustained 'modal' spaces rather than rapidly changing, complex harmonies; shifting from an emphasis on virtuosity and soloist/accompaniment to a more egalitarian approach to interaction; adopting a gentler 'cool' texture rather than the fiery histrionics of early styles. From this perspective, too, *Blue* (the MOPDtK simulacrum) might at first blush be read as an example of what Federico Reuben calls 'imaginary musical radicalism', in that it could be 'characterised by a lack of creativity in proposing new ways of distributing sensible forms and practices that can produce radical change' by simply (and egregiously) reproducing the structures, processes and literal sounds of the original, radical act.[72] But that would miss the critical nature of the 2014 recording. From the perspective of MOPDtK, it is the legions of contemporary jazz musicians, in their uncritical valorisation of the police distributions of jazz's sensible, that represent Reuben's imaginary radicalism, echoing guitarist Derek Bailey's scathing indictment: 'The mechanics of the style are everywhere; of the restlessness, the adventurousness, the thirst for change which was a central characteristic of the jazz of that period there seems to be no sign at all.'[73] *Blue* exaggerates what its creators see as *the* fundamental problem of mainstream contemporary jazz, its failure to do the very thing that it needs to do to matter politically, which is to shake things up, to redistribute sensoria, to introduce noise that disturbs dominant codes, to liberate music from its police counts.

But of course, the very narrative that locates *Kind of Blue* as a radical epistemic rupture is grossly simplistic – it is exactly the unidimensional historicist account that Rancière warns us against. It ignores the proliferation of minoritarian usages of jazz syntax, it constructs any number of false binaries (*we did* that; *now we're doing* this) and faulty ontologies (*there's a circumscribable thing called 'modal jazz'*). As Ethan Iverson states,

> Everyone knows the form of 'So What' is on two scales, D dorian and E-flat dorian. However: Miles Davis, John Coltrane, Cannonball Adderley, and Bill Evans ... do four different things with those two scales. Miles plays abstract songful melodies. Coltrane fills in every corner with a primeval roar. Cannonball deals out some blues. Bill dances like a swinging Ravel.[74]

Each contributor brings his own genealogy, his own mode of affect attunement, to the constitution of the improper place of *Kind of Blue*'s creative enunciation. The conventional story about *Kind of Blue*'s radicality, as an epistemic rupture, *miscounts*, in a word: *Kind of Blue* is much more appropriately read in Rancière's dissensual terms, as the enunciatory redistribution of the sensible, working from within and refiguring what is possible in jazz's own terms. *Blue*, from the perspective of the post-*Kind of Blue* culture machine, makes this point manifest by calling into question jazz's reifying actions, by forcing us to think carefully about long-held assumptions about right and wrong ways to do jazz, including right and wrong ways to break into new expressive spaces.

Because the jazz community is such a radically self-policing body, and because of its interlocking narratives of attending to one's roots, paying one's dues, knowing one's role and understanding where the boundaries are between 'correct' and other-than-correct, talking about music and talking about pedagogy are not far removed from one another. Nor is talking about politics. Perhaps it is through talking – through problematising the distinction between speech and noise – that we can begin to draw clearer lines between how dissensus can erupt within musical structures, how the enactment of a new police count can be avoided and how these can, following Attali, foreshadow new social structures outside of music.

Rancière writes that 'the world is divided between those who can and those who cannot afford the luxury of playing with words and images. Subversion begins when this division is contested ...'[75] Rancière describes a kind of interplay between fact and fiction that foregrounds a double division: between who can or cannot afford to be creative with words and concepts, and between the speaker and the hearer (or the artist and the spectator):

This very constructed, at times playful, relationship to ... history addresses a spectator whose interpretive and emotional capacity is not only acknowledged but called upon. In other words, the work is constructed in such a way that it is up to the spectator to interpret it and to react to it affectively.[76]

This comes to the forefront in many aspects of musician/poet/activist Sun Ra's public persona. When Sun Ra says to an audience 'I come from somewhere far away, and I have many names. Some call me Mr. Ra. Some call me Mr. Re. You may call me Mr. Mystery'; or, elsewhere, 'But history is his story. It's not my story – my story is mystery'; or when he calls for a vision of black identity-formation and liberation through attention to ancient Egyptian history and interstellar travel respectively – the listener is charged with making sense of Sun Ra's words and thinking through possible relations between his verbal expressions and the music that follows.[77] Sun Ra was a creative lexicologist, inventing connections between words and meanings based on loosely homonymous relations, rhymes and puns – deterritorialising meanings and reterritorialising them as new constellations of relationships. Likewise with musical structures: Sun Ra's music earned some of its radicality from its very closeness to mainstream jazz's expressive structures. I see no reason not to think of a frenetic, multilayered riff on a Fletcher Henderson tune as a complex pun or series of analogising gestures that signify (in Henry Louis Gates's sense) on the original, or as a deterritorialisation that expresses the original's rhizomatic potential, virtual until its actualisation in performance or imagination.

Or, following Rancière, a series of actions that problematise the hierarchy of the police count, opening up spaces where an equality, there latently in and around the original, can be expressed. While the police count 'structures perceptual space in terms of places, functions, aptitudes, etc., to the exclusion of any supplement', politics consists *solely* in 'the set of acts that effectuate a supplementary property ... the equality of speaking beings'.[78] Politics, therefore, involves a reconfiguration (redistribution) over and above the existing structures – that 'refigure the common of a "given world"'. Subjects here, which emerge through their positions, actions and capacities for enunciations, 'do not affirm another type of life but configure a different world-in-common'. Like Sun Ra's future instantiated by refabulating the past, the new age that Sanders announces through his performative claim to the expressive potential of *phōnē* is not a utopian otherworld but a reconfiguration of the possibilities of this world. This is jazz improvisation's (im)proper emancipatory claim, and as Monk, Sanders and MOPDtK demonstrate in widely divergent ways, it begins immanently, by revealing and refiguring its own counts.

Notes

1. Jacques Rancière, *Disagreement: Politics and Society*, trans. Julie Rose (Minneapolis: University of Minnesota Press, 2009), 16.
2. Friedrich Nietzsche, *Twilight of the Idols, or How To Philosophise With a Hammer*, in *The Portable Nietzsche*, trans. Walter Kaufmann (New York: Penguin, 1968), 519–20.
3. Nina Simone, in the documentary film *What Happened, Miss Simone?* (Netflix, 2015).
4. Davide Panagia, *Rancière's Sentiments* (Durham, NC: Duke University Press, 2018), 3.
5. For example, in *Disagreement*, Rancière insists that 'politics, in its specificity, is rare. It is always local and occasional' (139). He refines this statement some years later: 'Today I would revisit these formulations about political rarity ... By that I wanted to say that the political does not always exist ... From my point of view, the political is present in all forms of struggle, action and intervention that reassert decision making over public affairs as anyone's concern, and as the expression of anyone's equal capacity. Of course, these days, the so-called political scene is occupied by a machine to suppress the political.' Jacques Rancière, *Moments Politiques: Interventions 1977–2009*, trans. Mary Foster (New York and Oakland: Seven Stories Press, 2014), 157–8. This statement comes from a 2008 interview. Ioana Pribiag compares Rancière's position in *Disagreement* with that found in Homi Bhabha's contemporaneous work, and notes that, for the latter, 'political becoming is not a rare or ephemeral event, but rather an ongoing process of negotiation occurring in everyday life'. Ioana Pribiag, 'Politics and Its Others: Jacques Rancière's Figures of Alterity', *Philosophy Today* 63.3 (2019), 453.
6. Rancière, *Disagreement*, 35.
7. Luciano Berio, 'Meditations on a Twelve-Tone Horse', *Christian Science Monitor*, 15 July 1968.
8. Panagia, *Rancière's Sentiments*, 10.
9. Brian Massumi, *Parables for the Virtual: Movement, Affect,*

Sensation (Durham, NC: Duke University Press, 2002), 36. See also p. 27.
10. Henri Bergson, *Matter and Memory*, trans. Nancy M. Paul and W. Scott Palmer (New York: Zone Books, 1988), 37; Gilles Deleuze, *Difference and Repetition*, trans. Paul Patton (New York: Columbia University Press, 1994), 119–20.
11. Panagia, *Rancière's Sentiments*, 11.
12. Panagia, *Rancière's Sentiments*, 31.
13. Both Spinoza and Nietzsche account for the impingements of constraining forces on a body's capacity to affect and be affected: for Spinoza, this is the negative affect that forecloses 'joy' (increases in a body's capacity to act); for Nietzsche, it is the *ressentiment* that is paired differentially against the will to power. See Baruch Spinoza, *Ethics*, trans. Edwin Curley (Harmondsworth: Penguin, 1996), 70, and Friedrich Nietzsche, *The Will to Power*, trans. Walter Kaufmann and R. J. Hollindale (New York: Vintage, 1968), 104.
14. Rancière, *Disagreement*, 22–6; Jacques Rancière, 'Ten Theses on Politics', trans. Rachel Bowlby and Davide Panagia, *Theory & Event* 5.3 (2001), ¶23. See also Samuel Chambers, *The Lessons of Rancière* (Oxford: Oxford University Press, 2013), 96–7, as well as the Introduction to this volume.
15. Chambers, *Lessons of Rancière*, 58.
16. Davide Panagia borrows the term 'affective pragmatics' from Brian Massumi: see *Rancière's Sentiments*, 107 n. 3, and Brian Massumi, *Politics of Affect* (Hoboken, NJ: John Wiley, 2015). Panagia's invocation of Rancière's aesthetic sensorium as affective was instrumental in my drawing together of these themes in the way I am doing in this essay.
17. I make this case in Stover, 'Jazz Theory's Pragmatics', in Rachel Lumsden and Jeremy Swinkin (eds), *The Norton Guide to Teaching Music Theory* (New York: Norton, 2017), 234–51, in which I also take care to mitigate what might seem like an overly stark binary that misrepresents both terms.
18. The status of the identity of a musical 'work' remains an open question; see, for example, Lydia Goehr, *The Imaginary Museum of Musical Works: An Essay in the Philosophy of Music*, rev. edn (Oxford: Oxford University Press, 2007), and Chris Stover, 'Time, Territorialization, and Improvisational Spaces', *Music Theory Online* 23.1 (2017), <http://mtosmt.org/issues/mto.17.23.1/mto.17.23.1.stover.html> (last accessed 22 November 2019).
19. Examples of these three modes of dissemination include,

respectively, 1) George Russell's *Lydian Chromatic Concept* (1953) (Brookline, MA: Concept Publishing Company, 2001), Anthony Braxton's *Composition Notes* (Hanover: Frog Peak Music, 1988) and Leo Smith's *notes (8 pieces)* (1973) (Corbett vs. Dempsey and the Renaissance Society, 2015); 2) Steve Coleman's 'Symmetrical Movement Concept', <www.m-base.com>, and Miles Okazaki's 'Four Pulse Study', <www.milesokazaki.com> (both last accessed 23 October 2019); and 3) John Coltrane's *Giant Steps* (1960) (Atlantic/Warner CD 8122736102, 2002) and *Interstellar Space* (1974) (Impulse CD 5434152, 2000) and Braxton's *For Alto* (1969) (Delmark DE 420, 2000). A similar line of inquiry has seen jazz musicians engaging with what I would call minoritarian music theories: those that fall outside the traditional music theory lineage as taught and learned in, for example, university and conservatory settings; for instance, John Coltrane valorising Nicolas Slonimsky's *Thesaurus of Scales and Melodic Patterns* (New York: Schirmer, 1975), or Jacob Collier introducing a generation of jazz musicians to Ernst Levy's mystical/metaphysical conception of harmony, *A Theory of Harmony* (Albany: State University of New York Press, 1985).

20. Important early accounts of the relationship between progressive jazz and Black American activism include Philippe Carles and Jean-Louis Comolli, *Free Jazz/Black Power* (1971), trans. Grégory Pierrot (Jackson, MS: University of Mississippi Press, 2016); LeRoi Jones (Amiri Baraka), *Black Music* (1968) (New York: Akashi Classics, 2010); Frank Kofsky, *Black Nationalism and the Revolution in Music* (New York: Pathfinder, 1970); and Val Wilmer, *As Serious as Your Life: Black Music and the Free Jazz Revolution, 1957–1977* (1977) (London: Serpent's Tail, 2018). A more recent source that focuses specifically on late 1940s bebop is Eric Lott, 'Double V, Double-Time: Bebop's Politics of Style', in Krin Gabbard (ed.), *Jazz Among the Discourses* (Durham, NC: Duke University Press, 1995), 243–56.
21. John Szwed, 'Josef Skvorecky and the Tradition of Jazz Literature', *World Literature Today* 54.4 (1980), 588.
22. Fred Ho, 'What Makes "Jazz" the Revolutionary Music of the Twentieth Century, and Will it be Revolutionary for the Twenty-first Century?', in *Wicked Theory, Naked Practice: A Fred Ho Reader*, ed. Diane C. Fujino (Minneapolis: University of Minnesota Press, 2009), 95.
23. Abdullah Ibrahim, in Maya Jaggi, 'The Sound of Freedom', *The Guardian*, 7 December 2001.

24. Jacques Rancière, *Aisthesis: Scenes from the Aesthetic Regime of Art*, trans. Zakir Paul (London: Verso, 2013), 142. Rancière goes on to describe the virtues of 'decorative art' as a 'vital double function: habitation and expression', which I will elaborate below as the doubled status of jazz as artistic expression *and* as the pragmatic fulfilment of an entertainment function.
25. Jacques Rancière, *Dissensus: On Politics and Aesthetics*, trans. Steven Corcoran (London: Bloomsbury, 2010), 219.
26. Rancière, *Dissensus*, 219.
27. Jacques Attali, *Noise: The Political Economy of Music*, trans. Brian Massumi (Minneapolis: University of Minnesota Press, 1985), 23.
28. Attali, *Noise*, 24.
29. Attali, *Noise*, 29.
30. One polemical takeaway from this is that, contrary to how it is often characterised (by 'New Musicology' for example), music theory's practices are actually profoundly engaged with the social, cultural and political contexts in which music occurs.
31. Attali, *Noise*, 32.
32. From this perspective, the early stirrings of opera that Susan McClary describes in her Afterword to the English translation of *Noise* could be fruitfully characterised as a series of aesthetic eruptions that shook up and ultimately reconfigured the representational logic of their time. See McClary, 'Afterword: The Politics of Silence and Sound', in Attali, *Noise*, 154–6.
33. Attali, *Noise*, 32.
34. Attali, *Noise*, 33.
35. Attali, *Noise*, 33.
36. Attali, *Noise*, 34.
37. Eric Drott, 'Rereading Jacques Attali's *Bruits*', *Critical Inquiry* 41 (2015), 741.
38. On Thelonious Monk, *Thelonious Himself* (1957) (Original Jazz Classics OJC20 2542, 2001). A recording is readily available through all of the usual digital sources.
39. Evan Ziporyn and Michael Tenzer, 'Thelonious Monk's Harmony, Rhythm, and Pianism', in Michael Tenzer and John Roeder (eds), *Analytical and Cross-Cultural Studies in World Music* (Oxford: Oxford University Press, 2011), 147–86.
40. See, for example, Gilles Deleuze, *Expressionism in Philosophy: Spinoza*, trans. Martin Joughin (New York: Zone Books, 1990), 226.
41. See Chris Stover, 'The Improvisational Moment', <www.chrisstover

music.com/improvisational-moment> (last accessed 22 November 2019), for more on jazz tunes as 'bodies'.
42. See Benjamin Givan, 'Thelonious Monk's Pianism', *Journal of Musicology* 26.3 (2009), 404–42, for more on Monk's technique and its reception history. See especially p. 441 for examples of Monk defending his playing against characterisations of its being 'weird' or 'wrong'.
43. Robin James, '"These.Are.The Breaks": Rethinking *Disagreement* Through Hip Hop', *Transformations: Journal of Media & Culture* 19 (2011), 1, <http://www.transformationsjournal.org/wp-content/uploads/2017/01/James_Trans19.pdf> (last accessed 22 November 2019).
44. Jones, *Black Music*, 40.
45. Cf. this partial list of characteristics from jazz pedagogue David Baker: 'longer melodic phrases', 'a sound instrumental technique', 'chords [that serve] as the improvisation referential rather than melody', 'fast, intense, impassioned' improvisation, 'clean [melodic] execution' and more. David Baker, 'Bebop Characteristics' (2000), 37, <https://www.jazzbooks.com/mm5/download/FQBK-handbook.pdf> (last accessed 22 November 2019). Monk's music eschews all of these tendencies. See also Ziporyn and Tenzer's similar claim about bebop: 'groove, swing, speed, heat, cool, polyrhythm, conversational interaction among players ... antiphonal call and response, and more ... all but absent in ['I Should Care']' ('Thelonious Monk's Harmony', 164).
46. See Givan, 'Thelonious Monk's Pianism', 408–14. The flip side of this story is a faction of advocates who 'concede [Monk's] technical shortcomings but ... dismiss them as inconsequential' (414).
47. I am extending a small pun here, since jazz musicians refer to the way the notes of a chord are distributed when played as a 'voicing' of that chord.
48. I draw up on Erin Manning and Jane Bennett's work for this formulation. See Manning, *The Minor Gesture* (Durham, NC: Duke University Press, 2016), and Bennett, *Vibrant Matter: A Political Ecology of Things* (Durham, NC: Duke University Press, 2010).
49. Attali, *Noise*, 140.
50. For example, Attali suggests that 'free jazz, a meeting of black popular music and the more abstract theoretical explorations of European music, eliminated the distinction between popular music and learned music, broke down the repetitive hierarchy' (*Noise*, 139). See also Eugene Holland, 'Studies in Applied Nomadology: Jazz

Improvisation and Post-Capitalist Markets', in Ian Buchanan and Marcel Swiboda (eds), *Deleuze and Music* (Edinburgh: Edinburgh University Press, 2004), 29–30. I am interested in extending Attali's thoughts into the actual musical structures and processes themselves.
51. 'Now the musical components are also revolutionary. It changes everything we understand about music. Our understanding of time, strong beats 1 and 3 become weak beats, weak beats 2 and 4 become strong beats. That's a paradigmatic shift where the weak becomes the strong.' Fred Ho and Nora Ritchie, 'Fred Ho: Music as a Revolutionary Force?', <http://www.revive-music.com/2011/01/21/fred-ho-music-as-a-revolutionary-force/> (last accessed 16 May 2019). Amiri Baraka, Frank Kofsky and others have made similar arguments about the radical musical expressions of John Coltrane, Archie Shepp and others.
52. Ho is citing musician and activist Charles Stephens, from 'an interview [Ho] did with him the late 1980s'; 'The Damned Don't Cry', in *Wicked Theory, Naked Practice*, 147.
53. One of Massey's best-known compositions, 'Quiet Dawn', appears on Archie Shepp's 1972 record *Attica Blues*, and features Massey's then 7-year-old daughter Waheeda on vocals. Waheeda Massey's spirited but untrained singing lends a populist spin to the recording, which we might describe as an expression, if not of *the people*, then at least of 'a people to come'. I should also mention that I do not entirely agree with Stephens's/Ho's characterisation of Sun Ra as being somehow outside the activity of everyday activism. I discuss this in a forthcoming essay.
54. Rancière, *Dissensus*, 36.
55. Katherine Wolfe, 'From Aesthetics to Politics: Rancière, Kant and Deleuze', *Contemporary Aesthetics* 4 (2006), <https://digitalcommons.risd.edu/liberalarts_contempaesthetics/vol4/iss1/12/> (last accessed 22 November 2019).
56. Elvis Costello, 'This is Hell', from *Brutal Youth* (Warner Brothers CD 9362-45535-2, 1994).
57. Whitney Balliet, 'Newport 1966', in Whitney Balliet, *Collected Works: A Journal of Jazz 1954–2001* (New York: St. Martins Griffin, 2002), 272.
58. Imran Khan, 'Meditations in Sound: The Jazz Africana of Pharoah Sanders', *PopMatters*, 22 June 2015 <https://www.popmatters.com/194180-meditations-in-sound-the-jazz-africana-of-pharoah-sanders-2495522581.html> (last accessed 22 November 2019); Will Schube, 'The Cosmos is Still Catching Up to Pharoah Sanders'

Earliest Recordings', *Noisey*, 14 November 2017, <https://www.vice.com/en_uk/article/59y4xq/pharaoh-sanders-tauhid-impulse-records-essay> (last accessed 22 November 2019).

59. Nat Hentoff, album notes to John Coltrane, *Live at the Village Vanguard Again!* (Impulse! A-9124, 1966). The second citation is from Coltrane, quoted in Hentoff's text.

60. Jason Bivins, *Spirits Rejoice! Jazz and American Religion* (Oxford: Oxford University Press, 2015), 33.

61. See Michael Heller, *Loft Jazz: Improvising New York in the 1970s* (Oakland: University of California Press, 2017), 12, 89–92.

62. Jacques Rancière, *The Politics of Aesthetics: The Distribution of the Sensible*, trans. Gabriel Rockhill (London: Bloomsbury, 2004), 17.

63. Jacques Rancière with Fulvia Carnevale and John Kelsey, 'Art of the Possible', *ArtForum* 45.7 (2007), 263.

64. A seldom noted irony here is that quite a large number of aesthetically oriented jazz and improvising musicians have ended up being rewarded with substantial funding (in terms of grants, university positions, festival headlining appearances, and so on) for sticking steadfastly to the 'art' side of the art/market dichotomy.

65. Unattributed; quoted in David Berkman, *The Jazz Harmony Book* (Petaluma, CA: Sher Music Publications, 2013), 78.

66. While unusual, *Blue* is not unique: for one example, pianist Bill Dobbins has performed note-for-note recreations of entire Ahmad Jamal records as concert recitals, and as Tracy McMullen notes, trumpeter Charles Tolliver recently recreated Thelonious Monk's 1959 Town Hall concert – see McMullen, 'Approaching the Jazz Past: MOPDtK's *Blue* and Jason Moran's "In My Mind: Monk at Town Hall, 1959"', *Journal of Jazz Studies* 11.2 (2016), 13.

67. See Phil Zampino, 'Review: Mostly Other People Do The Killing', 22 September 2014, <http://www.squidco.com/cgi-bin/news/newsView.cgi?newsID=1705> (last accessed 23 October 2019).

68. See McMullen, 'Approaching the Jazz Past', for an engagement with some of *Blue*'s reception history. An egregious misinterpretation of an infamous quote from Moppa Elliott has animated some extraordinarily off-base critiques. Elliott's suggestion that 'standing on the shoulders of giants makes it easier to kick them in the teeth' has led several reviewers to suggest that Elliott was positioning himself as the one doing the kicking, missing the crucial point that he was criticising the pervasive practice in jazz of lionising the great performers of the past by copying and codifying their innovations (through a form of mimicry) into a regime of 'correct' practices. See especially

Keir Neuringer, 'Slinging Mud & Kicking in Teeth: MOPDtK & When Irony Becomes Racism', weblog Keir Neuringer, 20 February 2015, <http://keirneuringer.blogspot.com/2015/02/slinging-mud-kicking-in-teeth-why.html> (last accessed 22 November 2019), for an especially misguided response, which McMullen unfortunately echoes. It is imperative to understand that MOPDtK's ironic position operates along or against aspects of the contemporary jazz community's self-policing rather than being directed towards icons of jazz's history.

69. See Mark Laver, 'Freedom of Choice: Jazz, Neoliberalism, and the Lincoln Center', *Popular Music and Society* 38 (2014), 538–56.
70. Gary Peters, *The Philosophy of Improvisation* (Chicago: University of Chicago Press, 2009), 37.
71. See especially Theodor Adorno, 'On Jazz' (1936), trans. Jamie Owen Daniel, *Discourse* 12.1 (1989–90), 45–69, originally published in *Moments musicaux* (Frankfurt am Main: Suhrkamp, 1964).
72. Federico Reuben, 'Imaginary Musical Radicalism and the Entanglement of Music and Emancipatory Politics', *Contemporary Music Review* 34.2–3 (2015), 239–40.
73. Derek Bailey, *Improvisation: Its Nature and Practice in Music* (New York: Da Capo Press, 1992), 50.
74. Ethan Iverson, 'Received Wisdom (Jeff Goldblum, chord scales, the iReal Book, and Kamasi Washington)', *Do the M@th* (2018), <https://ethaniverson.com/received-wisdom-jeff-goldblum-chord-scales-the-ireal-book-and-kamasi-washington/> (last accessed 16 May 2019).
75. Rancière et al., 'Art of the Possible', 263.
76. Rancière et al., 'Art of the Possible', 263.
77. See Chris Stover, 'Sun Ra's Mystical Time', *The Open Space Magazine* 21 (2018), 106–13.
78. Rancière, *Dissensus*, 92.

Part IV Encounters and Challenges

11

Rancière, Resistance and the Problem of Commemorative Art: Music Displacing Violence Displacing Music
Sarah Collins

'It is a metaphor which has misled and confused you,' said Eduard. 'Here, to be sure, it is only a question of soil and minerals; but man is a true Narcissus: he makes the whole world his mirror.'[1]

This passage is from Goethe's celebrated novella *Elective Affinities* (1809), where it serves the narrative function of signalling the moment when the link between the title and the central theme of the story becomes explicit. In this part of the story, the subject of discussion between a married couple and their male guest is the meaning of the term 'affinity'. The guest explains that the term refers to the phenomenon in chemistry and physics where substances (such as water, oil or quicksilver) tend to 'adhere to themselves', and even if they are forcibly separated they slide back into each other and create a unity as soon as the external force is removed. By contrast, other materials, such as oil and water, refuse to combine even with force applied. The character of Charlotte observes that the same may be said of social circles, such as where members of certain classes and professions tend towards each other but are repelled by members of other groups. There ensues a discussion of the likeness of these chemical and social tendencies, including the fact that substances that repel one another can be brought together with a mediating substance (as with alkaline salt in the case of oil and water), just as laws and customs can bind together socially disparate individuals.[2]

Observing the likeness between chemical and human activity is, of course, not merely a case of mistaken metaphor or the egotistical projection of human personality on to inanimate objects, as the character of Eduard suggests in the quotation above. Rather, it intimates two claims that will become important for our discussion below. The first is that substances not only come together as a partnership, but rather that in coming together they relinquish the differences that make them individual. An example might be when a raindrop joins a puddle, or when later in Goethe's story the characters of Eduard and Ottilie begin to exhibit the same handwriting, the same idiosyncrasies in musical performance and simultaneous thought processes – they come to mirror each other so closely that it seems as if they were a single character.

More broadly still, the same claim has informed critiques of multiculturalism, such that the activity of bringing different groups and values into equal relation creates a veil of consensus that renders political difference impossible, leaving only what Rancière has called a 'homogeneous continuum of indifferent differences'.[3] This problem can also be seen in debates about the political recognition of indigenous groups, between the supposedly divergent agendas of representation on the one hand and sovereignty on the other.

The same paradox has been observed of the status of both contemporary art and the activity of critique – that is, in anxiously attempting to unveil the complicity of forms of resistance in the very forces and ideologies that they work against, art and critique only affirm the disempowerment of difference by consensus. Likewise commemorative artworks (including artworks of mourning and monuments of remembrance) face the difficulty that in lending an aesthetic sheen to their historical subject they risk mirroring the same activity of distancing that was required of the perpetrators of the original act of violence. By bringing the original act forward and joining it with a pacifist message, or one of universal peace, for example, the commemorative artwork makes a consensual manoeuvre that offers political recognition and equal footing to the original act of violence. So the practice of bringing different things on to the same plane sometimes has the effect of joining them together in a way that papers over their incommensurability and negates the political potential of difference to engender new forms of experience and social organisation.

The second claim in Goethe's discussion of 'affinities' in his novella is that attractions and repulsions are not necessarily 'elective' or a matter of choice, and that they can be diverted or strengthened by the presence of a mediating force. In the course of the story the intervening force comes in the form of other characters who provoke a realigning of partnerships, but it could equally signal the possibility, with respect to the broader readings just mentioned, that art might provoke a similar redistribution – the possibility, in other words, of art disrupting consensus and resisting its exclusions.

The two claims may be usefully explored through the idea of mirroring. The opening quotation, in which man 'makes the whole world his mirror', describes a situation where man's understanding of the world is entirely defined by the limits of his self-understanding. This is the proposition that when man observes something different from himself, his egotism allows him only to see his mirror image, and nothing is changed through the process of his encounter. In this context, mirroring is not only a missed opportunity but it can also be a wilful form of myopia. Art and critique attempt to offer the possibility of change or newness against this blindness, but more often they replicate and mirror that which they seek to disrupt. The second claim can therefore refer to the matter of heteronomy, which will be extrapolated here as pertaining to art's capacity for resistance.

There is, of course, a paradoxical character to the idea that difference tends towards sameness, or that resistance eventually lapses into assimilation, but identifying the tendency should not simply be a cynical exercise. Rather it asks us to consider practices of resistance in a different way. Typically, we are inclined to view aesthetic and political practices of resistance in terms of what they push against – for example tradition, progress, the status quo, violence, homogeny, injustice or inequality – leading to an ethical view of art. Under this view, when a project of resistance becomes assimilated, such as when modernist art is commodified for a 'middlebrow' market, when punk subculture goes mainstream, or when revolutionary action receives institutional recognition, it often appears bleakly ironic or concessionary. By contrast, the following discussion will invite us to construe practices of resistance as a dynamic involving strategies that draw different things into relation while also struggling against their tendency to become the same.

The category of commemorative music offers us a 'hard case' that can help us home in on questions that pertain to the condition of music more generally. When music is understood to perform a commemorative function it is called upon to make meaning of actual and specific historical events. At the same time it must evoke something of the unrepresentable quality of those experiences. In addition, it has the tendency to invite ethically inflected aesthetic judgements on the basis of its capacity to appropriately balance these conflicting desiderata. It is the interaction between three registers – the representational, the aesthetic and the ethical – that concerns us when we speak of art's capacity or incapacity for resistance, or its capacity to bring newness into the world. This interaction will concern us primarily in what follows, as it does Rancière in his own work on aesthetics and politics.

In the course of this chapter I will draw from Rancière's work and bring it into contact with selected scholarship on musical commemoration. The first two sections deepen the discussion of the impulse of things that are different to tend towards sameness, with a view to extrapolating the problem of commemorative art and its implications for an increasingly ethical view of music. The remainder of the chapter examines devices that have been used to address this problem in musical commemoration. This discussion begins to recast the problem of art's resistance not in terms of its ironic complicity in that which it resists, but instead in terms of the aesthetic strategies for holding forms of resistance aloof from assimilation.

Equality and mirroring

> [A]n artwork resists a social act only by refusing to mirror that for which the act stands.[4]

The problem of commemorative art may be fruitfully explored through a discussion of mirroring, or the possibility of 'refusing to mirror'. Mirroring describes the risk involved in bringing things that are different into relation on the same plane – the risk that they will become indistinguishable through being made equivalent or equal. This tendency can be the result of a rhetorical manoeuvre of some kind, such as the use of analogy, metaphor, homonymy or comparison. For example, to use a term from fine art such as 'impressionistic' or a term from movement such as 'heavy' or 'swift' to describe music is to posit a resonance between music and the spheres of activity to which these terms usually belong. This process may be useful heuristically (and for other reasons, as we shall see), but it does tend to make the relationship seem natural and inevitable, devaluing their specificity. Equally, analogy involves a process of abstraction, akin to the creation of a symbol, and therefore has a distancing function which may in some circumstances act as a form of concealment.

The commemorative artwork or monument functions in just this way and harbours similar potentials and dangers. On the one hand it holds the potential of the aesthetic to elide explicitly political gestures and fixed conceptual determinations, and on the other it risks being complicit in keeping the realities of violence and social oppression at a polite distance – burying any sense of immediate experience under layers of collective memory and forgetting. Likewise, as music is drawn into relation with other spheres of activity, its aesthetic specificity – its difference or incommensurability – is neutralised, and with it its capacity to resist or present something new, alternative or Other. The same might be said of the practice of comparison, which in its effort to draw things together under an overarching understanding has been associated with the imperialist mindset of Enlightenment cosmopolitanism. As Bruce Robbins summarises,

> Comparison presupposes common norms; common norms, which by definition impose sameness on difference, presuppose a view from outside or above; the view from outside or above presupposes that the viewer is a holder of power. Thus both comparison and cosmopolitanism can be assimilated to capitalist globalization, which is understood to rule by reducing difference to homogeneity.[5]

The activity of bringing two things that are different into some kind of relation on the same plane is premised on the possibility of equivalence or even equality. Rancière has cast literary realism in just this way. He describes literary realism (which he refers to using the more general term 'literature') as a form of writing that brings together two realms of experience that were formerly viewed as being separate – namely poetry and 'prosaic life' – writing that 'this new art of writing makes any subject matter equal to any other'.[6] The basis of the former difference was the Aristotelian idea that poetry, like philosophy, was active in combining concepts, whereas life passively flowed on, as it were, moment by moment.[7] The impulse to equalise art and life against this presupposition was a democratic impulse, according to Rancière. This does not, of course, imply that literature was inherently sympathetic towards democratic values, but that the form of writing was itself only made possible by a particular 'redistribution of the sensible' associated with social changes and shifting modes of perception in the late eighteenth and nineteenth centuries. Yet the bringing together or equalising of art and life prompted other problematic types of indistinction.

In his celebrated article 'Why Emma Bovary Had to be Killed' (2008), Rancière read the work of Flaubert as seeking to distinguish between two different art–life paradigms. The first was the practice of bringing art into everyday life, associated with the political aesthetics of aestheticism and decadence, and ultimately, via Adorno, with kitsch. The second was the cultivation of an aesthetic mode of perception. Put simplistically, Emma Bovary's 'crime', according to Rancière's interpretation of Flaubert, was that she pursued the first paradigm, drawing art into life, rather than drawing life closer to art. In this account, her bringing art and life together in a way that led to an assimilation of art's products into everyday life through self-conscious acquisition and performance was why the character 'had to be killed' by Flaubert – 'her suicide happened to be the last consequence of a chain of causes that reached back to a first mistake: she had too much imagination, she had mistaken literature for life'.[8]

The alternative strategy of bringing art and life into relation was by cultivating aesthetic perception. This involved a stance of disinterestedness, a means of perceiving 'sensations ... released from the chains of individuality', aloof from desire.[9] This mode of perceiving, akin to cosmopolitanism, is a mode of bringing form to disparate matter, joining things in commonality. Rancière cites the advice of the Devil in Flaubert's *Temptation of Saint Anthony* in this regard:

> The Devil reminded the saint that he had already felt that experience of fusion between the inside and the outside: 'Often, because of anything at all, a drop of water, a shell, a strand of hair, you have stopped short, your eyes fixed and your heart open. The object you were gazing at seemed to encroach upon you, as you bent toward, and new ties were found: you clutched each other, you touched each other by subtle innumerable embraces.'[10]

The 'new ties' that are found in combining art and life in this second formulation bring causality and poetics to a life previously only lived moment by moment, and allow one to partake of democratic redistribution.

Rancière viewed Flaubert's project as pointing out that 'it is the task of literature, as a new regime of writing, to inscribe the difference between two ways of making art similar to nonart'.[11] In other words, it was the task of the very form of writing born of the democratic impulse – an impulse to equalise and bring difference into relation – to delineate the terms of the relation, endorsing particular ways in which art may be brought on to an equal plane with life, while excluding others. In Rancière's formulation, literature (and perhaps art more generally) performs a regulatory function with respect to what I am calling the problem of mirroring. It draws things that are different together while working against the tendency of this activity to result in them becoming one and the same thing. It does this by revealing what Walter Benjamin called in his essay on Goethe's *Elective Affinities* a work's 'truth content' and 'material content', respectively, where the most enduring and significant works exhibit an almost total enmeshing of the two. Benjamin uses the example of a seal to describe the relationship between the two types of content to much the same ends as our distinction between analogy and metaphor above:

> just as the form of a seal cannot be deduced from the material of the wax or from the purpose of the fastening ... so the content of the matter cannot be deduced by means of insight into its constitution or through an exploration of its intended use ... rather, it is graspable only in the philosophical experience of its divine imprint ... In this way the achieved insight into the material content of subsisting things finally coincides with insight into their truth content.[12]

Rancière accords a similar regulatory function to commemorative art in its capacity to hold in tension two meanings of the word 'resistance'. He notes how 'resistance' refers both to the 'passive resistance of the stone' (namely 'a thing that persists in its own being'), or the 'active opposition of men' (namely 'people who refuse to remain in their situation').[13] Homonymy is a rhetorical category that is, of course, different from analogy and metaphor, but the category offers a similar sense in which the sameness and difference between the things in question may coexist in some way. It holds out a similar promise that things might be made equivalent while still remaining incommensurable. And indeed this is precisely Rancière's point. He offers a quotation from Gilles Deleuze that draws upon the metaphorical relationship between an artist's labour in transforming sensuous perceptions into an object of perception on the one hand, and a people's labour in transforming individual struggles into collective revolutionary action, on the other.[14] Both forms of labour result in a fixed, stone-like monument that is a trace or record of a moment of transcendence (that is, the artwork and the revolution, respectively). At the same time they also carry forward the 'vibrations' of that moment to the 'ear of the future', in a way that makes it less a work of art than an ongoing act of politics. This account thereby marks out an equivalence between art and revolutionary resistance that Rancière finds troubling yet productive. He terms this form of relation 'dissensus'.[15]

This proposed linking of the passive resistance of a stone and the active resistance of people is no mere analogy, according to Rancière. The conditions that make this link persuasive are the conditions of post-Kantian thought, which disrupted the representational regime wherein art functioned as a demonstration of people's ability to submit 'passive matter' to 'active form'[16] in a way that supposedly revealed the concordance between the laws of nature and human beings' sensuous perception of beauty. By contrast, Kant proposed that aesthetic experience was disconnected from both conceptual determination and desire. Aesthetic experience is a sensory experience that remains separate from other types of sensory experience, and nor is it geared towards ethical ends. Recognising the specificity of aesthetic experience means acknowledging that our pleasure in art cannot be explained by its closeness to natural laws, as in the 'representative regime of art'. In the 'aesthetic regime', which sees a disjuncture between the natural and the cognitive elements of human nature, art regulates the character of this link. Art must serve the paradoxical function of being a materialisation of 'thought outside of itself' while also denying its character as thought and retaining its character of the un-thought which defines the conditions of its existence, namely its art-ness:

> To say that art resists thus means that it is a perpetual game of hide-and-seek between the power of sensible manifestation of works and their power of signification. Now, this game of hide-and-seek between thought and art has a paradoxical consequence: art is art, that is, it resists in its nature as art, insofar as it is not the product of a will to make art, insofar as it is something other than art.[17]

To say that art must be neither a product of intellectual conceptualisation nor a product of a 'will to make art' means replacing art with an aesthetic mode of perception. This mode of perception relies on sensation, as we have seen, and in the language of post-Enlightenment thinking this shift had implicit egalitarian connotations. It was a type of egalitarianism that did not rely on the intelligibility of concepts such as equality and liberty or on the institutional changes to politics wrought by revolution. Rather it relied on a shared function of perception, and therefore held direct potential to shape new social formations. The aesthetic thus occupies the paradoxical position of being fundamentally isolated (from all other modes of sensation and cognition) and, because of this isolation, being capable of reshaping the sensorium. To wit, art and politics dissolve into one another. Rancière's point here is not to show that art must maintain autonomy from politics in order to remain resistant, but rather to show how a commitment to art's resistance in political terms (that is, in terms of the 'opposition of men') leads to an ethical conception of art that eradicates its other form of resistance (namely the 'passive resistance of the stone'): 'To prevent the resistance of art from fading into its contrary, it must be upheld as the unresolved tension between two resistances.'[18]

The problem of commemorative art

In rationalising the scope of what should be considered a 'Holocaust artwork', Henry W. Pickford observed a pattern in historical critiques of literature about atrocities that circulated around the conflicting requirements of presenting both 'historical fact' and 'imaginative truth'.[19] He noted how the strength of a Holocaust work has largely been seen to rest upon its ability to balance these two imperatives – too much historical material and the work becomes 'merely informative'; too aesthetically autonomous and it becomes 'merely formal'.[20] These criteria are explicitly normative in the sense that they suppose that it is possible to make a judgement about a work's success or failure as a commemorative monument – they ask, what *ought* a commemorative artwork to be or do – and accordingly they engage a longer history of normative theories of art.

As Pickford noted, thinkers such as Hegel and Adorno viewed art as bearing some kind of relation to things beyond its purely sensual or expressive qualities, even as their view of its 'ought' differed – the former imbued art with the potential to harmonise conceptual content and sensuous form, while the latter prized art's ability to exhibit the impossibility of such a reconciliation. The nature of this relation may characterise the problem of art in general, but in commemorative art this problem is laid bare in a particularly acute manner. The commemorative work must, by definition, bear some relation to the historical event that it commemorates, but if it were to breach the barrier of semblance and somehow replicate or carry forward its violence, it would mean perhaps relinquishing its status as an artwork. Rancière refers to this moment as the 'political becoming of art', which 'becomes the ethical confusion in which, in the name of their union, art and politics both vanish'.[21] While the possibility of this shift demonstrates to Rancière how art and politics are drawn towards each other, he warns that when art is subsumed into the political or vice versa, they suppress and neutralise each other in a way that gives cause for concern, as we have seen.

In a collection of essays under the Goethean title *Elective Affinities*, Lydia Goehr gives voice to a similar unease about the consequences of mirroring and the ethical confusion that correlates to the conflation of art and life. Yet rather than relating this problem to the aesthetic regime of art, she views it as illustrative of what she calls the 'challenge of indiscernibility',[22] including the need to preserve difference in the process of bringing things into relation. In commemorative art, according to Goehr, there is a danger of being both 'too distant' and 'too close':

> there is something inherently problematic in what commemorative art is both able and wants to do. Like Greek tragedies, commemorative works face a grave difficulty. To generate an adequate response, they must promote the illusion of reality, for without the feeling of reality we wouldn't be moved. Yet, given the painfulness of the reality implied by commemorative works, the works must maintain an appropriate distance.[23]

Here the stance of distance is the force that keeps two different substances from becoming one and the same, in the language of elective affinities. It is the force that resists assimilation, and working together with the levelling forces of analogy and comparison, distance sustains the inherently resistant quality of the aesthetic. Distance is the tool of the critic attempting to alchemically extract the 'truth content' from the 'material content' of a work, in Benjamin's terms.

There are several ways in which commemorative artwork might replicate the violence of the original act, according to Goehr. The first is the possibility of the commemorative artwork serving to aestheticise violence, offering a voyeuristic pleasure to the audience that dehumanises it to the point where agency, accountability and blame become moot. Goehr cites two practices of distancing in this regard – the first is to make the violent act seem a merely administrative matter (as in Viktor Ullmann's *Der Kaiser von Atlantis, oder Der Tod dankt ab*, 1943–44), or to represent it in an overly stylised manner (as in Jean Genet's *Les Bonnes*, 1947). Mass violence committed under the aegis of a set of religious, ethnic or secular ideals is a form of aestheticised violence, according to Goehr, and producing artwork that commemorates the tragedy presents a replication of that process. The second way in which commemorative works may replicate their violent subject is when they are positioned as value-free healing agents in a way that covers over ongoing claims to suffering. Goehr describes this and other similar manoeuvres as practices of 'displacement'. They are also practices of distancing that aim to address the balance between historical allusion and imaginative truth that Pickford identified as defining features of commemorative art.

A third form of aestheticising violence is what Goehr identifies as 'temporal displacement', which is when a commemorative work uses historical analogy to avoid the need to explicitly represent a violent event that is too recent. Displacement in this sense reminds the audience that they are in the presence of a work of art rather than a lived event of violence, requiring them to temper their emotional responses. Once again, here we are referring to art being an act of perception – one that requires a disinterested awareness of sensations without cognition or other senses engaged, as in the discussion of Emma Bovary above. This distanced position conceals the reality of the violence but it also calls up a different set of responses special to the aesthetic faculty that ensure that it does not slip into merely didactic or ethical art, or the undeniably political.

In delineating these and other practices of displacement and distancing, Goehr uses examples from commemorative films, oratorio-operas and chamber works, focusing on the role that music plays in intensifying or subverting the practices in question. She notes, for example, how music can provide 'false consolation' when it is depicted as a mode of resistance to violence. Rather than resist in these circumstances, it more often serves to ameliorate and distract, in her view – to promise humanity in inhuman situations, such as in accounts of musical performances in concentration camps – and to legitimise a universal vision of commonality in the face of the attempted annihilation of difference.

There is, of course, a long history of criticism related to commemorative artworks (and especially Holocaust art) that raise concerns that seem at first glance to bear a resemblance to these. Commemorative artworks are routinely either valorised for remembering or criticised for forgetting – for lending a voice to the voiceless victims and encouraging understanding and empathy, on the one hand, or for packaging trauma into a medium for voyeuristic consumption, on the other. The specific category of 'musical witness' has also been a part of these discussions. Music in this context is sometimes perceived as offering an immediacy of experience by virtue of its non-figural character or the visceral nature of sound.

Amy Lynn Wlodarski has reflected upon composers' struggles to do justice to the trauma of the Holocaust while also rendering it communicable to an audience that may be historically removed from the trauma.[24] She discusses a number of works that were criticised by some for being too explicit, and by others for being too abstract or too consumable – including Schoenberg's *Survivor from Warsaw* and Hans Eisler's music in Alain Resnais's *Nuit et brouillard*, a French documentary about the Holocaust, which Wlodarski interprets as a combination of these forces (referring to Eisler's 'practical strategy of empathic unsettlement').[25] Despite the merits of this approach, there is perhaps something of the too-easily metaphorical about equating harmonic dissonance and musical disjunction with trauma, and melodramatic or sentimental musical features with communicability, construed either as problematic compromise or empathy (both of which are implicated in forgetting).

Charting a way between these two poles is not the same as Rancière's injunction to hold different things in relation without allowing them to assimilate, nor about regulating the relationship between art and politics, or between art and life. Rancière is not concerned with communicability or overt resistance in the process of bearing witness, but rather with the possibility that art by its very nature engenders redistribution, and with how commemorative art (as a subset of art in general) faces a particularly difficult struggle to hold these things aloft:

> The form apprehended by aesthetic judgement is neither that of an object of knowledge nor that of an object of desire. It is this *neither . . . nor . . .* that defines the experience of the beautiful as the experience of a kind of resistance. The beautiful is that which resists both conceptual determination and the lure of consumable goods.[26]

In other words, while discussions of commemorative art measure successful and unsuccessful works by the extent to which they can balance historical and aesthetic features, for Rancière a commemorative artwork that breaches the barrier of semblance and becomes pure politics is simply not art (and therefore not resistance) at all.

In addition, ideas about testimonial aesthetics limit the types of musical works that can be considered commemorative, favouring those works that incorporate personal testimony – either recorded or in poetic form, but in any case verbal and vocal, with the music being only one of a number of elements. Accordingly, studies of specifically *musical* forms of witness have often focused on mapping common tropes and techniques of, for example, Holocaust representation in musical works, rather than on interrogating what it is about musical or sonic forms that may in some way carry the original act of violence forward, or alternatively resist in a variety of ways.[27] This type of mapping is an empirical project involving the description of musical devices and contextualising these within the composer's biography and the historical context of production and reception. The approach often draws attention to instances of musical fragmentation, fissure, disjunction and the like, relying once again on metaphors that assume an alignment between these devices and traumatic themes. This problematic alignment occurs even when comparatively tonal and even sentimental music is coupled with images or words evoking trauma, with this combination in turn being viewed as resistant in the sense of engendering a kind of ironic defamiliarisation (as in the case of the Eisler/Resnais documentary). The commemorative artwork is thereby held up to the criterion of testimony in order for it to be determined normatively legitimate. It is charged with the responsibility of bringing emotional force to the memory of a 'real' historical event; offering representation to the unrepresentable through a self-consciously conflicted aesthetic medium; or mediating or bringing meaning to experience.

This process of attributing an ethical function to particular musical strategies by virtue of their commemorative context leads to a fetishisation of voice, text, narrative and concept, and assumes that 'musical beauty' is merely a subset of beauty more generally, as opposed to being *sui generis*. It occludes the extent to which the experience of music can itself be an experience of resistance because of its paradoxical combination of sensation and form. The unmediated quality of sensory impact grates against the mediated quality of musical style in such a way that it allows music to be perceived as meaningful without conveying any determinate meaning.[28]

In her study of musical culture and British reconstruction efforts after the Second World War, Heather Wiebe considers the question of whether music and sound might have a special purchase on the problem of commemorative art.[29] She offers two possibilities in this regard. First, music is both ritual and event, as well as gesturing towards the canonical permanence of a monument. Ritual, event and monument all have 'amnesiac effects'. Yet Wiebe also offers the possibility that the sheer 'materiality of sound' and the 'ephemerality of performance' together achieve the requisite degree of both distance and closeness: 'Music's advantage ... might be that it necessarily avoids the permanence and solidity of the monument, participating, rather, in that play of repetition that [Walter] Benjamin recommended as a truer form of commemoration.'[30] On the other hand, music's disadvantage is its technological reproducibility, and this indeed was the case with Britten's *War Requiem* – as a popular LP recording, it could be listened to entirely abstracted from the conditions of ceremony.[31]

Cultures of commemoration (and so also the function of a commemorative artwork) change over time, and even though the collective memory of a generation that is more historically distant from the event is mediated by the symbols and commemorative practices of earlier generations, the aesthetic implications of this historical distance are sometimes expressed via a displacement of individual experience into universal themes of hope or suffering. This is different from the move from personal to collective remembrance that is associated with public monuments.[32] Public monuments engage a complex combination of personal and collective memory almost by definition, yet our concern here is with the aesthetic contortions required both to pay heed to individual suffering and to draw broader reflection from the particular.

Moving from the individual to the communal or universal results in a range of indistinctions, some of which may be problematic, others not. It has the effect of relativising the actions and interests of victims and perpetrators, refusing to take sides, such as in John Adams's controversial 1991 oratorio-opera *The Death of Klinghoffer*. It also places all suffering on the same plane, equalising the experiences of oppressed peoples across historical time and geopolitical space, and drawing links between groups that have suffered oppression, such as in Michael Tippet's oratorio *A Child of Our Time* (1939–41), which contains both anti-Nazi themes and the music of African-American spirituals. Almost by its very nature, this strategy of commemoration neutralises the event of violence through the process of abstraction, generalisation and comparison. And just as comparison has been linked with the conceptual and material forms of domination associated with Enlightenment rationality, as noted above, a similar characterisation would apply to any practice that places the immediacy of individual experience at the service of an abstract concept in commemoration. The universal acts as a form of consensus and closure, and even though sound and music may be able to hold this closure in tension with immediacy, still 'the ghostly presence of sound [tends to] lay ghosts to rest'.[33]

Consensus and the ethical turn

Consensus and closure may be viewed as echoing Enlightenment forms of domination that are similar to those attributed to the act of comparison. This similarity takes us back to the notion of analogy, metaphor, homonym and equivalence – of bringing things that are different under the banner of sameness. Consensus is a totalising action that has rightly attracted a great deal of criticism, and as we have seen it is also a tendency that critics of commemorative monuments are keen to view with caution. Consensus tends towards monumentality, easy closure, a return to an imagined natural order – all things that no serious critic since the early twentieth century would dare endorse as desirable aesthetic desiderata; and indeed works that have presented these features have required of critics almost unfathomable contortions so as to rationalise why they should not be construed in this way.

The task of theory has been purportedly to uncover these power struggles and inequities lying under the smooth surface of consensus – to extract the realities of difference from the abstract veil of sameness. This activity is an ethical (and even at times metaphysical) project, and one that accords to the critic or artist a suprasensible or priestly role with respect to common understanding. Rancière sees this move as part of an essentially theistic tendency that attributes special power to the Other, which he associates with the 'ethical turn'.

Democracy, as it is usually understood (and which Rancière pejoratively renames 'postdemocracy' or 'consensus democracy'), makes 'a people' of different individuals and groups through the process of consensus. Yet the consensus of democracy is not simply the coming together of different groups. It is an agreed-upon order of things – of which claims are visible and audible. The act of drawing parties or claims into the same field and expressing them in the shared language of debate has its own internal logic of visibility. In democracy, therefore, there is no realm of appearances or representation, with the putative real or true lying behind it, there is only a weighing of merits – the merits of contingent identities, defined by class, race, sexuality and so on. Democracy is then a particular 'regime of the perceptible' in which there is nothing uncounted, 'nothing left over'.[34] Rancière, however, sees democracy proper as the opposite of consensus – it is 'disagreement', not in the sense of either a misunderstanding or a failure to reach consensus, but in the sense of the becoming visible of the uncounted – 'floating subjects' – via a process of subjectification. This new visibility is once again not simply an entrance into the realm of democratic debate, akin to political recognition. It is a disruption in the perceived order of things that results is a reordering of what is visible and audible.

For Rancière, consensus is the ordering of things and ideas into different domains – things and ideas that are substitutable through the operation of metaphor. This radical substitutability – which is also Rancière's vaunted radical equality – is not akin to the difference-into-sameness of elective affinities. Rather, it is the ability to replace, be replaced or be reordered. Some have viewed Rancière's political thought as being akin to 'post-structuralist utopianism' by reason of his commitment to our capacity to provoke redistribution through blazing interventions. These interventions – indeterminate practices of transgression, disturbance or rupture – have the appearance of issuing from a source outside the existing order, pointing to a form of utopianism.[35] Yet there is a distinct difference here in the sense that, for Rancière, the only newness that is possible is from a reordering of consensus. Newness does not come from an external source, such as a political group or subject that was previously excluded from the community, nor is it the reconciliation of class divides or the cooperation of interest groups, because subjects without recognition are not subjects, according to Rancière – they are prior to the political subject and only come into being when the reordering allows them to become visible and audible. The becoming visible of a subject is what constitutes politics. This is what Samuel Chambers calls the element of 'surprise' that defines Rancière's conception of politics as dissensus.[36] If there is a utopian element to Rancière's work, then it is a utopianism of actions and the movement of bodies (for example, bodies occupying spaces from which they were formerly excluded), rather than a utopianism of thought, words or imagination. He writes that

> the thing that breaks with consensus in exercising the power of the one-in-addition is substitutability. It is, in art, the possibility that a metaphor or a play of light and shadow be no more than a metaphor or a play of light and shadow or that it may be the power of a love or a testimony of a specific time and world. It is the possibly that a thing be a work *and* a commodity.[37]

This move is against the moralising of art and the confusion of ethics that Rancière associates with art becoming political. Discussions of equality and justice mistake a type of regulation for a natural attribute, marking what he calls a failure to distinguish between 'law and fact'. It is the same problem that attends international calls for intervention based on human rights, with the arbiter of human rights assuming a suprasensible power, of thought outside of itself. This suprasensible power, just like the power of the Other that Lyotard and several others attribute to art, seeks to replace the flatness of democracy and egalitarianism, but instead simply introduces a theistic premise of ontological difference. It does not result in a substantive reordering of consensus.

In working against the reintroduction of a suprasensible figure to bring newness into the world, Rancière has sought to draw attention to the process of dissensus, which rests on 'the power of the equality of intelligences and the exigency of its verification, the democratic dispersion of the circular logic of the *arkhe* and the tension of contraries within the aesthetic regime of art'.[38] On one view, the critical purpose of this manoeuvre might be seen in terms of avoiding the tendency of elective affinities, of different things that are brought into relation being subsumed – of avoiding the

> way in which the apparently most radical forms of affirmation of artistic and political difference were transformed into their contrary, namely radical ethical indistinction: the inversion of modernist radicality in the nostalgic cult of the image and of testimony; the inversion of the proclaimed purity of the political into pure consent to the management of economic necessity, and indeed into the legitimation of the most brutal forms of warring imperialism.[39]

The point of Rancière's radical equality and substitutability is to avoid believing that we have achieved mastery of truth or of the Other. He and others call on commemorative art to be a play of both the actions of 'a people' and the stillness of a stone – a work of both voice and silence. In the tension between the stone and the people in a sphere of absolute substitutability we find the dissensual possibilities of the aesthetic mode of perception. What would this type of commemorative work look or sound like?

An interlude

Letná Hill overlooks the city of Prague. It is occupied by an extensive expanse of parkland, with the famous Prague Castle off to one side, and the Vltava river in front. It is a central point of reference for the city, and at the very pinnacle of the hill, on a massive stone plinth, stands a dark-red, 25-metre-high metronome, which slowly moves back and forth, 'ticking', as it were, though without any sound. When I visited Prague some years ago, although you could clearly see the metronome from any high point in the city, there was little indication that it was a landmark of any kind. It did not at that time appear on tourist maps, it was not touted as a 'must-see' curiosity nor as an especially significant part of the history of the city. Even as you approach its location there are few signs to direct you, and when you get there the site is littered with piles of rubble, a supporting plinth that has been turned into a well-used skateboarding area, and a wire with pairs of shoes hanging from it. The metronome swings very slowly, and seems rather wobbly at the top when the wind blows.

The metronome – a kinetic sculpture designed by the Czech artist Vratislav Novak (1942–2014) – was erected in 1991 as a temporary monument on the previous site of the largest statue of Stalin in Europe. The Stalin statue had taken five and a half years to build and was unveiled in 1955, just as the process of de-Stalinisation had begun. In other words, the statue arrived too late. The sculptor who designed this statue of Stalin, Otakar Švec (1892–1955), committed suicide a month before its unveiling, and the whole project was immediately an embarrassment and a terrible looming reminder. The statue was demolished using 800 kilogrammes of explosives in 1962. It stood for only a year and a half longer than it took to build.[40]

There is a mixture of devastating trauma and humorous absurdity bound up with the site, and discussions about what to replace the temporary metronome with have ranged from a water sculpture to a church or an aquarium. In 1996 there was a 10-metre-high, water-filled statue of Michael Jackson positioned on the plinth, to herald the musician's European tour. There has been no discussion of placing a memorial to the victims of Communism on the empty plinth.[41] Such a memorial does exist in Prague – a sculpture depicting a naked male figure whose body becomes gradually erased as he descends a set of stairs – but it is in a far less prominent location. The site of the Stalin statue on the other hand, the most prominent location in the city, is a site of forgetting, and of non-commitment – an eerie erasure of history.

Meanwhile the metronome silently 'ticks' away, gesturing neither forward towards new possibilities or new troubles, nor backward towards a remembered tragedy or a golden age of the past. It remembers nothing, it memorialises nothing, it is silent and voiceless. Accordingly, and notwithstanding that the sculpture is itself a moving timepiece, it in fact has no time, and indicates no movement; it exists only in the present and signifies nothing but a series of present moments, a series of nows. It is in this way a marker of the 'contemporary', and shares with the contemporary a withdrawal from history that aestheticises a particular attitude towards consensus in the politics of internationalism, as I have noted elsewhere in relation to the International Society for

Contemporary Music.[42] It also shares with the category of the contemporary a refusal to take sides or make a judgement.

Yet the metronome can nevertheless be seen to resist in a number of ways – it resists satisfying explication, interpretation, blame, accountability, meaning, resolution, false closure or indeed a sense of semblance with what it purportedly memorialises. In not naming an act, an effect, a victim or a perpetrator, the sculpture does two opposing things at once – on the one hand, it avoids merely aestheticising suffering and violence, while on the other it might be said to replicate the very same practices of erasure associated with the period that it commemorates, and to further ingrain the voicelessness of victims. The Prague metronome is therefore an apt example of the problem of commemoration. It points to the areas of concern that pervade considerations of commemorative art, as we have seen – the degrees of individual and universal themes and the degrees of aesthetic and historical material.

Despite having no sound, the metronome is also a useful device in the context of a discussion about musical commemoration, not because it replicates, in gargantuan proportions, an object that is familiar to musicians, but because its withdrawal from representation and its equivocal stance towards commitment (and the implications for the question of resistance that this entails) are gestures in which music is thought to have a special investment. Music has the capacity to hold in tension the conflicting requirements of the monument – it is at once fixed (as a work) and transient (as a performance), tangible and intangible, specific and universal, and it can provoke intensity of feeling even in the absence of representation or overt meaning. We might even say that in this way the statue is 'musical' as a way of indicating its ability to hold these things in tension. It suggests that the strategies for approaching the problem of commemorative art and art's resistance more generally – namely that of giving a stone monument an ongoing dynamic – may be, in effect, 'musical' strategies.

The non-work

In their respective discussions of commemorative artwork both Goehr and Rancière gesture towards the power of the non-work or fragment. Goehr recommends Adorno's solution of a 'residual art of the fragment' and draws a similar point from Benjamin's essay on Goethe's *Elective Affinities*.[43] She sees this notion exemplified in Schoenberg's *Survivor from Warsaw*.[44] The fragment is akin to the ruin – recalling the bombed church debate in post-war Britain[45] – in that it resists the amnesiac qualities of commemoration. But even fragments and ruins are only distant reminders of a tragedy, and they do not inherently call for completion or restitution, nor do they inherently unsettle – in other words, they do not necessarily prompt action, and in this way are like the stone. Goehr calls for an 'aesthetics of displacement, worked out under the conditions of the negative dialectic' which ensures that 'art's quieter violence' is preserved as a means of political resistance:

> an art of mourning does not require artists to decide how best to portray the horror of a specific act, because this would be to think about the art in terms of its copying or representing the world as it appears. Rather, the demand is for an art that, in its formal or expressive capacity as art, reveals something about the concealed violence of a society that allows explicitly violent acts to be performed without objection in its name.[46]

It has not been my intention to align Goehr's thinking directly with Rancière's on the question of commemorative art, but rather to draw them into productive discussion. There may be something of a resonance between the oscillation of Goehr's 'aesthetics of displacement' (for example, between realist and 'dissonant' sound–image relationships) and Rancière's celebration of art which maintains the 'unresolved tension between two resistances', though this may be drawing out the analogy – or affinity – a little too far.

Rancière's scheme is profoundly secular in every sense. There is no redemption, no salvation, no transcendence. And equally the role of those figures formerly occupied with these functions – such as the philosopher, artist or critic – becomes contested. Rancière acknowledges the difficulties in maintaining the 'very tension by which a politics of art and a poetics of politics tend towards each other, but cannot meet up without suppressing themselves',[47] and indeed keeping the possibility of suppression and annihilation close at hand is a key refrain in the discussions described in the foregoing: Goehr cites Karlheinz Stockhausen's infamous comment in an interview after the 9/11 terrorist attacks when he seemed to cast the attacks as the ultimate work of art, perfected by the creators' death through its creation;[48] the character whose individuality is most subsumed in partnership in Goethe's *Elective Affinities*, Ottilie, starves herself to death in a similar process of self-annihilation; Emma Bovary, who mistakes life for art, takes her own life; and this too was the fate of Otakar Švec, the artist who designed the statue of Stalin in whose rubble ruins the Prague metronome stands.

Needless to say, Rancière's discussion of commemorative art, resistance and dissensus more generally leaves the matter of agency open to question. There are, however, glimpses of a normative mandate for a 'dissensual practice of philosophy' in his approach, and this revolves, once again, around how we are to approach rhetorical modes of comparison or 'de-classification':

> there are two ways to deal with homonyms. One is to proceed to purify them, to identify the good name and the good sense and disperse the bad ... The other way considers that every homonymy arranges a space of thought and of action, and that the problem is therefore neither to eliminate the prestige of homonymy, nor to take names back to a radical indetermination, but to deploy the intervals which put the homonymy at work.[49]

Rancière's aim is thus both diagnostic and reparative. He is in fact more generous than others regarding art's capacity for resistance, affirming its significance and outlining the conditions of its possibility even as he concedes the near impossibility of its aim and the problematic tendencies of its associated practices.

The scholarly problem of how to recognise the relationship between art and non-art without simply substituting one for the other (a problem that is brought to the surface in the case of commemorative art) may be one that music is uniquely predisposed to address. Music's potential in this regard issues from its capacity to be meaningful without determinate meaning; its capacity to speak and narrate without a determinate 'voice'; to be mediated by its formal qualities while at the same time having an immediate sensory impact; and perhaps most significantly, to elicit just the type of emotional intensity that underpins all political sentiment without itself being explicitly political.

Notes

1. Johann Wolfgang von Goethe, *Elective Affinities*, trans. R. J. Hollingdale (Harmondsworth: Penguin, 1971), 50. Originally published as *Die Wahlverwandtschaften* in 1809.
2. Goethe, *Elective Affinities*, 50–7.
3. Jacques Rancière, 'What Does it Mean to be *Un?*', *Continuum* 21.4 (2007), 566.
4. Lydia Goehr, 'The Musicality of Violence: On the Art and Politics of Displacement', in *Elective Affinities: Musical Essays on the History of Aesthetic Theory* (New York: Columbia University Press, 2008), 202. This remark is followed by an explanation: 'In this resistance, the artwork becomes antirepresentational both artistically and politically, and art begins to serve a politics of displaced representation by raising anew the question on behalf of whom an artwork now speaks.'
5. Bruce Robbins, *Perpetual War: Cosmopolitanism from the Viewpoint of Violence* (Durham, NC: Duke University Press, 2012), 47. Robbins goes on to distinguish the comparative practices of Noam Chomsky on this point.
6. Jacques Rancière, 'Why Emma Bovary Had to be Killed', *Critical Inquiry* 34.2 (2008), 233–48.
7. Elsewhere Rancière describes the Hegelian notion that poetry was the most superior art form in a similar way: 'the superiority of the intrigue, that of causality constructed on the basis of empirical succession, that is, of action subjected to fortune and misfortune, over life which is forever identical to itself'. Here life stands for mute nature and animals, whereas poetry embodies the human intellect. Jacques Rancière, 'Metamorphosis of the Muses', in *Sonic Process: A New Geography of Sounds*, ed. Mela Dávila (Barcelona: Actar, 2002), 23.
8. Rancière, 'Why Emma Bovary Had to be Killed', 233.
9. Rancière, 'Why Emma Bovary Had to be Killed', 241.
10. Rancière, 'Why Emma Bovary Had to be Killed', 241–2, citing Gustave Flaubert, *La Tentation de saint Antoine* (Paris: E. Fasquelle, 1910), 418.
11. Rancière, 'Why Emma Bovary Had to be Killed', 243.
12. Walter Benjamin, 'Goethe's Elective Affinities', in *Selected Writings: 1913–1926, vol. 1*, ed. Marcus Bullock and Michael W. Jennings (Cambridge, MA: Belknap Press of Harvard University Press, 1996), 298–300.

13. Rancière was concerned here specifically with literary realism, and there have been criticisms that he saw this form less in terms of representation and more in terms of what it exemplified or offered – which Arne De Boever calls Rancière's 'performative realism'. Arne De Boever, 'The Politics of Realism in Rancière and Houellebecq', in Grace Hellyer and Julian Murphet (eds), *Rancière and Literature* (Edinburgh: Edinburgh University Press, 2016), 226–48.
14. Jacques Rancière, 'The Monument and Its Confidences; or Deleuze and Art's Capacity of "Resistance"', in *Dissensus: On Politics and Aesthetics*, ed. and trans. Steven Corcoran (London: Bloomsbury, 2015), 178. The quotation in question is from Deleuze and Guattari's *Qu'est-ce que la philosophie?*
15. Rancière, 'The Monument and Its Confidences', 181.
16. Rancière, 'The Monument and Its Confidences', 183.
17. Rancière, 'The Monument and Its Confidences', 182–3.
18. Rancière, 'The Monument and Its Confidences', 191.
19. Henry W. Pickford, *The Sense of Semblance: Philosophical Analyses of Holocaust Art* (New York: Fordham University Press, 2013), 2.
20. Pickford, *The Sense of Semblance*, 4.
21. Rancière, 'The Monument and Its Confidences', 190.
22. Goehr, 'The Musicality of Violence', 182.
23. Goehr, 'The Musicality of Violence', 182.
24. Amy Lynn Wlodarski, *Musical Witness and Holocaust Representation* (Cambridge: Cambridge University Press, 2015).
25. Wlodarski, *Musical Witness*, 60.
26. Rancière, 'The Monument and Its Confidences', 181.
27. Wlodarski's scope is limited to what she calls 'secondary musical witness', being different from more direct forms of musical testimony or response (*Musical Witness*, 2–3).
28. For a recent discussion of the philosophical lineage of this notion, see Michael Gallope, *Deep Refrains: Music, Philosophy, and the Ineffable* (Chicago: University of Chicago Press, 2017).
29. Heather Wiebe, *Britten's Unquiet Pasts: Sound and Memory in Postwar Reconstruction* (Cambridge: Cambridge University Press, 2012).
30. Wiebe, *Britten's Unquiet Pasts*, 202–3.
31. Wiebe, *Britten's Unquiet Pasts*, 202–3.
32. As described in Jay Winter and Emmanuel Sivan (eds), *War and Remembrance in the Twentieth Century* (Cambridge: Cambridge University Press, 1999), though see Martin Jay's chapter in that

volume – 'Against Consolation: Walter Benjamin and the Refusal to Mourn' – which highlights how the divide is not so easily drawn.
33. Wiebe, *Britten's Unquiet Pasts*, 14.
34. Jacques Rancière, *Disagreement: Politics and Philosophy*, trans. Julie Rose (Minneapolis: University of Minnesota Press, 1995), 102–3.
35. Paul Patton, 'Rancière's Utopian Politics', in Jean-Philippe Deranty and Alison Ross (eds), *Jacques Rancière and the Contemporary Scene* (London: Continuum, 2012), 129–44.
36. See Samuel A. Chambers, *The Lessons of Rancière* (Oxford: Oxford University Press, 2013), Introduction.
37. Jacques Rancière, 'The Use of Distinctions', in *Dissensus: On Politics and Aesthetics*, ed. and trans. Steven Corcoran (London: Bloomsbury, 2015), 221.
38. Rancière, 'The Use of Distinctions', 225.
39. Rancière, 'The Use of Distinctions', 225.
40. Mariusz Czepczyński, *Cultural Landscapes of Post-socialist Cities: Representation of Powers and Needs* (Farnham: Ashgate, 2008), 94.
41. See Hana Pichova, 'The Lineup for Meat: The Stalin Statue in Prague', *PMLA* 123.3 (2008), 614–31. See also Czepczyński, *Cultural Landscapes*.
42. Sarah Collins, 'What Was Contemporary Music? The New, the Modern and the Contemporary in the ISCM', in Björn Heile and Charles Wilson (eds), *The Ashgate Research Companion to Modernism in Music* (Farnham: Ashgate, 2019), 56–85.
43. Goehr, 'The Musicality of Violence', 197.
44. Though it must be said that there are certain practical challenges that arise from a fragment of a work. See Joy H. Calico, *Arnold Schoenberg's* A Survivor from Warsaw *in Postwar Europe* (Berkeley: University of California Press, 2014).
45. Wiebe, *Britten's Unquiet Pasts*, 204–5.
46. Goehr, 'The Musicality of Violence', 201.
47. Rancière, 'The Monument and Its Confidences', 183.
48. Stockhausen's comment, which has been translated in various ways, is cast in the following terms by Goehr (more for its representative quality rather than as an exact translation): 'The terrorists brought about in one act what composers can only dream of – to practice madly for ten years, completely, fanatically, for a concert and then die. That would be the greatest work of art for the whole cosmos. Against this, composers are nothing' (Goehr, 'The Musicality of Violence', 176–7).
49. Rancière, 'The Use of Distinctions', 226.

12

Stain
Murray Dineen

Excursus 1: Shopping Malls I. Some of us haunt shopping malls late into the evening after the stores have closed. We do so in part for the music. During the day, shopping mall music constitutes a normally unobtrusive backdrop for the hard labour of commerce and capital. But mall music is transformed fundamentally when commerce ends, along lines comparable to Rancière's 'double heteronomy'. Shoppers having parted, mall music emerges from its unobtrusive backdrop, and this is its first heteronomy. Oh, how it reverberates in empty halls devoid of footfalls and chatter. It works its way into every mall corner, chasing us down to insist upon its legitimacy, worthy of attention. Its normal pleasantries become an insistent liturgy: can you not hear how soothing and attractive it is? But in being so insistently pleasant, it emphasises its customary dependence upon commerce. Who, after all, needs pleasantries, when the customary irritants of shopping are removed. Mall music thus reverberates in an emphatic solitude not as an autonomous and absolute thing but instead as lonely and incomplete, as if tinted or stained by commerce and by capital. Thus it serves in its lonely solitude to reveal, as its second heteronomy, how truly unpleasant mall shopping and the spectre of capital can be.

This essay frames Rancière's concepts of the *stain* and the *count* by reference first to Adorno's concept of *remainder* and later to Derrida's writings on *aporia*. I shall frame this in terms of dialectics. In essence, the substance of dialectics is not synthetic. As a student of Marx, I mean *substance* in two senses of the term: a physical, material matter, as opposed to an insubstantial illusion; and ultimately the substance of physical labour as part of all human constructions. Substance lies in that which is left behind as a remainder in synthesis, and which in turn puts synthesis into question. Since all three philosophers are concerned with humans and humanity, I shall phrase this remainder in human terms, as a state of affairs suffered by humans, this under the aegis of capitalism.

Capital is based on the abstract transformation of original labour into congealed labour time and exchange value. For a capitalist, such a transformation is synthetic, producing capital. The synthesis is attained, however, at the expense of use value and original labour on the part of an individual worker, who is not taken into account in the accumulation of exchange value as capital. Where capital is accumulated, use value and original labour in the person of the worker are remaindered, cast aside. Neither use value nor original labour disappears entirely, however. Instead, they reappear in human form as the worker's proletarian consciousness remaindered by accumulated capital.

As remainders, use value and original labour give Marxists a material substance for the critique of capital. In the context of capitalism, use value and original labour form a remainder, a residue – a pain in the gut of every worker who clocks in. This residue is the real substance of dialectics. To elucidate this, I turn to Adorno, Rancière and, ultimately, Derrida. Adorno makes this clear by reference to music, and thus I shall start with him.

Adorno's remainder

In my 2011 book *Friendly Remainders: Essays in Music Criticism after Adorno*, I discussed the notion of a negative remainder produced by dialectics. The term *remainder* is in truth a mistranslation. Translating *Negative Dialectics*, E. P. Ashton, like most translators, amends from time to time the German original so as to add some expressive term, and thus arrives at a felicitous insertion, such as the phrase 'without leaving a remainder', in the following passage. Ashton's translation is followed here by its German original:

> The name of dialectics says no more, to begin with, than that objects do not go into their concepts without leaving a remainder, that they come to contradict the traditional norm of adequacy. [Ihr Name sagt zunächst nichts wieder, als daß die Gegenstände in ihrem Begriff nicht

aufgehen, daß diese in Widerspruch geraten mit der hergebrachten Norm der adaequatio.]

A more literal translation might read as follows:

> Its name says to begin with no more than that objects do not go into their concept, that these get into (go into, produce a) contradiction with the traditional norm of adequacy.

In this literal version, the result is merely a contradiction [*Widerspruch*]. Ashton, however, gives negation the full-fledged status of a 'remainder', more substantial than a simple contradiction. The translation is fortuitous, for it seems that Adorno is always on the lookout for such remainders, those aspects of things that don't fit into their concepts.[1] The term *remainder* means thus a residue produced in excess of synthesis: 'the name of dialectics says ... objects do not go into their concepts without leaving a remainder'.

Two examples shall suffice here for clarification: Engels's Herr Dühring, from the text commonly referred to as *Anti-Dühring*,[2] and Adorno's Mahlerian jackass, from the Schoenberg essay in the collection *Prisms*.[3] We begin with Engels's dynamic conception of dialectics. In any equation used to describe the human condition where x is purported to equate to y, there are aspects of the variables that do not equate. Their very equation transforms our understanding of the variables and thus the equation. Herein lies the dynamic quality in Marxist dialectics: the formulation of a dialectic equation transforms the very terms equated. Equation is thus dynamic rather than static. Dühring, on Engels's account, rails against such a dynamic thesis. For Dühring, anything that exceeds the simple equation of x equals y is beyond comprehension: all variables in rational mechanics equate precisely; why should they not be so in human affairs?

The nub of Dühring's argument is a polemic against *contradiction*, the contradiction implied in dialectics between the static and the dynamic. Engels says that, for Dühring, 'there is no bridge in rational mechanics from the strictly static to the dynamic'.[4] On this account, all variables unite in a complete and exhaustive assertion: x always equals y and nothing more, and thus their relationship is one of stasis, *tout court*. Thus Dühring denies contradiction as incomprehensible. For Engels, however, Dühring concedes its existence, albeit as a thing lying beyond his comprehension.

Comprehension of the incomprehensible: this is the stuff of Marxist dialectics as critique of class consciousness. It is the basis of the unquiet bourgeois mind, which senses the tenuous nature of its class existence. Blinded by the commodity fetish, the bourgeoisie cannot fully comprehend their situation, but sense the presence of a dangerous incomprehensible that contradicts their very being. As Lukács puts it in *History and Class Consciousness*:

> The resistance offered to historical materialism by bourgeois thought was by no means simply a matter of narrow-mindedness. It was the expression of the bourgeoisie's correct class instinct ... It would be suicidal for the bourgeoisie to grant recognition to historical materialism. Any member of the bourgeoisie who admitted the scientific truth of historical materialism would thereby abandon his own class consciousness and with it the strength needed to defend the interests of his own class effectively ... The survival of the bourgeoisie rests on the assumption that it never obtains a clear insight into the social preconditions of its own existence.[5]

In order to understand Dühring's insistence that all matters pertaining to humankind equate precisely and nothing more, we must understand the threat a Marxist dynamic poses to him. Like the bourgeoisie recoiling from the possibility of materialism, Dühring understands intuitively the threat posed by the possibility of contradiction. The situation is like the child before the cookie jar: 'Mother says there are no cookies for me in that jar. And yet cookie jars exist to hold cookies, *ergo* there must be cookies in the jar. To remain a good child, I must deny the possibility that there are cookies in the jar: there are no cookies in the cookie jar, there are no cookies in the cookie jar.' Thus the hand moves towards the cookie jar. Bourgeois metaphysics insists upon the exhaustive truth of its present state, but in denying anything beyond such metaphysics it opens up intuitively the possibility. The bourgeois mind tells itself: 'Metaphysics asserts that there is nothing beyond my complete and inalienable comprehension. And yet metaphysics exists to defend against the incomprehensible. *Ergo*, there must be an incomprehensible, something to defend against as a metaphysician.' Thus the metaphysical mind moves towards the incomprehensible, that which is remaindered by metaphysics. Engels says the following about Dühring:

[he] asserts that up to the present there is absolutely 'no bridge, in rational mechanics, from the strictly static to the dynamic'. The reader can now at last see what is hiding behind this favourite phrase of Herr Dühring's – it is nothing but this: the mind which thinks metaphysically is absolutely unable to pass from the idea of rest to the idea of motion, because the contradiction pointed out above blocks its path. To it, motion is simply incomprehensible because it is a contradiction. And in asserting the incomprehensibility of motion, it thereby against its will admits the existence of the contradiction, and in so doing admits the objective presence of a contradiction in things as processes themselves, a contradiction which is moreover an actual force.[6]

At the heart of Engels's critique lies the following passage from *Capital* wherein Marx speaks of capital exploiting capital. The exploitation of capital by capital is a contradiction, for normally capital merely exploits labour:

> That which is now to be expropriated is no longer the labourer working for himself, but the capitalist exploiting many labourers. This expropriation is accomplished by the action of the immanent laws of capitalist production itself, by the centralization of capitals. One capitalist always kills many ... Hand in hand with this centralization, or this expropriation of many capitalists by few ... the monopoly of capital becomes a fetter upon the mode of production ... Centralization of the means of production and socialization of labour at last reach a point where they become incompatible with their capitalist integument. This integument is burst asunder ... The expropriators are expropriated.[7]

Contradiction, the bringing together of two things normally kept separate, is essential to Marxist dialectics. Dühring senses the potential for class revolution in Marx's dynamic thought, and by denying dynamics would thereby deny revolution.

There are two stages at work in capitalism. Only one of these is truly contradictory, however. The first stage is that of original labour ('the labourer working for himself')[8] transformed into congealed labour time, and thereby expropriated and turned into capital. Essential here is a contradiction between forms of actual labour and labour's abstraction as time – between original labour and labour congealed as labour time. Ultimately, as Marx puts it, capital expropriates other forms of capital. This constitutes a second stage and brings about a crucial transformation in fundamental terms.

Original labour differs from congealed labour time in terms of quality: sweat is transformed into the calculations on a spreadsheet. The two contradict each other in material terms: physical sweat versus abstract operations on numbers. But in the second stage, exploited capital differs from exploiting capital only in terms of quantity, the quantitative relationship of one to the other. From his capitalist understanding, Dühring is correct: the static nature of capital contains within itself no contradiction. Capital exploiting capital is stasis, two quantities of the same abstract thing.

In this second stage, where capital is exploited by capital, there is no material constraint, no worker's sweat. Labour (and sweat) is remaindered, alongside material truth. Capital's relationship to capital is as fictive and immaterial as the commodity fetish. The equation of exploiting to exploited capital is a redundancy, if not a tautology, y equals y. Exploited capital is merely another form of capital.

For capitalism to work, two contradictory variables (original labour versus congealed labour time) must be kept separate and discrete. Engels's point is that in monopoly capitalism two forms of capital are confounded, and labour is simply brushed to one side. The result befuddles capitalists (certainly Herr Dühring), and leads ultimately to the spiralling inflation of abstracted value.

In Engels's equation, the worker's labour has a symbolic content; it is a touchstone, *Wegweiser*. It testifies to the central problem of capitalism, that monopoly capital bears no necessary and thus material relationship to actual effort. Remaindered by capital exploiting capital, original labour becomes the point of reference for a critique of capital. This is as true of Adorno's thought as it is of Engels's.

Adorno's critical task is twofold. He looks for false equations (such as that implicit in the relationship between exploited and exploiting forms of capital). These are often expressed as tautologies in his hands. In order to do so, he seeks out remainders, the truths left out of fetishistic equations. Implicit in Adorno's critical method is a manoeuvre that I call *hinge* (the German is *das Scharnier*). Adorno states one thing (x), then hinges – flips the statement around – so as to put its contrary in the form of a contradiction (y). He does so in such a fashion, however, that the original (x) is transformed. The result is not a static synthesis or a placid accommodation reached between x and y. It embodies instead the very dynamic motion that Engels finds lacking in Dühring. In Adorno's hands, this hinge-like turn of sense points to something immanent, a latent content hidden in any apparently exhaustive assertion.

As noted above, in Marx's equation 'the expropriators are expropriated', original labour is remaindered, erased from the equation when capital exploits capital. At play in monopoly capitalism is capital pitted against capital. Just how either form of capital was accumulated is a matter of the past, and thus irrelevant to the present. And yet the original act of expropriation (original labour transformed into capital) returns to haunt monopoly capitalism. In a twist upon the old master versus slave dialectic, Adorno might have said the following: the absence of original labour in monopoly capitalism is [hinge] the means of its ultimate revenge and the latter's demise at the hands of the proletariat.

More a cultural theorist than Marxist economist, Adorno sets out in search of hinges in the cultural realm. My favourite example is a passage on sublime understanding and Mahler found in *Prisms*, wherein Adorno refers to an inimitable kind of listener he calls a 'jackass': 'If one does not understand something, it is customary to behave with the sublime understanding of Mahler's jackass, and project one's own inadequacy on to the object, declaring it to be incomprehensible.'[9] Implied here is the following logic: (x) the jackass does not understand Mahler, then [hinge] (y) the jackass understands that he does not understand Mahler. This leads back to (x) revised: in coming to know that he does not understand Mahler, the jackass understands Mahler sublimely; he understands the existence of a Mahler beyond the limits of jackass understanding. The original proposition (x) is followed hinge-like by its contradiction (y), and this produces a remaindered insight: the jackass is a Mahler expert – his understanding of the jackass is sublime. In effect the hinge-like juxtaposition of 'not understanding' to 'understanding' produces a remaindered 'sublime understanding of misunderstanding'.

I find this hinge-like construction all through Adorno. It is not merely the technique of polished irony so admired by Adorno's opponents. Its meaning is fundamental to Adorno's dialectics: it produces a thing, a *res facta*, the negative remainder. It produces a sublime understanding of matters lying completely beyond one's understanding.

As a music theorist in a field that takes little or no account of labour in the Marxist materialist sense, I am intrigued with the notion of a substantive remainder. The substance of our musical world, both inside and outside academia, is labour, as both an objective presence and an actual force. Rare, however, is music-theoretical work that takes this into account (despite the ever-growing awareness of academic labour and its exploitation in the new university). Instead some music theorists (certainly many in North America) have preferred to analyse musical artefacts in absolute terms devoid of relation to labour, analysing them instead as works in and of themselves, for example as works of an interior organic unity. The usually tacit decision to ignore labour in music and in music theory (like the decision to avoid skin colour or ethnicity) constitutes a remainder for me. It is substantial, a presence that clings (with rare exception) to music theoretical thought in our day. This is one of the reasons I turn to Rancière.

Excursus 2. Out-takes. The practice of including hitherto suppressed tracks as supplements on reissued recordings raises two issues. On the one hand, it draws attention to musical labour, normally ignored by the music industry. By presenting the listener with two versions of the musician's output, it emphasises that original musical labour can be multifaceted, can produce many musical performances whose differences lie in the variability of individual musician's abilities. Thus out-takes point to musical labour as individual effort and point ultimately to the individual musician. On the other hand, these same out-takes obscure musical labour by packaging them as musical commodities equivalent to their authorised counterparts. It is as if musical capital, not content with the release of authorised performances, must work its way back closer and closer to the musician's original labour and alienate the latter by commodification. The proliferation of out-takes demonstrates that capital's thirst for music is not to be quenched.

Stain

One of the basic elements in Rancière's notion of equality is the non-equation implicit in equation. As Gabriel Rockhill summarises it: 'The essence of equality is not to be found in an equitable unification of interests but in the acts of subjectivization that undo the supposedly natural order of the sensible.'[10] I shall examine this notion of an 'equitable unification of interests' as undone by 'subjectivization', and compare it with Adorno's remainder.

To describe subjectivisation, Rancière uses the term *stain* in two essays where he cites Adorno: 'The Aesthetic Revolution and its Outcomes', from 2002, and 'The Monument and its Confidences', presented at a colloquium in Brazil in 2004. The two are reproduced in English in *Dissensus: On Politics and Aesthetics*.[11] I shall focus on the word *stain* here.

Rancière states the following: 'Adorno said that art must be entirely self-contained, the better to make the stain of the unconscious appear and denounce the lie of autonomised art.'[12] He catches something of Adorno's hinge here: art must be entirely self-contained, [hinge] for thus it will make clear its necessary relationship to the unconscious. Related of necessity to the unconscious, [hinge] the self-contained nature of art will be revealed as a lie.

In a reading of Schoenberg's path towards twelve-tone music, Rancière paraphrases Adorno by reference to a double heteronomy: to render clear the abstraction of human labour into capital (the first heteronomy), Schoenberg had to transform the labour of music into a more perfected form of abstraction (the second heteronomy – Schoenberg's system of composition with twelve notes). The effect, however, was to make perfectly clear the repression of labour in his music:

> The autonomy of Schoenberg's music, as conceptualised by Adorno, is a double heteronomy: in order to denounce the capitalist division of labour and the adornments of commodification, it has to take that division of labour yet further, to be still more technical, more 'inhuman' than the products of capitalist mass production. But this inhumanity, in turn, makes the *stain* of what has been repressed appear and disrupt the work's perfect technical arrangement.[13]

Following Rancière, Schoenberg's music must be perfect technically, which it achieves by the abstraction of labour. But, hinge-like, by the absence of labour in its perfection, Schoenberg's music makes clear its inhumanity. Repressed humanity in the form of absent labour thus appears as a *stain* upon Schoenberg's perfect work.

As it proceeds further and further along the axis of the inhuman commodification of labour, Schoenberg's music becomes ever more human in this regard. The more it proceeds towards technical perfection distanced from labour, the more its stain becomes visible and audible. The humans in his concert hall protest – stuff up their ears, cry out in pain: 'This is inhuman.' And thus Schoenberg, by the most abstract technical means, elicits a human response from his audience. The perfect technical work is stained by an immanent element of humanity. Thus it renders service to humanity [hinge] by repression.

Rancière frames the stain by referring to 'Adorno's expression: "art's social function is not to have one"'.[14] Stained art takes upon itself the function of refuting the customary function of art in capitalism. In capitalism, art is produced by the division of labour, but the goal of music production in capitalism is to forget that fact. The goal is to attribute to music a 'functionless' state of being. Music's social function is to forget the very division of labour that produced it (and thus music is a *simulacrum* for commodity fetishism in general).

> On this view, art does not resist purely by ensuring its distance. It resists but its closure itself shows itself to be untenable, because it occupies the site of an impassable contradiction. For Adorno the solitude of art does not cease to present the contradiction between its autonomous appearance and the reality of the division of labour, symbolised by the famous episode from the *Odyssey* in which, tied to his mast, Ulysses' mastery is separated from the work of the sailors, their ears covered, and the song of the sirens. To denounce the capitalist division of labour and the commodity embellishment more effectively, Schoenberg's music must be even more mechanical, even more 'inhuman' than the Fordist assembly line. But its inhumanity in its turn makes the stain of the repressed appear, the capitalist separation of labour and enjoyment.[15]

Reading this quotation, we remember the following passage on Schoenberg from Adorno's *Prisms*, which is a touchpoint surely for the neologism *playbour*: 'The more [Schoenberg's music] gives its listeners, the less it offers them. It requires the listener spontaneously to compose its inner movement and demands of him not mere contemplation but praxis.'[16]

Rancière's use of *stain* here supplements Adorno's remainder. There is a dynamic quality to Rancière's thought, a quality missing in Adorno. In Adorno the Wrong is still palpable in a static form of capitalism: ultimately all remainders, as I call them, refer to the problems implicit in capital and are thus restricted to the critique of capital. In other words, Adorno's criticism is still fraught with the ease of dialectic thought. Presupposed is the possibility of a correct form of dialectics, correctly dialectic even if it is attained only by a negative dialectics.

Rancière reads Adorno's insights as stains, as something untoward, unwanted, extraneous – rising autonomously, immanently, sublimely in the work of art. Rancière's stain is an attestation to a continual process of dirtying, of accidental disruption. (To anticipate Derrida, it is a prosthesis, both a crutch for an incurable ailment and a shield against the limitations of purity.) There can be no reconciliation, no negation of an accidental process. No remainder can shine forth as a beacon of dialectic hope. There can be only a constant and ongoing process of staining, which no form of dialectics can reconcile.

Excursus 3. Under the rubric of idleness, in The Arcades Project, *Walter Benjamin notes the following about 'modern beauty' as expounded by Poe, Baudelaire and Berlioz. Sensation transforms experience by making it immediate, but in doing so sensation poisons experience: 'It was a matter of injecting experience ... with the poison of sensation; that is to say, highlighting within ordinary experience [*Erfahrung*] the character of immediate experience'.*[17] *Thus Benjamin posits two kinds of experience: ordinary versus sensual. And he treats the latter as toxic, or at the very least sensually intoxicated.*

On these lines, we can say that Beethoven the revolutionary symphonist and symphonic revolutionary was content with ordinary experience. Revolutionary ends were served in his time simply by making his orchestration transparent, so as to make the rationality of the sonata form available to the declining aristocracy and the rising bourgeoisie and working classes alike. As revolutionaries, the musicians in Beethoven's orchestra strove for a musical experience of class equality based on clarity of design and purpose. Their musical labour was material in the Marxist sense of dispelling class divisions. By Berlioz's day, this had become an ordinary experience, in need of sensual supplement in keeping with bourgeois class distinctions and sensual excess.

In Dissensus, *Rancière writes: 'The power of the Juno Ludovisi [is] transferred to the vegetables, the sausages and the merchants* of *Les Halles* by Zola and Claude Lantier, the Impressionist painter he invents, in *Le Ventre de Paris*.'[18] *The Juno Ludovisi is a Greek statue*, he tells us. In Schiller, she stands in for the notion of free and unfettered appearance. Being self-contained, she is idle, removed from care, duty, purpose, or volition. In Zola, the goddess takes the form of an extreme description of the idle sensuality of food in Les Halles, the grand food market of Paris, a detailed enumeration of the contents of market stalls, and of shops – the cheese and the butcher shop, the sweet shop. Zola devotes pages and pages to the static riches of food piled high as it waits for purchase and consumption. And in Zola, the market vendors, largely women, are equally idle. They become for him a veritable army of Juno Ludovisi types, with heaving bosoms and rustling skirts.

We shall compare this to Berlioz's *Fantastic Symphony*, to its excesses of orchestral riches, and to the theme referred to as the idée fixe, which winds itself through the various movements. While the specific formation of the theme depends upon its given context – now soft and languorous, now shrill and irritating – the theme by its very ubiquity assumes a kind of autonomy, as if it were like the Juno Ludovisi, ultimately free and unfettered by any particular application. The theme stands as outside the customary rationale of classical sonata form, and thus it demands both a new compositional technique in orchestration and a new and special kind of listening – irrational and sensual. By its sensual presence, Berlioz's theme creates a musical autonomy devoid of the sonata conventions that hitherto guaranteed a form of musical autonomy (and elided class difference). Listening to Berlioz in this regard is a dispassionate experience, as if it were unmotivated by anything rational as experienced in music before, as if, slack jawed, we stood back in amazement at sounds that make no sense and yet sound so very good.

Rancière describes the Juno Ludovisi as a new kind of sensorium of an artwork that is not an artwork, a new kind of 'free appearance', without contingency:

> Correspondingly, the spectator who experiences the free play of the aesthetic in front of the 'free appearance' enjoys an autonomy of a very special kind. It is not the autonomy of free Reason, subduing the anarchy of sensation. It is the suspension of that kind of autonomy. It is an autonomy strictly related to the withdrawal of power.[19]

In similar ways, listening to Berlioz is a withdrawal of the revolutionary power given the composer, the musician, and the listener by the sonata form. The power withdrawn is worthy of note, for, as noted above, the sonata form transformed the privilege of music, moving it from an aristocratic context to the arena of the bourgeoisie and briefly the working classes. The sonata form articulates the thesis that any rational spectator can listen to music and in doing so become the equal of all humankind – kings and commoners. Berlioz suspends this rationale of autonomy. By his errant theme and by the luxurious orchestration whereby he illuminates the sensuous variety of the new orchestral instruments at his disposal, Berlioz comes to resemble the ladies of Les Halles. At hand is sheer ripeness: this is no longer autonomous art but art pushed beyond the bounds of autonomy to posit a new sensuality. As the idée fixe *disrobes, we stand powerless and singular before it:*

> The goddess and the spectator, the free play and the free appearance, are caught up together in a specific sensorium, cancelling the oppositions of activity and passivity, will and resistance. The 'autonomy of art' and the 'promise of politics' are not counterposed. The autonomy is the autonomy of the experience, not of the work of art. In other words, the artwork participates in the sensorium of autonomy inasmuch as it is not a work of art.[20]

When alluding to Zola, Rancière omits the transformation of the sensual in Le Ventre de Paris *that occurs at the book's end, where the protagonist Florent, about to foment revolution, is betrayed by these selfsame market ladies of Les Halles, the petit bourgeoisie. As the betrayal takes its final shape, the sensual nature of the market is changed, from appetite to disgust. Zola turns briefly to musical metaphor in this regard:*

> All around them the cheeses were stinking ... each adding its own shrill note in a phrase that was harsh to the point of nausea ... The cheeses seemed to stink even more. They all seemed to stink together, in a foul cacophony: from the oppressiveness of the heavy Dutch cheeses and the gruyères, to the sharp alkaline note of the olivet. From the cantal, Cheshire, and goat's milk came the sound of a bassoon, punctuated by the sudden, sharp notes of the neufchâtels, the troyes, and the mont-d'ors. Then the smells went wild and became completely

jumbled, the port-salut, limbourg, gérômé, marolles, livarnot, and pont-l'évèque combining into a great explosion of smells. The stench rose and spread, no longer a collection of individual smells, but a huge, sickening mixture.[21]

In Zola, the analogy between rot and betrayal is never addressed directly, but the cause and effect is made perfectly clear. The petit bourgeoisie of Les Halles are as rotten as they come. Oppressed by their labours in the service of bourgeois excess, the ladies of the market destroy the one entity – Florent – that might produce liberation. In this regard the market stall owners are made truly autonomous, for in the service of sensuality by their own hands they put themselves beyond redemption.

There is an overripe sensuality to Berlioz's orchestration. As the symphony builds and its orchestral richness unfolds, we are aware of anonymous musical labour as never before. Who were these musicians? Their names are lost to us, much as are the names of the market stall vendors of Les Halles. In Berlioz's time, through the spread of opera and concert music such as the symphony, a new class of musician arose in great numbers and to great sensual effect to meet rising bourgeois appetites for distraction. And being thus distracted, the bourgeoisie took little or no interest in these orchestral musicians and their alienated labour. In Berlioz's day, orchestral musicians became a kind of collective Juno Ludovisi, idle in the bourgeois mind and yet something to be contemplated, gazed at, and, as goddess of poisonous sensuality, feared.

A stain lies on Berlioz's Fantastic Symphony. On the one hand as an ordinary musical experience, it blends homogeneously with the concept of advanced musical creation. But over all that sensuous richness spreads the stain of alienated musical labour. From its first notes, it begins to ripen and to stink.

Nothing counts

A dynamic process of staining is implied in Rancière's notion of the count. As tidy census takers, we want to know the sum of entries in any given category. But that is merely one type of count. The other type is the enumeration of the entries – the varieties contained within a category, which, as varieties, undermine the very notion of a unified category. (We might think of this in simple semiotic terms leading back to Saussure. The use of a given word in practical speech is comfortably unitary: 'toast, please'. But the use of the term enumerates a host of other words, synonyms, 'grilled, browned on the outside, crisped lightly', and antonyms, 'buttered or dry, white or brown, hot or, heaven forbid, cold', all of which work to aggravate the unity. Ordering breakfast becomes thus a task both Protean and Procrustean.)

Rancière thus speaks of the 'count' of the uncounted in what I shall call here *ontological* terms, after Lukács: the very being of the bourgeois consciousness depends upon a strictly limited counting – an account of a definite and exhaustively defined class capable of strict enumeration. But when the bourgeois accounts for itself as a class, it does so without accounting for the proletariat; thus its count is incomplete, requiring supplement. Lukács's point is that, should the bourgeois mind take into account the existence of something beyond itself, a whole supplementary class, it senses its tenuous existence, its weakness, and having done so, the bourgeois mind implodes. Ontologically, the bourgeoisie exist as an incomplete count.

Rancière's count is a thing that adds up, but not simply as a definite 'social category' or 'original structure', or even an 'originary difference'. The count is a supplement to an originary structure, in truth two counts. And what matters is the effect of the supplement, the second count, upon the whole:

> When I introduce the notion of the count of the uncounted, this notion should not be understood as meaning the social category of poor wretched people, homeless and so on, but it should be understood, rather, in a structural meaning as designating a supplement to any count of individuals, groups, and identities. I did not, for that, intend to ground politics in an originary structure, an originary ontological difference. The count of the uncounted doesn't mean that the parties of the society cannot add up to a total sum, because they do add up.[22]

The sum of this reckoning is the dynamic political community – *political* in Rancière's sense of the word, the *polis*. Reckoning – the process of addition – puts into relief the 'distinction' between things added. The full scope of poverty is not attained by summing up the numbers of the impoverished, but rather by enumerating the varieties of poverty that accrue to that sum, and in their variety call into question the tidy work of summing poverty. The aim of counting is not exhausted by a single sum; the aim of counting is to draw distinctions between the things counted in a summation, even if these differences are set aside by the sum. Enumeration is both a supplement and the actual count, encompassing both equation and non-equation:

> What I call 'polis' is this addition – the identification of the political community with the sum of the components of the population. The count of the uncounted means that there is an overcount, a polemical count separating the whole from the sum of its parts. So I do not refer to politics as an original and structural void in metalinguistic fashion. I said that the demos of democracy is an empty part. It is empty, first, in terms of census, of an enumeration of parts. And it is empty, second, because it is the part of those who are nothing. But what matters to me is not the void, it is the distinction between two counts.[23]

Adorno plays a cameo role here. The sum is both a thing and its remainder. As good statisticians, we sum up matters: the number of children, y, in circumstances below the poverty line is x. Thus x, the number of children in poverty, $= y$, the sum of child poverty in our community. We arrive thus at a tautology from which no action proceeds.

But as a remainder left out of this sum, each child is to be counted individually; each child presents its own case to be remedied on its own terms. Thus poverty is not simply a unit to be tallied. To remedy each and every case of child poverty, we must break down their grand equation and deal individually with their particular circumstances, in particular our incapacity to deal with impoverished children on an individual basis.

For Rancière, the count becomes praxis, a vehicle for instructing the minority whose individuality is remaindered by the sum of equality:

> Equality turns into the opposite the moment it aspires to a place in the social or state organization. Intellectual emancipation accordingly cannot be institutionalized without becoming instruction of the people, in other words, a way of organizing the eternal minority. The two processes must remain absolutely alien to each other, constituting two radically different communities even if composed of the same individuals, the community of equal minds and that of social bodies lumped together by the fiction of inequality. They can never form a nexus except by transforming equality into the opposite.[24]

Thus, like Adorno, equation produces a dialectic remainder, the thing – *res facta* – that is made by being left out. Unlike Adorno, the application of Rancière's count is not exhausted by dialectics under the aegis of capitalism. Rather it is continuous and ongoing.

Excursus 4. It is impossible to define the 'jazz voice', since so many jazz singers, certainly in the years of swing and bebop, sang jazz standards taken from non-jazz repertoires such as Tin Pan Alley, and did so in a style that became less and less distinguishable from 'standard' music. The jazz singer Blossom Dearie is a case in point. Her vocal talents are prodigious and she demonstrates considerable ability as a jazz pianist. But the often saccharine tone with which she enunciates equally saccharine lyrics detracts from the seriousness of jazz as a vehicle for the expression of a social content in the music; for example, jazz as an icon for alternative forms of life in an era of grand conformity. Her antipode is the trumpeter Miles Davis, not a singer, whose voice appears interjecting from time to time on recordings, included by the producer to add a smudge of verisimilitude – real life – to Davis's often arcane and obscure improvisations. Davis's voice was scarred, it is thought, by an accident early in his career, and thus it sounds raspy and hoarse. It would be unthinkable to fuse Blossom Dearie and Miles Davis together as emblems of 'jazz voice'. And yet as twinned vocalists they articulate perfectly the material nature of the 'jazz voice' as a thing incapable of articulation.

On the border of aporia

In *Aporias*, Derrida speaks of the borders of truth. Crossing Derridean borders of truth is, to us, like calling across the river Styx. From the living side of this antique river, we cannot understand the stranger on the distant shore; to us they are as good as dead. We can merely stand and wave our tear-stained handkerchiefs.

Derrida says, in effect, that truth, like life, is a finite thing:

> By itself, the expression 'limits of truth' can certainly be understood – and this would be an *indication* – as the fact that the truth is precisely limited, *finite*, and confined within its borders. In sum, the truth is not everything, one would then say, for there is more, something else or something better: truth is finite [*finie*]. Or worse: truth, it's finished [*c'est fini*].[25]

But Derrida overturns this definition immediately. Truth is observed by exceeding (if not by breaking). The term *truth's borders* is a law: it 'can signify – and this time it would not be an indication but the law of a negative prescription – that the limits of truth are borders that must not be exceeded'.[26]

Derrida calls this the 'shibboleth effect: it always exceeds meaning and the pure discursivity of meaning'.[27] He says thus (without reference to Adorno's identity and non-identity paradigm): 'The identity of a language can only affirm itself as identity to itself by opening itself to the hospitality of a difference from itself or of a difference with itself.'[28]

This is akin to Adorno's remainder. Derrida's borders identify that which should need no identity, one's sense of self and land – *Heimatland* – a peaceful terrain without threat of division or dispersal. And yet borders arise only when that sense of self and land is under threat. Thus, the customary peaceful notion of self and land is remaindered when, anxiously, we drive up to the border, and the foreign guard asks 'What is your purpose?' or their domestic counterpart asks 'Are you bringing back anything?' Either question raises issues of integrity that do not haunt us when safely at home. And yet, like remainders, our home depends upon their existence, upon such questions being posed daily at borders.

Let us say that identity operates as if it were in-different (the hyphen is intentional), as if it could do without difference, indeed had never given the notion of difference any thought. At face value, Adorno's Mahlerian jackass is in-different to any difference with regard to Mahler: he knows what he likes, and he doesn't like Mahler. On this account, the mind of the jackass is an indivisible territory without border, stretching as far as the jackass can see or hear. But the jackass senses Mahler – as that thing he doesn't like and is thereby not encompassed by knowing what he likes. Mahler is a challenge to his in-difference and to his sense of the indivisible unity of jackass taste. Mahler creates in the jackass's mind a Derridean border, and in doing so Mahler transgresses the jackass's borders so as to make him uncomfortable at home.

Rancière's count is like a border. A census affirms what is to be encompassed by its terms against that which is not. Affirming the unity of a community, it creates a border. But having done so, the census is stained by all the uncounted aspects of its community, those entities to which the census takers are in-different.

Derrida describes this process of affirmation of borders as a problem: there 'is a problem as soon as this intrinsic division divides the relation to itself of the border and therefore divides the being-one-self of anything'.[29] In this regard he speaks of a contradiction in the word *problem* itself. On the one hand, its trajectory is outward and expansive (*project*). On the other hand, it is inward, centripetal, contraction (*prosthesis*).

> In sum, *problema* can signify *projection* or *protection*, that which one poses or throws in front of oneself, either as the projection of a project, of a task to accomplish, or as the protection created by a substitute, a prosthesis that we put forth in order to represent, replace, shelter, or dissimulate ourselves, or so as to hide something unavowable – like a shield (*problema* also means shield, clothing as barrier or guard-barrier) behind which one guards oneself in secret or in shelter in case of danger. Every border is problematic in these two senses.[30]

We might paraphrase Derrida as follows: a border is, on the one hand, something to project oneself over; on the other hand, something by which to deflect projections on to one's own territory. Implicit here is a Rancièrean stain: having created a border for the purposes of crossing over into someone else's territory, one immediately creates a border requiring one to stay home and defend it. Implicit here too is a Rancièreian double count: having created a border (or merely a wall) by which to enumerate those within, one creates a border to be filled thus by those without. Thus one creates a within and a without, where before there was only unity. The border to the Garden of Eden was drawn with the juice of an apple freshly bitten.

Derrida's border implies an immanent non-border. What good is a border, after all, if there is nowhere to go? If everything beyond the border is beyond the pale? In such a state of peripatetic innocence, border is not a problem. There is no problem for those content to live at home – *Heimat*. Nothing is problematic for those content never to look beyond the wall.

But we are all bordered: as members of a community among other communities, indeed as persons with the rights of individuals, since we must defend our individuality from the commonplace. Derrida describes in sensual terms – *passionné* – the contradiction of being at home and not being at home, at one and the same time. He describes this with the Greek term *aporia*, meaning thus the unresolved and unresolvable assertion (the author of this essay is a liar). But he goes beyond the simple logical stalemate by giving it sensuality, the *passionné*.

> I keep the word *problem* for another reason: so as to put this word in tension with another Greek word, *aporia*, which I chose a long time ago as a title for this occasion, without really knowing where I was going, except that I knew what was going to be at stake in this word was the 'not knowing where to go'. It had to be a matter of the nonpassage, or rather from the experience of the nonpassage, the experience of what happens [*se passe*] and is fascinating [*passionné*] in this nonpassage, paralyzing us in this separation in a way that is not necessarily negative: before a door, a threshold, a border, a line, or simply the edge or the approach of the other as such. It should be a matter of . . . what, in sum, appears to block our way or to separate us in the very place where *it would no longer be possible to constitute a problem*, a project, or a projection, that is, at the point where the very project or the problematic task becomes impossible and where we are exposed, absolutely without protection, without problem, and without prosthesis, without possible substitution, singularly exposed in our absolute and absolutely naked uniqueness, that is to say, disarmed, delivered to the other, incapable even of sheltering ourselves behind what could still protect the interiority of a secret. There, in sum, in this place of *aporia*, *there is no longer any problem*, or fortunately, the solutions have been given, but because one could no longer even find a problem that would constitute itself and that one would keep in front of oneself, as a presentable object or project, as a protective representative or a prosthetic substitute, as some kind of border still to cross or behind which to protect oneself.[31]

Derrida touches upon substance here, in ways similar to Adorno and Rancière. There is a place, a *locus*, really a state of paralysis, lying immanent in a contradiction. That place is a state of mind, a remainder left over from normal patterns of thought, but nonetheless substantial for being of mind. I will venture to suggest, in closing, that a person suffering Derrida's *aporia* might compare with Rancière's *polis*, who, like Adorno's jackass, is possessed immanently of a sublime insight not their due.

Excursus 5: Shopping Malls II. To return to our original conceit: shopping malls are like a grand subterranean cavern through which the river Styx pours. During opening hours, the mall is situated on the Hades shore, in the heat, its inhabitants prodded by the devils of commerce and of capital, lost to anything but the travails of ever-increasing work and consumption. After hours, we stand alone on the opposite shore, and the only sound that issues to us from across the waters is a distant music of pleasantries and soothing. The fabric of this distant music is stained by the memory of shopping, like a faint cry of suffering. Hearing this music and these faint cries, we come to understand that shopping is our inescapable destiny in Late Capitalism; we shall be borne across the Styx. In the music of the deserted shopping mall, we recognise that there is no escaping a commerce from which not even Orpheus can extract our lost souls.

Notes

1. Murray Dineen, *Friendly Remainders: Essays in Musical Criticism after Adorno* (Montreal: McGill-Queen's University Press, 2011), 13. Internal quote from Theodor W. Adorno, *Negative Dialectics*, trans E. B. Ashton (New York: Continuum, 1973), 5; translated from Theodor W. Adorno, *Negative Dialektik* (Frankfurt am Main: Suhrkamp, 1973), 16–17.
2. See Frederick Engels, *Herr Eugen Dühring's Revolution in Science (Anti-Dühring)*, trans. Emile Burns, ed. C. P. Dutt (New York: International Publishers 1939).
3. See Theodor W. Adorno, *Prisms*, trans. Samuel and Shierry Weber (Cambridge, MA: MIT Press, 1967).
4. Engels, *Anti-Dührung*, 133.
5. Georg Lukács, *History and Class Consciousness: Studies in Marxist Dialectics*, trans. Rodney Livingstone (Cambridge, MA: MIT Press, 1971), 225.
6. Engels, *Anti-Dührung*, 133.
7. Engels, *Anti-Dührung*, 146. Compare with Karl Marx, *Capital: A Critique of Political Economy*, vol. 1, trans. Ben Fowkes (London: Penguin Books and New Left Review, 1976), 928–9.
8. See Marx, *Capital*, ch. 32.
9. Adorno, *Prisms*, 149.
10. Jacques Rancière, *The Politics of Aesthetics: The Distribution of the Sensible*, ed. and trans. Gabriel Rockhill (London: Bloomsbury, 2004), 86.
11. Jacques Rancière, *Dissensus: On Politics and Aesthetics*, ed. and trans. Steven Corcoran (London: Bloomsbury, 2013).

12. Rancière, *Dissensus*, 116.
13. Rancière, *Dissensus*, 129.
14. Rancière, *Dissensus*, 178. No citation provided for internal quote. Compare Theodor Adorno, *Aesthetic Theory*, ed. and trans. Robert Hullot-Kentor (Minneapolis: University of Minnesota Press, 1997), 277: 'Insofar as a social function can be predicated for artworks, it is their functionlessness.'
15. Rancière, *Dissensus*, 178.
16. Adorno, *Prisms*, 149–50.
17. Walter Benjamin, *The Arcades Project*, trans. Howard Eiland and Kevin McLaughlin (Cambridge, MA: Harvard University Press, 1999), 803.
18. Rancière, *Dissensus*, 126.
19. Rancière, *Dissensus*, 117.
20. Rancière, *Dissensus*.
21. Émile Zola, *The Belly of Paris*, trans. Brian Nelson (Oxford: Oxford University Press, 2007), 210–11, 215–16.
22. Jacques Rancière, 'Comment and Responses', *Theory and Event* 6.4 (2003), n.p.
23. Rancière, 'Comment and Responses'.
24. Jacques Rancière, *Disagreement: Politics and Philosophy* (Minneapolis: University of Minnesota Press, 1999), 34.
25. Jacques Derrida, *Aporias*, trans. Thomas Dutoit (Stanford: Stanford University Press, 1993), 1.
26. Derrida, *Aporias*.
27. Derrida, *Aporias*, 10.
28. Derrida, *Aporias*.
29. Derrida, *Aporias*, 11.
30. Derrida, *Aporias*, 10–12.
31. Derrida, *Aporias*, 12.

13

On Shoemakers and Related Matters: Rancière and Badiou on Richard Wagner

Erik M. Vogt

Jacques Rancière's *The Philosopher and His Poor* narrates the history of the separation between philosophy and artisans and workers. This separation is articulated paradoxically in philosophy's endeavour to make time for the poor, while the poor are identified as those who, according to philosophy's judgement, do not have time for philosophy since they are allegedly consumed by work. Moreover, philosophy's assertion of a division of manual and intellectual labour is based on supposedly strictly separated, hierarchically structured natures codifying artisans (and workers) as simply lacking the capacity for philosophical reflection. This naturalisation of the division of labour proves to be a kind of internal exclusion of artisans through and in philosophy: an internal exclusion that serves not only as the condition of the possibility for pure philosophy, but at the same time as a restriction obliging artisans to a monotechnics, imbuing them with a capacity to do only one thing and to be only in one place, implying that artisans cannot and must not participate in other activities.[1] Thus, artisans cannot and must not be anything else but artisans, and their identity as artisans bars them from participating in other practices of sensemaking such as philosophy or politics.

However, the utility of artisans consists not only in illustrating one of the lessons of philosophy, according to which one can do one and only one thing at a time, but also in complying with the necessity of differentiating philosophy from its doubles. This task is assigned not simply to the artisan in general, but rather to the 'shoemaker' who, according to Rancière, 'is the generic name for the man who is not where he ought to be if the order of estates is to get on with the order of discourse'.[2] The shoemaker serves thus as what is at stake for, and the supplement of, a position that is supposed to guarantee that the philosopher can be strictly distinguished from the sophist, the poet and the artist. The shoemaker embodies not only the fundamental principle that one can do one and only one thing at a time but also the principle that is to exclude the following evil:

> that two things be in one, two functions in the same place, two qualities in one and the same being. Only one category of people, then, finds itself *de facto* without employment, those whose specific occupation consists in doing two things in one – *the imitators*.[3]

Since the philosopher assigns to the shoemaker the role of the body in this division of labour and its underlying incomparability of natures, the shoemaker assists the philosopher in denouncing all mere imitators. At the same time, the shoemaker is relegated to 'the truth of his specific technique', consisting in the production of one thing and one thing only.[4] Since technics always harbours the capacity of doing something else with it, the shoemaker's technics must become a kind of monotechnics that prohibits 'play, lying and appearance'.[5] Consequently, the shoemaker is locked in the world of useful labour and excluded from the world of imitation. The shoemaker is thus arrested both at the threshold of philosophical thinking and common political causes and at the threshold of the polytechnic world of imitations and appearances. In a word, 'the world of imitations divides itself on the subject of the artisan, leaving to the philosopher the guarding of appearances'.[6]

The shoemaker must be kept at a distance from theatre and from 'theatrocracy', in so far as the latter carries within itself a kind of democratic disorder. This reveals the attempts of the philosopher to regulate imitation in an effort to establish a foundation for the division of labour. Since Plato, the theatrical stage has been perceived as a site in which a potential disintegration of the functional principle of the division of labour occurs by enabling artisans to question their singular status, that is, the exclusivity of their function, therefore opening up their potential to imagine doing more than one thing. In this context, in Rancière's assessment, Plato denounced the theatrical stage both as space of public activities and as site of the performance of illusions, in that it potentially allows for a distribution of the sensible that renders functional identities indeterminate, delegitimises positions of speaking that correspond to natures, and deregulates hierarchical distributions of space and time. Or more specifically, the way Plato's denunciation distributes the sensible along prescribed divisions of labour 'both excludes artisans from the political scene where they might do *something other* than their work *and* prohibits poets from getting on the artistic stage where they might assume a character *other* than their own'.[7] Thus, 'Plato simultaneously excludes both democracy and theatre so that he can construct an ethical community, a community without politics'.[8] If artisans are allowed to be present in the theatre, they can only do so as representatives of the crowd chasing after cheap, popular, aesthetic pleasures, thereby reduplicating aesthetically their sociological confinement. That is to say:

> The shoemaker or carpenter must be merely one of the *polloi* who make up the noisy multitude. As if this were a matter of exorcizing the phantasm of an even more formidable anarchy: suppose the shoemaker or carpenter had forgotten the difference between useful work and a simulacrum, and decided to occupy himself not with judging theatre but – supreme folly – the Beautiful in itself.[9]

A shoemaker on the stage

Does the figure of Hans Sachs, who appears on the stage in Richard Wagner's *Die Meistersinger von Nürnberg*, not mark something like a rupture of the sociological and aesthetic exclusion of artisans from the political and artistic public realm? Is the figure of Sachs not evidence of Wagner's unwillingness to reduce the shoemaker to a mere bearer of a popular aesthetics? The unprecedented nature of Sachs's proposal consists not only in entrusting once a year the judgement regarding musical matters to the people, but above all in choosing a knight as 'the first singer he wants to name as one of the masters'.[10] If the first aspect could still be reduced to the affirmation of a popular aesthetics, the choice of a knight who, moreover, is a poet and not a singer is indicative of a confusion in which 'everything seems to get scrambled: weapons, tools, and meters; trade, science and inspiration; gold, silver, and iron'.[11] In order to keep this threat at bay – a threat which, due to the confusion of natures and the unregulated entry of the shoemaker into the world of art and philosophy, not only confounds the hierarchical order of estates but also creates a political and aesthetic disorder – a solution is offered 'that will satisfy simultaneously the government, the people and the poets: return popular culture to the people, return to them the rationality of the myth first confiscated and then abolished by the philosopher'.[12] It is precisely this solution that, according to Rancière, is staged in *Die Meistersinger*. For this work represents 'a farewell performance' reiterating the previous suppression of the insurrection of shoemakers and returning to the artist 'full possession of the attributes of nature and genius' that Wagner, 'in the turmoil of the 1840s', had 'entrusted to the people's care'.[13] The seeming triumph of the shoemaker-poet at the end of *Die Meistersinger* is really Sachs's abdication, that is, the restitution of artistic inspiration briefly usurped by the shoemakers to the 'aristocratic *Minnesaenger*'.[14]

Rancière draws the following conclusion: 'The alliance of shoemaker and poet in the cult of the people is over as soon as it began. It was power for a single day, the royalty of carnival exercised just long enough to restore the supremacy of genius over technique, inspiration over mnemonics.'[15] This represents the elevation of the inspired artist-knight baptised by the people over the mere mnemotechnician who, in the figure of Beckmesser,[16] is (also physically) vilified as 'petty bourgeois' and denounced as a 'discount sophist'. Wagner's seeming glorification of craftmanship is sustained by a logic of 'tit for tat' that can be described in the following manner:

> The inspired artist attributes to the popular *ethos* a genius, a *daïmon*, that the people immediately cede back to him, thereby consecrating the artist of the people, worker and knight, in his difference from the mechanical imitator. This consecration of the artist is then proposed in turn as a model for the politician and expert.[17]

Although the carnival staged in *Die Meistersinger* seems to disrupt the old Platonic order, it is followed by a 'popular art' that offers 'the guardians and those inspired by the modern age a new legitimacy based on the only powers that now are said to matter, the ones from below'.[18] In other words, the disruption staged by *Die Meistersinger* suspends the existing order so as to institute another order characterised by a new police count whose central watchword is *the people*: that is, a substantial category claiming unity, homogeneity and strict self-identity.

Die Meistersinger inscribes itself in the tradition of popular art in which *the people* functions as political and aesthetic legislator and fuses with the cult of the collective stage and the collective enjoyment of artworks. At the same time, the artist is assigned the task of aesthetic education; that is, the task of educating the people by means of its own legends. This task can, however, only be realised by sublating the contradiction between the aristocratic stage of opera characterised by 'unnatural' performances of folk melodies, and a people that, alienated from its own essence, has been degraded to the status of mere consumers of a mass spectacle. According to Wagner's aesthetic theory of the music drama, the mission of the artist consists in restoring a lost unity of the people:

> That unity lay in myth, the poem of a collective conception of life, or the popular unconscious. Drama was the elaboration of myth, the primitive language rediscovered for telling the essential conception of life ... The author of the music drama, a unity of the poet's male egoistic understanding with music's female liberating love, was himself the prototype of this essential individuality.[19]

Wagner's aesthetics of the music drama is based on the phantasm of a people whose essence could be restored by means of a return to a living popular culture, and this return rests on the artist-educator.

One (Sachs) divided into two (Wagners)

Rancière's brief excursus on some central moments from Act III of Wagner's *Die Meistersinger* is submitted to a critical interrogation by Alain Badiou. Badiou, too, sees as the central theme of this music drama the relation between art and the people that, moreover, addresses the necessity of transforming art in the moment of the encounter between the musical tradition represented by Hans Sachs and a new art of song inaugurated by the young aristocrat Walther von Stolzing. It is Sachs who faces the task of instituting between art and the people the relation of a non-relation – a task that requires not only the rejection of the 'horrible Beckmesser' who embodies 'the most entrenched advocates of tradition obviously opposed to the new song', but above all the mediating 'reconstruction of the relation where the non-relational dimension of the new song could be inscribed'.[20] Walther's victory in the competition, made possible by Sachs, reveals itself as 'a public construction of a new internal relation interweaving art, tradition, the people and invention'.[21] Against Rancière's claim that Wagner ultimately deprives the people of the power of artistic inspiration in order to return it to Walther – who, precisely through this expropriation of the people, is consecrated as artist – Badiou argues that Rancière's elaboration of the logic of tit for tat between the people and the artist fails to recognise the role that Wagner ascribes to Sachs. For it is only through Sachs that Walther realises that his inclusion among the mastersingers amounts to the institution of a non-relation as relation by means of which art as 'a new *organon* of the collective' becomes possible. Furthermore, the end of *Die Meistersinger* clearly shows that the people recognise in 'the miserable cobbler' the true 'master of the whole process'.[22] What is more, Badiou also rejects Rancière's interpretation of *Die Meistersinger* as a kind of farewell performance, for it neither has a nostalgic function nor is it a testimony for the 'complete disjunction between the arts of the avant-garde and the collective of the people'.[23] Rather, the figure of Hans Sachs must be grasped as the theatrical-musical representation of the anticipatory 'Idea of a great art which is neither reserved for the educated bourgeois nor degraded as booming sing-a-longs'.[24] Finally, the music of *Die Meistersinger* acts not only as 'prospective, anticipatory, and a temporal beacon of the becoming-eternal of the Idea', but it also generates 'a generic figure of *artistic discipline as an analogy of political discipline*'.[25]

Badiou's *Five Lessons on Wagner*, published several years after his critical reply to Rancière's interpretation of *Die Meistersinger*, reiterates many of these points. If the finale of this music drama is viewed from what Badiou believes to be the only legitimate perspective, that is, the perspective of music, it can be grasped in terms of the necessary synthesis of tradition and innovation. While Walther represents the creative genius of innovation and the guild of mastersingers represents tradition, it is the dual sacrifice of Hans Sachs – the sacrifice of his love and of his authority – that produces the very synthesis by means of which the rules for judging Walther's song are transformed. Badiou describes this synthesis in the following manner:

> The master of art is he who is able to sacrifice himself in a timely manner so that the new can be incorporated into the old, so that artistic innovation can be synthesised with tradition. It is consequently he who becomes the *people's* master precisely because he is the master of art.[26]

For Badiou, then, the lesson of Hans Sachs is that art is a dialectic 'of genius and mastery' unfolding via the following three main figures:

> The genius, Walther, who introduces something new into singing. The typical reactionary, Beckmesser. He is the Jew, when you come right down to it . . . And, finally, the master, who occupies a singular position that . . . is a position in which genius is accepted, acknowledged, and incorporated into the synthetic power of art.[27]

Furthermore, the militant task of Sachs, a representative of the proletarian aristocracy of masters, consists precisely in synthesising artistic innovation and tradition in such a manner that the new fundamental relation between the people and its historicity is established in the medium of art – a task that is accomplished through separating the avant-gardist forces (Walther) from the reactionary forces (Beckmesser) and by generating some temporary inequality (Sachs as master; Walther as fellow) that is then to be transformed into some structured avant-garde. Consequently, Badiou's elaboration of the finale of *Die Meistersinger* has recourse both to the Platonic question of education and to the modernist question of the avant-garde as forefront of artistic innovation.

Platonism and modernism constitute the two poles of Badiou's *inaesthetic* reading of Wagnerian art.[28] That is to say, the novel character of Wagner's musical art can be identified only under the premise that a space is opened for Wagnerian music that is not contaminated by traditional aesthetic schemata (and aesthetic theories) nor by non-art, and in which configurations of an art become visible that must not be confused with any kind of musical romanticism that, according to Badiou, signifies music's problematic entanglement in both philosophical thought and in politics. Consequently, Wagnerian musical art must be extricated inaesthetically from the ideology of the total artwork and its aspirations to a multi-sensorial art. Although the Wagnerian music drama is a mixture of different arts and can therefore be grasped as an impure form, the function of music in the Wagnerian music dramas is precisely to purify impurity. This hypothesis affects the traditional interpretation of the relationship between music and drama; for against its claim that music is ultimately subordinated to the dramatic scenario, Badiou's inaesthetic purification aims to demonstrate that, 'in Wagner, *dramatic possibilities are created through the music*', and not by the text or the drama.[29]

Badiou's inaesthetic project of the purification of the impurity of the music drama through and in music emerges most clearly in his reading of *Parsifal*, which explicitly examines the issue of 'how something pure is crafted out of the impure'.[30] *Parsifal* seems to be an exemplary representation of a heterogeneous multiplicity 'composed of chance and nothingness', that is, a strange hodgepodge of Christian elements, racial and even racist clichés and dubious sexual symbols.[31] On the other hand, the effects of this work have often been attributed to a type of nothingness constituted by an excessive system of leitmotifs, a 'decorative affectation' and a 'somewhat sugary sort of sublime'.[32] In this context, Badiou suggests that we examine the question as to whether *Parsifal* succeeds in 'changing chance into the infinite and nothingness into purity' in light of the figure of Parsifal.[33] For Badiou, Parsifal does not represent a character or an identity, but rather embodies 'the pure signifier' undergoing a transformation 'from the powerlessness of purity's ignorance to purity as power or force, purity as a force of knowledge'.[34] Moreover, the decisive moments articulating 'the connection between infinity and purity as an index of the Idea, as the struggle against the contingency of the material and the nothingness of its effects'[35] are to be found in those scenes of *Parsifal* that are concerned with the ceremony in the castle and are rendered 'by some exceptionally beautiful orchestral music'.[36] Consequently, the subject of *Parsifal* concerns the question of ceremony in the castle and its interpretation in light of the difference between these two scenes that Badiou describes in terms of the transition from the old to the new ceremony. However, what is the difference enabling this transition? It neither consists in the setting, nor in the '*formal* protocol of the ceremony', nor in the 'symbolic objects (the Grail and the Spear)', nor in the 'crowd';[37] rather, this difference is exclusively articulated in and by music, that is, through the striking contrast 'between Amfortas's howling and Parsifal's soothing music',[38] although the latter remains in some state of indeterminacy.

Although Badiou acknowledges that aesthetic mixture is constitutive for the Wagnerian music drama, he intends to safeguard music as the essence of Wagnerian art against the encroachments of Wagner's own aesthetic discourse on art and against the transgressions of the borders between the arts and of the border between art and non-art. His insistence on the strict separation between Wagnerian art and Romantic aesthetics reveals a modernist conception of autonomous, anti-mimetic art rejecting any notion of similarity or representation and radically purifying all heterogeneous moments connecting autonomous art with forms of life and with aesthetic discourses on art for the sake of some essence of art. However, since Badiou's inaesthetics is less interested in elaborating the immanent materialities of the different arts, and more in conceptualising the specificity of their ideas, its specific modernism is linked to what Rancière describes as a kind of 'ultra-Platonism, most succinctly encapsulated in the idea of a Platonism of the multiple'.[39] In a word, Badiou's inaesthetics constitutes a defensive enterprise that safeguards the eternity of the Idea from losing itself in the texture of the sensible and from being deprived of its educational value. The normative reference to modernism sustains the Platonic imperative of ethical art. That is to say:

> Badiou needs to affirm several things: that there is a specificity of art ... exposed in its purity only with the advent of modernity; that this specificity is the manifestation of a self-sufficient truth wholly separate from any discourse whatsoever about art's finality; and, lastly, that the 'specificity of art' is always the specificity of *an* art.[40]

But is it not the case that the constant negotiations and identifications of the borders between the arts – music, dance, poetry, architecture, sculpture, painting, stage design – of the borders between art and non-art, as well as the promise of an aesthetic revolution of the forms of art and the forms of life, are characteristic of both Wagner's aesthetic writings and his music dramas? Do not Wagner's music dramas, as impure genres that confound and blur modernist separations and oppositions, exemplify the kinds of redistributions that characterise Rancière's aesthetic regime? Are they not also expressions of the problematisation of the modernist separation between the arts, between art and non-art, between art and life? Do they not manifest the impure 'art of mixture in general, that which is made up of an admixture of other arts (the novel, music, painting, theatre)'?[41] Therefore, as an aesthetic rupture, does the Wagnerian conception of the music drama not enact a break with the representative regime? For Wagner's critique of traditional opera not only brings to light the hierarchical relation operative between opera's internal principles of form and construction, but it also examines this relation in its analogy to societal hierarchy. His conception of music drama expands not only the scope of art by transforming material previously excluded from art into art, but it also sets in motion an admixture of genres by confronting the representative model of opera, consisting of aggregate actions and of expressive modes coded according to subject matters and situations, with an original force of art that, by abolishing the norms that regulate the distance between the arts in the representative regime, mixes the different materialities in a direct manner. For this reason, Rancière can claim that 'Wagner could celebrate the carnal union of male poetry and female music in the same physical materiality' and therefore can be grasped as a 'great indifferent melange of significations and materialities'.[42] Wagner dissolves the representative norm into a commonality testifying to a more fundamental relation of mutual belonging; that is, to a common world in which the heterogeneous elements of language and music belong to the same sensible fabric. What is more, the dramaturgy of the Wagnerian music drama includes not only the 'male'-conscious materiality of language and the 'female'-unconscious materiality of music, but also attempts to integrate materialities such as stage and stage design, body and lighting, whose admixture is not possible without frictions and even conflicts.[43]

Since the Wagnerian music drama is part of the aesthetic revolution, it also shares in the constitutive paradox of the aesthetic regime that consists in the fact that the music drama is an autonomous form and at the same time goes beyond itself to merge into social life. Wagner conceptualises this moment of music drama's self-transcendence in the idea of the 'artwork of the future'[44] or total work of art, and this 'artwork of the future' is presented as the medium and site of the sublation of the divided aesthetic and social existence of the human being in capitalist society. The task of the 'artwork of the future' consists in the fulfilment of the destiny of modernity, that is, in the destruction of the reality of a collective based on the division between manual and intellectual-artistic labour. Against this background, one could claim that *Die Meistersinger* presents a notion of art that operates as a symbol of work. Art as material production 'anticipates the end – the elimination of oppositions – that work is not yet in a position to attain by and for itself ... Art anticipates work because it carries out its principle: the transformation of sensible matter into the community's self-presentation.'[45] Hence, Wagner's notion of art defines on the one hand an autonomous aesthetic realm, and at the same time aims at the destruction of the border between this aesthetic realm and the general social realm of life, in so far as the aesthetic realm and its attendant experience are elevated to the form of an integral experience encompassing the human community.

Wagner's 'artwork of the future' expresses the indistinctness of art and social life. But Wagner insists that the artwork of the future can realise its promise only if the aesthetic experience that it articulates negates its specificity and creates forms of a common life that no longer knows the distinction between art and politics, work and leisure, public life and private existence. In a word, the Wagnerian 'artwork of the future' defines the project of an aesthetic metapolitics that aims at the transformation of the forms of collective life and not only of the laws and forms of the state.[46] The 'artwork of the future' demarcates the specific and isolated space of aesthetic experience, and at the same time posits this as the promise of a common space that would no longer articulate any differentiation into specific spheres of experience. However, the self-cancellation of art thus implied, by means of the realisation of a new art–politics amalgamation, entails at the same time the self-cancellation of politics. The 'artwork of the future' knots art and politics together in terms of an aesthetic metapolitics that causes the practice of political dissensuality to vanish in favour of the formation of a consensual community. This disappearance of political dissensuality is made possible by the elimination of the autonomous 'aesthetic state' or 'aesthetic appearance' carried out by the 'activity of a conquering human mind' which transforms 'all sensible appearance into the manifestation of its own autonomy'.[47] The consensual nature of the Wagnerian aesthetic metapolitics appears above all in two constructive moments in the 'artwork of the future': in its theatrical frame, and in its hypostatisation of the audience as *the* people.

The theatrical frame of the 'artwork of the future' reproduces the Platonic opposition between chorus and theatre but is reformulated into the opposition 'between the truth of the theatre and the simulacrum of the spectacle'.[48] For Wagner, the truth of the theatre consists essentially in the idea of theatre as the exemplary form of the community, and this aesthetically constituted community is to occur exclusively in the temporal mode of self-presence.

In sum, the Wagnerian theatre serves the purpose of the restoration of the communal essence or as 'assembly or ceremony of the community':[49] a ceremony in which the audience transcends its position as mere passive spectator and enters directly into the theatrical ceremony to find its proper place in the community. The theatrical form commensurate with the 'artwork of the future' is a type of representation that can erase its own aesthetic distance by merging the theatrical stage with the communal stage and by transforming the theatre audience into the people that presents and celebrates itself as a living and acting community. But the Wagnerian theatrical art without representation replaces the representative stake, which consists of the improvement of behaviour, with an 'archiethical paradigm', according to which 'all living bodies directly embody the sense of the common' and which jettisons 'both art and politics in the same stroke, fusing them together by framing the community as artwork'.[50]

According to Wagner, the 'artwork of the future', as an aesthetic structure of collective life, is directly rooted in the collective life of the people, in so far as the 'artwork of the future' is to be created out of the spirit of the people. What is more, the increasingly nationalistically charged idea of the people that is also manifest in *Die Meistersinger* suggests that the 'artwork of the future' ultimately corresponds to the imaginary embodiment of the (German) people that pretends to already exist and that the artist simply must discover.[51] Wagner supposes the existence of a 'true' people with a real body and a substantial identity; in short, he identifies the people 'as *ethnos*, as the tangible collective of those who share the same origins, blood, god etc.',[52] whereas Rancière claims that *the people* does not exist and that it therefore cannot find its self-presence or self-presentation in the 'artwork of the future'. In other words, the 'artwork of the future' cannot provide a rationale as to why the political people that, according to Rancière, does not exist in a substantialist, unitary and homogeneous manner, should find its corresponding presentation in an artwork. Consequently, while the people should be conceptualised as '*demos*, that is, as a division of the *ethnos*, as a supplement of every counting of the parts of the collective',[53] it has to be insisted at the same time that the 'artwork of the future' cannot be political as such; although it can give rise to new possible experiential areas that dissolve existing subjectivations and provoke new ones, it cannot guarantee political subjectivations.

Mallarméan dissociations

Badiou's inaesthetic reading of Wagnerian music presents Wagner as hero of a type of anti-mimetic, Platonic modernism that deviates from conventional modernism in that it sets itself the task of investigating ideas or local truths in the context of the music dramas that are conceived as specific artistic configurations. By contrast, Rancière explicitly situates Wagnerian aesthetic theory and art in the context of the aesthetic regime of art and its corresponding aesthetic-political projects in the nineteenth century.[54] Therefore it may be surprising that these two different, even opposed readings of Wagner's art begin to overlap in their respective inscriptions of Stephane Mallarmé into the Wagnerian project of the 'artwork of the future' – inscriptions intended to address the difficult question of whether the Wagnerian 'artwork of the future' is ultimately to be interpreted as a problematic restitution of a 'properly religious art'.[55]

Badiou's claim that the subject of *Parsifal* must be identified in terms of the relation and transition between the two ceremonies in the castle occurs in the context of the question of whether a new ceremony is (still) possible; that is, a new ritual that must no longer be religious and that must account for the impossibility of celebratory festivals of the collective impacting modernity after the saturation of the revolutionary sequence. To examine closely the relation between these two ceremonies, Badiou refers to a line from Mallarmé – 'A magnificence, of one sort or another, will unfold, analogous to the Shadow of yore'[56] – that is supposed to aid in illuminating the Wagnerian ceremonial problematic. While 'the Shadow of yore' names 'the exhausted nature of nineteenth-century Christianity' and 'magnificence' designates the modern ceremony's sublation of all the elements contained in the demise of Christianity, the 'of one sort or another' announces the entry into democracy, that is, the impossibility of submitting the ceremony to any type of (religious) particularity, as well as the necessity of 'a ceremony of the generic'.[57] But the last point reveals the fundamental difference between Mallarmé and Wagner in that Mallarmé's 'magnificence' is subject to the future tense, whereas Wagner implies that this 'magnificence' already exists. Here, a decisive indeterminacy comes into play that deeply affects the status of the ceremony in Wagner, arousing the suspicion that the Wagnerian ceremony is ultimately nothing but a 'ceremony of ceremony', a 'representation of representation', a bourgeois spectacle rejecting or undoing the work of emancipation, that is, the project of conferring some ideal consistency upon emancipatory efforts – the very project that, in Mallarmé, is kept open via the use of the future tense.[58]

But this Wagnerian indeterminacy regarding the possibility of a new ceremony, and its oscillation between restoration and rupture, defines also Wagner's actuality, for the uncertainty regarding the possibility of a new ceremony characterises our present that can no longer rely on the new as revolutionary rupture and that therefore faces the question of whether there can be 'a modern form of ceremony that would exist by virtue of true *creation* rather than mere indeterminacy between restoration and innovation'.[59] Wagner's lesson for our present consists not only in pointing to the difficult choice between restoration and renovation, but also in insisting on the necessity of ceremony for the self-declaration of the collective that must not be restricted to mere forms of political revolt. Even though *Parsifal* fails to introduce a new ceremony, its indeterminate presentation of the relation between old and new ceremony contains nonetheless the task of preparing for the 'intrusion into future celebrations'[60] – a task that, according to Badiou, regards as imperative the assumption of the future existence of ceremony.

Rancière, too, establishes an explicit connection between the problematic of the Wagnerian ceremony and Mallarmé's reflections about the relationship between the pure poem and the ceremonial constitution of a new community in the context of the social, political and religious efforts of the nineteenth century; that is, about the poem as form of life and of art sharing in the political-religious consecration of the human abode. He even references the very same line from Mallarmé that is already at the centre of Badiou's thoughts regarding the possibility or impossibility of transition from the old to the new ceremony: 'A magnificence, of one sort or another, will unfold analogous to the Shadow of yore'.[61] Like Badiou, Rancière recognises in the 'shadow of yesteryear' a Christianity that is to be replaced by 'a human grandeur that would be constituted by anything whatsoever, by assembling objects and elements taken at random in order to confer on them an essential form, the form of a type'.[62] Without being able here to examine Rancière's interpretation of Mallarmé's type in more detail, one can say that Mallarmé's world of types is characterised by the task of consolidating a new human space that, because of the untenability of the old religion and the destruction of the monarchic political order, had become questionable. Mallarmé's reflections on the relationship between poem and human community occur in the time of an interval, that is, in a time of transition from the destroyed old representative order to a postrevolutionary social order that, if it is to lead to the bonds of a new community doing justice to a symbolic economy separate from the political economy of circulation, requires a new mission of the poem that, by celebrating the sensible community, could supplement the formalism of the political community. Mallarmé's idea of a new mission for poetry in the wake of religion is, however, marked by a distance both from mythological discourse and from a conception of Christianity that posits the Eucharist as its centre and thus worships some incarnated presence. For the 'grandeur' of Christianity consists precisely in its consecration of absence which ultimately can only be accomplished by the 'religion' of artworks, that is, by the 'institution of artifacts and rituals that transfer to the community'.[63] Mallarmé's 'new religion' turns out to be a human religion, and it is a new form of the sensible bond between human beings that exceeds the limits of the political community, which is traditionally conceived of in statist terms, by supplementing the latter.

The elaboration of this 'new religion' occurs in a time of transition. This means that the enactment of a new texture of communal life has to confine itself to the preparation of the celebrations of the 'future crowd'; it has to insist that the glorious hour of the new community has not yet arrived, and it has to strongly reject the opposite claim (enacted in *Parsifal*), according to which the existence of the new community can already be brought on stage, as phantasm. At this point, Mallarmé's confrontation with Wagner's 'musical religion' reaches its crucial moment. Although Wagner's 'artwork of the future' marks the end of the old theatre of representation by accomplishing 'the absorption of the poem and its politics into music',[64] it also preserves the theatre of representation by continuing to offer both a fable and a set of consistent figures through its system of leitmotifs. Moreover, the Wagnerian 'artwork of the future' transports in its conception of the total work of art what Rancière describes as a 'specific idea about the poem's function of community' that is tantamount to a phantasmic fusion of 'nature and music, representation and mystery, the gods of myth and the god of absence'.⁶⁵ This phantasmic fusion results in Wagner's problematic transformation of the 'communion "through the vacant space" into the people's real presence to itself, invited to the celebration of community origin', in which music is 'consecrated as the religion of the people, the Eucharist of the real presence to self of a people defined as a community of origins, of a people called itself to become the total work of art'.⁶⁶ Mallarmé opposes to Wagner's dual identitarian framing of music and the crowd both a 'Cartesian poetics of imaginative abstraction' and a 'revolutionary politics of justice' that, by remaining faithful to the accomplishments of the French Revolution, refuses to fill up the void of power with some real body of the people.⁶⁷ If the Mallarméan poem has the task of preparing the splendour of the future community by withdrawing from any embodiment of anonymous power, the distance between the poem and the future community must be maintained so that the future of both is not sacrificed for some phantasmic fusion. The very distance that the poem inscribes allegorically both towards itself and towards the people interrupts Wagner's archiethical model by attesting to a mode of aesthetic efficacy that consists in the reality of separation itself, that is, in the rupture of the very continuum of a causal relation that, according to Wagner's problematic assumption, is operative between the 'artwork of the future' and the people effected by it.

The accomplishment of Wagner's 'artwork of the future' is certainly the elaboration of new and differently sensible collective forms of experience that distance themselves from the canon of artistic configurations of the given and that interrupt the canonical relation between sense and the sensible. His supposition of the aesthetic rupture with the representative canon enacted by the 'artwork of the future' corresponds at the same time with an immediate, effective relationship between artwork and the people as the former's experiential body. However, the unique mode of efficacy taking place in the aesthetic rupture is one that performs two modes of decoupling, namely 1) the decoupling of artistic products from particular social ends, and 2) of their sensible forms both from the meanings that can be extracted from them and from the effects that they can generate. In a word, this mode of aesthetic efficacy is that of a dissensus by means of which art touches politics, in so far as politics itself is 'a dissensual reconfiguration of the common experience of the sensible'.⁶⁸ But art and politics touch each other in dissensus only if the distance and separation between these two forms of dissensus is maintained, and the pretence of a direct identification of the forms of art and the forms of politics – a pretence that, after all, accounts for the archiethical closure of Wagnerian aesthetic metapolitics and its production of a phantasmic consensus – is suspended.[69]

Notes

1. Jacques Rancière, *The Philosopher and His Poor*, trans. Andrew Parker (Durham, NC: Duke University Press, 2004), 22.
2. Rancière, *The Philosopher and His Poor*, 48.
3. Rancière, *The Philosopher and His Poor*, 8 (italics in original).
4. Rancière, *The Philosopher and His Poor*, 16.
5. Rancière, *The Philosopher and His Poor*, 17.
6. Rancière, *The Philosopher and His Poor*, 45.
7. Jacques Rancière, *Aesthetics and Its Discontents*, trans. Steven Corcoran (Cambridge: Polity, 2009), 26 (italics in original).
8. Rancière, *Aesthetics and Its Discontents*, 26.
9. Rancière, *The Philosopher and His Poor*, 48.
10. Rancière, *The Philosopher and His Poor*, 57. Briefly, the plot of *Die Meistersinger* revolves around the real-life shoemaker-poet Hans Sachs and the guild of mastersingers – poets and musicians who pursue their craft according to the strict rules of their tradition. Eva, the daughter of the goldsmith Pogner, and Walther von Stolzing, a knight, fall in love with each other, but Pogner has promised his daughter to the winner of the forthcoming song contest. Under the tutelage of Sachs and against the opposition of the town clerk Beckmesser, Walther acquires the mastersinger's art and succeeds in winning the song contest and therefore also Eva. Sachs's proposal is remarkable not only because, by speaking up for the young aristocrat Walther, he deliberately blurs existing class distinctions, but also because he seems to dissolve these class distinctions into (the judgement of) the people.
11. Rancière, *The Philosopher and His Poor*, 57.
12. Rancière, *The Philosopher and His Poor*, 60.
13. Rancière, *The Philosopher and His Poor*, 61.
14. Rancière, *The Philosopher and His Poor*, 61.
15. Rancière, *The Philosopher and His Poor*, 61.
16. Beckmesser is the town clerk whose task consists in preserving the existing singing tradition; moreover, he is Walther's rival in the

song contest who ends up in utter disgrace and is excluded from the celebration of German art headed by Sachs. There is no doubt that Wagner's representation of Beckmesser contains antisemitic features. Rancière critically alludes to these features when he shows that Wagner reduces the figure of Beckmesser to a mere functionary of technique and mnemonics, lacking the 'German' qualities of genius and inspiration.

17. Rancière, *The Philosopher and His Poor*, 62.
18. Rancière, *The Philosopher and His Poor*, 62.
19. Jacques Rancière, *The Intellectual and His People: Staging the People*, vol. 2, trans. David Fernbach (London: Verso, 2012), 18. As to Wagner's conceptualisation of music as female and of poetry as male, the following passages from his *Opera and Drama* must suffice here as illustrations of Rancière's point:

> *Music is a woman.* The nature of Woman is *love*: but this love is a *receiving* . . . and in receival . . . an unreservedly *surrendering*, love . . . *Who* then must be *the Man*, whom this Woman is to love so unreservedly? . . . Let us closely view *the Poet*! . . . If we now pry a little closer into the Poet's business, we shall see that the realisement of his Aim consist solely in the making possible an exhibition of the 'strengthened actions' of his characters . . . through an exposition of their motives to the Feeling; and that this, again, can only be effectuated through an *Expression* which shall in so far claim his active aid, as *its invention and establishment first makes possible the displaying of those motives and actions* . . . The Understanding is therefore driven by necessity to wed itself with an element which shall be able to take-up into it the poet's Aim as a fertilising seed, and so to nourish and shape this seed by its own, its necessary essence, that it may bring it forth as a realising and redeeming utterance of Feeling. This element is the same mother-element, the womanly, from whose womb . . . there issued Word and Word-speech, so soon as it was fecundated by the actual outward-lying objects of Nature; just as the Understanding throve from out of Feeling, and is thus the condensation of this womanly into a manly, into an element fitted to impart. Now, just as the Understanding has to fecundate in turn the Feeling . . . just so is the intellectual Word impelled to recognise itself in Tone, the Word-speech to find itself justified in Tone-speech. The stimulus which rouses this impulse and whets it to the highest agitation, lies outside the one impelled, and in the object of yearning; whose

charm is ... the influence of the 'eternal womanly', which draws the manly Understanding out of its egoism. (Richard Wagner, *Opera and Drama*, trans. W. Ashton Ellis (Lincoln: University of Nebraska Press, 1995), 111, 115, 235f.)

20. Alain Badiou, *The Adventure of French Philosophy*, ed. and trans. Bruno Bosteels (London: Verso, 2012), 127–8.
21. Badiou, *The Adventure of French Philosophy*, 128.
22. Badiou, *The Adventure of French Philosophy*, 128.
23. Badiou, *The Adventure of French Philosophy*, 129.
24. Badiou, *The Adventure of French Philosophy*, 129. In this context, Badiou claims that 'this opera, from the spring-like architecture of its overture onwards, is *artistically* the opera of constructive gaiety'. Badiou, *The Adventure of French Philosophy*, 129.
25. Badiou, *The Adventure of French Philosophy* (italics in original).
26. Alain Badiou, *Five Lessons on Wagner*, trans. Susan Spitzer (London: Verso, 2010), 109 (italics in original).
27. Badiou, *Five Lessons on Wagner*, 109–10.
28. See Alain Badiou, *Handbook of Inaesthetics*, trans. Alberto Toscano (Stanford: Stanford University Press, 2005). For a detailed introduction to Badiou's inaesthetic reading of Wagner, see Erik M. Vogt, *Aesthetisch-Politische Lektueren zum 'Fall Wagner'* (Vienna and Berlin: Turia + Kant, 2015).
29. Badiou, *Handbook of Inaesthetics*, 89 (italics in original).
30. Badiou, *Handbook of Inaesthetics*, 136.
31. Badiou, *Handbook of Inaesthetics*, 137.
32. Badiou, *Handbook of Inaesthetics*, 138. Badiou claims that these criticisms of Wagner's *Parsifal* can be found in the writings of Nietzsche, Adorno, Lacoue-Labarthe and even Boulez.
33. Badiou, *Handbook of Inaesthetics*, 139.
34. Badiou, *Handbook of Inaesthetics*, 140.
35. Badiou, *Handbook of Inaesthetics*, 142.
36. Badiou, *Handbook of Inaesthetics*, 147.
37. Badiou, *Handbook of Inaesthetics*, 153.
38. Badiou, *Handbook of Inaesthetics*, 155.
39. Rancière, *Aesthetics and Its Discontents*, 70.
40. Rancière, *Aesthetics and Its Discontents*, 74 (italics in original).
41. Rancière, *Aesthetics and Its Discontents*, 83.
42. Jacques Rancière, *The Future of the Image*, trans. Gregory Elliott (London: Verso, 2007), 42–3.
43. Rancière examines the question of different sensible regimes in the

Wagnerian music dramas with reference to Adolphe Appia's conception of an art of staging that attempts to do justice to the aesthetic-revolutionary kernel of the Wagnerian music drama by giving a spatial form to music as the force of unconscious life. However, Appiah is confronted with the difficulty that Wagner's idea of the music drama still relies on the mimetic space of the old spoken drama. See Jacques Rancière, *Aisthesis: Scenes from the Aesthetic Regime of Art*, trans. Zakir Paul (London: Verso, 2013), 120–31. For a more detailed account of Rancière's interpretation of Appia's conception of staging, see Erik M. Vogt, *Zwischen Sensologie und aesthetischem Dissens* (Vienna and Berlin: Turia + Kant, 2019).

44. Richard Wagner, *The Art-Work of the Future and Other Works*, trans. W. Ashton Ellis (Lincoln: University of Nebraska Press, 1993).
45. Jacques Rancière, *The Politics of Aesthetics: The Distribution of the Sensible*, trans. Gabriel Rockhill (London: Continuum, 2004), 44. See also Udo Bermbach, *'Bluehendes Leid': Politik und Gesellschaft in Richard Wagners Musikdramen* (Weimar: Metzler, 2003), 264, 269.
46. Aesthetic metapolitics designates 'the principle of a politics ... which, against the upheavals of state forms, proposes a revolution of the forms of the lived sensory world' (Rancière, *Aesthetics and Its Discontents*, 99). Elsewhere, Rancière claims that 'Schiller's notion of the *aesthetic education of man* constitutes an unsurpassable reference point' for aesthetic metapolitics – see Rancière, *The Politics of Aesthetics*, 27. It is this Schillerian notion that

> defined a neutral state, a state of dual cancellation, where the activity of thought and sensible receptivity become a single reality. They constitute a sort of new region of being – the region of free play and appearance – that makes it possible to conceive of the equality whose direct materialization, according to Schiller, was shown to be impossible by the French Revolution. It is this specific mode of living in the sensible world that must be developed by 'aesthetic education' in order to train men susceptible to live in a free political community ... It can be said, regarding this point, that the 'aesthetic revolution' produced a new idea of political revolution: the material realization of a common humanity still only existing as an idea. This is how Schiller's 'aesthetic state' became the 'aesthetic programme' of German Romanticism, the programme summarized in the rough draft written together by Hegel, Hölderlin and Schelling: the material realization of

unconditional freedom and pure thought in common forms of life and belief. (Rancière, *The Politics of Aesthetics*, 27)

Incidentally, the 'material realization of a common humanity' is at play also in Wagner's conception of the relation between 'female' music and 'male' poetry, between 'feeling' and 'understanding'. For this relation does not represent a dualism that would be in need of deconstruction, but rather the neutralisation or cancellation of this dualism for the sake of bringing into material existence a new type of (human) being.

47. Rancière, *Aesthetics and Its Discontents*, 37.
48. Jacques Rancière, *The Emancipated Spectator*, trans. Gregory Elliott (London: Verso, 2009), 5.
49. Rancière, *The Emancipated Spectator*, 6.
50. Jacques Rancière, *Dissensus: On Politics and Aesthetics*, ed. and trans. Steven Corcoran (London: Continuum, 2010), 137.
51. As to the nationalist overdetermination of *Die Meistersinger*, see Stefanie Hein, *Richard Wagners Kunstprogramm im nationalkulturellen Kontext* (Würzburg: Könighausen & Neumann, 2006), 176–7.
52. Jacques Rancière, *Dissenting Words*, ed. and trans. Emiliano Battista (London: Bloomsbury, 2017), 144.
53. Rancière, *Dissenting Words*, 144.
54. These include, to name a few, Schiller's 'aesthetic education', Hölderlin's 'aesthetic church', as well as the 'mythology of reason' articulated in *The Oldest Systematic Program of German Idealism*.
55. The question of whether the Wagnerian music drama must be grasped as the artistic attempt to reinstate ancient Greek tragedy as the religious, that is, political art *par excellence* guides – and haunts – Philippe Lacoue-Labarthe's readings of Wagner. See Philippe Lacoue-Labarthe, *Musica Ficta (Figures of Wagner)*, trans. Felicia McCarren (Stanford: Stanford University Press, 1994), xv. What is more, Lacoue-Labarthe also examines in detail Mallarmé's critical response to Wagner's art.
56. Badiou, *Five Lessons on Wagner*, 150.
57. Badiou, *Five Lessons on Wagner*, 150.
58. Badiou, *Five Lessons on Wagner*, 151.
59. Badiou, *Five Lessons on Wagner*, 156 (italics in original).
60. Badiou, *Five Lessons on Wagner*, 159.
61. However, the English translation speaks of the 'shadow of yesteryear' and of 'some splendour'. See Rancière, *The Future of the Image*, 96.

62. Rancière, *The Future of the Image*, 96–7.
63. Jacques Rancière, *Mallarmé: The Politics of the Siren*, trans. Steven Corcoran (London: Continuum, 2011), 30–1.
64. Rancière, *Mallarmé*, 39.
65. Rancière, *Mallarmé*, 39.
66. Rancière, *Mallarmé*, 40.
67. Rancière, *Mallarmé*, 40.
68. Rancière, *Dissensus*, 140.
69. At this point, one could briefly point to both affinities and differences between Badiou's and Rancière's respective inscriptions of Mallarmé into the Wagnerian corpus on the one hand, and Lacoue-Labarthe's readings of Wagner on the other. All three oppose the danger of a 'new mythology' and a 'national aestheticism' giving figure to and celebrating the community of the German people that haunts Wagner's religious art – see Lacoue-Labarthe, *Musica Ficta*, xxi. All three also ask for that which could have the potential of interrupting religion. But these affinities between Badiou, Rancière and Lacoue-Labarthe ultimately give way to profound differences between them. Although I cannot enumerate all these differences, let me briefly point to a few. While Lacoue-Labarthe's final word seems to concern the question of the interruption or caesura of religion, both Badiou and Rancière attempt to press beyond this point in order to address the question of a post-religious ceremony of/for the modern political collective. Furthermore, Lacoue-Labarthe claims that 'ultimately Wagner saturated opera' or brought about a 'closure of opera' (Lacoue-Labarthe, *Musica Ficta*, 117, 118). This claim seems to imply that Wagnerian art is nothing but a false totalisation and thus 'beyond redemption'; for Badiou, however, Wagnerian art still contains possibilities that are relevant both for our present and for our future. Although Rancière does not share Badiou's conviction that Wagnerian art contains the contours of a future 'great art', he also does not subscribe to Lacoue-Labarthe's imposition of a kind of 'prohibition of graven images' on Wagner's work; rather, he seems to engage in a reading of Wagner that turns against him the Wagnerian accomplishment of the paradox of the aesthetic rupture of both the representative regime and the archiethical regime. If the dissensus of Wagnerian art afforded by the aesthetic rupture is not to disappear in its very opposite, it must remain the unresolved tension between art's resistance and the resistance of politics.

14

Roll Over the Musical Boundaries: A Few Milestones for the Implementation of an Equal Method in Musicology

Danick Trottier

> I think that 'the rest is up to you' is an essential maxim in my work.
> Jacques Rancière[1]

The notion of equality pervades Rancière's philosophy at every level. From his earliest works such as *Proletarian Nights: The Worker's Dream in Nineteenth-Century France* to his current writing and collections such as *The Method of Equality*, with interviews by Laurent Jeanpierre and Dork Zabunyan, equality features as a presupposition. Whereas some scholars try to divide Rancière's philosophical output into territories marked in turn by a historical moment (labour movements, Joseph Jacotot), a political moment (the declaration of equality within a police logic, disagreement, etc.) and an aesthetic moment (engagements with film, literature and so on),[2] others – such as Jeanpierre and Zabunyan – reject this division in favour of a unity premised on equality across his career. Indeed, Rancière has argued for this unity several times recently, insisting that the themes that thread through his entire body of work are vastly more significant than the differences that might be found between writings from different decades. The publication of *The Method of Equality* has been a kind of revelation in this direction: equality is addressed specifically as a working method present throughout Rancière's career; to this end the interviewers aspire 'to restore the unity of Rancière's philosophical project'.[3]

Equality therefore finds a twofold application in Rancière's thinking: it is both a philosophical principle and a working method. As a philosophical principle, equality is 'a starting point', to use Rancière's words, based on 'the Jacotist side of [his] thinking',[4] which begins with the axiom that 'intelligence is the same for everyone'[5] and that a non-hierarchical disposition can be the basis for intellectual emancipation.[6] As a methodological starting point, equality is grounded in epistemological concerns: how do we approach the objects at the basis of our scientific work and how do we build our scientific discourses? We find a good example in Rancière's archival investigation into the labour movements of the nineteenth century, in that *Proletarian Nights* reveals the ways in which workers subverted the different hierarchical relations within which they found themselves. To reach this goal, in contrast to the vertical, Marxist approach based on deducing the nature of the alienation of the masses, Rancière's attention is directed towards the workers themselves, 'through the glances and the words, the dreams and the nightmares' they produced as historical actors.[7] As such, *Proletarian Nights* was 'made up essentially of equivalences and displacements: a text cited, a commentary in the form of a paraphrase that displaces it and starts a movement towards another scene'.[8] In doing so, the heuristic goal is to foster a renewed scientific posture, based on epistemological considerations:

> It's a principle of egalitarian writing: doing away with the hierarchy between the discourse that explains and the discourse that is explained, and bringing out a common texture of experience and reflection on that experience which crosses the boundaries between disciplines and the hierarchy of discourses. It's a quasi-syntactical problem.[9]

How can these epistemological considerations be extended to musicology? More broadly, how, where and at what cost could equality be introduced as a method of working in the study of music? The question could also be framed retrospectively: where are glimpses of the method of equality already found in the history of musicology? While Rancière's work has been decidedly 'indisciplinary',[10] musicologists have a specific object of study, which should be the focus of a possible implementation of equality as a working method: music, or let us say the totality of possibilities that the word music invokes. Therefore, musicologists are concerned in the first place with an object that is situated at the core of sense perception: music doesn't circulate in a vacuum; rather, it is governed by the distribution of the sensible, another concept central to Rancière's philosophy. In *The Politics of Aesthetics*, he argues that the concept 'establishe[s] at one and the same time something common that is shared and exclusive parts', which amounts to a kind of regulation or mapping of constraints on sense experience, the *sine qua non* of the ongoing distribution in human life.[11] Henceforth, what is at stake in the distribution of the sensible is the whole scene in which it takes place, namely 'a distribution of spaces, times and forms of activity that determines the very manner in which something in common lends itself to participation and in what way various individuals have a part in this distribution'.[12] In the case of music, musicologists take part in that distribution as producers both of cultural activity and of discourses that affect how distributions are formed, for example in the way some works gain attention at the expense of others, and how canons are formed.

Some key concerns here include how music is used, the ways in which it is appropriated and the spaces in which it takes form. In Rancièrean terms, these concerns foreground how music comes to make sense for the people who practise it, listen to it and make use of it. These concerns centre specifically around different kinds of artistic practices, which Rancière describes as an inquiry into 'what they "do" or "make" from the standpoint of what is common to the community'.[13] I would suggest that we summarise this idea through two questions: 'What makes art?' and 'What does art do?'[14] These Rancierian questions provide occasions to underscore what is included and what is excluded in the word 'music', namely in the way it is distributed through the labels given to different kinds of music. As musicologists, we must admit it: the very notion of music is fragmented in its essence by the words we use, which have been transmitted by and within social and cultural traditions; for example, through the categories and related constellations of descriptive words we use for speaking of music and arranging the phenomena linked to it. Popular genres such as hip-hop or metal are persuasive cases. We can easily imagine all the stereotypes that are associated with these genres: hip-hop is violent, gangsterish, misogynist, ostentatious, etc. (or, positively, culturally expressive, poetic, politically incisive); metal is loud, noisy, dangerous, macho (or liberating, cathartic, etc.).[15] The use of language to understand and give sense to music is intricately wrapped up in processes of qualification. Therefore, if we agree that the ways we use words to describe musical phenomena function as mediations that inscribe particular kinds of culturally and socially specific meanings, we must also admit that words are a way by which we enclose music in hierarchical principles, such as when it comes to questions of 'art music', 'serious music', 'world music', 'popular music', 'entertainment music' and so on. In short, there are many qualifiers that uphold hierarchies. And as we saw above with hip-hop and metal, these qualifiers can have overtly deleterious effects. Music, as a cultural form governed by the distribution of the sensible, inevitably engenders forms of inclusion and exclusion.[16]

It is worth bringing a Rancièrean perspective to bear on this issue. Beginning with the distribution of the sensible and the ways in which discursive mediations influence our perception of music, I sketch here the beginning of a possible application of the method of equality in the study of music by drawing attention to traces that can already be found in musicology's history. What is at stake in the implementation of equality as a method of working in musicology? To answer this question, I will focus on some key moments in the recent history of musicology: the so-called 'new musicology' and its afterlife. I will also show how musicology and popular music studies have only quite recently been in contact, the implications of which will reveal important aspects of how musical hierarchies are constructed, genre boundaries are drawn, and evaluative language is deployed. In sum, the discussion that follows will take the form of a brief disciplinary overview focusing on the presence of an equal method, particularly in relation to the new musicology and the related development of the study of popular music. My hope is that, in developing the following concepts, I can bring to attention some of the ways in which musicology's discursive practices have covered over or suppressed an underlying equality that precedes hierarchical inscriptions. Furthermore, I hope to provide the foundations for a Rancièrean equal method (drawing on methodological precedents in popular music studies) through which we can continue to engage the disciplinary forces that reiterate and reconstitute musicological hierarchies through practices of redistributing the sensible.

Epistemological issues in musicology: what does music do?

Rancière's discussion of Pierre Bourdieu's sociology of distinction in *The Philosopher and His Poor* is a good starting point to see what is at stake in equality as a method, and to begin to locate its echo in music.[17] Before arriving at an example that he develops through the intermediary of the Argentinian pianist Miguel Angel Estrella, Rancière outlines the work that Bourdieu accomplished in *The Inheritors* (co-written with Jean-Claude Passeron) and *Distinction: The Social Critique of Judgment*.[18] In those texts, Bourdieu famously developed his theories of legitimacy and domination regarding the capitalist aesthetic that the upper classes possess in their relation to culture and works of art – that capital is legitimised by official institutions such as the school, the museum and so on. Rancière's critique lies with the methodological game played by Bourdieu: the sociologist repeatedly questioned the French citizens who comprised his quantitative research study (with questions centred on their cultural tastes), until he ended up at the system of domination that he already perceived as the foundation of the social world. What had already been assumed as legitimate culture is therefore always relegitimised in any act that poses as an unsurpassable social reality, which social and individual judgement dissimulates at every step. For Bourdieu, therefore, only the sociologist has the power to reveal social reality.

In contrast, the pianist Estrella's experimental method is comparable to Rancière's own thought, and is more promising in the ways in which it plays on forms of appropriation that permit listening in real time: the fact that he played classical music to the people and workers in a rural Argentinian villages led to results in which Debussy is kept at a distance, Mozart is appreciated and Bach is 'adopted as the son of the people by the village community'.[19] Even though this example is not supported by rigorous empirical observation, instead drawing on Estrella's personal experience, what is important is Rancière's conclusion: the way that people engage with music is more complex than is revealed in Bourdieu's sociology of domination, which limits citizens by proceeding through questionnaires far removed from actual acts of listening. In an article in which they propose the idea of an *equal music*, Jairo Moreno and Gavin Steingo summarise what is at stake in that discussion:

> Rancière disagrees with Bourdieu's methodology and the results derived from it. For him, Estrella's informal experiments with music were 'dissensual.' They assumed the fundamental equality of all people to engage music . . . Prior to cultural proclivities and aesthetic competences, any formation (community, culture, society) has the sensorial as its common.[20]

Here equality is given as a presupposition in so far as the relation with a work of art such as music can be engaged with by everyone through sense experience: once the work is distributed, the sensorial disposition to listen to it is the prerequisite to have a relation to it, whatever the nature of that relation. Thus, the idea is to claim the foundation of an active sensibility shared by everyone through sense perception in any event of engaging in a relation with a work of art.

The idea that everyone can relate to a work in terms of an active, shared sensibility goes, to some degree, against the epistemological foundations on which musicology is formed. Musicology, to the extent that it attempts to be a scientific discipline, was born of the will to give sense to musical objects and to composers' intentions: this is the sense of the scientific heritage of the nineteenth century, where the field of action focuses on the exegesis and explanation of the work of 'great' composers (for example, Johann Nikolaus Forkel's work on J. S. Bach and Gustav Nottebohm's engagement with Beethoven's music), as well as on the lexicography of music (for example, François-Joseph Fétis) and the history of European art music (for example, Guido Adler), especially the Austro-German canon that coincided with the long history of positivism.[21] The ideology of 'serious music' which evolved from writing on Beethoven similarly determines modes of apprehending, understanding and listening to music.[22] This entanglement of scientific engagement with the explanation of a musical work is perceived in other instances as an act of musical criticism, as undertaken by a number of aestheticians and musicologists, first among them Eduard Hanslick, with his virulent critique of the aesthetics of feeling.[23] Musicology has travelled a long way since then and has adopted a more critical posture that has cleared the way for a more comprehensive musicology that has engaged in the deconstruction of certain acquired ideas. Among them, we can sketch a few examples where the goal was to displace the way we study music and return to the question 'What does music do?' from new critical perspectives: introducing issues around the role of the body and of sociocultural meaning, deconstructing the authority of the Austro-German canon, developing critical considerations about the music analyst's posture regarding music signification and discourse or musical representation in acts of listening, criticising the overwhelming presence and idealisation of the musical score, and much more.[24] Each of these disparate modes of engagement suggests in its own way a mediating lens through which to come to understand music, and each presumes its own kind of authority that polices how we ought or ought not to listen, and what we ought or ought not to listen to. This is wrapped up in the very notion of critique around which North American musicology was reforming itself in the 1980s and 1990s, as well as in the return to positivist scientific positions – drawing both on formalist methodologies and on appeals to structural cohesion stemming from Schenker and Adorno – that the comparatively new discipline of music theory was assuming. Both disciplines assumed that critical tools could be brought to bear that would determine musical quality in some important way, even if the specific methods of their diverse practitioners diverged greatly. As Moreno and Steingo suggest, an equal method such as that proposed in Rancière's account of Estrella's performative engagement, where listening participants are revealed to have the authority to make their own decisions, might be said to reveal the constructedness of these mediated forms of listening and valuing.

It is important to remember this journey because it also follows a path towards the study of popular music, which was considered to lack value in musicology until surprisingly recently. A good example of this path was the way scholars in the 1980s and 1990s developed a critical view of the way music education was shaped through a division between classical music (mostly the European variety) and popular music, which I consider a Rancièrean turn with a displacement from the top to the bottom, namely in how people engage with a cultural practice such as music. Lucy Green's work was at the forefront of this critical view, especially on the side of the music education given to children in schools: the dichotomy between what children hear in their everyday lives (popular music) and what they learn in class (classical music) was never addressed as a major issue in music education before the arrival of the new millennium. As Green explains, regarding her research in British schools, '[t]he education system is based on certain implicit values, and educational success depends on the acceptance of and familiarity with those values'.[25] Those values that she points out (for example, universality, complexity and originality linked to classical music) are reified as if they were obvious. What is at stake for Green and other scholars who have discussed these issues is the way demarcations are legitimised by institutions, and then ideologised, with the consequence of excluding other musics.

During the same period, the path to the inclusion of popular music in the field of musicology was similar, regarding the institutions that needed to be built and the critical views that had to be developed. We must remember that popular music studies did not emerge within musicology, but was first formed alongside cultural studies, most notably at the Birmingham School of Cultural Studies, which focused in large part on the study of youth culture, including its music. The International Association for the Study of Popular Music (IASPM) was founded in 1981, followed by the launch of the journal *Popular Music* the same year. The two first issues give a clear indication of what was at stake for the musicologists who plunged into popular music studies: volume 1, 'Folk or Popular? Distinctions, Influences, Continuities', sought to circumscribe the new object of study through discussions on subjects such as 'the goal of true folk' or 'the ideology of folk and the myth of the rock community',[26] while volume 2, 'Theory and Method', laid the scientific foundations for the study of popular music with analytical goals grounded in semiotics, stylistic study, aesthetic study and more.[27]

Popular music was not the only cultural practice to gain institutional value, epistemologically speaking. In the years that followed, this same transformation displaced the musical 'work' as a centre of interest in favour of new objects, for example the reception of musics, their social and cultural usages, interpretative frameworks and other perspectives. From there, the passage from a traditional musicology to a critical musicology – qualified sometimes as a *new musicology* – put to rest the idea that the musicologist must be an exegete who paves the way for listeners by capturing the meaning or the message of a musical work. In doing so, the idea that music is a sensible activity that can be perceived and appreciated by one and all has made its way into musicology and has created a situation in which an explosion of scientific approaches and objects of study can be seen at every stage. A book such as Susan McClary's *Feminine Endings: Music, Gender, and Sexuality* – an essay in which the author questions the cultural significance behind musical creators as diverse as Monteverdi, Beethoven and Madonna, from a variety of analytic perspectives – testifies to the degree to which musicology had come under the influence of postmodernity and the development of humanities and new forms of social knowledges. Moreover, McClary pursues the idea that music is a sensible activity, insisting that any music, whether popular, jazz, experimental, classical or otherwise, can carry value and sense for an individual listener in a sociocultural context.

To an extent, through the importance she gives to cultural signification and the sensible form that music is, McClary reaches some Rancièrean goals. By focusing on the way European art music has developed a gendered dimension or even a phallic posture in her characterisation of how it is conceptualised in traditional music theory, she sheds light on the way music has been thought through 'sensible delimitation', namely 'the forms of its visibility and of its organization'.[28] Critical musicology in this sense can be viewed as a dissensual practice that reveals the distributions animated by dominant hierarchies and points to an underlying equality of practices of engagement. Conversely, a problem arises in the way that she deploys a rapprochement between different musics according to the same experience of listening; in other words, how she digs into all kinds of musical objects from music history to foster a critical perspective based on analytical, cultural and feminist considerations, for example her interpretation of Beethoven's Ninth as a prototype of masculine domination in European art music.[29] By doing so, McClary puts all musical phenomena on the same level in excluding the specificity of each object's context, for example the tumultuous cultural reception of the Ninth from its creation until today.[30] This is far from equality insofar as her approach is delimited by the scientific endings she seeks to reach. In other words, from a Rancièrean perspective, McClary is reifying the scientific as the power to reveal, just as Bourdieu did with his own vertical inquiry approach. At the same time, McClary's approach is an important step towards the possibility of displacing borders to see what is shared in common across multiplicities of musical objects and disciplinary and discursive perspectives.

Feminine Endings was, therefore, an important catalyst for redefining the object and practice of musicological study in an overtly plural way, bringing cultural, social, economic and political (in addition to more traditionally empirical, structural and hermeneutic) perspectives into the methodological picture. Music as a cultural activity governed by the distribution of the sensible has continued to be addressed by musicologists who, while refining and using various scientific tools, take as given the notion that music is a multiple and plural practice.[31] Nicholas Cook's *Music: A Very Short Introduction* presents itself as a concentration of this epistemological posture, the English musicologist having tried to engage the multiple usages through which music circulates in the world, for example in audio-visual media including advertising, cartoons and children's shows, movies, television and so on. An example that illustrates this approach well is Cook's discussion of the classical violinist Vanessa Mae, who was aggressively marketed as a kind of pop star by foregrounding her youth, trendy image and sex appeal.[32] Like McClary, Cook demonstrates that the heuristic themes chosen by musicologists have unifying power for thinking the common elements according to which musics are distributed and make sense for listeners, for example the use of vocabulary or representations, the role of academics and institutions, and sexual divisions to the benefit of phallic authority. In doing so, Cook displaces the attention given to music by combining production with reception, questioning the usages, functions and experiences that musical acts such as Vanessa Mae reveal. By focusing his scientific interest on these usages, functions and experiences, Cook newly considers the question of 'What does music do?'

In sum, through a kaleidoscopic approach to the study of music, Cook goes beyond hermetic works to focus on the deployment of music as a whole, which includes reception as well as production, distribution, mediation, qualification and many other modes of musicking. Music's sensibility is also at stake in such a scientific posture: 'If the continuity of history lies in the story of how people have perceived things, then we might reasonably expect interpretation – performance, listening, writing – to lie at the centre of music history, rather than on its margins.'[33] The consequences of Cook's posture could be summarised in Rancièrean terms: deploying the multiplicity of the musical on the basis of the principle of equality then becomes a priority to be in phase with the shared sensibility at the basis of the reception of many musics.

In this way we might understand why and how McClary and Cook were both positioning themselves at the centre of this discussion regarding the contemporaneous development of musicology: they open – of course, they are not the only ones – a space in which music is questioned in terms of 'what it does' through the multiple usages, functions and experiences it could engage. But how to unify that multiplicity under a common approach? Here again, I will suggest that Rancière's method of equality might be a fruitful tool for musicologists to consider.

Equality and the distribution of musics through musical genres

What would justify musicology taking into account the method of equality to make it a field of action? In an ideal world, the demarcations that separate the study of different musical realities into genres, places, time periods and so on would be absent because music would be thought as one and the same object, thus valuing all musics through the spectre of the sensible in the first place. We know that such a world is completely utopian; it does not exist, for the simple reason that a musicologist must become a specialist by choosing an object or a discipline to master: for some this is music theory, for others ethnomusicology, and so on; for some this is the classical style, for others the historical avant-garde, and so on. That does not mean that dialogue or cross-over is impossible between the disciplines, but such a specialisation follows inevitably from institutional and disciplinary conventions.

Considering this scholarly compartmentalisation in terms of objects of study, one of the problems posed by the transposition of equality into musicology is that of the one compared to the multiple; namely, the idea of *a music* as set into dialogue with a conception of *musics*. In other words, music is constantly taken between the fact of being an art in its own right (i.e. music) and the fact of decomposing into multiple phenomena (various musics). The notion of musical genres, as much in classical as in popular music, offers a situation typical of this reality across what I identified above as the process of qualification, namely the role that mediation through words plays in our relation to music. This is an important process because it is an operative classification in our understanding of music; for example, what makes the difference between progressive rock and punk in the 1970s, or what differentiates the classical concerto and the romantic concerto. The role of genres is also seen in the ways that they function as objects of debate and displacement, playing on borders that are undone and redone to the advantage of certain values or to the disadvantage of certain practices;[34] for example, the value that certain genres acquire through generational experience as in the case of commercial rock for the baby boomer cohort or grunge for Generation X.[35] As Roy Shuker states regarding the role that musical genres play in conjunction with the establishment of canons in popular music, the challenges are dictated both by the commercial constraints to sell music and cultural constraints that have to do with differentiations of various musics in terms of nationality, race, age and so on.[36]

For musicologists and sociologists, genres are often understood as objects of study that circumscribe and reify musical practices based on usage and reception. From this perspective, the music critic is a good example of a policing figure who performs the work of inscribing more or less fixed meaning through acts of genre classification. This becomes an important determinant of how a given (manufactured) genre is communicative, and for whom.[37] However, musical genres and the borders that they bring about should not be seen as barriers to the implementation of an equal method in musicology. Rather, they should be a means of understanding in what way the distributions that they enact reinforce or diminish our conceptions and perceptions of specific musical cases – thereby turning from the (policed) general to the (potentially politically vibrant) particular – which can be thought through as we theorise the forms of inclusion and exclusion that affect the ways we interact with and perceive different musics, as in the examples given above of the stereotypes sometimes associated with musical genres such as hip-hop and metal.

Needless to say, all musics deploy categorical concepts that put in place questions about issues, borders and values of all kinds, and these concepts are determined according to a wide range of critical participants: mass media taste-makers, cultural mediators, fans, the musicians themselves. This is where we find, for example, the largely constructed dichotomy in classical music between simplicity and complexity, or in popular music between commercialism and authenticity. An equal musicology will resist reproducing these dichotomies, or reinforcing them through practices of scientific legitimacy that reproduce predetermined values, as was the case when the musicologist's task was to provide an exegesis in the service of composers or works. The long road towards the implementation of equality in musicology has to be shaped through the displacement of old epistemic interests and the ongoing analysis and calling into question of musical boundaries. Nevertheless, it is important to recognise that a major thrust of Rancière's work is understanding that there is no need for a battle over what is *more* equal in specific scenes or events (that is, Rancière's is not an argument for a political correctness competition), but rather that we should treat equality as a *goal* for musicology to reach. What I hope to have shown is that elements of Rancière's method are already present in musicological scholarship of the last several decades. It is in drawing together these kinds of threads, recognising the presence of equality in all actions of the human intellect and disciplinary engagement, that we gain a glimpse of how an equal method is already present and can be developed as an influential and valuable practice.

In conclusion, we could ask whether the method of equality in the study of music could really exist, considering the requirements of scientific rigour that a discipline such as musicology ostensibly demands. To go beyond the boundaries delineated by musical genres and turn to the sensible as the only way to understand music: is this achievable or even desirable? Or is it naïvely utopian, considering the specialisation required of the many discrete musicological disciplines, and of individual musicologists? The overview of the history of musicology provided in this essay suggests otherwise, as the special case of popular music studies demonstrates, effecting a transformation in the ways in which 'the musical' as a multiplicity has been theorised since the end of the twentieth century. This might be interpreted as a Rancièrean displacement. So there is every reason to think and hope that in addressing questions such as 'What does music do?', the study of music will further resist incursions from boundary inscriptions, qualifications and other kinds of valuations that affect how music is distributed and received.

Notes

1. Jacques Rancière, *The Method of Equality: Interviews with Laurent Jeanpierre and Dork Zabunyan*, trans. Julie Rose (Cambridge: Polity, 2016), 90.
2. That is the case with Anders Fjeld's book *Jacques Rancière. Pratiquer l'égalité* (Paris: Michalon, 2018).
3. Rancière, *The Method of Equality*, viii.
4. Rancière *The Method of Equality*, 102.
5. Rancière, *The Method of Equality*, 115.
6. See also Fjeld, *Jacques Rancière*, 40–8.
7. Jacques Rancière, *Proletarian Nights: The Workers' Dream in Nineteenth-Century France*, trans. John Drury (London: Verso, 2012), vii.
8. Rancière, *The Method of Equality*, 30–1.

9. Rancière, *The Method of Equality*, 31.
10. See 'Jacques Rancière and Indisciplinarity', trans. Gregory Elliott, *Art & Research* 2.1 (2008), <http://www.artandresearch.org.uk/v2n1/jrinterview.html> (last accessed 23 October 2019).
11. Jacques Rancière, *The Politics of Aesthetics: The Distribution of the Sensible*, trans. Gabriel Rockhill (London: Continuum, 2004), 12.
12. Rancière, *The Politics of Aesthetics*, 12.
13. Rancière, *The Politics of Aesthetics*, 13.
14. Dork Zabunyan, 'Préface', in *Les grand entretiens d'artpress: Jacques Rancière. Patrice Blouin, Maxime Boidy, Yan Ciret, Dominique Gonzalez-Foerster, W. J. T Mitchell, Stéphane Roth* (Paris: Artpress, 2014), 5. These two questions are my English translation of those that Dork Zabunyan posed in his preface to this collection of interviews: 'ce *que* fait l'art?' and 'ce *qui* fait art?' Actually, those questions are a way to summarise Rancière's aesthetics project since they are at the core of *The Politics of Aesthetics*: 'Artistic practices are "ways of doing and making" that intervene in the general distribution of ways of doing and making as well as in the relationships they maintain to modes of being and forms of visibility.' Rancière, *The Politics of Aesthetics*, 13.
15. For a discussion of genre differentiation in popular music and the ideological role it plays in our conception of music, see Roy Shuker, *Understanding Popular Music Culture* (London: Routledge, 2013), 95–110.
16. As Gabriel Rockhill summarises in his 'Glossary of technical terms' at the end of *The Politics of Aesthetics*, 'The distribution of the sensible thus produces a system of self-evident facts of perception based on the set horizons and modalities of what is visible and audible as well as what can be said, thought, made, or done. Strictly speaking, "distribution" therefore refers both to forms of inclusion and to forms of exclusion' (8).
17. Jacques Rancière, *The Philosopher and His Poor*, trans. John Drury (Durham, NC: Duke University Press, 2003), 165–202.
18. Pierre Bourdieu, *Distinction: A Social Critique of the Judgment of Taste*, trans. Richard Nice (Cambridge, MA: Harvard University Press, 1984); Pierre Bourdieu and Jean-Pierre Passeron, *The Inheritors: French Students and their Relation to Culture*, trans. Richard Nice (Chicago: University of Chicago Press, 1979).
19. Rancière, *The Philosopher and His Poor*, 185.
20. Jairo Moreno and Gavin Steingo, 'Rancière's Equal Music', *Contemporary Music Review* 31.5–6 (2012), 488.

21. See Joseph Kerman, *Contemplating Music: Challenges to Musicology* (Cambridge, MA: Harvard University Press, 1985), 31–7, and James Deaville and H. Wiley Hitchcock, 'Musicology in the United States', in *Grove Music Online* (Oxford: Oxford University Press, 2013), <https://www.oxfordmusiconline.com/grovemusic/view/10.1093/gmo/9781561592630.001.0001/omo-9781561592630-e-1002242442> (last accessed 22 November 2019).
22. Tia DeNora, *Beethoven and the Construction of Genius: Musical Politics in Vienna, 1792–1803* (Berkeley: University of California Press, 1995), 11–36.
23. See Eduard Hanslick, *On the Musically Beautiful*, trans. Lee Rothfarb and Christopher Landerer (New York: Oxford University Press, 2018).
24. On the role of the body in musicology, see Richard Middleton, *Studying Popular Music* (Milton Keynes: Open University Press, 1990). For investigations of sociocultural meaning and the deconstruction of the authority of the Austro-German canon, see Susan McClary, *Feminine Endings: Music, Gender and Sexuality* (Minneapolis: University of Minnesota Press, 1991), and Marcia J. Citron, *Gender and the Musical Canon* (Urbana: University of Illinois Press, 1993), respectively. For critical consideration of the music analyst's posture regarding music signification and discourse, see Kofi V. Agawu, 'Analysing Music under the New Musicological Regime', *The Journal of Musicology* 15.3 (1997), 297–307. On musical representation in acts of listening, see Lawrence Kramer, *Classical Music and Postmodern Knowledge* (Berkeley: University of California Press, 1995), and for a critique of the overwhelming presence and idealisation of the musical score, see Philip Tagg and Bob Clarida, *Ten Little Title Tunes* (New York and Montreal: The Mass Media Music Scholar's Press, 2003).
25. Lucy Green, 'Ideology', in Bruce Horner and Thomas Swiss (eds), *Key Terms in Popular Music and Culture* (Malden, MA: Blackwell, 1999), 14.
26. John Blacking, 'Making Artistic Popular Music: The Goal of True Folk', *Popular Music* 1 (1981), 9–14; Simon Frith, '"The Magic That Can Set You Free": The Ideology of Folk and the Myth of the Rock Community', *Popular Music* 1 (1981), 159–68.
27. Philip Tagg, 'Analyzing Popular Music: Theory, Method and Practice', *Popular Music* 2 (1982), 37–67; Franco Fabbri, 'What Kind of Music?', *Popular Music* 2 (1982), 131–43; Peter Wicke, 'Rock Music: A Musical-Aesthetic Study', *Popular Music* 2 (1982), 219–43.

28. Rancière, *The Politics of Aesthetics*, 18.
29. McClary, *Feminine Endings*, 112–31.
30. Tracked most recently and most comprehensively by Alexander Rehding, *Beethoven's Symphony No. 9* (New York: Oxford University Press, 2018).
31. Perhaps most important here is Christopher Small's *Musicking: The Meanings of Performing and Listening* (Hanover: University Press of New England, 1998).
32. Nicholas Cook, *Music: A Very Short Introduction* (Oxford: Oxford University Press, 1998), 11–14.
33. Cook, *Music*, 83.
34. David Brackett's recent work is valuable here. See David Brackett, *Categorizing Sound: Genre and Twentieth-Century Popular Music* (Oakland: University of California Press, 2016), 1–40.
35. Andy Bennett, *Cultures of Popular Music* (Buckingham: Open University Press, 2001), 152–61.
36. Shuker, *Understanding Popular Music Culture*, 95–110.
37. See Fabbri, 'What Kind of Music?'

Afterword

A Distant Sound
Jacques Rancière

I am well aware of the challenge raised by the organisers of this volume, which is devoted to the relationship that an author who has never or almost never taken music for an object entertained with this art and the thought regarding it. Responding to this challenge supposes two operations more or less knotted together: showing by example that its problematic finds in this domain a privileged application, and analysing the reasons why the author has not proceeded on his own behalf in this application. The contributions in this volume have generously responded to the first requirement and I thank the authors wholeheartedly. It is necessary that I attempt to respond to the second.

How is it that I have not spoken, or have spoken so little, about music? It is necessary first of all – and many contributions have done this – to sensibly relativise this diagnostic. It assumes that one looks for music where it should normally be: in works that clearly announce that they are occupied with art or aesthetics. It does not figure in *Aisthesis* or barely so – only in the detour of Appia and his *mise en scène* for the *Ring*, which itself remained on paper. But the other great canonical art, painting, only appears by way of the detour of Hegel's gaze on two paintings by Murillo for which I have no particular affection. Nor do I have any for the Belvedere Torso with which the book starts and which is present more or less explicitly in a number of these scenes. My personal tastes have no bearing on the choice of these episodes. Katharina Clausius playfully suggests an explanation of the absence of music in *Aisthesis* as due to an insensitivity or a secret hatred that I have inherited from Fénelon via Jacotot. And she reminds us that the latter's book *Musique* does not speak about music at all. But in fact, I have not frequented Fénelon's texts apart from what was strictly necessary to understand Jacotot's usage. This is to say that he hardly had the capacity to communicate these sentiments on music to me – sentiments all the more complex because the same Mentor who condemns, in keeping with the Platonic tradition, softening music, takes, in another episode, the Orphic lyre to charm the Phoenician sailors by singing of the misfortune of Narcissus or the death of Adonis. And if Jacotot's book called *Musique* does not speak about music, neither do the books entitled *Mathématiques* and *Langue étrangère* speak to the matters that they announce. What I share with Jacotot is not a love or hatred of this or that art but a practice of displacement that does not find things where they *should* be. And, in fact, music is present throughout my work where it would not be expected specifically, or not at all.

It is present more than once when I speak about another art, which is also an art of mixing the arts – cinema. It is present throughout the short book that I devoted to Béla Tarr where it is essential either as the subject of a film (*The Outsider* or *Werckmeister Harmonies*) or as a form structuring its construction, as is in the case in all the music of Mihaly Vig, beginning of course with *Satantango*, which owes its narrative structure to the rhythm of tango and is traversed by the obsessive presence of the accordion. But it is there also, more or less discreetly, in the analyses I have devoted to other films where I study music's capacity to occupy several places, to fill many roles and to metaphorise itself. It can enter discreetly into the composition of an affect accompanying the narrative, like the slow waltz in *Suspicion* that accompanies Cary Grant as he mounts the stairs with the criminal glass of milk in his hand. On the contrary, it abandons this role to become a structuring element that explodes the narrative in *First Name: Carmen*, where a whole game of correspondences is organised around a Beethoven quartet that Godard substitutes for Bizet's music. Music becomes in a way the cipher of a character in *Mouchette*, where the heroine stubbornly struggles with the B♭ of a mediocre scholastic cantata before appropriating it to make it her own music. I have studied as well the way that the cracking of assonances of a chorale by Bach comes to resonate with the chorale structure of a film whose title is borrowed from the song of workers (*Workers, Peasants* by Jean-Marie Straub and Danielle Huillet). I find it as a silent presence in Murnau's *Tartuffe* where the visual translation of two arias from *The Marriage of*

Afterword: A Distant Sound 355

Figaro contributes to the transformation of a seventeenth-century theatre piece into a silent film of the twentieth. And in *The Future of the Image* I use the sound of a Schubert sonata blended with the braying of a donkey at the beginning of *Au hasard Balthazar* to illustrate a relational thinking of the image that subtracts it from its visual evidence.[1] In all these examples – and I am probably forgetting some[2] – music is taken out of its consensual role as affective intensifier of the events of the narrative. It does not simply supplement the cinematographic story. It introduces, on the contrary, the mark of heterogeneity. It comes to disturb the idea of a purity of the language of images and, more broadly, the 'modernist' vision that presents to us autonomous arts in their proper language with their proper material.

This double role of music – to unite and separate, separating in unifying – is, in fact, consubstantial with the idea of music, which, we should remind ourselves, before being the art of sounds, is the art of the muses, the *liberal* art that says which forms of sensible performance and sensible pleasure are suitable to which category of individuals. This question of the consonance between a sensible performance and a category of human beings is at the heart of a body of texts that have apparently little to do with the musical art, from the articles in *Les Révoltes logiques* to *Proletarian Nights* and *The Philosopher and His Poor*. The reality or the metaphor of music is constantly present there. My article 'Pleasures at the Barriere' follows the history of so-called popular song in the nineteenth century, from the time of Béranger and *la goguette* to the appearance of the gramophone and the unionisation of musicians. There I show how popular song is perceived by the police order as the carrier of a double peril: uniting the people by collective entrainment to the rhythms that push them to disorder or, on the contrary, separating the people from itself through the mode of hedonistic consumption.[3] To this double peril responds the dream of a musician people instructed and moralised by *les orphéons*, discussed in another article in *Révoltes logiques* dedicated to the theatre of the people.[4]

I also returned in many texts to the quarrel around the worker poets whom all well-intentioned souls of the time counselled to abandon the pomp of grand poetry, which did not suit them, to instead consecrate themselves to the more authentic rhythms of the popular song that rhymes and enchants the work and celebrations of the people.[5] I later systematised this question of music that suits or does not suit the people around the relationship between the partition of *nemeïn* [*distribution*] and the melody of *nomos* in Platonic archipolitics, whose importance Patrick Nickleson rightly emphasises. But this is already at the heart of *The Philosopher and His Poor*. This book addressed in many ways the scene of what I would later call *le partage du sensible*, around the figure of the Platonic artisan whose survival I demonstrate in the modern forms of Marxism or the sociology of Bourdieu. Music is constantly present in this book, from the song of the cicadas, which the philosophers listen to when the workers take a nap, to the sociologist's questionnaires aimed at unmasking the men of the people who would like to believe that they love 'great music'. Erik Vogt rightly looked into the central scene around which my demonstration pivoted, that at the end of *Die Meistersinger von Nürnberg*. Eva there takes the crown of the knight Walther to give it to the cobbler/musician Hans Sachs, but I tried to show that this homage to the worker-poet is the turn by which is effectuated the inverse operation. It is in fact the knight – and Wagner through him – who himself appropriates the power of 'popular' song.[6] Music's power as unifier/separator functions indeed in two complementary ways by preventing the poor from hearing the divine cicadas so as to assign them to the song of the earth, and also by keeping the people rooted in their identity.

It is this double game of music that is found so often frustrated in *Proletarian Nights*. There is little talk of music in this book, but it was partly structured, albeit unintentionally on my part, by certain operatic scenes, the arias of which I had in my head while writing it: arias that confuse the frontier between elitist and popular, from the barcarolle in *Tales of Hoffmann* which shares responsibility with Shakespeare's *Twelfth Night* for the title of the book, up to those Verdi scenes through which I perceived and told the equivocal stories of love between proletarians and bourgeois apostles that subvert for a time – but only for a time – the sharing of conditions: Saint-Simonian scenes of fraternisation but also homage paid to Supreme Father Enfantin, the echo of which I heard in the scene from *The Sicilian Vespers* where the rebellious son Arrigo, to save his accomplices, is summoned to greet with the name of father the French governor Montfort ('Dimmi sol, di' "Mio Padre"'); and the rebellion of Icarian workers against their 'Father' Cabet, who signs the end of utopian love between bourgeois and proletarian, and where I heard the resonance of the final

Afterword: A Distant Sound 357

aria of *Simon Boccanegra*, a story of open hatred and clandestine love between plebeians and patricians ('Come passò veloce/ L'ora del lieto amore'). Yet another music concludes this book dedicated to 'missed encounters of bourgeois apostles with popular dreams and aspirations',[7] since it is through the song of Marguerite in *La Damnation de Faust* ('D'amour l'ardente flamme') that I perceived and attempted to make ring out the vivacious love letter addressed by an octogenarian worker to the Fourierist lover who had seduced and abandoned her sixty years earlier.

These scenes of a music that one might call 'democratic' have structured the perspective that I have carried and that I have wanted to share regarding a history of workers' emancipation whose content of sensible experience was so radically ignored by the dominant Marxist doxa. This is without doubt because the period when I was immersed in the workers' archives was also when I saw or heard all these Verdi operas, considered vulgar during periods of structuralist rigour, but which took on a new virtue after the events of '68 that aimed to put to an end the separation between workers and intellectuals. It is partly from opera that my manner of proceeding by scenes came: by concrete sensible blocks in which one can see at work a symbolic distribution of relationships between sensible presence and significance, which is also a symbolic distribution of positions and competences. Far from being indifferent or hostile to music, one could say that it has never ceased to play a double role in my method. On the one hand, it emblematises the forms of separation, reunion and distribution of roles which define my object, the partition of the sensible; on the other, it taught me to concentrate on the forms of condensation through which this partition might be made sensible but also evaded: the many ways that the *nomoi* efface the work of the *nemein*. Loïc Bertrand says that music is for me another name for the aesthetic regime of art. In fact, I have never said nor thought this. On the other hand, it is very true that music could be another name for the distribution of the sensible, and that it is its capacity to symbolise this distribution that explains the role it has been given for thinking this regime and its immanent politics, from Schopenhauer to Wagner, or from Nietzsche to Adorno.

Still it remains to explain that, in my work, music distributes and disperses at the same time between two poles where its proper materiality tends to disappear: on the one hand, it becomes central as a dominant metaphor of the partition of the sensible and not as a singular art; on the other, it stands out, incarnated in these tunes, these timbres and these scenes which turn in my head and inspire my modes of looking and listening or my forms of writing. As an art of the muses, music becomes a name for the distribution of the sensible. But the scenes where this distribution is shown at work are borrowed from other arts. We might be surprised by this setting offstage of an art that gives the very idea of the theatre on which the scenes unfold. It seems that the history of music presents a great number of scenes – real or virtual – where the partition of genres of art involves the partition of sensible worlds. One could easily find a multitude of comparable scenes to the tableau of beggar boys, acrobatic clowns, musical hall dances or performances of the mechanical eye, which exemplify in *Aisthesis* the transgression of frontiers between noble and vulgar genres, art and non-art, or art and life. And, in fact, it is on such scenes that most of the interventions in this volume lean and which focus on what I could have done and on what I did not. They demonstrate how my concepts and methods could be applied to these boundary cases. They show, for example, the audacities of romantic music where two notes stand at the limit of consonance and dissonance. It is remarkable that João Pedro Cachopo and Martin Kaltenecker both concentrate on similar events related to Berlioz, the man of programme music: he who explored the limits of harmony to introduce into music the equivalent of the noise of bells, but who also blurred the identities of music and theatre by making one contralto voice recount the story of Romeo and Juliet while the two lovers disappear in the wordless melody of the violins. These two references made me think of a scene that I could have done, departing from another Berlioz piece which puts in place the frontier between art and popular musics. I am speaking of the 'Sérénade d'un montagnard des Abruzzes à sa maitresse' which echoes from the pages consecrated by Berlioz to the *pifferari*, which he heard for the first time in Rome before going to hear them in their mountains. I could have confronted this transfer with other contemporary appropriations of popular musics, but also polemical texts from *Opera and Drama*, evoked in *The Philosopher and His Poor*, where the young Wagner mocks the popular passion of his colleagues and especially Rossini's imitation of alpine melodies.

It would without doubt have been possible to construct, around these cases of the encounter of art music with the noises of the world and the songs of the people, a scene illustrating a central thesis of *Aisthesis* by showing how this music that ruins the representative system of art also poses a future threat to its own autonomy, in the same way that it sought to assure it. Berlioz is at once he who was inspired by Shakespeare, Byron or Gautier, and he who delivered the art of sounds from the classical paradigm that submitted it to the legislation of the poem. But he is also the one who, to assure the power of emancipated music, must affirm that 'any sonorous body employed by a composer is a musical instrument'.[8] Daniel Frappier rightly emphasises the logic that leads from the romantic emancipation of symphonic music towards the poem that would come to pass in the next century: the emancipation of 'musics of noise' from the musical tradition. And it is entirely natural that many of the interventions in this collection deal with the diverse artistic enterprises that have in the twentieth century transgressed or displaced the frontier between music and noise – and eventually between the human and the non-human.

This is evidently the case in *musique concrète*: Loïc Bertrand shows the dream of a language of things in the work of Pierre Schaeffer, which evokes the one that Jean Epstein dreams in the art of the camera; he shows as well the way that this language is taken into the tension between the two forms of 'mute speech' that I had studied in the art of words. Martin Kaltenecker shows in the evolution between two rewritings of Beethoven by Pierre Henry a step in the transformation that makes the musical work no longer an autonomous organism but an instrument for knowing the world of sound and its relations with the functions of our world. It is clear that these analyses define a form of intelligibility of music called modern or contemporary which converges with my own attempt to question the 'modernist' dogma.

It is clear as well that other contributions are consonant with my attempt to complicate the relationship between aesthetics and politics. Thus Dan DiPiero rejects the oversimplified identification of musical improvisation with political equality by taking up the question of forms of community that connect the practice, reception and diffusion of this music. Chris Stover shows the diversity of strategies at work in an improvisation by Thelonious Monk or Pharaoh Sanders, by crossing two oppositions central in my work. He shows in effect how the gap between politics and police can be carried out through the opposing ways of putting into play the relation between *logos* and *phōnē*. Kjetil Klette Bøhler focuses on the play through which Roberto Carcassés transformed a patriotic song of revolutionary Cuba into a dissensual demonstration and the construction of another sensible community. There is also the question of the type of community forged by music which is in play in the reflections of Sarah Collins on commemorative music, while the chapter by William Fourie and Carina Venter addresses a scene of transgression of frontiers reminiscent of that of the worker poets, while in turn posing a question that is not treated in my work: what happens when the frontier separating the cobblers from the art of the muses becomes a racial barrier? How does this further complicate the question of disidentification?

In brief, the diverse interventions in this volume show that music occupies a decisive place in the relationship between speech and noise, an essential object of my reflection, and that one finds in the notions that I have advanced the elements that permit thinking this place. They pose as well – explicitly or tacitly – the question of why I did not do this myself. The response is simple: if I did not stage the boundaries of music, it is because of the barrier that separates me from music or, if we prefer, that separates music from itself in me. Music has accompanied my entire life and in a way fashions my relationship to the world. Sadly I still do not know much about how it is made. I never learned it, nor do I play an instrument, and my knowledge of *solfège* does not extend beyond a few snatches absent-mindedly heard in high school. If I do not speak or rarely speak about music, it is simply because I do not have the knowledge that would permit me to speak about it in my own language. The only time when I tried to be a bit more precise, in the book on the films of Béla Tarr in which music plays a structural role, I had to ask my son, who is himself a musician, to translate what I heard.

One could retort that I speak about painting, dance or cinema without practising these arts, and my knowledge of the methods required to make them is no better than my knowledge of music. We could add that there are many ways of speaking about music as a practice and social institution and of the relationships with the lines of demarcation of society and art, before which initiates and non-initiates alike are equal. Jacques Attali is known to have, among other things, competence as a pianist and conductor. But his book *Noise: The Political Economy of Music* could have been written by someone no more knowledgeable than me in the practice of this art. He does not include any internal analyses

Afterword: A Distant Sound 361

of works but rather concentrates entirely on the relationships of power that preside over the social existence of music. But this problem, apparently accessible to a non-musician like me, is not mine. That's what makes the difference in the parallel that Chris Stover establishes between these two approaches. Attali considers music within the large problematic of the role of noise in the symbolic economy of power. And it is from this point of view that he studies the way in which a new noise has effects in the symbolic systems through which power relations play out. But politics for me is not about relationships of power, it is about conflicts of worlds, and this conflict is fundamentally played on the frontier where music is distinguished from noise. That which I seize is therefore singular cases where this frontier is put into play. The problem that I encounter then does not concern the necessary conditions for speaking about music in general. It concerns that which is needed to speak of music from my own perspective and according to my own method, to make a scene of the aesthetic regime of art.

A scene from *Aisthesis*, in effect, is not an internal analysis of a work or a performance. I certainly find fascinating Stover's method of directly transposing the opposition between politics and police to think about practices of improvisation in jazz. But, besides not having the capacity to discern how it operates in a piano or saxophone solo, what occupies me in *Aisthesis* is the seizure of the relationship between the performance and its thinkability. I do not mean the analysis of the context in which it appeared, the social or political conditions that permitted its birth and eventually its ulterior lives, as has been done by Esteban Buch for Beethoven's Ninth Symphony, nor the signification of the same symphony in relation to masculine power as has been made by Susan McClary, whose approach is discussed by Danick Trottier in his investigation of the 'method of equality' in musicology. Nor is it the revelation, in the content of the work, of the social fracture that it testifies to or the lost unity that it maintains a promise of, in the manner of Adorno, which Murray Dineen uses to mark my separation with him. A scene is a specific device that highlights the way that an artistic performance, understood not as an organism but as an event, is understood within a certain mode of perception, and how this perception itself presupposes a certain sensible world held in common.

It is for this reason that each of the scenes dedicated to an artistic event is introduced by a text contemporary to the event: not a text that tells the truth nor a text that testifies to its 'reception', but a text that questions the idea of art that it implicates and that renders this idea itself thinkable. What makes it possible to see what a text designates? What makes it possible to think that which is given to thought by its subject? In what type of world is this thinkability itself thinkable? These are the questions that are contained within the relationship that the texts opening the chapters of *Aisthesis* entertain with their object. It is these that the method of the scene seeks to untangle in a game of translations and displacements. It is about seizing, in the relationship between a singular performance and the textual network that renders it perceptible and thinkable as an artistic event, the inscription of performances of art in the configuration of a way of making a world. It is within this crossing that I think I can seize the 'politics' of music, and not in the direct relationship of a musical performance with existing social relationships.

But the seizure of this circulation supposes that I myself can circulate without frontier between inside and outside: between what the text said of the performance in question and what I can say myself in perceiving it. The condition of operation is that nothing hinders the translatability. I can speak of what Hegel said of Murillo, of what Mallarmé said of Loïe Fuller, or Ismaïl Urazoc of Dziga Vertov, because I have the language that permits me to say what I see in the works they tell me about. The same does not apply if I have to say what I heard in the *Sérénade* from *Harold en Italie*: what exactly did Berlioz get from *pifferari* music? What exact transformations did he subject them to? This problem of translation/transgression is basically symmetrical to the one I approach in *Proletarian Nights*, showing how, in the 1830s, a floor layer appropriated the verses of the 'great poet' Victor Hugo. Conversely, what would be at stake would be studying the way in which, at the same time, a laureate of the Paris Conservatory, sent to Rome, listened to the popular music of the Italian mountains and worked later to transpose it. But for that, I would have to translate into my language the significant traits by which Berlioz's composition appropriates and transforms this popular music. Lacking this minimum knowledge, it is impossible for me to do what my own project would require: disentangle the regime of listening and sensibility that is mobilised by such a scholarly appropriation of popular music.

At the time I was planning *Aisthesis*, I thought that I could turn the difficulty around by treating a question easier to phrase in my language: that of the introduction of noise as such into art music. I had by chance heard on the radio in my childhood the famous concert when Varèse's *Déserts* created a memorable uproar. I had the idea that it should be possible to create a scene based not on this scandalous episode but on the first works in which Varèse had introduced the noises of the American city. I sadly did not find the text that would give me the primary elements needed to construct the scene. This is without doubt because I did not look for it thoroughly enough. But it was also that I sensed that replacing the cor anglais with the boat or factory siren would not solve the problem. Indeed, Berlioz's formula is reversible: the introduction of any sonorous body into the musical tissue falls within a science of harmony that opposes all over again its barrier to the layman who believes the border abolished.

The cor anglais will not have a scene until I have acquired a little more knowledge about harmony. Until then it will remain a timbre: 'its tones are melancholy, dreamy, noble, somewhat veiled – as if played in the *distance*'[9] as Berlioz says of this oboe of the poor, whose simple melodies come from time to time to suspend the refined combinations of the orchestration as if to make resonate this distant song of a people's musician that art music does not want to give up. It is the cor anglais, in fact, that introduces the romance of Marguerite which inspired the final scene of *Proletarian Nights* that I spoke of above. The same lends its voice to the shepherd's song of *Tristan and Isolde* evoked, thirty-five years later, at the end of the chapter dedicated to dance in *Modern Times*. It is the distant timbre, a little veiled, that colours a writing dedicated to making resonate in each other the texts of workers and those of philosophers, the phrases of great writers and the refrains of popular songs. It may be that I will speak one day 'directly' on music. It may be that it has to stay in its place: that of an untranslatable text whose mute power sustains the energy of translations.

Translated by Patrick Nickleson

Notes

1. See, in order, Jacques Rancière, *Béla Tarr: The Time After* (Minneapolis: University of Minnesota Press, 2013), 'A Fable without a Moral: Godard, Cinema, Histories', in *Film Fables* (New York: Berg, 2006), 172; 'The Indecisive Affect', in *Dissenting Words*, ed. and trans. Emiliano Battista (London: Bloomsbury, 2017), 213; 'Mouchette and the Paradoxes of the Language of Cinema', in *The Intervals of Cinema* (London: Verso, 2014), 52, 63; 'La Pensée sensible', in *Cinéma 05* (spring 2003), 767–77; 'A Silent Tartuffe', in *Film Fables*, 40; *The Future of the Image*, trans. Gregory Elliott (London: Verso, 2007), 3.
2. Two of these omissions occurred to me at proofreading: the analysis of the role of music in *Listen to Britain*, a documentary by Humphrey Jennings dedicated to the English resistance to German bombardment in the Second World War (Jacques Rancière, *Figures of History* (Cambridge: Polity, 2014), 26); and the place of an aria from *Così fan tutte* ('Come scoglio') in *Drancy Avenir*, a film by Arnaud des Pallières dedicated to an episode during the extermination of the Jews (*Figures of History*, 54–5, and Jacques Rancière, 'La constance de l'art', *Trafic* 21 (spring 1997), 40–3).
3. Jacques Rancière, 'Good Times or Pleasure at the *Barrière*', in *Staging the People: The Proletariat and his Double* (London: Verso, 2011), 175–232.
4. Jacques Rancière, 'The People's Theatre: A Long-drawn Affair', in *The Intellectual and His People: Staging the People*, vol. 2, trans. David Fernbach (London: Verso, 2012), 1–40.
5. See notably Jacques Rancière, 'Ronds de fumée. Les poètes ouvriers dans la France de Louis-Philippe', *Revue des sciences humaines* 190 (1983), 31–47.
6. Erik Vogt analyses the implications of the critical remarks that I addressed to Alain Badiou on the interpretation of this episode. It is interesting to recall that these remarks responded at a distance to a private text that I had written about the implicit presence of opera in Badiou's *Theory of the Subject*, and that I had entitled 'Sull'ali dorate' in reference to the celebrated chorus from *Nabucco*.
7. Jacques Rancière, *Proletarian Nights: The Workers' Dream in Nineteenth-Century France*, trans. John Drury (London: Verso, 2012), 425.
8. Hector Berlioz, *A Treatise Upon Modern Instrumentation and Orchestration*, trans. Theodore Front (New York: Kalmus, 1948),

1. Rancière cites *Grand traité d'instrumentation et d'orchestration modernes* (Paris: Henry Lemoine, 1844), 2.
9. Berlioz, *A Treatise Upon Modern Instrumentation and Orchestration*, 184; Rancière cites the 1844 edition, 122. Rancière's note highlights that in Berlioz's original French, *Lointain* [distant] is capitalised and italicised [translator's note].

Works Cited

Abrams, M. H., *The Mirror and the Lamp. Romantic Theory and the Critical Tradition* (Oxford: Oxford University Press, 1971).

Adès, Thomas, and Tom Service, *Thomas Adès: Full of Noises. Conversations with Tom Service* (New York: Farrar, Straus and Giroux, 2012).

Adhikari, Mohamed, *Not White Enough, Not Black Enough: Racial Identity in the South African Coloured Community* (Athens: Ohio University Press, 2005).

Adler, Guido, 'Umfang, Methode und Ziel der Musikwissenschaft', *Vierteljahrschrift für Musikwissenschaft* 1 (1985), 5–20.

Adorno, Theodor W., *Prisms*, trans. Samuel and Shierry Weber (Cambridge, MA: MIT Press, 1967).

Adorno, Theodor W., *Negative Dialectics*, trans. E. B. Ashton (New York: Continuum, 1973).

Adorno, Theodor W., 'On Jazz' (1936), trans. Jamie Owen Daniel, *Discourse* 12.1 (1989–90), 45–69.

Adorno, Theodor W., *Aesthetic Theory*, ed. and trans. Robert Hullot-Kentor (Minneapolis: University of Minnesota Press, 1997).

Adorno, Theodor W., 'The Aging of the New Music' (1955), trans. Robert Hullot-Kentor and Frederic Will, in *Essays on Music*, ed. Richard Leppert (Berkeley: University of California Press, 2002), 181–202.

Adorno, Theodor W., 'Art and the Arts' (1967), trans. Rodney Livingstone, in *Can One Live After Auschwitz? A Philosophical Reader* (Stanford: Stanford University Press, 2003), 368–87.

Agawu, V. Kofi, 'Analysing Music under the New Musicological Regime', *The Journal of Musicology* 15.3 (1997), 297–307.

Ahmed, Sara, *Queer Phenomenology* (Durham, NC: Duke University Press, 2006).

Ahmed, Sara, *Willful Subjects* (Durham, NC: Duke University Press, 2014).
d'Alembert, Jean le Rond, *Mélanges de littérature, d'histoire et de philosophie*, ed. Martine Groult (Paris: Classiques Garnier, 2017).
Althusser, Louis, 'Reply to John Lewis', in *Essays in Self-Criticism*, trans. Grahame Lock (London: NLB, 1976).
Althusser, Louis, 'Student Problems', *Radical Philosophy* 170 (November/December 2011), 11–15.
Althusser, Louis, *On the Reproduction of Capitalism: Ideology and the Ideological State Apparatuses*, trans. G. M. Goshgarian (London: Verso, 2014).
Arendt, Hannah, *The Human Condition* (1958) (Chicago: University of Chicago Press, 1998).
Aristotle, *Poétique*, trans. Barbara Gernez (Paris: Les Belles Lettres, 2001).
Arnheim, Rudolf, *Radio*, trans. Margaret Ludwig and Herbert Read (London: Faber and Faber, 1936).
Attali, Jacques, *Noise: The Political Economy of Music*, trans. Brian Massumi (Minneapolis: University of Minnesota Press, 1985).
Babbitt, Milton, 'Who Cares if You Listen?', anthologised as 'The Composer as Specialist' in *The Collected Essays of Milton Babbitt*, ed. Stephen Peles (Princeton: Princeton University Press, 2003), 48–54.
Badiou, Alain, *Handbook of Inaesthetics*, trans. Alberto Toscano (Stanford: Stanford University Press, 2005).
Badiou, Alain, *Five Lessons on Wagner*, trans. Susan Spitzer (London: Verso, 2010).
Badiou, Alain, *The Adventure of French Philosophy*, trans. Bruno Bosteels (London: Verso, 2012).
Bailey, Derek, *Improvisation: Its Nature and Practice in Music* (New York: Da Capo Press, 1992).
Baker, David, 'Bebop Characteristics' (2000), <https://www.jazzbooks.com/mm5/download/FQBK-handbook.pdf> (last accessed 22 November 2019).
Baker, Geoffrey, 'Cuba Rebelión: Underground Music in Havana', *Latin American Music Review* 32.1 (2011), 1–38.
Balliet, Whitney, 'Newport 1966', in Whitney Balliet, *Collected Works: A Journal of Jazz 1954–2001* (New York: St. Martins Griffin, 2002), 272–5.
Balzac, Honoré de, *Histoire et physiologie des boulevards de Paris* (1845), <http://www.bmlisieux.com/curiosa/balzac02.htm> (last accessed 15 May 2019).

Balzac, Honoré de, *Illusions perdues* (1837–43) (Paris: Gallimard, 1977).
Balzac, Honoré de, *Letters to Madame Hańska, born Countess Rzewuska, Afterwards Madame Honoré de Balzac*, trans. Katherine P. Wormeley (London: Forgotten Books, 2016).
Barbey d'Aurevilly, Jules A., *Œuvre critique*, ed. Catherine Mayaux and Pierre Glaudes (Paris: Les Belles Lettres, 2004–06).
Barthes, Roland, 'The Reality Effect' (1968), in *The Rustle of Language*, trans. Richard Howard (Berkeley: University of California Press, 1986).
Barzun, Jacques, *Berlioz and the Romantic Century*, vol. 1 (Boston: Little, Brown and Company, 1950).
Bataille, Georges, 'The Psychological Structure of Fascism', trans. Carl R. Lovitt, *New German Critique: An Interdisciplinary Journal of German Studies* 16 (1979), 64–87.
Bedriomo, Emile, *Proust, Wagner et la coïncidence des arts* (Tübingen and Paris: Gunter Narr Verlag and Jean-Michel Place, 1984).
Bell, David F., 'Writing, Movement/Space, Democracy: On Jacques Rancière's Literary History', *SubStance* 33.1 (2004), 126–40.
Benjamin, Walter, *Selected Writings: 1913–1926*, vol. 1, ed. Marcus Bullock and Michael W. Jennings (Cambridge, MA: Belknap Press of Harvard University Press, 1996).
Benjamin, Walter, *The Arcades Project*, trans. Howard Eiland and Kevin McLaughlin (Cambridge, MA: Harvard University Press, 1999).
Benmayor, Rina, 'La "Nueva Trova": New Cuban Song', *Latin American Music Review/Revista de Música Latinoamericana* 2.1 (1981), 11–44.
Bennett, Andy, *Cultures of Popular Music* (Buckingham: Open University Press, 2001).
Bennett, Jane, *Vibrant Matter: A Political Ecology of Things* (Durham, NC: Duke University Press, 2010).
Bergson, Henri, *Matter and Memory*, trans. Nancy M. Paul and W. Scott Palmer (New York: Zone Books, 1988).
Berio, Luciano, 'Meditations on a Twelve-Tone Horse', *Christian Science Monitor*, 15 July 1968.
Berkman, David, *The Jazz Harmony Book* (Petaluma, CA: Sher Music Publications, 2013).
Berlioz, Hector, *Grand traité d'instrumentation et d'orchestration modernes* (Paris: Henry Lemoine, 1844).
Berlioz, Hector, *Mémoires*, vol. 2 (Paris: Garnier-Flammarion, 1969).
Berlioz, Hector, *A Critical Study of Beethoven's Nine Symphonies with a Few Words on His Trios and Sonatas, a Criticism of 'Fidelio', and an*

Introductory Essay on Music, trans. Edwin Evans (Urbana: University of Illinois Press, 2000).
Berlioz, Hector, *Critique musicale*, vol. 3 (Paris: Buchet-Chastel, 2001).
Berlioz, Hector, *Harold en Italie, New Edition of the Complete Works*, vol. 17, ed. Paul Banks and Hugh Macdonald (Kassel: Bärenreiter, 2001).
Berlioz, Hector, *The Memoir of Hector Berlioz* (1870), trans. and ed. David Cairns (New York: Alfred A. Knopf, 2002).
Berlioz, Hector, *Berlioz on Music: Selected Criticism*, ed. Katherine Kolb, trans. Samuel N. Rosenberg (New York: Oxford University Press, 2015).
Bermbach, Udo, *'Bluehendes Leid': Politik und Gesellschaft in Richard Wagners Musikdramen* (Weimar: Metzler, 2003).
Bertrand, Loïc, 'The Language of Things: An Archaeology of *musique concrète*', *Organised Sounds* 22.3 (2017), 254–61.
Bivins, Jason, *Spirits Rejoice! Jazz and American Religion* (Oxford: Oxford University Press, 2015).
Blacking, John, 'Making Artistic Popular Music: The Goal of True Folk', *Popular Music* 1 (1981), 9–14.
Bøhler, Kjetil Klette, 'Grooves, Pleasures, and Politics in Salsa Cubana: The Musicality of Cuban Politics and the Politics of Salsa Cubana', PhD dissertation, University of Oslo, 2013.
Bøhler, Kjetil Klette, 'How Live Cuban Popular Dance Music Expresses Political Values in Today's Cuba', *Danish Musicology Online* (2015), 55–75, <http://www.danishmusicologyonline.dk/arkiv/arkiv_dmo/dmo_saernummer_2015/dmo_saernummer_2015_musikcensur_03.pdf> (last accessed 3 May 2019).
Bøhler, Kjetil Klette, '"Somos la mezcla perfecta, la combinación más pura, cubanos, la más grande creación": Grooves, Pleasures, and Politics in Today's Cuba', *Latin American Music Review* 37.2 (2016), 165–207.
Bøhler, Kjetil Klette, 'Theorizing Musical Politics through Case Studies: Feminist Grooves against the Temer Government in Today's Brazil', *International Journal of Gender, Science and Technology* 9.2 (2017), 118–40.
Boever, Arne de, 'The Politics of Realism in Rancière and Houellebecq', in Grace Hellyer and Julian Murphet (eds), *Rancière and Literature* (Edinburgh: Edinburgh University Press, 2016), 226–48.
Bonds, Mark E., *Wordless Rhetoric. Musical Form and the Metaphor of the Oration* (Cambridge, MA: Harvard University Press, 1991).

Bonds, Mark E., *After Beethoven: Imperatives of Originality in the Symphony* (Cambridge, MA: Harvard University Press, 1996).

Booth, Douglas, *The Race Game: Sport and Politics in South Africa* (London: Frank Cass, 1998).

Born, Georgina, *Rationalizing Culture: IRCAM, Boulez, and the Institutionalization of the Avant-Garde* (Berkeley: University of California Press, 1995).

Born, Georgina, 'After Relational Aesthetics: Improvised Music, the Social, and (Re)Theorizing the Aesthetic', in Georgina Born, Eric Lewis and Will Straw (eds), *Improvisation and Social Aesthetics* (Durham, NC: Duke University Press, 2017), 33–58.

Born, Georgina, 'On Nonhuman Sound – Sound as Relation', in James A. Steintrager and Rey Chow (eds), *Sound Objects* (Durham, NC: Duke University Press, 2019), 185–210.

Born, Georgina, Eric Lewis and Will Straw (eds), *Improvisation and Social Aesthetics* (Durham, NC: Duke University Press, 2017).

Bourdieu, Pierre, *Distinction: A Social Critique of the Judgment of Taste*, trans. Richard Nice (Cambridge, MA: Harvard University Press, 1984).

Bourdieu, Pierre, and Jean-Pierre Passeron, *The Inheritors: French Students and Their Relation to Culture*, trans. Richard Nice (Chicago: University of Chicago Press, 1979).

Bourriaud, Nicolas, *The Radicant* (Berlin: Sternberg/Merve Verlag, 2009).

Brackett, David, *Categorizing Sound. Genre and Twentieth-Century Popular Music* (Oakland: University of California Press, 2016).

Braxton, Anthony, *Composition Notes* (Hanover, NH: Frog Peak Music, 1988).

Breen, Walter, 'Apollo and Dionysus', *Crawdaddy!* 18 (1968), 11–15.

Brouwer, Marianne (ed.), *Dan Graham: Works 1965–2000*, trans. Brian Holmes, Peter Ingham and Victor Joseph (Düsseldorf: Richter Verlag, 2001).

Browne, David, *Goodbye 20th Century: A Biography of Sonic Youth* (Boston: Da Capo Press, 2008).

Calico, Joy H., *Arnold Schoenberg's* A Survivor from Warsaw *in Postwar Europe* (Berkeley: University of California Press, 2014).

Cannone, Belinda, 'Le Lecteur y mettra le titre: un pamphlet de Mirabeau en faveur de la musique instrumentale', *Dix-huitième siècle* 20.1 (1988), 403–14.

Carducci, Joe, *Rock and the Pop Narcotic: Testament for the Electric Church* (Centennial, CO: Redoubt Press, 2005).

Carles, Philippe, and Jean-Louis Comolli, *Free Jazz/Black Power* (1971),

trans. Grégory Pierrot (Jackson: University of Mississippi Press, 2016).
Castro, Fidel, 'Nuevo Lineamientos VI Congreso del Partido Comunista de Cuba' (2010), <http://www.cubadebate.cu/congreso-del-partido-comunista-de-cuba/informe-central-al-vi-congreso-del-partido-comunista-de-cuba-v/> (last accessed 15 May 2019).
Chabanon, Michel Pierre Guy de, *De la musique considérée en elle-même et dans ses rapports avec la parole, les langues, la poésie et le theatre* (Paris: Pissot, 1785).
Chambers, Samuel, 'Jacques Rancière's Lesson on the Lesson', *Educational Philosophy and Theory* 45/46 (2013), 637–46.
Chambers, Samuel, *The Lessons of Rancière* (Oxford: Oxford University Press, 2013).
Chanter, Tina, *Whose Antigone? The Tragic Marginalization of Slavery* (Albany: State University of New York Press, 2011).
Chanter, Tina, *Art, Politics and Rancière: Broken Perceptions* (London: Bloomsbury, 2017).
Chastagner, Claude, 'Rock: le paradoxe', in *Le Corps dans tous ses états*, ed. Marie-Claire Rouyer (Bordeaux: Presses Universitaires de Bordeaux, 1995), 107–14.
Chastagner Claude, *La Loi du rock: ambivalence et sacrifice dans la musique populaire anglo-américaine* (Castelnau-le-Lez: Climats, 1998).
Chor, Ives, 'Microtiming and Rhythmic Structure in Clave-Based Music: A Quantitative Study', in Anne Danielsen (ed.), *Musical Rhythm in the Age of Digital Reproduction* (Farnham: Ashgate, 2010), 37–50.
Citron, Marcia J., *Gender and the Musical Canon* (Urbana: University of Illinois Press, 1993).
Citton, Yves, 'Le Percept noise comme registre du sensible', *Multitudes* 28.1 (2007), 137–46.
Clausius, Katharina, 'Translation ~ Politics', *Philosophy Today* 61.1 (2017), 1–21.
Cobussen, Marcel, *The Field of Musical Improvisation* (Leiden: Leiden University Press, 2017).
Cohen, Jonathan D., 'Rock as Religion', *Intermountain West Journal of Religious Studies* 7.1 (2016), 46–86.
Cohn, Nik, *Awopbopaloobop Alopbamboom: The Golden Age of Rock* (New York: Grove, 2001).
Coleman, Steve, 'Symmetrical Movement Concept', <www.m-base.com> (last accessed 15 May 2019).
Collins, Sarah, 'Nationalism, Modernisms, and Masculinities: Strategies

of Displacement in Vaughan Williams's Reading of Walt Whitman', *Nineteenth-Century Music Review* 14.1 (2017), 65–91.

Collins, Sarah, 'What Was Contemporary Music? The New, the Modern and the Contemporary in the ISCM', in Björn Heile and Charles Wilson (eds), *The Ashgate Research Companion to Modernism in Music* (Farnham: Ashgate, 2019), 56–85.

Cook, Nicholas, *Beethoven: Symphony No. 9* (Cambridge: Cambridge University Press, 1993).

Cook, Nicholas, *Music: A Very Short Introduction* (Oxford: Oxford University Press, 1998).

Courbet, Gustave, *Peut-on enseigner l'art?* (1861) (Caen: L'Échoppe, 1986).

Currie, Scott, 'The Other Side of Here and Now: Cross-Cultural Reflections on the Politics of Improvisation Studies', *Critical Studies in Improvisation/Études critiques en improvisation* 11.1–2 (2016), <https://www.criticalimprov.com/index.php/csieci/article/download/3750/3980> (last accessed 22 November 2019).

Czepczyński, Mariusz, *Cultural Landscapes of Post-socialist Cities: Representation of Powers and Needs* (Farnham: Ashgate, 2008).

Dahlhaus, Carl, *Esthetics of Music* (Cambridge: Cambridge University Press, 1982).

Dahlhaus, Carl, *The Idea of Absolute Music* (1978), trans. Roger Lustig (Chicago: University of Chicago Press, 1991).

Daniel, Yvonne, *Rumba: Dance and Social Change in Contemporary Cuba* (Bloomington: Indiana University Press, 1995).

Dasgupta, Sudeep, 'Art is Going Elsewhere, and Politics Has to Catch It. An Interview with Jacques Rancière', *Krisis: Journal of Contemporary Philosophy* 1 (2008), 70–6.

Deaville, James, and H. Wiley Hitchcock, 'Musicology in the United States', in *Grove Music Online* (Oxford: Oxford University Press, 2013), <https://www.oxfordmusiconline.com/grovemusic/view/10.1093/gmo/9781561592630.001.0001/omo-9781561592630-e-1002242442> (last accessed 22 November 2019).

Deleuze, Gilles, *Foucault* (Paris: Minuit, 1986).

Deleuze, Gilles, *Expressionism in Philosophy: Spinoza*, trans. Martin Joughin (New York: Zone Books, 1990).

Deleuze, Gilles, *Difference and Repetition*, trans. Paul Patton (New York: Columbia University Press, 1994).

DeNora, Tia, *Beethoven and the Construction of Genius. Musical Politics in Vienna, 1792–1803* (Berkeley: University of California Press, 1995).

Derrida, Jacques, *Aporias*, trans. Thomas Dutoit (Stanford: Stanford University Press, 1993).

Dikeç, Mustafa, 'Beginners and Equals: Political Subjectivity in Arendt and Rancière', *Transactions of the Institute of British Geographers* 38.1 (2013), 78–90.

Dineen, Murray, *Friendly Remainders: Essays in Musical Criticism after Adorno* (Montreal: McGill-Queen's University Press, 2011).

DiPiero, Dan, 'Improvisation as Contingent Encounter, Or: The Song of My Toothbrush', *Critical Studies in Improvisation/Études critiques en improvisation* 12.2 (2018), <https://www.criticalimprov.com/index.php/csieci/article/view/4261/4863> (last accessed 22 November 2019).

Dömling, Wolfgang, *Hector Berlioz und seine Zeit* (Laaber: Laaber-Verlag, 1986).

Drott, Eric, 'Rereading Jacques Attali's *Bruits*', *Critical Inquiry* 41 (2015), 721–56.

Du Bos, Charles, *Réflexions critiques sur la poésie et la peinture* (Paris: Mariette, 1719).

Dufourt, Hugues, *Musique, pouvoir, écriture* (Paris: Bourgois, 1991).

Eidsheim, Nina Sun, *Sensing Sound: Singing and Listening as Vibrational Practice* (Durham, NC: Duke University Press, 2015).

Engels, Frederick, *Herr Eugen Dühring's Revolution in Science (Anti-Dühring)*, trans. Emile Burns, ed. C. P. Dutt (New York: International Publishers, 1939).

Eoan History Project, *Eoan: Our Story*, ed. Wayne Muller and Hilda Roos (Johannesburg: Fourth Wall Books, 2013).

Epstein, Jean, *L'intelligence d'une machine*, in *Écrits sur le cinéma, 1921–1953*, vol. 1 (Paris: Seghers, 1974).

Fabbri, Franco, 'What Kind of Music?', *Popular Music* 2 (1982), 131–43.

Faydit, Pierre Valentin, *La Télémacomanie, ou La Censure et critique du roman intitulé, Les Aventures de Télémaque Fils d'Ulysse, ou suite du quatrième Livre de l'Odyssée d'Homère.* (Paris: Pierre Philalethe, 1700).

Fénelon, François, *Telemachus, Son of Ulysses*, trans. Patrick Riley (Cambridge: Cambridge University Press, 1994).

Fjeld, Anders, *Jacques Rancière. Pratiquer l'égalité* (Paris: Michalon, 2018).

Flaubert, Gustave, *La Tentation de saint Antoine* (Paris: E. Fasquelle, 1910).

Flaubert, Gustave, *Madame Bovary*, trans. Eleanor Marx-Aveling (2006), <https://docs.google.com/document/d/1NuohloTov7FZg_gtd_WEFyNR_4EGy_z1pDk9k7l-exY/edit#> (last accessed 15 May 2019).

Flaubert, Gustave, 'Lettre à Louise Colet, 26 août 1853', in *Correspondance*, II, ed. Jean Bruneau (Paris: Gallimard, Bibliothèque de la Pléiade, 2007).

Foege, Alec, *Confusion Is Next: The Sonic Youth Story* (New York: St. Martin's Press, 1994).

Foucault, Michel, 'L'Inquiétude de l'actualité', *Le Monde*, 19–20 September 1975.

Fowles, Ian W., *A Sound Salvation: Rock 'n' Roll as a Religion* (Huntington Beach, CA: Sonic Mystic, 2011).

Frappier, Daniel, '"Ici rien n'est silencieux": reconfigurations de l'audible sous le régime esthétique des arts', MA thesis, Université de Montréal, 2016.

Frith, Simon, '"The Magic That Can Set You Free": The Ideology of Folk and the Myth of the Rock Community', *Popular Music* 1 (1981), 159–68.

Frith, Simon, 'Why Do Songs Have Words?', in *Music for Pleasure: Essays in the Sociology of Pop* (Cambridge: Polity, 1988), 105–28.

Frith, Simon, *Performing Rights: On the Value of Popular Music* (Cambridge, MA: Harvard University Press, 1998).

Gallope, Michael, *Deep Refrains: Music, Philosophy, and the Ineffable* (Chicago: University of Chicago Press, 2017).

Game, Jérôme, and Aliocha Wald Lasowski (eds), *Jacques Rancière: Politique de l'esthétique* (Paris: Éditions Archives Contemporaines, 2009).

Gámez Torres, Nora, '"Rap is war": Los Aldeanos and the Politics of Music Subversion in Contemporary Cuba', *Trans. Revista Transcultural de Música* 17 (2013), 2–23.

Gaztambide-Fernández, Rubén, 'Decolonial options and artistic/aestheSic entanglements: An interview with Walter Mignolo', *Decolonization: Indigeneity, Education & Society* 3.1 (2014), 196–212.

Genette, Gérard, 'Frontières de la narration', in *L'Analyse structurale du récit* (Paris: Seuil, 1981), 158–69.

Givan, Benjamin, 'Thelonious Monk's Pianism', *Journal of Musicology* 26.3 (2009), 404–42.

Goehr, Lydia, *The Imaginary Museum of Musical Works: An Essay in the Philosophy of Music*, rev. edn (Oxford: Oxford University Press, 2007).

Goehr, Lydia, *Elective Affinities: Musical Essays on the History of Aesthetic Theory* (New York: Columbia University Press, 2008).

Goethe, Johann Wolfgang von, *Elective Affinities* (1809), trans. R. J. Hollingdale (Harmondsworth: Penguin, 1971).

Goldman, Albert, 'The Emergence of Rock', *New American Review* 3 (1968), 118–39.
Goldstein, Richard (ed.), *The Poetry of Rock* (Toronto: Bantam, 1969).
Gordon, Kim, *Girl in a Band: A Memoir* (New York: Dey Street, 2015).
Grabócz, Márta, and Makis Solomos, 'New Musicology. Perspectives critiques', *Filigrane* 11 (2010).
Graham, Dan, 'My Religion', *Museumjournaal* 27.7 (1982), 324–9.
Graham, Dan, *Rock My Religion*, ed. Xavier Douroux, Franck Gautherot and Maryvonne Bégon, trans. Patrick Joly and Sylvie Talabardon (Villeurbanne and Dijon: Institut d'Art Contemporain and Les Presses du Réel, 1983).
Green, Lucy, 'Ideology', in Bruce Horner and Thomas Swiss (eds), *Key Terms in Popular Music and Culture* (Malden, MA: Blackwell, 1999), 5–17.
Greenberg, Clement, 'Towards a Newer Laocoon', *Partisan Review* 7 (1940), 296–310.
Gropas, Maria, 'The Repatriotization of Revolutionary Ideology and Mnemonic Landscape in Present-Day Havana', *Current Anthropology* 48.4 (2007), 531–49.
Guerra, Lillian, 'Gender Policing, Homosexuality and the New Patriarchy of the Cuban Revolution, 1965–70', *Social History* 35.3 (2010), 268–89.
Gueudeville, Nicolas, *Critique générale des aventures de Télémaque* (Cologne: Heretiers de Pierre Marteau, 1700).
Gusdorf, Georges, *Les Sciences humaines et la pensée occidentale* (Paris: Payot, 1966–88).
Gusdorf, Georges, *Le Romantisme* (Paris: Éditions Payot et Rivages, 1993).
Hamm, Charles, *Putting Popular Music in Its Place* (Cambridge: Cambridge University Press, 1995).
Hanslick, Eduard, *On the Musically Beautiful: A Contribution Towards the Revision of the Aesthetics of Music*, ed. and trans. Geoffrey Payzant (Indianapolis: Hackett, 1986).
Hanson, Howard, 'The Challenge of the Modern Role of Arts', *American String Teacher* 12.4 (1962), 1–2.
Hayakawa, Samuel I., 'Popular Songs vs. the Facts of Life', *ETC.: A Review of General Semantics* 12.2 (1955), 83–95.
Hegel, Georg Friedrich Wilhelm, *Vorlesungen über Ästhetik*, vol. 2 (Frankfurt am Main: Suhrkamp, 1986).
Hein, Stefanie, *Richard Wagners Kunstprogramm im nationalkulturellen Kontext* (Würzburg: Koenighausen & Neumann, 2006).

Heller, Michael, *Loft Jazz: Improvising New York in the 1970s* (Oakland: University of California Press, 2017).

Hellyer, Grace, and Julian Murphet (eds), *Rancière and Literature* (Edinburgh: Edinburgh University Press, 2016).

Henao Castro, Andrés Fabián, 'Slavery in Plato's Allegory of the Cave: Alain Badiou, Jacques Rancière and the Militant Intellectual from the Global South', *Theatre Survey* 58.1 (2017), 86–107.

Henry, Pierre, liner notes to *Pierre Henry remixe sa dixième Symphonie* (Philips CD 462821-2, 1998).

Hentoff, Nat, liner notes to John Coltrane, *Live at the Village Vanguard Again!* (Impulse! A-9124, 1966).

Herder, Johann Georg, *Viertes Kritisches Wäldchen* (Erlangen: Bläsing, 1846).

Highmore, Ben, *Michel de Certeau: Analysing Culture* (London: Continuum, 2006).

Hinch, John, 'Stravinsky in Africa', *Muziki* 1.1 (2004), 71–86.

Ho, Fred, *Wicked Theory, Naked Practice: A Fred Ho Reader*, ed. Diane C. Fujino (Minneapolis: University of Minnesota Press, 2009).

Ho, Fred, and Nora Ritchie, 'Fred Ho: Music as a Revolutionary Force?' (2011), <http://www.revive-music.com/2011/01/21/fred-ho-music-as-a-revolutionary-force/> (last accessed 16 May 2019).

Holland, Eugene, 'Studies in Applied Nomadology: Jazz Improvisation and Post-Capitalist Markets', in Ian Buchanan and Marcel Swiboda (eds), *Deleuze and Music* (Edinburgh: Edinburgh University Press, 2004), 20–35.

Honig, Bonnie, 'Antigone's Two Laws: Greek Tragedy and the Politics of Humanism', *New Literary History* 41.1 (2010), 1–33.

Hugo, Victor, *The Essential Victor Hugo*, trans. E. H. and A. M. Blackmore (Oxford: Oxford University Press, 2004).

Huyssen, Andreas, *After the Great Divide: Modernism, Mass Culture, Postmodernism* (Bloomington: Indiana University Press, 1986).

Iverson, Ethan, 'Received Wisdom (Jeff Goldblum, chord scales, the iReal Book, and Kamasi Washington)', *Do the M@th* (2018), <https://ethaniverson.com/received-wisdom-jeff-goldblum-chord-scales-the-ireal-book-and-kamasi-washington/> (last accessed 16 May 2019).

Iyer, Vijay, 'Improvisation, Temporality and Embodied Experience', *Journal of Consciousness Studies* 11.3–4 (2004), 159–73.

Jacotot, Joseph, *Enseignement universel: musique, dessin, peinture*, 2nd edn (Paris: Bureau du Journal de l'émancipation intellectuelle, 1830).

Jaggi, Maya, 'The Sound of Freedom', *The Guardian*, 7 December 2001.

James, Robin, '"These.Are.The Breaks": Rethinking *Disagreement* Through Hip Hop', *Transformations: Journal of Media & Culture* 19 (2011), <http://www.transformationsjournal.org/wp-content/uploads/2017/01/James_Trans19.pdf> (last accessed 22 November 2019).

Jones, LeRoi [Amiri Baraka], *Black Music* (1968) (New York: Akashi Classics, 2010).

Joubert, Joseph, *Pensées* (Paris: Christian Bourgois, 1966).

Kaltenecker, Martin, 'L'Hypothèse de la continuité. Variations à partir de Jacques Rancière', in Martin Kaltenecker and François Nicolas (eds), *Penser l'oeuvre musicale au XXe siècle: avec, sans ou contre l'Histoire?* (Paris: Editions du CDMC, 2006), 7–38.

Kaltenecker, Martin, *L'Oreille divisée. Les discours sur l'écoute aux XVIIIe et XIXe siècles* (Paris: Musica falsa, 2010).

Kaltenecker, Martin, 'Résonances théologiques de l'écoute chez Pierre Schaeffer', *Droit de Cités* 4 (October 2010).

Kaltenecker, Martin, 'The Discourse of Sound', *Tempo* 70 (2016), 1–10.

Kaltenecker, Martin, 'De l'effrangement à la connexion', in Wilfried Laforge and Jacinto Lageira (eds), *À la frontière des arts: lectures contemporaines de l'esthétique adornienne* (Paris: Minerve, 2019), 125–54.

Kane, Brian, *Sound Unseen: Acousmatic Sound in Theory and Practice* (Oxford: Oxford University Press, 2014).

Kawabata, Maiko, 'The Concerto That Wasn't: Paganini, Urhan and *Harold in Italy*', *Nineteenth-Century Music Review* 1.1 (2004), 67–114.

Kerman, Joseph, *Contemplating Music: Challenges to Musicology* (Cambridge, MA: Harvard University Press, 1985).

Khan, Imran, 'Meditations in Sound: The Jazz Africana of Pharoah Sanders', *PopMatters*, 22 June 2015, <https://www.popmatters.com/194180-meditations-in-sound-the-jazz-africana-of-pharoah-sanders-2495522581.html> (last accessed 22 November 2019).

Kofsky, Frank, *Black Nationalism and the Revolution in Music* (New York: Pathfinder, 1970).

Kramer, Jonathan D., *Postmodern Music, Postmodern Listening* (London: Bloomsbury, 2016).

Kramer, Lawrence, *Classical Music and Postmodern Knowledge* (Berkeley: University of California Press, 1995).

Kramer, Lawrence, 'Like Falling Leaves: The Erotics of Mourning in Four *Drum-Taps* Settings', in Lawrence Kramer (ed.), *Walt Whitman and Modern Music* (New York: Garland, 2000), 151–65.

Kreidler, Johannes, Harry Lehmann and Claus Steffen Mahnkopff (eds),

Musik, Ästhetik, Digitalisierung. Eine Kontroverse (Hofheim: Wolke, 2010).

Kruttge, Eigel, 'Aus den Reisetagebüchern des Grafen Ludwig von Bentheim-Steinfurt (1756–1817)', *Zeitschrift für Musikwissenschaft* VI.1 (1923–24), 16–53.

Kurth, Ernst, *Selected Writings*, ed. and trans. Lee A. Rothfarb (Cambridge: Cambridge University Press, 1991).

Lacoue-Labarthe, Philippe, *Musica Ficta (Figures of Wagner)*, trans. Felicia McCarren (Stanford: Stanford University Press, 1994).

Lampert, Matthew, 'Beyond the Politics of Reception: Jacques Rancière and the Politics of Art', *Contemporary Philosophical Review* 50 (2017), 181–200.

Laver, Mark, 'Freedom of Choice: Jazz, Neoliberalism, and the Lincoln Center', *Popular Music and Society* 38 (2014), 538–56.

Lazkano, Ramon, *La Ligne de craie* (Champigny-sur-Marne: 2e2M, 2009).

Le Brun, Jacques, '*Les Aventures de Télémaque*: destins d'un *best-seller*', *Littératures classiques* 70.3 (2009), 133–46.

Lehmann, Hans Thies, *Postdramatic Theatre* (London: Routledge, 2006).

Lehmann, Harry, *Die digitale Revolution in der Musik. Eine Musikphilosophie* (Mainz: Schott, 2012).

Levy, Ernst, *A Theory of Harmony* (Albany: State University of New York Press, 1985).

Lott, Eric, 'Double V, Double-Time: Bebop's Politics of Style', in Krin Gabbard (ed.), *Jazz Among the Discourses* (Durham, NC: Duke University Press, 1995), 243–56.

Lukács, Georg, *History and Class Consciousness: Studies in Marxist Dialectics*, trans. Rodney Livingstone (Cambridge, MA: MIT Press, 1971).

Macciocchi, Maria-Antonietta, *Letters from inside the Communist Party to Louis Althusser*, trans. Stephen M. Hellman (London: NLB, 1973).

Manning, Erin, *The Minor Gesture* (Durham, NC: Duke University Press, 2016).

Marks, Shula, and Stanley Trapido, 'The Politics of Race, Class and Nationalism', in Shula Marks and Stanley Trapido (eds), *The Politics of Race, Class and Nationalism in Twentieth-Century South Africa* (London: Routledge, 2014), 1–70.

Marx, Karl, *Capital: A Critique of Political Economy* (1867), vol. 1, trans. Ben Fowkes (London: Penguin Books and New Left Review, 1976).

Massumi, Brian, *Parables of of the Virtual: Movement, Affect, Sensation* (Durham, NC: Duke University Press, 2002).
Massumi, Brian, *Politics of Affect* (Cambridge: Polity, 2015).
Mattheson, Johann, *Der Vollkommene Kapellmeister* (Hamburg: Christian Herold, 1739).
May, Todd, *The Political Thought of Jacques Rancière: Creating Equality* (Edinburgh: Edinburgh University Press, 2008).
McClary, Susan, 'Afterword: The Politics of Silence and Sound', in Jacques Attali, *Noise: The Political Economy of Music*, trans. Brian Massumi (Minneapolis: University of Minnesota Press, 1985), 149–58.
McClary, Susan, *Feminine Endings: Music, Gender and Sexuality* (Minneapolis: University of Minnesota Press, 1991).
McMullen, Tracy, 'Approaching the Jazz Past: MOPDtK's *Blue* and Jason Moran's "In My Mind: Monk at Town Hall, 1959"', *Journal of Jazz Studies* 11.2 (2016), 1–39.
Mecchia, Giuseppina, 'Mute Speech: The Silence of Literature in Rancière's Aesthetic Paradigm', in Patrick M. Bray (ed.), *Understanding Rancière, Understanding Modernism* (New York: Bloomsbury, 2017), 97–110.
Meiksins Wood, Ellen, *Peasant-Citizen and Slave: The Foundations of Athenian Democracy* (London: Verso, 2015).
Meltzer, Richard, *The Aesthetics of Rock* (Boston: Da Capo Press, 1987).
Menger, Pierre-Michel, *Le Paradoxe du musicien: le compositeur, le mélomane et l'etat dans la société contemporaine* (Paris: Harmonique/Flammarion, 1983).
Mercer, Michelle, 'How Norway Funds a Thriving Jazz Scene', *A Blog Supreme*, NPR online, 6 April 2013, <https://www.npr.org/sections/ablogsupreme/2013/03/26/175415645/how-norway-funds-a-thriving-jazz-scene> (last accessed 22 November 2019).
Middleton, Richard, *Studying Popular Music* (Milton Keynes: Open University Press, 1990).
Mombelet, Alexis, 'La musique metal: des "éclats de religion" et une liturgie', *Sociétés: Revue des Sciences Humaines et Sociales* 88.2 (2005).
Mondrian, Piet, *The New Art – The New Life: The Collected Writings of Piet Mondrian* (Boston: G. K. Hall, 1986).
Monson, Ingrid, 'From the American Civil Rights Movement to Mali: Reflections on Social Aesthetics and Improvisation', in Georgina Born, Eric Lewis and Will Straw (eds), *Improvisation and Social Aesthetics* (Durham, NC: Duke University Press, 2017), 78–90.
Moreno, Jairo, and Gavin Steingo, 'Rancière's Equal Music', *Contemporary Music Review* 31.5–6 (2012), 487–505.
Mousie, Joshua, 'Rancière, Resistance and Improvisation', *Improvisation,*

Community and Social Practice, Online Research Collection (2010), <http://www.improvcommunity.ca/research/ranciere-resistance-and-musical-improvisation> (last accessed 22 November 2019).

Muller, Stephanus, '*An Inconsolable Memory*: Ethical and Methodological Challenges for Music Historiography in Traumatic and Post-Totalitarian Contexts', paper presented at Royal Holloway, University of London, 25 November 2014.

Murail, Tristan, *Modèles et artifices* (Strasbourg: Presses Universitaires de Strasbourg, 2004).

Nattrass, Nicoli, and Jeremy Seekings, *Class, Race, and Inequality in South Africa* (New Haven, CT: Yale University Press, 2005).

Negus, Keith, *Popular Music in Theory* (Malden, MA: Polity, 1996).

Neset, Anne, 'All Shook Up', *Wire* 304 (June 2009), 32–3.

Nietzsche, Friedrich, *The Birth of Tragedy and The Case of Wagner* (1872), trans. Walter Kaufmann (Harmondsworth: Penguin, 1967).

Nietzsche, Friedrich, *Twilight of the Idols, or How To Philosophise With a Hammer* (1889), in *The Portable Nietzsche*, trans. Walter Kaufmann (Harmondsworth: Penguin, 1968).

Nietzsche, Friedrich, *The Will to Power* (1906), trans. Walter Kaufmann and R. J. Hollindale (New York: Vintage, 1968).

Nietzsche, Friedrich, *The Dionysian Vision of the World*, trans. Ira J. Allen (Minneapolis: University of Minnesota Press, 2012).

Padel, Ruth, *I'm a Man: Sex, Gods and Rock 'n' Roll* (London: Faber and Faber, 2000).

Palmer, Robert, *Dancing in the Street: A Rock and Roll History* (London: BBC Books, 1996).

Panagia, Davide, 'Rancière's Style', *Novel* 47.2 (2014), 284–300.

Panagia, Davide, *Rancière's Sentiments* (Durham, NC: Duke University Press, 2018).

Patton, Paul, 'Rancière's Utopian Politics', in Jean-Philippe Deranty and Alison Ross (eds), *Jacques Rancière and the Contemporary Scene* (London: Continuum, 2012), 129–44.

Perna, Vincenzo, *Timba: The Sound of the Cuban Crisis* (New York: Routledge, 2017).

Peters, Gary, *The Philosophy of Improvisation* (Chicago: University of Chicago Press, 2009).

Pichova, Hana, 'The Lineup for Meat: The Stalin Statue in Prague', *PMLA* 123.3 (2008), 614–31.

Pickford, Henry W., *The Sense of Semblance: Philosophical Analyses of Holocaust Art* (New York: Fordham University Press, 2013).

Pierret, Marc, *Entretiens avec Pierre Schaeffer* (Paris: Pierre Belfond, 1969).
Pistorius, Juliana M., 'Coloured Opera as Subversive Forgetting', *Social Dynamics* 43.2 (2017), 230–42.
Plato, *Republic*, trans. G. M. A. Grube, rev. C. D. C. Reeve (Indianapolis: Hackett, 1992).
Pribiag, Ioana, 'Politics and its Others: Jacques Rancière's Figures of Alterity', *Philosophy Today* 63.3 (2019), 447–70.
Proust, Marcel, *À la recherche du temps perdu*, ed. Pierre Clarac and André Ferré (Paris: Gallimard, 1978).
Proust, Marcel, *Contre Sainte-Beuve précédé de Pastiches et mélanges et suivi de Essais et articles*, ed. Pierre Clarac and Yves Sandre (Paris: Gallimard, 1978).
Quiros, Oscar, 'Critical Mass of Cuban Cinema: Art as the Vanguard of Society', *Screen* 37.3 (1996), 279–93.
Rancière, Jacques, 'Ronds de fumée. Les poètes ouvriers dans la France de Louis-Philippe', *Revue des sciences humaines* 190 (1983), 31–47.
Rancière, Jacques, *The Ignorant Schoolmaster: Five Lessons in Intellectual Emancipation*, trans. Kristin Ross (Stanford: Stanford University Press, 1991).
Rancière, Jacques, *The Names of History: On the Poetics of Knowledge*, trans. Hassan Melehy (Minneapolis: University of Minnesota Press, 1994).
Rancière, Jacques, *Disagreement: Politics and Philosophy*, trans. Julie Rose (Minneapolis: University of Minnesota Press, 1995).
Rancière, Jacques, *On the Shores of Politics*, trans. Liz Heron (London: Verso, 1995).
Rancière, Jacques, 'Politics, Identification, Subjectivization', in *The Identity in Question*, ed. John Rajchman (London: Routledge, 1995), 63–72.
Rancière, Jacques, *Mallarmé. La politique de la sirène* (Paris: Hachette, 1996).
Rancière, Jacques, 'La constance de l'art', *Trafic* 21 (spring 1997), 40–3.
Rancière, Jacques, *La Chair des mots: politiques de l'écriture* (Paris: Galilée, 1998).
Rancière, Jacques, *Politique de la littérature* (Paris: Galilée, 1998).
Rancière, Jacques, 'Dissenting Words: A Conversation with Jacques Rancière' (with Davide Panagia), *Diacritics* 30.2 (2000), 113–26.
Rancière, Jacques, *Le Partage du sensible* (Paris: La Fabrique, 2000).
Rancière, Jacques, *La Fable cinématographique* (Paris: Galilée, 2001).
Rancière, Jacques, *L'Inconscient esthétique* (Paris: Galilée, 2001).

Rancière, Jacques, 'Ten Theses on Politics', trans. Rachel Bowlby and Davide Panagia, *Theory & Event* 5.3 (2001).

Rancière, Jacques, 'La Métamorphose des muses', in *Sonic Process: une nouvelle géographie des sons* (Paris: Centre Pompidou, 2002), 25–35.

Rancière, Jacques, 'Metamorphosis of the Muses', in *Sonic Process: A New Geography of Sounds*, ed. Mela Dávila (Barcelona: Actar, 2002), 17–29.

Rancière, Jacques, 'Autonomie et historicisme: la fausse alternative (Sur les régimes de l'historicité de l'art)', presented at the seminar 'Penser la musique contemporaine avec/sans/contre l'histoire?', École normale supérieure, December 2003.

Rancière, Jacques, 'Comment and Responses', *Theory and Event* 6.4 (2003), n.p.

Rancière, Jacques, *Le Destin des images* (Paris: La fabrique, 2003).

Rancière, Jacques, 'La Pensée sensible', *Cinéma 05* (spring 2003), 767–77.

Rancière, Jacques, *The Philosopher and His Poor*, trans. John Drury, Corinne Oster and Andrew Parker (Durham, NC: Duke University Press, 2003).

Rancière, Jacques, *Short Voyages to the Land of the People*, trans. James B. Swenson (Stanford: Stanford University Press, 2003).

Rancière, Jacques, 'Is There a Deleuzian Aesthetics?', *Qui Parle* 14.2 (2004), 1–14.

Rancière, Jacques, *Malaise dans l'esthétique* (Paris: Galilée, 2004).

Rancière, Jacques, *Film Fables* (New York: Berg, 2006).

Rancière, Jacques, *The Future of the Image*, trans. Gregory Elliott (London: Verso, 2007).

Rancière, Jacques, 'What Does it Mean to be *Un*?', *Continuum* 21.4 (2007), 559–69.

Rancière, Jacques, 'Why Emma Bovary Had to be Killed', *Critical Inquiry* 34.2 (2008), 233–48.

Rancière, Jacques, *The Aesthetic Unconscious*, trans. Debra Keates and James Swenson (Cambridge: Polity, 2009).

Rancière, Jacques, *Aesthetics and its Discontents*, trans. Steven Corcoran (Malden, MA: Polity, 2009).

Rancière, Jacques, 'Afterword/The Method of Equality: An Answer to Some Questions', in Gabriel Rockhill and Philip Watts (eds), *Jacques Rancière: History, Politics, Aesthetics* (Durham, NC: Duke University Press, 2009), 273–88.

Rancière, Jacques, *The Emancipated Spectator*, trans. Gregory Elliott (London: Verso, 2009).

Rancière, Jacques, *Et tant pis pour les gens fatigués: entretiens* (Paris: Éditions Amsterdam, 2009).
Rancière, Jacques, 'A Few Remarks on the Method of Jacques Rancière', *Parallax* 15.3 (2009), 114–23.
Rancière, Jacques, 'Politique de l'indétermination esthétique', in Jérôme Game and Aliocha Wald Lasowski (eds), *Jacques Rancière: Politique de l'esthétique* (Paris: Éditions des archives contemporaines, 2009), 157–76.
Rancière, Jacques, *Dissensus: On Politics and Aesthetics*, trans. Steven Corcoran (London: Bloomsbury, 2010).
Rancière, Jacques, *Aisthesis: scènes du régime esthétique de l'art* (Paris: Galilée, 2011).
Rancière, Jacques, *Althusser's Lesson*, trans. Emiliano Battista (London: Continuum, 2011).
Rancière, Jacques, *Mallarmé: The Politics of the Siren*, trans. Steven Corcoran (London: Continuum, 2011).
Rancière, Jacques, *Mute Speech: Literature, Critical Theory, and Politics*, trans. James Swenson (New York: Columbia University Press, 2011).
Rancière, Jacques, *The Politics of Literature*, trans. Julie Rose (Cambridge: Polity, 2011).
Rancière, Jacques, *Staging the People: The Proletariat and his Double* (London: Verso, 2011).
Rancière, Jacques, *The Intellectual and His People: Staging the People*, vol. 2, trans. David Fernbach (London: Verso, 2012).
Rancière, Jacques, *Proletarian Nights: The Workers' Dream in Nineteenth-Century France*, trans. John Drury (London: Verso, 2012).
Rancière, Jacques, *Aisthesis: Scenes from the Aesthetic Regime of Art*, trans. Zakir Paul (London: Verso, 2013).
Rancière, Jacques, *Béla Tarr: The Time After* (Minneapolis: University of Minnesota Press, 2013).
Rancière, Jacques, *The Politics of Aesthetics: The Distribution of the Sensible*, trans. Gabriel Rockhill (London: Bloomsbury, 2013).
Rancière, Jacques, *Figures of History* (Cambridge: Polity, 2014).
Rancière, Jacques, *Le Fil perdu. Essais sur la fiction moderne* (Paris: Galilée, 2014).
Rancière, Jacques, *The Intervals of Cinema* (London: Verso, 2014).
Rancière, Jacques, *Moments Politiques: Interventions 1977–2009*, trans. Mary Foster (New York: Seven Stories Press, 2014).
Rancière, Jacques, *The Lost Thread: The Democracy of Modern Fiction*, trans. Steven Corcoran (London: Bloomsbury, 2016).
Rancière, Jacques, *The Method of Equality: Interviews with Laurent*

Jeanpierre and Dork Zabunyan, trans. Julie Rose (Cambridge: Polity, 2016).

Rancière, Jacques, *Les Bords de la fiction* (Paris: Galilée, 2017).

Rancière, Jacques, *Dissenting Words*, ed. and trans. Emiliano Battista (London: Bloomsbury, 2017).

Rancière, Jacques, *En quel temps vivons-nous? Conversation avec Eric Hazan* (Paris: La fabrique, 2017).

Rancière, Jacques, *Les Temps modernes: art, temps, politique* (Paris: La fabrique, 2018).

Rancière, Jacques, 'Autonomy and Historicity', trans. Patrick Nickleson, *Perspectives of New Music* 57.1–2 (2019).

Rancière, Jacques, with Fulvia Carnevale and John Kelsey, 'Art of the Possible', *ArtForum* 45.7 (2007), 256–69.

Rehding, Alexander, *Beethoven's Symphony No. 9* (New York: Oxford University Press, 2018).

Reuben, Federico, 'Imaginary Musical Radicalism and the Entanglement of Music and Emancipatory Politics', *Contemporary Music Review* 34.2–3 (2015), 232–46.

Rihm, Wolfgang, *Ausgesprochen, Schriften und Gespräche*, vol. 1 (Winterthur: Amadeus, 1997).

Riley, Patrick, 'Introduction', in François Fénelon, *Telemachus, Son of Ulysses*, trans. Patrick Riley (Cambridge: Cambridge University Press, 1994).

Rimbaud, Arthur, *Œuvres complètes*, ed. Pierre Brunel (Paris: Le Livre de Poche, 1999).

Rinzler, Alan, 'A Conversation with Charles Reich: Blowing in the Wind', *Rolling Stone* 75 (4 February 1971), 31–4.

Robbins, Bruce, *Perpetual War: Cosmopolitanism from the Viewpoint of Violence* (Durham, NC: Duke University Press, 2012).

Robertson, Sandy, 'Behind the Wall of Sleep with the Patti Smith Group', *Sounds*, 25 March 1978, 16–18.

Rockhill, Gabriel, and Philip Watts (eds), *Jacques Rancière: History, Politics, Aesthetics* (Durham, NC: Duke University Press, 2009).

Rodgers, Stephen, *Form, Program, and Metaphor in the Music of Berlioz* (Cambridge: Cambridge University Press, 2009).

Roos, Hilde, 'Opera Production in the Western Cape: Strategies in Search of Indigenization', PhD dissertation, Stellenbosch University, 2010.

Roos, Hilde, 'Remembering to Forget the Eoan Group – The Legacy of an Opera Company from the Apartheid Era', *South African Theatre Journal* 27.1 (2014), 1–18.

Ross, Alex, *The Rest Is Noise: Listening to the Twentieth Century* (New York: Farrar, Straus and Giroux, 2007).
Ross, Alex, *Listen to This* (New York: Farrar, Straus and Giroux, 2010).
Ross, Kristin, *May '68 and Its Afterlives* (Chicago: University of Chicago Press, 2006).
Ross, Richard van der, *In Our Own Skins: A Political History of the Coloured People of South Africa* (Cape Town: Jonathan Ball, 2015).
Rouby, Bertrand, 'Le Rock à l'épreuve du canon', *Études britanniques contemporaines: Revue de la Société d'Études Anglaises Contemporaines* 24 (2003), 97–109.
Rudy, Dario, and Yves Citton, 'Le lo-fi: épaissir la médiation pour intensifier la relation', *Écologie & Politique* 48.1 (2014), 109–24.
Russell, George, *Lydian Chromatic Concept* (1953) (Brookline, MA: Concept Publishing, 2001).
Rutherford-Johnson, Tim, *Music after the Fall* (Berkeley: University of California Press, 2017).
Salewicz, Chris, 'Oy Lemmy, Is It True You Were a Hippie??', *New Musical Express*, 25 August 1979, 18–21.
San Juan, Rebecca, 'Cuba's Unresolved UMAP History: Survivors' Struggles to Counter the Official Story', PhD dissertation, Mount Holyoke College, 2017.
Sangild, Torben, *The Aesthetics of Noise* (Datanom, 2002).
Saunders, James, 'Interview with Rebecca Saunders', <http://www.james-saunders.com/interview-with-rebecca-saunders/> (last accessed 20 November, 2019).
Schaeffer, Pierre, 'L'élément non-visuel au cinéma (I): analyse de la bande "son"', *La revue du cinéma* 1 (1946), 45–8.
Schaeffer, Pierre, 'L'élément non-visuel au cinéma (II): psychologie du rapport vision-audition', *La revue du cinéma* 2 (1946), 62–5.
Schaeffer, Pierre, 'L'élément non-visuel au cinéma (III): conception de la musique', *La revue du cinéma* 3 (1946), 51–4.
Schaeffer, Pierre, *À la recherche d'une musique concrete* (Paris: Seuil, 1952).
Schaeffer, Pierre, 'Notes sur l'expression radiophonique', in *Machines à communiquer 1: genèse des simulacres* (Paris: Seuil, 1970), 89–118.
Schaeffer, Pierre, *De la musique concrète à la musique même*, La Revue musicale, vols 303–5 (Paris: Richard-Masse, 1977).
Schaeffer, Pierre, *Essai sur la radio et le cinéma: esthétique et technique des arts-relais, 1941–1942* (Paris: Allia, 2010).
Schmidt, Lothar, *Organische Form in der Musik. Stationen eines Begriffs 1795–1850* (Kassel: Bärenreiter, 1990).

Schoenberg, Arnold, *Schönbergs Verein für musikalische Privataufführungen*, Musik-Konzepte 36, ed. Heinz-Klaus Metzger and Rainer Riehn (Munich: text+kritik, 1984).

Schopenhauer, Arthur, *The World as Will and Representation* (1819), trans. E. F. J. Payne (New York: Dover, 1969).

Schube, Will, 'The Cosmos is Still Catching Up to Pharoah Sanders' Earliest Recordings', *Noisey*, 14 November 2017, <https://www.vice.com/en_uk/article/59y4xq/pharaoh-sanders-tauhid-impulse-records-essay> (last accessed 22 November 2019).

Scott, Derek B., 'Postmodernism and Music', in Stuart Sim (ed.), *The Routledge Companion to Postmodernism*, 3rd edn (London: Routledge, 2011), 182–93.

Scudo, Paul, *Critique et littérature musicales*, vol. 2 (Paris: Hachette, 1859).

Shank, Barry, *The Political Force of Musical Beauty* (Durham, NC: Duke University Press, 2014).

Shannon, William J., 'The Presley Plague', *The Catholic Sun*, 25 October 1956, 1.

Shuker, Roy, *Understanding Popular Music Culture*, 4th edn (London: Routledge, 2013).

Sisario, Ben, 'A Brief, Noisy Moment that Still Reverberates', *The New York Times*, 12 June 2008, E1.

Slonimsky, Nicolas, *Thesaurus of Scales and Melodic Patterns* (New York: Schirmer, 1975).

Smith, Adam, 'Of the Nature of Imitation', *Essays on Philosophical Subjects*, vol. 3 (Oxford: Clarendon Press, 1980).

Smith, Leo, *notes (8 pieces)* (1973) (Corbett vs. Dempsey and the Renaissance Society, 2015).

Solie, Ruth, 'Living Work: Organicism and Musical Analysis', *Nineteenth-Century Music* 4.2 (1980), 147–56.

Sparks, Holloway, 'Quarrelling with Rancière: Race, Gender and the Politics of Democratic Disruption', *Philosophy and Rhetoric* 49.4 (2016), 420–37.

Spinoza, Baruch, *Ethics* (1677), trans. Edwin Curley (Harmondsworth: Penguin, 1996).

Stearn, Jess, 'Rock 'n' Roll Runs into Trouble: Disgusted Adults Battling Music of Delinquents', *Daily News*, 11 April 1956, 34.

Stearn, Jess, 'Rock 'n' Roll Runs into Trouble: More Youngsters Ignore That Primitive Beat', *Daily News*, 12 April 1956, 42.

Stearns, Matthew, *Daydream Nation* (New York: Continuum, 2007).

Stevens, Ruth W., 'Editorially Speaking...', *Music Journal* 16.2 (1958), 3.

Stover, Chris, 'Jazz Theory's Pragmatics', in Rachel Lumsden and Jeremy Swinkin (eds), *The Norton Guide to Teaching Music Theory* (New York: Norton, 2017), 234–51.
Stover, Chris, 'Time, Territorialization, and Improvisational Spaces', *Music Theory Online* 23.1 (2017), <http://mtosmt.org/issues/mto.17.23.1/mto.17.23.1.stover.html> (last accessed 22 November 2019).
Stover, Chris, 'Affect and Improvising Bodies', *Perspectives of New Music* 55.2 (2018), 5–66.
Stover, Chris, 'Affect, Play, and Becoming-Musicking', in Markus Bolhmann and Anna Catherine Hickey-Moody (eds), *Deleuze and Children* (Edinburgh: Edinburgh University Press, 2018), 145–61.
Stover, Chris, 'Sun Ra's Mystical Time', *The Open Space Magazine* 21 (2018), 106–13.
Stover, Chris, 'Politicking Musical Time', in Mark Doffman, Emily Payne and Toby Young (eds), *The Oxford Handbook of Time in Music* (Oxford: Oxford University Press, 2020).
Street, John, '"Fight the Power": The Politics of Music and the Music of Politics', *Government and Opposition* 38.1 (2003), 113–30.
Sweezy, Stewart, 'Sonic Youth: The Sound and the Fury', *Option* G2 (March and April 1986), 29–31.
Sulzer, Johann Georg, *Allgemeine Theorie der Schönen Künste* (Berlin: Directmedia, Digitale Bibliothek, 2004).
Szwed, John, 'Josef Skvorecky and the Tradition of Jazz Literature', *World Literature Today* 54.4 (1980), 586–90.
Tagg, Philip, 'Analyzing Popular Music: Theory, Method and Practice', *Popular Music* 2 (1982), 37–67.
Tagg, Philip, and Bob Clarida, *Ten Little Title Tunes* (New York and Montreal: The Mass Media Music Scholar's Press, 2003).
Tahbaz, Joseph, 'Demystifying las UMAP: The Politics of Sugar, Gender, and Religion in 1960s Cuba', *Delaware Review of Latin American Studies* 14.2 (2013), <http://www.udel.edu/LAS/Vol14-2Tahbaz.html#_ednref19> (last accessed 22 November 2019).
Tanke, Joseph J., *Jacques Rancière: An Introduction* (New York: A&C Black, 2011).
Tovey, Donald Francis, '*Harold in Italy*, symphony with viola obbligato, Op.16' (1937), in *Symphonies and Other Orchestral Works: Selections from Essays in Musical Analysis* (Mineola, NY: Dover, 2015), 171–8.
Trottier, Danick, 'Music, History, Autonomy and Presentness: When Composers and Philosophers Cross Swords', in Martin Kaltenecker and François Nicolas (eds), *Penser l'oeuvre musicale au XXe siècle:*

avec, sans ou contre l'histoire? (Paris: Centre de documentation de la musique contemporaine, 2006), 70–85.

Truong, Nicolas, 'Il n'y a jamais eu besoin d'expliquer à un travailleur ce qu'est l'exploitation', *Philosophie Magazine* 10 (June 2007), 54–9.

Valéry, Paul, 'Poésie et pensée abstraite', in *Variété V* (Paris: Gallimard, 1944), 151–5.

Varèse, Edgard, and Chou Wen-chung, 'The Liberation of Sound' (1936), *Perspectives of New Music* 5.1 (1966), 11–19.

Ventura, Michael, *Shadow Dancing in the USA* (Los Angeles: J. P. Tarcher, 1986).

Vitali, Luca, *The Sound of the North: The Norwegian Jazz Scene* (Milan: Mimesis International, 2016).

Vogt, Erik M., *Aesthetisch-Politische Lektueren zum 'Fall Wagner'* (Vienna and Berlin: Turia + Kant, 2015).

Vogt, Erik M., *Zwischen Sensologie und aesthetischem Dissens* (Vienna and Berlin: Turia + Kant, 2019).

Wackenroder, Wilhelm H., *Confessions and Fantasies*, trans. Mary H. Schubert (University Park: Penn State University Press, 1971).

Wagner, Richard, *Sämtliche Schriften und Dichtungen*, vol. 10 (Leipzig: Breitkopf & Härtel/Siegel, n.d.).

Wagner, Richard, *Beethoven*, trans. Edward Dannreuther (London: Reeves, 1903).

Wagner, Richard, *The Art-Work of the Future and Other Works*, trans. W. Ashton Ellis (Lincoln, NE: University of Nebraska Press, 1993).

Wagner, Richard, *Opera and Drama*, trans. W. Ashton Ellis (Lincoln: University of Nebraska Press, 1995).

White, Charles, *The Life and Times of Little Richard: The Quasar of Rock* (New York: Da Capo Press, 1994).

Wicke, Peter, 'Rock Music: A Musical-Aesthetic Study', *Popular Music* 2 (1982), 219–43.

Wiebe, Heather, *Britten's Unquiet Pasts: Sound and Memory in Postwar Reconstruction* (Cambridge: Cambridge University Press, 2012).

Williams, Paul, 'Rock Is Rock: A Discussion of a Doors Song', *Crawdaddy!* 9 (May 1967), 42–6.

Wilmer, Val, *As Serious as Your Life: Black Music and the Free Jazz Revolution, 1957–1977* (1977) (London: Serpent's Tail, 2018).

Wlodarski, Amy Lynn, *Musical Witness and Holocaust Representation* (Cambridge: Cambridge University Press, 2015).

Wolfe, Katherine, 'From Aesthetics to Politics: Rancière, Kant and Deleuze', *Contemporary Aesthetics* 4 (2006), <https://digitalcommons.

risd.edu/liberalarts_contempaesthetics/vol4/iss1/12/> (last accessed 22 November 2019).

Woolf, Virginia, *Le Cinéma et autres essais* (Paris: Les Éditions de Paris, 2012).

Zabunyan, Dork, 'Préface', in *Les grand entretiens d'artpress: Jacques Rancière. Patrice Blouin, Maxime Boidy, Yan Ciret, Dominique Gonzalez-Foerster, W. J. T Mitchell, Stéphane Roth* (Paris: Artpress 2014), 5–13.

Ziporyn, Evan, and Michael Tenzer, 'Thelonious Monk's Harmony, Rhythm and Pianism', in Michael Tenzer and John Roeder (eds), *Analytical and Cross-Cultural Studies in World Music* (Oxford: Oxford University Press, 2011), 147–86.

Zola, Émile, *The Belly of Paris*, trans. Brian Nelson (Oxford: Oxford University Press, 2007).

Index

acousmatic, 38, 40
Adam, Adolphe, 106
Adams, John, 279
Adès, Thomas, 132
Adorno, Theodor W., 2, 19, 103,
    132, 250, 270, 273, 284, 290–2,
    295–6, 298–300, 305–7, 309,
    340, 357, 361
  and the Mahlerian jackass, 292,
    296, 307, 309
  Prisms, 292, 296, 299
  and remainder, 290–2, 295–300,
    305–9
aesthetic education, 316, 331, 332
aesthetic regime (of art), 2, 5–8,
    10–12, 14–17, 19–20, 27, 29–33,
    36, 42, 48, 78, 97–8, 100–1, 103,
    119–20, 125–6, 131–4, 210, 228,
    236, 239, 272, 274, 282, 320–1,
    324, 357, 361
  and Attali's compositional stage,
    239
aesthetic revolution, 11, 48, 119–20,
    126, 298
affect, 5, 7, 30, 102, 118, 179, 191,
    193, 198, 214, 221–2, 224,
    229–33, 241–4, 255, 355
Ahmed, Sara, 228–9
Althusser, Louis, 10, 14, 71–6, 78–9,
    81–5, 88–9, 90, 91
Aristotle, 5, 9, 48, 52, 83, 97, 101,
    102
Armstrong, Louis, 235
Art Ensemble of Chicago, the, 244
artistic modernity, 11, 15, 17,
    117–20

Association for the Advancement
    of Creative Musicians, the,
    210
Attali, Jacques, 22, 233, 235, 238–40,
    243–4, 252, 259, 360–1
autonomy, 2, 6, 13, 37, 42, 64, 118,
    120, 128, 131–2, 273, 298,
    301–2, 322, 359
avant-garde, 7, 15, 18, 19, 101, 108,
    120, 208, 209–10, 218, 228, 235,
    246, 317–18, 344
Ayler, Albert, 246–7

Babbitt, Milton, 15
Badiou, Alain, 19, 316–20, 324–5,
    333, 364
  inaesthetics, 318–20
Bailey, Derek, 251
Baker, David, 258
Balzac, Honoré de, 17, 52, 98–9, 101,
    126
Banville, Théodore de, 99
Baraka, Amiri (LeRoi Jones), 242,
    259
Barthes, Roland, 79, 91, 126–7,
    128
Barzun, Jacques, 127–8, 132
Bataille, Georges, 59
Bayreuth, 108
beauty, 48, 50, 99, 104, 181–2, 191,
    216, 217, 227, 242, 272, 278,
    300
Beethoven, Ludwig van, 6, 7, 8, 52,
    102, 106, 107, 108–9, 128, 131,
    132, 300, 339, 342, 354, 359,
    361

390

Benjamin, Walter, 117, 271, 275, 278, 284, 300
  The Arcades Project, 300
Bergson, Henri, 2, 232
Berio, Luciano, 231
Berlioz, Hector, 18, 21, 51, 100, 101, 106, 120–34, 135, 137, 300–3, 358–9, 362–3
  Harold en Italie, 18, 120–1, 123, 125–9, 132–3, 135–7, 362
  'Marche de pèlerins chantant la prière du soir', 121, 123–4, 127, 137
  Mémoires, 120–1, 125, 135
  Roméo et Juliette, 100, 358
  Symphonie Fantastique, 121, 133
Berry, Chuck, 54
Bhabha, Homi, 254
Bildungsroman, 103
Blanqui, Auguste, 17, 166, 167–9
bodies, 30, 33, 37–8, 77, 163, 166, 168, 169, 214, 221, 224, 228, 231, 232, 233, 239, 281, 305, 323
Borges, Jorge Luis, 250
Born, Georgina, 23, 213–14, 215, 216–18
Bourdieu, Pierre, 160–1, 216, 337–8, 342
Bourriaud, Nicolas, 110
Brackett, David, 3, 21
Byron, Lord, 121, 359

Cage, John, 41, 62, 114, 137, 210
Carcassés, Roberto, 177, 185–6, 187–98, 199
Castelluci, Romeo, 101
Castro, Fidel, 180, 193, 196, 197
Chabanon, Michel Paul Guy de, 102
Chambers, Samuel, 80, 83, 233, 281
Charles, Ray, 55
Christianity, 73, 143, 324–6
cinema, 34–7, 38, 133, 354–5
Citton, Yves, 68–9
Clarke, Kenny, 235
Coleman, Ornette, 235
Coltrane, John, 233
  Live at the Village Vanguard Again!, 233, 245–7, 252, 259
commemorative art and music, 19, 266, 267–8, 269, 273–8, 281, 284–6, 360
communism, 283

community, 19, 38, 86, 88, 104, 107, 108, 110, 161–2, 165, 166–8, 169, 177, 178–9, 182, 183, 186, 193, 198, 199, 215, 216–17, 225, 227, 241, 245, 248–52, 261, 304–5, 307, 308, 314, 322–3, 325–7, 333, 336, 341, 359, 360
Conrad, Joseph, 29
consensus, 172, 194, 215, 217, 220, 237–8, 243–4, 248, 250–1, 266–7, 279–81, 283, 328
contingency, 100, 207, 215, 219–23, 229, 301, 319
Cook, Nicholas, 342–3
Courbet, Gustave, 50
Cuarón, Alfonso, 133
Cuba, 177–200
'Cuban police order', 195, 196, 198–9

Darmstadt, 14, 15
Davis, Miles, 235, 249–52, 306
  Kind of Blue, 249–52
Dearie, Blossom, 306
Debussy, Claude, 106, 338
decadence, 270
Deleuze, Gilles, 2, 40, 103, 225, 232, 242, 271
democracy, 31, 49, 78, 87, 160, 178, 191, 200, 280, 281, 305, 314, 324
demos, 305, 323
Derrida, Jacques, 290, 300, 306–9
dialectics, 130, 215, 235, 290–3, 294, 296, 300, 306, 318
  negative, 285, 291, 296, 300
disfiguration, 36–7
dis-identification, 13, 19, 157–8, 166, 168–9, 231, 234, 235, 242, 243, 360
displacement, aesthetics of, 285
dissensus, 18, 125, 162, 165, 178, 185, 191, 215, 230, 237, 249, 251, 252, 281, 282, 286, 327–8
distribution of the sensible, 3, 9, 10, 12, 17, 19, 29–30, 31, 32, 38, 40, 42, 126, 134, 163, 165–6, 178, 210, 217, 231, 233, 237, 242, 243, 245, 251, 252, 269, 313–14, 320, 335–7, 342, 357–8
Dömling, Wolfgang, 127, 135
Dostoevsky, Fyodor, 125
Dufourt, Hugues, 102

Eisler, Hans, 276, 277
Ellington, Duke, 235, 250
Elliott, Moppa, 250, 260
emancipation, 10, 139, 143, 144, 147, 148–9, 150–2, 168, 325, 357, 359
  intellectual, 139, 142, 305, 335
Engels, Friedrich, 292, 293–6
  Anti-Dühring, 292
  and dialectics, 292, 294
Enlightenment, 49, 52, 64, 144, 152–3, 269, 273, 279
enunciation, 32, 33, 37, 158, 179, 231, 253
Eoan Group, the, 18, 156, 157–8, 161–9, 170, 172
Epstein, Jean, 35, 36–7, 41, 359
equal music, 3, 338
equality, 4, 8, 11, 12, 20, 21, 50, 81, 85–6, 100, 129, 151–2, 153, 157, 158–9, 160–1, 163, 165, 166, 178, 180, 193, 196, 198, 209–10, 215, 227, 232, 236, 238, 244, 253, 269, 273, 280, 281–2, 297, 305, 331, 334, 335, 337, 338–9, 342, 343, 344–6, 359
  method of, 79, 229, 334, 335, 344–6, 361
erosion of the arts, 117, 132
ethical regime (of art), 2, 11, 17, 86, 97, 119, 147, 239
ethnomusicology, 216, 344
ethnos, 323

Faydit, Pierre Valentin, 143–5, 148
Fenélon, François-Joseph, 18, 139–53, 154, 155, 353–4
fiction, 30, 31, 35, 42, 110–11, 252, 305
figuration, 125–6
Five Cuban Heroes, the, 186–7, 188, 189, 191
Flaubert, Gustave, 4–5, 7, 14, 17, 29, 31, 48, 105, 125–6, 127, 128, 129, 270–1
  Coeur simple, Un, 127, 128, 129
  Emma Bovary, 5, 48, 62, 105, 270, 275, 286
Foucault, Michel, 17, 44, 101
Fuller, Loïe, 5, 92, 362

Gates Jr., Henry Louis, 253
Genet, Jean, 275

genre in music, 35, 57–8, 336, 344–6
Givan, Benjamin, 272
Godard, Jean-Luc, 110, 354
Goehr, Lydia, 19, 274–6, 284–6
Goethe, Johann Wolfgang von, and *Elective Affinities*, 265–6, 286
Gordon, Kim, 58, 60
Graham, Dan, 56, 60
grand opera, 100
Green, Lucy, 340
Greenberg, Clement, 131
groove, in Cuban music, 187–9
  'locked' groove on records, 40
Guerra, Digna, 195–6

Hegel, Georg Wilhelm Friedrich, 2, 6, 7, 17, 99–100, 287, 331, 353, 362
Henry, Pierre, 108–9, 359
  Dixième Symphonie, 108
Hentoff, Nat, 246
Herder, Johann Gottfried, 102
Ho, Fred, 244

'I Should Care' (Cahn and Stordahl), 241–2
IASPM, 341
Ibrahim, Abdullah, 244
improvisation, 4, 18–19, 41, 78, 177, 186, 194, 207–9, 215, 219–23, 233–7, 244–5, 250, 306, 359, 361
  and contingency, 19, 207, 208, 209, 215, 216, 219–23
  ideological commitments of, 208
Interactivo, 177, 179, 185, 186–93, 194, 198, 199
  'Cubanos por el mundo', 177, 179, 182–6, 187, 193, 198
irony, 296
  and free indirect style, 75, 76, 78, 85, 142
  in jazz improvisation, 241, 250, 261

Jackson, Michael, 283, 101
Jacotot, Joseph, 18, 83, 139–43, 144, 148–52, 353–4
James, Robin, 242
Jarmusch, Jim, 47
jazz, 19, 58, 208, 210, 217, 218, 233, 240, 241, 244–5, 246, 247, 256, 306, 361

as emancipatory politics, 215,
    236–7, 256
  as self-policing community, 234–8,
    243, 247–52
Jazz at Lincoln Center, 250
Joubert, Joseph, 103
Juno Ludovisi, 300–3

Kane, Brian, 87
Kant, Immanuel, 104, 272
kitsch, 270
Kreidler, Johannes, 111
Kurth, Ernst, 106

labour, 157–9, 164, 165, 170, 272,
    290, 291, 294–300, 303, 312–14,
    334, 335
leitmotif, 319, 326
Letná Hill, 282
Ligeti, György, 133
listening, 9–12, 37, 38, 40, 84, 89,
    108, 133, 136, 137, 212, 227,
    338, 348
  as active, 212
  listening community, 216–17
literature, 5, 30–6, 105, 125–6,
    269–71
liveness, 220–1, 229
logos, 9–10, 13, 33, 49–50, 52, 76–8,
    180, 246–7, 359
Louis XIV, 141–4, 150
low music, the, 71–6, 82–5, 88–9
Lully, Jean-Baptiste, 98
Lyotard, Jean-François, 16, 281

Mae, Vanessa, 343
Mahler, Gustav, 106, 292, 296, 307
Maierhof, Michael, 111
Malick, Terrence, 133
Mallarmé, Stéphane, 4, 5, 6, 7, 14,
    92, 100, 324–7, 362
Marcus, Greil, 54–5, 58
Marx, Karl, 290, 294, 296
  and dialectics, 290–4, 300, 306
  and Marxism, 72, 74, 84, 89, 245,
    291–3, 297, 300, 335, 356, 357
Massey, Cal, 245, 259
Massumi, Brian, 221, 229, 255
Mattheson, Johann, 107
McClary, Susan, 257, 341–3, 361
McMullen, Tracy, 250, 260–1
Menger, Pierre-Michel, 23
mésentente; as mishearing, 9, 76, 139

metapolitics, 322, 328, 331
method of the scene, 8, 12, 17, 18, 20,
    27, 38, 88, 100, 104, 117–21,
    137, 156, 225, 230, 231, 233,
    235, 240, 245, 336, 345, 356,
    357–63
microphone, 36–7
Mignolo, Walter, 156–7
mimesis, 2, 6, 8, 30, 32, 36, 78, 102,
    104, 125, 234, 235, 238, 239,
    331
  anti-mimetic, 320, 324
Mirabeau, Honoré Gabriel Riqueti
    de, 102
mise en scène, 117–18, 353
modernism, 13, 15–16, 130–3
  and Platonism, 318–20, 324
modernity, 11, 13, 15–20, 117, 120,
    130–3, 137, 239, 320–1
Mondrian, Piet, 101
Monier, Conrad, 194–6
Monk, Thelonious, 21, 233, 241–5,
    247, 249, 254, 258, 359
montage, 4, 41
monument, 19, 266, 269, 272, 273,
    278, 279, 283–4
Moreno, Jairo and Gavin Steingo, 3,
    338, 340
Mostly Other People Do The Killing,
    233, 254, 261
  Blue, 249–52
Mr. K (band), 209
  Waves, 214–17, 219
multiculturalism, 266
multimedia, 111
music drama, 316–21, 324, 331, 332
musical modernity, 117, 120, 130–3,
    137
musical pleasure, 48, 145–7, 153,
    177–9, 183, 184, 187, 191, 193,
    355
musical score, 16, 73, 83, 212–13,
    339, 348
musicality, 1, 3–6, 8, 12, 16, 139,
    183
musicology, 3, 12, 16, 20, 88, 127,
    130, 257, 335, 337, 339–46,
    348, 361
musique concrète, 17, 27–35, 38–42,
    58, 359
muteness and mute speech, 1, 5, 6, 13,
    32–4, 48–50, 52, 55, 61, 62, 91,
    147, 151, 152, 287, 363

muthos, 4, 8, 12, 17, 27, 28–30, 36–7, 39, 40–2, 97–8
'My Favorite Things' (Rogers and Hammerstein), 245, 247
myth and mythology, 86, 98, 238, 315–16, 326–7, 332, 333, 341
   and jazz narratives, 237, 243
   pedagogic myth, 81–2, 87
   Pythagorean, 87

New Musicology, 20, 257, 337, 341
Nicolas, François, 13
Nietzsche, Friedrich, 2, 51, 61, 255, 330, 357
noise (and *phōnē*, *logos*, speech or meaning), 4, 7, 9, 10, 12, 16–17, 19, 22, 27, 28, 29, 30–5, 38–9, 41, 48, 50, 71, 73, 75, 86, 88–9, 91, 101, 103–5, 111, 129, 130–4, 137, 215, 233, 238, 240, 241, 243, 247, 251, 252, 358–61, 363
   bruit, 41, 82
   noise rock (genre), 57–61
   and silence, 76–80
non-art, 117, 286, 318, 320, 358
Novak, Vratislav, 283

opera, 18, 39, 98, 99, 100, 111, 142, 154, 156, 161–6, 169, 170, 172, 257, 275, 279, 303, 316, 320–1, 330, 333, 356, 357, 358, 364
opsis, 8, 27, 28, 29, 34–6, 39, 42
other, the, 38, 55, 59, 103, 111, 269, 280–2
Ott, Daniel, 111

Paganini, Niccolò, 121, 135
Paisiello, Giovanni, 98
Palestrina, Giovanni Pierluigi da, 106–7
Panagia, Davide, 14, 77, 81, 232
Parker, Charlie, 235
Pathos, 33, 59
pedagogic myth *see* myth
pedagogy, 18, 76, 80–2, 141–3, 146, 148, 150, 252
people, the, 14, 15, 19, 49, 76, 84, 88, 93, 99, 103, 178, 181, 195, 196, 259, 280, 282, 305, 314–18, 322, 323, 327, 328, 338, 355–6, 359, 363

peripeteia, 97, 110
phōnē, 9–10, 13, 78, 246, 247, 254, 359
phonograph, 40, 47
Pickford, Henry W., 273, 275
Plato, 48, 49, 85, 86, 93, 154, 159, 160, 161, 313–14, 318, 320
   and archipolitics, 86, 356
   the 'double lie', 159
   Republic, 157
   the slave in, 159–60
Platonism, 318–24, 354, 356
poesis, 32
poetics, 231, 270, 285, 327
   of knowledge, 16, 139
police, 6, 7, 10, 11, 12, 19, 72, 78, 80, 85, 88, 89, 100, 112, 117, 119, 126, 158, 162, 164, 165, 167, 168, 169, 177, 178–86, 198–200, 207, 210, 215–18, 219, 223, 224, 227, 229, 231–5, 237–9, 243–5, 247–53, 315, 340, 355, 359, 361
police logic, 7, 9, 10, 11, 18, 19, 86, 334
political art, 210–11, 332
politics, 7, 9–12, 71–80, 142, 147–9, 152–3, 156–7, 161, 163–9, 177–80, 186, 193, 196, 198–200, 207–23, 230–3, 237, 240, 243, 253, 272–3, 281, 283, 322, 327–8, 356, 361
   and aesthetics, 1–4, 11, 17, 19, 153, 156–7, 239, 251, 268, 359
   and improvisation, 207–23
politics, rarity of, 11, 210, 223, 231
politics of art, 11, 117, 119, 131, 274, 276, 285, 322–3, 327–8
politics of music, 16, 31, 117, 177–8, 198, 237, 244–5, 249, 362
Pop, Iggy, 21, 47, 62
popular culture, 131, 315–16
postmodern debate, 15, 120, 130–1
postmodernism, 15–16, 130–1
Presley, Elvis, 53, 55
Prins, Stefan, 111
   programme music, 18, 106, 109, 122–34, 358
Proust, Marcel, 50, 105, 125
Pythagoras and Pythagoreanism, 85–7

Quinault, Philippe, 98

Index 395

radio, 27–9, 32–9, 53, 58, 101, 111, 185, 210, 263
Rancière, Jacques
  Aesthetic Unconscious, 119
  Aesthetics and Its Discontents, 15, 119, 131
  Aisthesis: Scenes of the Aesthetic Regime, 8, 12, 18, 88, 118–20, 130, 211, 353, 358–9, 361–3
  Althusser's Lesson, 71–2, 81, 83
  'Autonomy and Historicism', 13
  Disagreement, 9, 17, 71, 76, 78, 85, 158, 166, 233
  Emancipated Spectator, The, 81, 156
  Future of the Image, The, 79, 355
  Ignorant Schoolmaster, The, 17, 71, 74, 81–3, 139–43, 148–52
  Les Révoltes logiques, 355
  Lost Thread, The, 127
  'Metamorphosis of the Muses', 4–5, 12–13, 85
  Method of Equality, The, 334
  on music, 4–8, 353–65
  On the Shores of Politics, 78
  Philosopher and his Poor, The, 157–60, 312, 337, 355–6, 358
  'Pleasures at the Barrière', 355
  Politics of Aesthetics, The, 211
  Proletarian Nights, 158, 334–5, 355–6, 362–3
  Short Voyages to the Land of the People, 14
  'Ten Theses on Politics', 9
  'The Aesthetic Revolution and Its Outcomes', 298
  'The Monument and Its Confidences', 298
  Temps modernes, Les, 125
  'Why Emma Bovary Had to be Killed', 270
rap, 183
regimes of art, 2–3, 11, 17, 97, 100, 117, 119, 126, 152
Reich, Charles I., 53
religion, 62, 107, 143, 183–4, 217, 326–7
representation, 5–8, 30, 35, 39, 42, 53, 61, 163, 198, 212, 230, 238–9, 266, 278, 280, 284, 319, 320, 323, 325, 326, 339

representative regime (of art), 5, 8, 11, 29, 32, 42, 51, 97–8, 101, 125–6, 239, 272, 320–1
resistance, 14, 51, 162, 265–8, 271–3, 276–8, 284–6, 293, 302
Resnais, Alain, 276
Reuben, Federico, 251
Rimbaud, Arthur, 14, 17, 99
Robbins, Bruce, 269
Rockhill, Gabriel, 2, 297
Rodríguez, Sílvio, 186, 196–7
Rolling Stone, 53
romanticism, 15, 18, 48–9, 318
Romitelli, Fausto, 110
Ross, Kristin, 17, 81–3, 142

Sanders, Pharoah, 233, 246–7, 254, 359
Sangild, Torben, 57, 59, 61
scene, 8, 12, 18, 27, 38, 80, 88, 100, 117–21, 209–10, 214–15, 230–1, 245, 247, 250, 314, 335–6, 356, 358–63
Schaeffer, Pierre, 17, 27–9, 31–42, 359
  Notes sur l'expression radiophonique, 28–9, 35
Schoenberg, Arnold, 19, 102, 108, 128, 231, 276, 285, 292, 298–9
  Survivor from Warsaw, 276, 285
Schopenhauer, Arthur, 2, 13, 51, 357
Schubert, Alexander, 111
Sebald, Winfried Georg, 110
Seidl, Hannes, 111
Serialism, 14, 102, 108, 132
Shakespeare, William, 100–1, 356, 359
Shank, Barry, 216
Shepp, Archie, 259
silence, 16, 29, 30, 32, 55, 73–80, 83, 88–9, 105, 107, 139, 146–53, 191, 210, 236, 242, 282
silent film, 37, 355
simulacrum, 234, 242, 251, 299, 314, 322
Smith, Adam, 102
Smith, Patti, 57, 59
Sonic Youth, 48, 57–61

sound, 1–2, 4, 9–10, 12, 16, 17, 27, 29–34, 36–41, 51, 57, 60, 62, 76–80, 88, 97, 101, 103, 105–7, 109–11, 121–2, 124, 128–30, 132–3, 139, 147, 179, 181, 198, 211, 213, 215, 222, 236, 238, 246–7, 250, 276, 278, 279, 282, 284, 285, 301–2, 310, 355, 359
Sousa, John Philip, 47
speech, 9, 13, 19, 28, 30, 32–4, 39, 41, 48–50, 52, 55–6, 59, 61–2, 76–7, 79–80, 86, 100, 103, 151–2, 180, 191, 193, 196–7, 215, 240, 252, 304, 359, 360; see also logos
Spinoza, Baruch, 255
staging see method of the scene
Stalin, Joseph, 283, 286
Stockhausen, Karlheinz, 4, 13–15
Street, John, 177
stultification, 17, 71, 80, 82, 84, 88, 150
subjectivisation, 297–8
sublime, 5, 61, 103, 110, 129, 132, 182, 296, 309, 319
Sulzer, Johann Georg, 107
Sun Ra, 4, 244–5, 253
Švec, Otakar, 283, 286
Szwed, John, 244

Tarr, Béla, 354, 360
Telemachus, 141, 143–9
testimony, 277, 281–2, 317
theatre, 12, 29, 37–8, 99, 101, 108, 162, 172, 313–14, 320, 322–3, 326, 355, 358
theatrocracy, 313
Thomas, Augusta Read, 133
timbre, 74, 106, 124, 363
Tippett, Michael, 19

Tovey, Donald Francis, 127
tradition, 19, 87–8, 131–2, 142, 150, 209, 234, 246, 267, 316–18, 354, 359
trauma, 276–7, 283

Ullman, Viktor, 275

Varèse, Edgard, 120, 133, 363
Verdi, Giuseppe, 161, 356–7
violence, 19, 55, 60, 156, 168–9, 238, 266–7, 269, 274–7, 279, 284–5
voice, 9, 11–12, 18, 28–9, 33–4, 38, 48–51, 55, 60–1, 76, 105, 130, 140, 143–7, 150–1, 157, 180, 182–5, 187, 195–6, 235–6, 238–40, 243, 276, 278, 282–4, 286, 306, 358, 363

Wackenroder, Wilhelm H., 51–2, 59, 61
Wagner, Richard, 12, 19, 21, 50, 52, 102, 105–8, 128, 131–3, 314–28, 356–8
  Meistersinger von Nürnberg, Die, 19, 314–18, 321–3, 328, 356
  Opera and Drama, 329–30, 358
  Tristan and Isolde, 50, 363
Webern, Anton, 231
Western art music, 8, 97, 132, 234
Wiebe, Heather, 278
Wolfe, Katherine, 245
Woolf, Virginia, 17, 29, 35, 105, 110, 125
Wordsworth, William, 17, 103–4, 110
Workers' strikes, 17, 76–7

Zani de Ferranti, Marco Aurelio, 18, 120–3, 130
Zola, Émile, 301–3

EU representative:
Easy Access System Europe
Mustamäe tee 50, 10621 Tallinn, Estonia
Gpsr.requests@easproject.com